Inside the Music Industry

Inside the Music Industry

Creativity, Process, and Business

SECOND EDITION

MICHAEL FINK

University of Texas at San Antonio

THOMSON

SCHIRMER

Australia • Canada • Mexico • Singapore • Spain

United Kingdom • United States

ISBN: 0-02-870764-8

Library of Congress Catalog Number: 96-10606

COPYRIGHT © 1996 by Michael Fink

Wadsworth Group/Thomson Learning
10 Davis Drive
Belmont CA 94002-3098
USA

For information about our products, contact us:
Thomson Learning Academic Resource Center
1-800-423-0563
http://www.wadsworth.com

For permission to use material from this text, contact us by
Web: http://www.thomsonrights.com
Fax: 1-800-730-2215
Phone: 1-800-730-2214

Printed in the United States of America
10 9 8 7 6 5 4 3

Fink, Michael
        Inside the music industry: creativity, process, and business / Michael Fink. —
    2nd ed.
        p. cm.
        Rev. ed. of: Inside the music business. 1989.
        Includes bibliographical references and index.
        ISBN 0-02-870764-8 (alk. paper)
        1. Music trade—United States.   2. Music—Economic aspects.
    I. Fink, Michael Inside the music business.   II. Title.
    ML3790.F56   1996
    780'.973—dc20   96-10606

Contents

PART 2
Music and Media

Preface and Acknowledgments

Inside the Music Industry is an introduction to music as it functions in the real world. In this book I describe musical life in the United States, with a special focus on the music industry and related fields. The contents are, therefore, extremely diverse. Each chapter is like a single tile in the large and complex mosaic that represents the workings of our musical industries and institutions. To make sense out of all this, I have grouped the chapters into four major parts: I. Music in Recording and Entertainment; II. Music and Media; III. Music in Business Settings; and IV. Music in Theatrical and Concert Traditions.

There are four chief objectives in *Inside the Music Industry*:

1. to provide a general introduction to the music industry and related fields;

2. to explore the main *structures, procedures, functions,* and *relationships* within and among the topics;

3. to provide brief histories of several of the fields discussed; and

4. to heighten the reader's awareness of the great variety of musical experiences available in everyday life.

In order to achieve the first two of these, I have stressed basic theory and process. I try to guide the reader to an understanding of how one thing affects or leads to another. For example, Chapters 2, 3, and 4 trace the business and artistic processes of popular music from songwriting through publishing, recording, marketing, and performing.

I believe that it is intrinsically important for a person to obtain a historical perspective in order to understand present circumstances. Thus, the third objective is carried out chiefly by the four chapters (1, 5, 11, and 13) devoted entirely to the "history and musical trends" of some particular field. I have provided shorter historical sketches elsewhere, principally in Chapters 7, 8, and 9.

To achieve the fourth objective, I have tried to take into account the ways in which we encounter music in our lives. For example, Part II focuses entirely on music in the communications media, while portions of Chapter 4 and all chapters in Part IV concern live performance.

Inside the Music Industry makes no attempt to cover all the repertoires of music currently performed in the United States. My main thrusts are industries and activities. Thus, there are several styles of American music which may appear to be shortchanged, notably jazz. The emphasis seems lopsided (from the musical repertoire point of view) because I have restricted my discussion to the styles of music which have fulfilled one or more of the following functions:

  making the greatest impact on the industries discussed and considered of prime importance within those industries (for example, rock);

  being an essential constituent in the structure of an industry (for example, any broadcast format); and

  having become an institution in itself (for example, musical theater, opera, and symphonic concert music).

If I have overlooked anyone's favorite musical style, I apologize—but it was a necessary omission.

Finally, the underlying strategy in much of *Inside the Music Industry* has been to take the reader from the known to the unknown. Key words and phrases in chapter titles and subheadings often focus on familiar topics (for example, songs, records, radio, and musical shows). From one of these points the discussion may lead into the arcane and sometimes complex details of behind-the-scenes operations, contracts, copyright law, and so forth. My purpose has been to clarify the basics of a topic and to give the reader a comfortable, general knowledge of it. If the reader desires more depth of information, the Further Reading list at the end of the book will be helpful. I also recommend looking up unfamiliar terms in the extensive glossary.

Several people have generously given their time, advice, and constructive criticism while I worked on this book. First, I wish to thank my wife and family for their patience and constant encouragement. I thank Nancy Lamb for her invaluable help with research and proofreading. I thank Gerald Warfield for his encouragement and his useful suggestions in the early chapters. I am grateful to Richard Blinn (Capitol Records, Inc.) for all his help. My gratitude goes to Daniel Roeder (Muzak of San Antonio), Beth Phillips, Jeff Cifka, and Leslie Ritter (Muzak Limited Partnership) for much valuable data on environmental music. I thank Alfredo Flores (Alamo Music Center) and Arthur Gurwitz (Southern Music Company) for their fine suggestions concerning retail music.

Finally, to Richard Broderick, Charles Suber, and the late David Baskerville, all of whom became my warmest friends through the Music & Entertainment Industry Educators Association (MEIEA), I owe a debt of gratitude for the extensive knowledge they have imparted to us over the years.

The Grammy® portion of this publication was printed by permission of the National Academy of Recording Arts & Sciences®. I wish to thank the following organizations for kindly providing information: American Music Conference (AMC), American Symphony Orchestra League (ASOL), National Association of Music Merchants (NAMM), National Music Publishers Association (NMPA), and the Recording Industry Association of America (RIAA).

For providing photographs and artwork, and for granting permission to reproduce them in this text, I am grateful to the Edison National Historical Site; Science Museum (London); RCA Records, Inc.; Capitol Records, Inc.; the American Society of Composers, Authors, and Publishers (ASCAP); Don Putnam Photographers; Broadcast Music, Inc. (BMI); Billboard Publications, Inc.; the National Academy of Recording Arts & Sciences®; Century 21 Programming, Inc.; the Theatre Arts Library of the Harry Ransom Humanities Research Center, The University of Texas at Austin; Muzak Limited Partnership; Broadcasting and Related Products Division/3M; the National Association of Music Merchants (NAMM); and the New York Public Library.

Michael Fink

Part 1

Music in Recording and Entertainment

1
The Record Business:
History and Musical Trends

When Thomas Edison invented practical phonograph recording in 1877 he could hardly have anticipated the powerful mass entertainment medium it would become. Edison's chief interests were in preserving classical music and the spoken word. He also foresaw the connection between motion pictures and sound recording as a method of historically documenting the "lives and the voices of the great men and women of the world," as Edison himself put it. The great inventor did not anticipate that audio phonograph recordings would become an entertainment medium, but when they did, he was pleased to make his contributions to that enterprise, too.

Early Commercial Recordings

The earliest experiments in Edison's laboratory utilized tinfoil wrapped around a cylinder, but the first commercially produced phonographs could play wax and shellac cylinders well before the turn of the century. Developments in producing the cylinders came quickly because of the need to compete with the newly introduced disc phonograph. Invented and developed by Emile Berliner, the new disc format appeared around 1896, and a standard speed of 78 revolutions per minute (rpm) was arrived at quite early (though apparently quite arbitrarily).

Edison's original cylinder phonograph. Photo courtesy of Edison Historical Site, National Park Service, U.S. Department of the Interior.

Disc and cylinder formats competed for about twenty-five years, but the disc finally won out, due to ease of manufacture, better sound quality, and better marketing.

In the early years of the twentieth century, recording in the United States was dominated by two companies that have continued to the present day to be two of the largest names in the recording industry. One, originally named the Victor

Emile Berliner's disc phonograph. British Crown copyright. Science Museum, London.

Early acoustical recording. Photo courtesy of Edison Historical Site, National Park Service, U.S. Department of the Interior.

Talking Machine Company, was an offshoot of the English Gramophone and Typewriter Company. The other was the Columbia Gramophone Company, which had been incorporated from a number of small manufacturers. The repertoire that these early companies recorded was largely operatic, and all the biggest opera stars of the day were persuaded to make recordings. The various recordings of Enrico Caruso singing "Vesti la giubba," first recorded in 1902, sold an aggregate total of over 1 million copies. (The first million-selling individual recording was Alma Gluck's "Carry Me Back to Old Virginny," released on the Victor label during this period.)

The recorded repertoire expanded relatively quickly. Instrumental music had been recorded from the earliest period. However, due to problems in loudness connected with the acoustic (nonelectrical) recording techniques in use at the time, recorded piano music was not satisfactory, and orchestral music was nearly nonexistent.

Classical music was not the only type recorded in the early twentieth century. Dance music was soon introduced, and popular songs were recorded. In the area of popular music the most prominent songwriter around World War I was Irving Berlin, and his song "Alexander's Ragtime Band" (1911) was a phenomenal success. Jazz also found its way into the recorded repertoire. In 1917 the first jazz recordings were made by The Original Dixieland Jazz Band and released under the Victor, Aeolian, and Columbia labels.

Between 1918 and 1922 the recording industry flourished. Leopold Stokowski and Arturo Toscanini conducted orchestral works, popular and operatic singers recorded, and jazz—the latest novelty in the United States and in Europe—was commercialized. For the first time the sale of records was outpacing that of sheet music for the most popular songs. However, this flush of success for the record business soon became severely curtailed by the popularization of radio.

The Period of Radio Domination

By 1922 radio had already stolen a great deal of attention from the phonograph. On the radio, listeners could hear constantly varying programs without relying on private record collections. And the best thing of all was that the programs were *free*!

In a few short years radio became a giant industry, at first dwarfing and later absorbing the record business. The Radio Corporation of America (RCA) originated in the years following World War I. Then, in 1926 RCA founded the National Broadcasting Company (NBC), which soon held a monopoly in network radio. RCA bought out the Victor recording label at the end of the decade. Through an odd sequence of financial events, a maverick rival network of twelve stations eventually became the basis of the Columbia Broadcasting System (CBS) in 1928. However, CBS did not own the Columbia record label until as late as 1938, when it purchased the American Record Corporation, owner of the Columbia, Brunswick, and Vocalion labels.

Although the business of phonograph records shrank to nearly nothing in the course of the 1920s, audio recording technology moved forward during that period. Microphones and amplifiers, developed for use in radio, were applied to recordings, and in 1924 Bell Laboratories developed an electrical recording process which brought to an end the acoustic period of recording.

There were several tangible advantages to the new method. The audible range of earlier recordings had been so restricted that bass instruments could not be heard, and there was a lack of high-frequency response. The new method allowed an expanded frequency range of 100–5,000 cycles per second, or Hertz (Hz). Bass instruments could now be heard, and the upper range was greatly improved. New developments in recording and disc manufacturing also enhanced the dynamic range of records.

An expansion of recorded repertoire during the 1920s was also significant. The first "race" records, mainly blues intended to be bought by the black population, began to appear. The commercial successes made by the historic "You Can't Keep a Good Man Down" and "That Thing Called Love" by Mamie Smith (1920) were followed by the release of numerous other black recordings.

Radio continued to dominate home entertainment during the Great Depression of the 1930s, and the big networks considered their record labels as something of a sideline. In contrast to this trend, the American Decca label, not owned by a network, was established during this time. Decca quickly became a force to be reckoned with as a result of two strategic moves. First, the label's new president, Jack Kapp, personally controlled the recording contracts of several Brunswick artists, including Bing Crosby, Guy Lombardo, and Louis Armstrong. These stars now became Decca's artists. Second, Kapp cut the retail price of a single record from 75 cents to 35 cents (or three for a dollar), which increased Decca's record sales tremendously. The other labels were forced to follow suit. In those economically depressed times records again became an affordable form of home entertainment.

Many of the top recording artists of the 1930s were also the radio stars of their day (see Chapter 5). Their repertoire came primarily from Tin Pan Alley (see below) and Broadway. While a few songs of the period were influenced by the Depression (for example, "Brother, Can You Spare a Dime?"), the majority of popular music was more optimistic, or at least sentimental. Examples of 1930s sentimentalism are "Smoke Gets in Your Eyes" (1933), "Stormy Weather" (1933), and "Blue Moon" (1934).

By the mid-1930s the first albums, (collections similar to boxed sets) of 78–rpm discs appeared. Most of these contained classical works broken up into segments that could fit on one side of a twelve-inch record (approximately four-and-a-half minutes). Despite these unfortunate divisions, entire concert works and operas were now made available.

From the mid-1930s until after World War II a recovery in the popular music record business took place, aided by two outside forces: jukeboxes and radio. Many restaurants and public recreational places had jukeboxes. Not only did jukebox operators purchase large numbers of records, but jukebox exposure seems to have stimulated consumer sales of records as well. Radio also helped to sell records by giving exposure to popular artists and new songs. Beginning in 1935, the most influential exposure was through the weekly radio show "Your Hit Parade," which presented live performances of the current top ten recorded songs.

Tin Pan Alley

During the two decades between the world wars, most of the repertoire of songs sung by pop artists came from one or another of the large New York music publishers known collectively as "Tin Pan Alley." Originating as far back as the 1890s, these publishers and the composers they represented were the most powerful single influence on popular style and, as a result, on popular taste. The lyrics of Tin Pan Alley songs followed a philosophy of escapism rather than realism, and the music used the forms, harmonic patterns, and melodic styles inherited from the lighter European traditions, such as operetta. Many Tin Pan Alley songs originated in Broadway shows. Examples of Tin Pan Alley tunes are "A Pretty Girl Is Like a Melody" (Irving Berlin, 1919), "Tea for Two" (Vincent

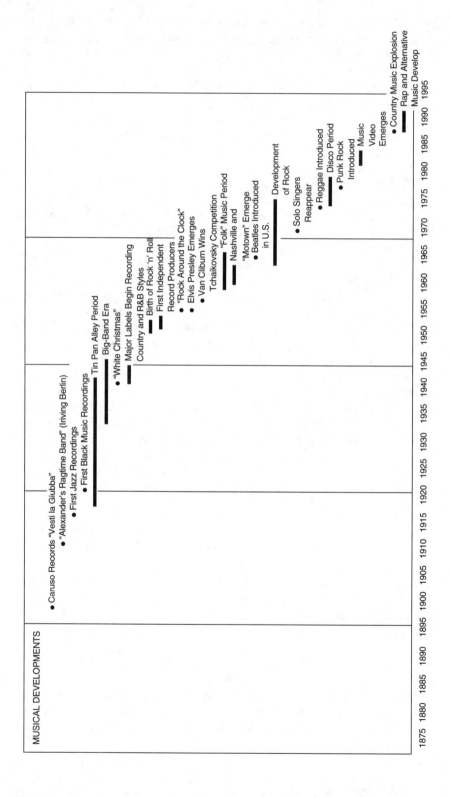

MUSICAL DEVELOPMENTS

1875 1880 1885 1890 1895 1900 1905 1910 1915 1920 1925 1930 1935 1940 1945 1950 1955 1960 1965 1970 1975 1980 1985 1990 1995

• Caruso Records "Vesti la Giubba"
• "Alexander's Ragtime Band" (Irving Berlin)
• First Jazz Recordings
• First Black Music Recordings
Tin Pan Alley Period
Big-Band Era
• "White Christmas"
Major Labels Begin Recording
Country and R&B Styles
Birth of Rock 'n' Roll
First Independent
Record Producers
• "Rock Around the Clock"
• Elvis Presley Emerges
• Van Cliburn Wins
Tchaikovsky Competition
"Folk" Music Period
Nashville and
"Motown" Emerge
• Beatles Introduced
in U.S.
Development
of Rock
• Solo Singers
Reappear
• Reggae Introduced
Disco Period
• Punk Rock
Introduced
Music
Video
Emerges
• Country Music Explosion
Rap and Alternative
Music Develop

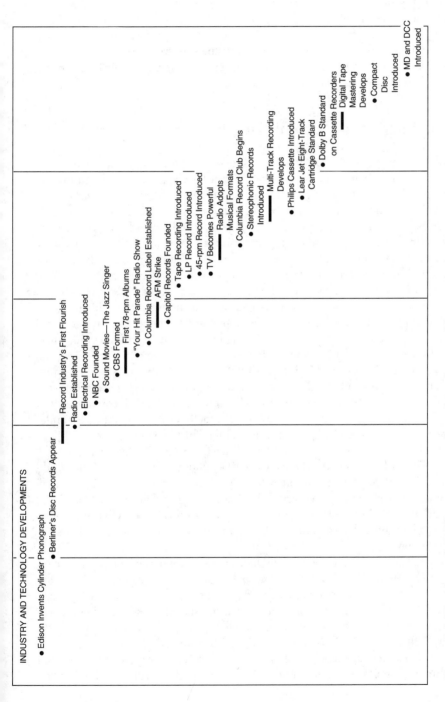

INDUSTRY AND TECHNOLOGY DEVELOPMENTS

- Edison Invents Cylinder Phonograph
- Berliner's Disc Records Appear
- Record Industry's First Flourish
- Radio Established
- Electrical Recording Introduced
- NBC Founded
- Sound Movies—The Jazz Singer
- CBS Formed
- First 78-rpm Albums
- "Your Hit Parade" Radio Show
- Columbia Record Label Established
- AFM Strike
- Capitol Records Founded
- Tape Recording Introduced
- LP Record Introduced
- 45-rpm Record Introduced
- TV Becomes Powerful
- Radio Adopts Musical Formats
- Columbia Record Club Begins
- Stereophonic Records Introduced
- Multi-Track Recording Develops
- Philips Cassette Introduced
- Lear Jet Eight-Track Cartridge Standard
- Dolby B Standard on Cassette Recorders
- Digital Tape Mastering Develops
- Compact Disc Introduced
- MD and DCC Introduced

Figure 1-1. Timeline of significant events and trends in the record business.

Youmans, 1924), "Blue Moon" (Richard Rodgers, 1934), and "That Old Black Magic" (Harold Arlen, 1943).

A Tin Pan Alley publisher's traditional means of promoting the sales of a printed song was to persuade one or more record companies to record it. However, after the advent of sound films (*The Jazz Singer*, 1927) the screen furnished a new alternative for introducing and promoting songs. Probably the movie song most successful on records was "White Christmas" by Irving Berlin, sung by Bing Crosby in the film *Holiday Inn* (1942). Its sentimentality was quite typical of the Tin Pan Alley songs of its day.

Big Bands and Wartime Trends

Although popular vocalists dominated the rosters of the major record labels during the early 1930s, public taste had begun to change drastically during the Depression, and the time grew ripe for a rebirth of enthusiasm for instrumental music. In imitation of black jazz bands, white regional bands like the Casa Loma Orchestra began to appear around the beginning of the decade. This trend grew rapidly, and by 1935 the ten-year "big-band era" had dawned. The popularity of names like Benny Goodman, Glenn Miller, Duke Ellington, Count Basie, Artie Shaw, Tommy and Jimmy Dorsey, and others not only affected what was recorded but influenced the pattern of the music business behind the scenes as well.

Tin Pan Alley music publishers had been accustomed to wielding a great deal of power in the matter of recorded repertoire. Within the existing system it was they who found new songs for the big labels' major artists to record. Thus, publishers had held the initiative. However, most of the new "Swing"-style tunes and arrangements played by big bands did not come from publishers but rather from the leaders and members of the bands themselves. The big bands were the first complete entertainment "packages" (forerunners to the self-contained Rock bands of the 1960s), and they had little need for Tin Pan Alley. Prime examples of swing tunes and their popularizers include "In the Mood" (Glenn Miller), "Let's Dance" (Benny Goodman), and "Take the A-Train" (Duke Ellington).

The big bands held sway from the late 1930s until after the U.S. entry into World War II. Unfortunately, a lethal blow to the popularity of big bands came when the American Federation of Musicians held a strike against the record companies between 1942 and 1944. Record labels countered this move by reissuing older recordings and making new releases from their large backlogs of unreleased masters. In the process, records by featured singers were generally promoted more than before, leaving big band records with little promotion and a dwindling audience.

The World War II military bases and defense plants caused much of the American work force to relocate in various parts of the country. These people carried with them their own regional tastes in music. As a result, during the war years two styles outside mainstream "popular" music gained more prominence: Hillbilly (Country and Western) and Race (Rhythm and Blues).

At first the major labels began making records for these growing markets, but a wartime shortage of shellac forced them to cut back to mainstream pop releases only. An exception to this pattern was Capitol Records, formed in 1943 by Johnny Mercer (songwriter), Glenn Wallichs (record retailer), and Buddy de Silva (movie executive). Capitol was sensitive to the demand for Country music and Rhythm and Blues and at various times prospered by spreading its releases more evenly between these fields and mainstream pop. (An early successful record on the Capitol label was "Cow Cow Boogie" by Ella Mae Morse.) After the war the newer styles flourished more fully, but the major labels were successful only with Country style. The relatively small Rhythm and Blues market was left to independent record companies.

Tape, the LP, and the 45–rpm Record

The years following World War II saw two technological advances which revolutionized the recording industry: the use of magnetic tape for recording and the invention of the long-playing (LP) record. Magnetic tape had been publicly introduced by the German BASF company as early as 1935. It was brought to the U.S. recording industry in 1947, and in less than two years tape completely replaced direct-to-disc wax master recording. The advantages of tape were irrefutable: ease of setup, almost unlimited length of record/play time, immediate playback, ease of editing, and the future possibility of multitrack recording.

Introducing the LP record was a laborious process. Over the years research divisions of the major American labels had made sporadic attempts at producing a record that would play at a slower speed than 78 rpm, but there were always more problems than the apparent gains could justify. Finally, in June 1948 Columbia Records introduced an LP record that would hold over twenty minutes of music on a twelve-inch side. A speed of 33 1/3 rpm was used, and most of the previous technical drawbacks were overcome by employing a microgroove cutting technique and making the final pressing on "unbreakable" vinyl rather than on shellac. In addition, the lower amount of friction involved during disc mastering and home playback allowed the LP's surface to be very quiet. Thus, the first major steps toward "high fidelity" had been taken.

For the listener a major advantage of the LP was the longer unbroken musical program it offered. This was particularly important on classical records. For example, an entire symphony could be stored on one disc, and individual movements did not have to be interrupted, as they had been on 78s. To promote the compactness of LPs, Columbia photographed a stack of 78 rpm records about eight feet high next to a pile of LP recordings of the same music which rose only fifteen inches.

RCA at first declined to adopt the LP format and instead introduced 45–rpm records in February 1949. At the same time the company began to market its own low-cost player to handle only 45s. There ensued the year-long "war of the speeds." Dealers were compelled to stock records that were variously released in 78, 45, and 33 1/3 rpm (LP) speeds, complicated further by the 78s and LPs being ten or twelve inches in diameter, while the 45s were seven-inch discs. The 45–rpm microgroove vinyl record easily proved to be superior to the 78–rpm for single recordings. However, in an attempt to compete with Columbia's LPs, RCA also packaged boxed albums of 45s, but that effort was not very successful. Ultimately, in early 1950 RCA acknowledged the superiority of the LP for longer programs of music, and Columbia adopted the 45 for single-record releases. Since many people still owned older players, the 78–rpm record was not completely phased out until a few years later.

Television's Impact

With the firm establishment of network television in the late 1940s came the transference of several music/comedy variety shows from radio. New TV variety shows also began to spring up. The most famous and longest running of these was "The Ed Sullivan Show," hosted by a former newspaper columnist, which ran from 1948 to 1971. Numerous top stars made their television debuts on that show, and it also introduced a huge amount of new musical talent to the American public. Variety shows built around singing artists also abounded, notably "The Perry Como Show" (1948–1963). Later shows were built around versatile contemporary artists, for example, "The Glen Campbell Goodtime Hour" (1969–1972), "The Sonny and Cher Comedy Hour" (1971–1974), and "Tony Orlando and Dawn" (1974–1976). The popularity of weekly variety shows waned, and they finally disappeared in the course of the 1970s, but TV "specials" in variety format are still occasionally produced.

The phenomenal growth of television as the favorite form of home entertainment in the early 1950s had profound influences on the other entertainment industries. The structure of the business of radio and the nature of radio programming (see below) were altered radically by the impact of TV. The onslaught of TV also affected record sales, but not as drastically as had been expected. It seems that the adverse affects on the recording industry were somewhat counterbalanced by two developments which made records attractive to the public.

One of these forces was the advent of new improvements in sound quality and playing time afforded by the LP and the 45. "High fidelity" became a new attraction, especially in the popular middle-of-the-road (MOR) and classical markets. The other development which aided the record business was the complex of changes which took place in radio during this period as the result of TV's damaging effects on radio. For economic reasons radio ceased to program live music. Its comedy shows and other live entertainment either died or were transferred to TV. Network radio, in the form into which it had grown, declined rapidly, replaced by network television. Following the lead of innovative independent stations, the central format for most of radio soon became "music and news," featuring phonograph records. By the mid-1950s numerous stations had adopted the very successful "Top 40" format. Frequency of airplay became one of the intrinsic measures of a new record's success. Radio, which in the early 1920s had nearly destroyed the record business, now owed its own recovery to its new role as something of a promotional tool for the recording industry.

Rock 'n' Roll

Besides the industry-wide revolution incited by TV, the 1950s experienced a revo- lution in popular music style that would reshape several aspects of the record business and give it new life: Rock 'n' Roll was born. (The term "Rock 'n' Roll" was taken from Rhythm-and-Blues lyrics and popularized by disc jockey Alan Freed in 1952.) Black rhythm and blues (R&B) had become a distinct and powerful force in records after 1950 and grew to have a white, teenage market around 1952. From R&B evolved early Rock 'n' Roll, and for a time there was only a thin line between them. Each had a crossover black and white audience, and each eventually incorporated both black and white musicians. Representative early Rock 'n' Roll records by black artists included "Rocket 88" by Ike Turner (1951), "Sh-Boom" by the Chords, and "Shake, Rattle, and Roll" by Joe Turner (both 1954).

The greatest mass popularizers of Rock 'n' Roll, Chuck Berry, Bill Haley, and Elvis Presley, emerged around 1955. Their backgrounds varied from R&B to Country Blues. Chuck Berry, though black, rose to popularity through his great sensitivity to the tastes of white youth, reflected in such hits as "Maybellene" and "Sweet Little Sixteen." Bill Haley's classic was "Rock Around the Clock," featured in the 1955 movie *The Blackboard Jungle*. The worldwide popularity of that movie and of its sequel, *Rock Around the Clock*, succeeded in making Rock 'n' Roll a sudden international sensation.

Elvis Presley is a chapter unto himself. Like Carl Perkins, Buddy Holly, and Jerry Lee Lewis, he was exposed to both black music (via radio) and to the white Country music of his southern upbringing. The new crossover style generated by such artists was at first called "Rockabilly," but was soon acknowledged to be an integral part of the Rock 'n' Roll movement. Presley's earliest records were made for Sun Records, an independent label in Memphis, but his contract was soon bought by RCA. From that point he became the most phenomenal single entertainer the recording industry has ever seen. Beginning with "Heartbreak Hotel," Presley's first recording for RCA, his records sold incredibly fast and stayed at the top of the charts for unheard-of lengths of time. Up to Presley's time there had been a general industry reluctance to accept Rock 'n' Roll, and some of the adult public considered Presley, his songs, and his body movements to be scandalous. However, his vast popularity finally forced even Ed Sullivan to schedule Presley to appear on his TV family variety show—but viewed only from the waist up. Elvis Presley's singing versatility became more apparent as his career broadened into films, and he maintained his popularity well into the 1970s.

Major Labels vs. Independents: The Shifting Market

The industry establishment's reaction to Elvis Presley was typical. Until RCA was bold enough to sign Presley, the major pop labels of the time (Columbia, RCA, Decca, Capitol, Mercury, and MGM) would not even consider contracting with Rock 'n' Roll artists. Although the companies were turning their backs on an obvious jackpot, there were reasons for ignoring the new phenomenon. One was

(a)   (b)

Elvis Presley. Photos courtesy of RCA Records, Inc.
(a) In the early days.
(b) Around 1970.

that the major labels all had "stables" of established popular middle-of-the-road artists in whom the companies had made sizable investments. Another reason was the record industry's connection with the Tin Pan Alley establishment, which traditionally supplied the songs on which these artists built their styles. Rock 'n' Roll songs, heavily controlled by the singers, were anything but Tin Pan Alley in style. The record industry's aversion to Rock 'n' Roll was reinforced by objections on the part of adult consumers (many of them parents). Record executives were fearful of losing their goodwill at a time when the future of the industry appeared uncertain.

Although large dollar volumes were being projected for LP records, the major labels failed to realize that in spite of the LP, there was still a huge market for single records. In fact, the biggest market transformation in the history of the industry was about to take place, and it would be focused on single records. Teenagers and college students now had money and were creating the record market of the future: the youth market.

This unprecedented state of affairs left the door open for entrepreneurs to create new labels built on newer styles. Among the most successful independent labels of this period were Atlantic, Chess, and Dot. The situation also nurtured a new breed of industry personality: the independent record producer. Two prominent early single record producers were Sam Phillips and Phil Spector. The independents felt freer to pioneer novelties in sound. Some of the more colorful early production techniques were reverberation effects achieved by recording in tiled bathrooms or singing into lengths of sewer pipe.

Ultimately, the major labels had to give in. Elvis Presley was with RCA, Decca signed Bill Haley and Buddy Holly, and in the mid-1950s the other major labels also began to attract and promote their own Rock 'n' Roll stars. The decision to serve the youth market, rather than resist it, completed a revolution in the record business and charted the path of its future history.

Record Clubs and Stereo Sound

Although the Rock 'n' Roll hysteria leveled off considerably from 1958 to 1963, there were other novel developments in the record industry during that period. This time they related to marketing. In 1955 the Columbia Record and Tape Club was introduced. Other companies soon imitated Columbia's innovation, and through the record club concept a new mail-order record business was created. (After the first ten years record club sales accounted for 14 percent of total record sales.)

Advances in technology came, too. In 1957 England and the United States were introduced to the first stereophonic LP records. The new recordings reproduced two channels of sound heard through speakers several feet apart or through a pair of headphones. Since stereo records sounded more "spacious" but were compatible with existing monaural equipment, the records sold briskly, and stereo was easily phased into the mainstream of home entertainment.

Record clubs and stereophonic sound each increased the public's awareness of classical music. In addition, when the American pianist Van Cliburn won the International Tchaikovsky Competition in Moscow in April 1958 (in the wake of the USSR's *Sputnik* satellite launch), it was both a musical and political triumph. One of the results was that Cliburn's recording of the Tchaikovsky Piano Concerto no. 1 became the first classical album to sell over 1 million copies.

Folk Music

All through the 1950s an underground movement known as "Folk" Music had developed, consisting of obscure artists recording for small, independent labels. When, beginning in 1957, a lull in public enthusiasm for Rock 'n' Roll developed, major labels tried introducing slick, commercial versions of Folk and Calypso Music. Capitol began recording the Kingston Trio in 1957, and Harry Belafonte's success with RCA dates from 1958. These and other artists were so successful that weekly TV variety shows that were produced around Folk and pseudo-Folk styles began to appear.

Bob Dylan was the not-so-slick superstar of urban folk music during the early 1960s. His albums and concert appearances were made up mostly of original songs. Several of these went on to become hits, notably "Blowin' in the Wind." Joan Baez had grown popular slightly earlier than Dylan, and throughout the Folk movement she was his strong female counterpart. The most durable purely folk group developing at this time was Peter, Paul, and Mary, who began recording in 1962. However, Paul Simon's early music was probably the consummation of urban Folk style. Simon and Garfunkel's recordings of "Scarborough Fair" and "Sounds of Silence" (both from 1966) are examples of their work.

Rock During the 1960s

In a few short months around late 1963 and early 1964 an event occurred which would impact upon all of American popular culture, including the recording industry, the style of popular music, clothing styles, and even the acceptable length of male hair: America discovered The Beatles. The immediate and universal success of records by this British group on the Capitol label (by then a subsidiary of the British EMI corporation) amounted to nothing less than a revolution in music and public taste. "Folk," per se, was out, and "Rock" (just "Rock" now, not "Rock 'n' Roll") was in. Throughout the rest of the decade The Beatles would be stylistic leaders. Although they did not break up until 1970, the age of "Beatlemania" is considered to have spanned the years 1963–1968. During that period The Beatles' records grossed over $150 million worldwide. Their most varied and influential album (and perhaps their greatest masterpiece) was *Sgt. Pepper's Lonely Hearts Club Band* (1967).

The new trend in rock in Britain and the United States, sometimes called "Progressive Rock," was characterized by a heavier, yet more complex beat and freer musical forms than those of Rock 'n' Roll. The Rock of the 1960s had lyrics that ranged from social protest, through love and explicit sex, to drug references and obscure philosophy. Rock made increased use of electric instruments and amplification. Following the lead of Dylan and the Beatles, most of the new Rock singers and bands wrote their own songs. Rock style soon affected all of the younger artists. Even Dylan began to use an electric guitar in the mid-1960s and, like other former "folkies," developed new types of songs and a new performance style.

A wide spectrum of Rock styles evolved in the 1960s, ranging from Soft Rock and Folk Rock to "Psychedelic," Hard Rock and Acid Rock (musically related to the later "Heavy Metal" style). In the recording industry widespread emphasis was placed on recording young acts. Also, many of the newer groups developed in urban centers like San Francisco that were relatively tolerant of unconventional life-styles. The Grateful Dead and the Jefferson Airplane (later, Jefferson Starship) are examples.

Rock was responsible for a tremendous upswing in the record business during the 1960s. With Rock the main product emphasis shifted from the single record to the album, and artwork on the album jacket became an important merchandising factor. On the artistic side, independent record producers became generally more successful than major label staff producers in discovering and developing new "underground" talent. As a result, independent producers became the wizards of the industry, responsible for an estimated 80 percent of

(a)

(b)

The Beatles. Photo courtesy of Capitol Records, Inc.
(a) "Magical Mystery Tour" (1968).
(b) "Let It Be" (1970). Clockwise from upper left: John Lennon,
Paul McCartney, George Harrison, Ringo Starr.

the Rock records released during the decade. One of the most successful independents was Lou Adler, producer of The Mamas and the Papas (among other acts) and founder of two independent record labels. The promotion of rock was aided greatly by the development of FM radio in the 1960s. With the advent of multiplex broadcasting, records could now be heard stereophonically and in FM's wide frequency-range. Many smaller FM stations concentrated on progressive rock, and some of these played entire albums without interruption.

Nashville and Motown

Rock was by no means the only style which flourished during this time. The 1960s also witnessed the emergence of Country and Black music styles, which had matured enough to be capable of competing on the pop charts as well as in their own, more-specialized markets. Named for the place where the recordings took place, the new styles were called "The Nashville Sound" and "The Motown [Detroit] Sound." By blending just the right proportions of traditional country-and-western melodic style with newer Rock beats and contemporary instrumental combinations, recording artists in Nashville (and, to a degree, Memphis) opened a new chapter in the field of Country music. Writer-performers like Hank Cochran ("Make the World Go Away"), Willie Nelson ("Touch Me"), and Bobby Russell ("Little Green Apples") typified recording in Nashville. This music drew so much attention and gained such an increased market share that before the end of the decade several major labels had established offices or even complete studios in Nashville.

In contrast with Nashville, Detroit did not become a major recording center, but it was the place where Motown Records, the monolith of Black music, was built. This was largely the work of one man, Berry Gordy, who founded Motown in 1960 when he produced Smokey Robinson's "Shop Around." Motown soon became a force to be reckoned with. Featuring tight-knit, highly disciplined groups like the Supremes and the Temptations, and with new "soul" singers like Marvin Gaye and Stevie Wonder, Gordy established the Motown sound. Motown concentrated on the single-record market, creating several new labels in the process. The enormous success by the late 1960s of labels under Motown is typified by a *Billboard* chart of the "Hot 100" single records from late 1968 showing five of the top ten single records to be Motown products (two of these by Diana Ross and the Supremes).

New Technology and New Marketing Methods

Technical developments in the 1960s made recordings more luxuriant sonically as well as more compact and portable. Multitrack recording was developed at this time. Four tracks were in use before 1965. Then came eight-, sixteen-, twenty-four-, and finally thirty-two-track studios. Extensive overdubbing was now possi-

The Supremes. Photo courtesy of Motown Record Corporation.

ble, and mixing down the many tracks to two became an art in itself. The Philips cassette made its debut in 1963, and its stereophonic-monoaural compatibility as well as its compactness gave it early and lasting popularity. The Lear Jet eight-track cartridge also became a standard in 1965, largely due to its promotion by major U.S. auto manufacturers. (However, eight-track cartridges all but disappeared before the mid-1980s.) In the late 1960s Dr. Ray Dolby developed an advanced form of encoding audio tapes to reduce hiss and distortion in the upper frequency range. The Dolby "A" system was adopted by professional recording studios, and in 1970 the consumer version, Dolby "B," became standard on home cassette recorders.

At the same time as the overall upswing in the record business during the 1960s (caused mainly by the popularity of Rock), the structure of the business went through some important changes. In the mid-1960s many independent labels merged with or were bought by major companies, which themselves were often owned by large conglomerates, such as Gulf and Western. Another change was the appearance of classical "budget" labels, featuring either rereleases of older masters deleted from catalogs of major labels or new recordings by lesser-known artists. Record distribution patterns were altered drastically during this time as well. Several major labels bought out local distributors and occasionally even retail chains in order to control the various levels of distribution. A new type of grass-roots marketing also developed successfully: rack jobbing. Display racks of records could now be found in previously unlikely places, such as supermarkets, drugstores, and variety stores.

Return of the Solo Singer

The realignment of the industry around 1970 also affected the ownership of artists' contracts. There were several cases of larger labels purchasing recording contracts from lesser labels, notably CBS's acquisition of Neil Diamond from MCA. Diamond was one of a new breed of singer-songwriters who became the recording superstars of the 1970s. In fact, there was a swing of interest toward solo singers in general about this time. In Black music James Brown and Aretha Franklin had become the king and queen of Soul. Counterparts of these were "White Soul" or "White Blues" singers, such as Rod Stewart and Janis Joplin.

Early Rock 'n' Roll had featured mainly male singers, and women artists had often been relegated to "girl groups." Folk artist Joan Baez had begun to blaze a path for the female singer, and in the course of the 1960s and 1970s women could be heard as the featured singers of several prominent rock bands (e.g., Stevie Nicks with Fleetwood Mac). Female soloists, such as Janis Joplin, Aretha Franklin, Helen Reddy, Carly Simon, and others, became giants in the Rock, Soul, and Pop fields. In the 1970s this trend reached a peak with the music of singer-songwriter Carole King, whose album *Tapestry* (1971) sold over 13 million copies by the end of 1975, making it the biggest-selling album up to that time. Women's time had come.

Trends in the 1970s

The decade of the 1970s was an age of crossover culture, and music with a crossover market was a significant part of it. Rock music with Country or Black appeal (for example, Creedence Clearwater Revival), or a Country hit with strong popular appeal (such as most of Glen Campbell's records), are examples of crossover styles which characterized the industry. There were two major instances of crossover in Black music during this decade. The first was Reggae, originating in the Caribbean in the mid-1960s but growing popular in the United States beginning in 1973 (especially Bob Marley and the Wailers). The second was Disco (or "Pop Soul"), which reached a crest of popularity extending from 1974 to 1978. Although Disco had definite black roots and many black artists (notably Donna Summer), the style was also picked up by white groups. Undoubtedly the most successful of these was a revitalized British group, The Bee Gees. The most successful exploitation of the Disco craze was the movie *Saturday Night Fever* (1977), featuring the music of The Bee Gees. The double-LP sound track album from this movie became the best-selling album up to that time, with over 25 million copies sold worldwide. (The biggest-selling album at this writing is Michael Jackson's *Thriller*, with over 60 million copies sold.)

The progressive trend of the late 1970s and early 1980s was Punk Rock and its immediate spin-off, New Wave. Introduced in Britain in 1977, Punk was not so much a new sound as a new development in theatrics and rebellious, insolent posing, following in the steps of earlier groups that had emphasized glitter and horror (for example, Kiss). But Punk Rock was more camp, static, and gruelingly repetitive than any previous white Rock style. Punk Rock's premiere artists were the Sex Pistols and its chief culture hero was Johnny Rotten. New Wave and "Art Rock" were each more serious and more adventurous in lyric content and in exploring electronic tone colors.

Trends toward Punk Rock and its derivatives abated in the mid-1980s, a period of general conservatism in the arts and politics. The focus of popular music and mainstream rock during this time veered somewhat away from musical groups ("bands") in favor of solo singers, such as Madonna and Bruce Springsteen.

The experiments of new wave, or mainstream rock for that matter, would not have been possible without significant advances in electronic technology. Gradually electronic organs had become more and more enhanced, then were finally replaced by electronic synthesizers. Some of these had computer capabilities for storing a large number of preprogrammed settings, or they could be interfaced to personal computers via MIDI technology. Synthesizers of all sorts opened the door to processing sound in ways far more sophisticated than previously possible with simple echo, delay, and so forth. Recorded sound had come a long way from the tile bathroom or sewer pipe "echo chamber."

Newer, Higher Technology

One industry development of the early 1970s was quadraphonic sound: four tracks of music played through speakers in four corners of the listening space. At first, it appeared that "quad" would be a success. It was naturally adaptable to eight-track cartridges. However, phonograph records presented their own special problems. Quad signals had to be encoded onto discs, and two rival systems of encoding-decoding developed. The large consumer expense to upgrade equipment to quad and the industry's failure to arrive at a single format were responsible for the ultimate demise of a home application for quadraphonic sound.

A technical quest which did have continuing discoveries and successes was the search for better noise reduction and wider dynamic range. Although the Dolby A and B methods were in common use throughout the 1970s and early 1980s, they reduced only high-frequency noise (like tape hiss). Other interference, such as record surface noise, was not affected. In the late 1970s compression/expansion systems like dbx were introduced to reduce overall noise and extend the dynamic range. A full-range Dolby C system was also developed.

Beginning in 1978, the state-of-the-art solution to noise reduction and expanded dynamic range became the *digital* recording of master studio tapes. At first this process was used only for classical masters made for independent "audiophile" labels. However, within a few years several recording studios boasted digital recording equipment used for all types of music. The phonograph records made from digital master tapes were playable on conventional stereo equipment.

In early 1983 a completely digital disc player was introduced in the United

States. It played a small, laser-read compact disc (CD). Noise and distortion were practically nonexistent on the CD, and its dynamic range was wider than that of any previous commercial recording system. By early 1987 CD players held a place among high-demand electronic equipment (alongside videocassette recorders), and record retailers devoted more and more space to CDs.

Classical Recordings

The tradition of recording concert music and opera was established in the earliest years of the industry, and CBS (now Sony), RCA (now BMG), and several other major U.S. labels have always maintained separate Classical divisions or affiliate Classical labels. Classical record producers have often held elite positions in their companies. However, in the United States Classical records generally do not make money. Few releases on even the large U.S. labels ever break even, but the income from a major label's popular records has usually been sufficient to offset these deficits. While classical sales in the United States are relatively small, Europe's tradition of listening to Classical music has contributed to the financial success of major European labels.

For budgetary reasons major domestic labels have threatened from time to time to close their Classical record operations. However, this has rarely happened, probably because the issue involves a desire on the part of major record companies for prestige and for credit for visible contributions to artistic culture. Though the number of Classical listeners in the United States is relatively small, it is more constant, stable, and loyal than the pop/rock market.

For a number of years Beethoven was the most recorded classical composer, with Mozart and Bach alternating in second and third places. At this writing Mozart recordings are in the lead. There have been numerous significant Classical recording artists over the years: conductors, instrumental soloists, and opera singers, only a few of whom can be mentioned here.

The most celebrated American conductor has been Leonard Bernstein, music director of the New York Philharmonic Orchestra from 1958 to 1969, and guest conductor with many orchestras around the world. His first recording of Beethoven's Symphony No. 5 was particularly successful, since it originally appeared in conjunction with his own noteworthy TV special on Beethoven. Austrian-born conductor Herbert von Karajan, with about nine hundred albums to his credit (mainly with the Berlin Philharmonic Orchestra and the Vienna State Opera), is the most recorded conductor in history. Sir Georg Solti, former music director of the Chicago Symphony Orchestra, has won over two dozen Grammy® awards, more than any other artist, popular or Classical.

Solo artists are even more visible as stars in the Classical field. Probably the most durable Classical recording artist was the late Artur Rubinstein, pianist, who began concertizing around 1900 and made his last appearance in 1976. His prodigious recorded output includes the complete piano music of Chopin and three LP versions of the five Beethoven piano concertos. In the field of vocal music the biggest sensation of recent years has been tenor Luciano Pavarotti. His career began in the early 1960s, and in the 1970s his international popularity snowballed. Pavarotti's recordings have consistently appeared among the top-selling classical albums since the late 1970s.

The 1980s

American taste and the U.S. market for records and tapes splintered and broadened to an extreme degree in the 1980s. A 1984 report issued by the Recording Industry Association of America (RIAA), covering the years 1979–1983, identified no fewer than ten distinct "music types": Rock, Country, Pop/Easy Listening, Black/Dance, Gospel, Classical, Shows/Soundtracks, Jazz, Children's, and other (Ethnic, Nostalgia, Folk, Latin, and so forth).

The fast-spreading popularity of the compact disc (CD) prompted some new trends since its introduction in 1983. CDs helped to revitalize a previously ailing audio industry by sparking new interest in recorded sound, encompassing all musical tastes. In addition, new markets for older recordings were opened by new digital remasterings, notably the 1987 reissue of the complete Beatles recordings.

In the CD's first four years, sales in the United States soared from 800,000 to 53 million units. This momentum increased even more in 1987 and contributed significantly to a total of $5.57 billion sales of all recorded audio products, the highest figure posted since 1978. A trend began in 1987 to shut down LP pressing plants and to construct new CD manufacturing facilities, both in the United States and abroad. By the end of 1988 over fifty U.S. CD plants were in operation. That figure more than tripled during the next five years. The acceptance of the CD was phenomenal.

The 1990s: Paving the Information Superhighway

Popular trends in music both regressed and progressed as the 1980s passed into the 1990s. As "baby-boomers" (people born between 1946 and 1964) aged, the market for older "Classic" Rock revived. The most audible evidence of this trend was in the proliferation of "oldies" radio stations.

The popularity of Country music continued to explode as the decade began. This growth was associated with a new generation of "Young Country" artists, led by Garth Brooks, including Clint Black, Reba McEntire, and Billy Ray Cyrus. The 1990s have also seen the rise of such artists as Mark Chestnutt, Brooks & Dunn, Kathy Mattea, and Mary Chapin Carpenter.

Although the early 1990s called its newest music "Modern Rock," the cutting edge among popular styles became "Rap" or "Hip-Hop." Originating among black artists, this half-spoken, half-played music spread to white artists as far afield as Christian music. A classic Rap artist has been MC Hammer, and among the

	1990	1991	1992	1993	1994
Rock	36.1	34.8	31.6	30.2	35.1
Country	9.6	12.8	17.4	18.7	16.3
Pop	13.7	12.1	11.5	11.9	10.3
Urban Contemporary	11.6	9.9	9.8	10.5	9.6
Rap	8.5	10.0	8.6	9.2	7.9
Classical	3.1	3.2	3.7	3.3	3.7
Jazz	4.8	4.0	3.8	3.1	3.0
Gospel	2.5	3.8	2.8	3.2	3.3
Soundtracks	0.8	0.7	0.7	0.7	1.0
Children's	0.5	0.3	0.5	0.4	0.4
Other	7.5	6.5	7.4	6.6	9.2

Figure 1-2. Five-year comparison: percent of sales (dollar volume) for various style on CD, CD single, cassette, cassette single, and music video software. (*Source: Recording Industry Association of America.*)

most controversial groups is 2 Live Crew. The RIAA created a category for Rap separate from other musical classifications, which include Rock, Country, Pop, Urban Contemporary, Classical, Jazz, Gospel, soundtracks, and children's music. Figure 1–2 is an illustration of consumer buying trends between 1990 and 1994.

In the early years of the 1990s one thing became clear: digital technology was here to stay and was to be the wave of the future. Consumers could see it in the disappearance of vinyl products from record racks. (Conventional LPs and vinyl single records continue to be manufactured, but in only minute quantities: in 1994, less than 2 million LPs and less than 13 million singles.)

It seemed natural that digital audio recorders for the home should follow closely behind the CD. However, due to conflicts between hardware manufacturers and coalitions of recording and copyright interests, the introduction of home digital media recorders was delayed until 1992. The chief issues were safeguarding the music industry against illegal copying and establishing royalties to cover home taping. (See Chapter 2.) Digital Audio Tape (DAT) machines, originally planned for consumers, came into more widespread use on the professional level, largely due to their higher price. In 1992 two competing consumer products entered the digital audio arena: the Sony MiniDisc (MD) and the Mitushita/Philips Digital Compact Cassette (DCC). Both the MD and the DCC are recordable on portable "Walkman"-size machines, using magnetic media. The DCC is a small tape cassette, and the MD is a minidisc similar to a computer floppy disk. Record companies have been quick to issue pre-recorded products in both formats.

Desktop CD recorders ("burners") also became a reality in the early 1990s, but hardware costs have been prohibitive to consumers thus far. In 1994 a new type of video "enhanced" CD was introduced. These can play audio on regular CD players, and on computers with CD-ROM drives they also offer graphics, music video, and written text.

Satellite-cable now delivers dozens of music channels featuring digital-quality sound, and digital television is just around the corner. It seems that the music and entertainment industries are about to embark on the fabled Information Superhighway. In a commentary column published in *Billboard* (July 9, 1994) AFTRA Executive Director Bruce York predicted:

> New digital technologies will entertain and excite us all in ways that we never dreamed possible, and the march of technology is not stopping or slowing. Music is, and will be, delivered to us through our computers, our phones, cable, and satellite. Soon new services will allow us to call up individual tracks or entire digital recordings on demand in our homes, or receive them in our cars, bypassing manufacturers of CDs and retail outlets altogether.

Review Questions

1. Who was the inventor of practical phonograph recording, and who developed the disc format for records?

2. What type of music predominated on records before 1920?

3. What connections did the major record companies have with radio starting in the 1920s?

4. Who was Jack Kapp, and what did he accomplish?

5. What was Tin Pan Alley?

6. Name two or three leaders of "big" bands in the 1930s.

7. Describe the "war of the speeds" and the events leading up to it.

8. What service did "music-and-news" radio formatting provide to the record business?

9. Name two or three recording artists of the 1950s who popularized Rock 'n' Roll.

10. Discuss how the youth market (beginning in the 1950s) has affected recording artists, record producers, and record companies.

11. When did stereophonic sound develop?

12. Describe some aspects of the record business that developed along with the rise of Rock music.

13. Who were some of Motown's top recording artists in the 1960s?

14. Describe two or three technological developments in recording during the 1960s and 1970s.

15. When did digital recording develop?

16. Name two or three major Classical recording artists (or conductors).

17. When did the Country music explosion occur? Name one of the artists involved.

18. What is the difference between a CD, a MD, and a DCC?

Songs: Songwriting, Publishing, Copyright, and Performing Rights

A song is the main starting point in the popular music recording industry. The original creation, like a spark with fuel, starts everything running—publishing, recording sessions, record sales, radio and TV airplay, promotion, concerts, and more. The song is the recording artist's vehicle of expression and emotion. Choosing songs for recording and making decisions on their musical treatment are always serious matters, but they also involve personal belief, aesthetic sensibilities, and almost as much intuition as was required to create the song itself. On the other hand, successful songs are also extremely valuable as commodities, enabling large profits and royalties to be earned by songwriters, publishers, record producers, performers, and record companies.

This chapter and the next will explain the process of the recording industry from writing songs to the purchase of records by the public. The present chapter concerns itself principally with the position of songs and other musical creations in the industry. However, before delving into the issue of songs, a short section on the recording industry as a whole will provide some general perspectives.

The Recording Industry: A Brief Overview

Unlike most industries outside the arts, the recording industry does not always follow established patterns of ownership, operation, and distribution. It is true that there are definite distinctions between the various functions and activities within the industry—songwriting, publishing, performing, producing, manufacturing, and marketing records. However, in the business itself these functions are not always operated as separate entities, or even by separate individuals. For example, a publishing firm may be an affiliate company of a record corporation or a motion picture studio. An independent record producer may also write songs, publish, and perhaps own a recording studio. Recording artists may publish their own songs and produce their own records. As an extreme example, in the late 1960s The Beatles established an entire music conglomerate, The Apple Corps, which included a record label (Apple Records), publishing companies, record production, film production, and artist management.

The recording industry is an intricate maze of activities. There is a considerable amount of crossover and integration between one activity and another. It is therefore helpful to learn about the industry by separating these various activities. For the sake of theory and clearer understanding, each activity, such as *songwriting, publishing,* or *record producing,* will be referred to as if it were handled by a different person from the others. Each activity will be explained in this chapter and the next. However, because of the industry's complexity, here is a brief overview of processes involving the main activities.

A songwriter writes a song and submits it to a publisher. Under contract with the songwriter, the publisher owns the copyright on the song. A record producer makes an agreement with the publisher to have his artist record the song. The producer makes all the necessary arrangements for a recording session, and the artist records the song. The record company manufactures compact discs (CDs) and cassettes from the recorded master tape. The distributors and rack jobbers place the CDs and cassettes in retail outlets. Promotion of the recording may include press releases, advertising, radio and TV airplay, live concerts, TV appearances by the artist, and a promotional music video of the song. (See Figure 2–1 for a flowchart of activities, extending from the original song to the consumer.)

Radio and TV make their profits from the sale of advertising time. The retailer, rack jobber, distributor, and record company make their profit from the sale of CDs and cassettes. The record company pays the artist a royalty on each unit sold. The record company gives the producer one or a combination of the following: outright payment, a salary (plus bonus royalties), a royalty. Through a licensing agency (or directly), the record company pays the publisher a royalty on each recording sold. The publisher pays the songwriter a portion (normally 50 percent) of royalties collected. A performing-rights organization collects fees for all performances of the song (principally radio and TV airplay), splits the income fifty-fifty between publisher and songwriter, and pays each of them separately. (See Figure 2–5.)

Songwriting

The recording industry places a premium on artists or acts that come as a package, a trend that has continued since the 1960s. That is, the artist or group writes

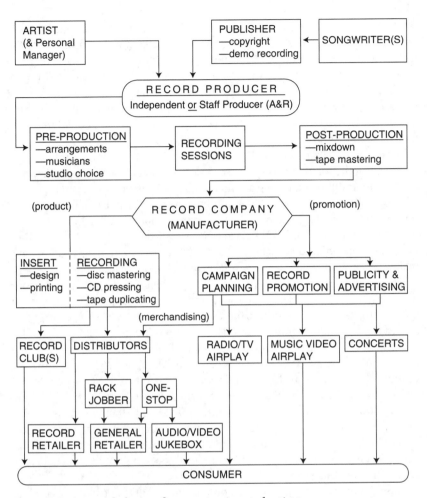

Figure 2-1. A recorded song, from songwriter and artist to consumer.

its own song material and performs it with little need for outside help. Many of the most popular artists in all styles of popular music fall into this category. But some singers write only a portion of what they sing, and many others are strictly performers. These artists are in constant need of new material for recordings, concerts, and club engagements. Likewise, there are many good songwriters who do not perform, at least not for a living. They compose and write, either on a full-time basis or as a sideline, and depend on prominent artists to record and make hits of their songs.

As with most creative endeavors, a formal education can help a songwriter but is not absolutely essential. Many successful songwriters neither read nor write musical notation. The classic example is Irving Berlin, who played piano by ear (in only one key) and had someone else write down all his songs. Sufficient talent to create a successful song is most important.

A song's two most basic elements are the tune (melody and implied harmony) and the lyrics (words). Some songwriters have the ability to compose both the tune and lyrics to their songs. More often a song is the product of a collaboration between two (or occasionally more) people. Both songwriters may work on the music and lyrics together, or they may function separately, one as composer and the other as lyricist. If composing and lyric writing are separate, either the tune or the lyric may be drafted first. Many composers prefer most or all of the lyrics to be written first, so that the lyrics can suggest a tune.

One goal of songwriters is to earn income from their songs, and that can come only if the songs receive public exposure. The best and most lucrative type of exposure results from having a song recorded by a major artist. But that is not always possible at first. Besides soliciting artists' managers, publishers, record producers, and record labels, songwriters will often try to establish a limited reputation at first and then build on that to open bigger doors. They may show their work to talented friends or local artists, who then perform the songs and perhaps make demonstration tapes of them. Songwriters may play the demonstration tapes for local music industry people, like disc jockeys, to get their reactions. Some songwriters try for semiprofessional recognition by entering a song contest.

Unfortunately for songwriters, there is usually much more involved in getting a song commercially recorded than whether it has the potential of being a hit. Some concerns are political and some are purely business. However, rarely can these problems be solved by the songwriter alone. They usually require the intervention of a function in the music industry known as publishing. Under the copyright law, ownership of all rights to a song resides initially with the songwriter. However, in order to have a song recorded and otherwise exploited it is usually necessary for a songwriter to turn ownership of the song over to a publisher. Publishers' livelihoods depend on their ability to find good new songs and to effectively promote and achieve commercial recordings of them. That is precisely what the songwriter needs.

If songwriters want their songs recorded, why can't they deal directly with an artist or a record company? They can, but if a song is accepted, they will sign a contract with the publishing arm (or affiliate) of the artist's business or that of the record company anyway. The reason for this is that when the first U.S. copyright law was written (1909), print music publishing was the dominant music industry. "Mechanical" performances, such as phonograph recordings, were treated in a subordinate manner, separate from the main business at that time. The music industry has continued to be structured to include an activity called "publishing," even though the meaning of the word—and the business itself—has changed drastically over the years.

Song Publishers in the Recording Industry

To most people the term "music publishing" connotes a business concerned with *print* music. Originally, before the player piano and the phonograph, print music was a publisher's sole concern. As the record industry grew, publishers continued to be powerful figures, chiefly because they supplied most of the new songs and they controlled the copyrights on them. However, over the years the importance of popular sheet music sales has declined in inverse proportion to the success of recordings. There are still music publishers whose main job is to produce print music, but most of them are not directly connected with the commercial recording industry. (See the section "The Print Music Business" in Chapter 10.)

Today there are several types of music publishers, and even the legal definition of the word "publishing" is far more general than it once was. Several thousand publishing businesses have less public visibility than the mainline companies but are still classifiable as publishers. These are the recording industry's song publishers, the ones with whom songwriters are most likely to become affiliated. A few of these are established purely as publishing operations, with little or no owned interest in record production or artist management. More prevalent is the independently named publishing company owned and controlled by one of the following: an independent record producer or production company; a record label or its parent company; a motion-picture studio or its parent company; or a songwriter, recording artist, or songwriter-artist, often in partnership with a personal or business manager.

One of the song publisher's functions is to promote and exploit the songs he has under contract, and sometimes it is possible to obtain a reasonably secure commitment to record as soon as a songwriter contract is issued. Most of the very active publishers are constantly bombarded with new material, and the songwriter fortunate enough to gain the attention of one of these insiders has moved closer to obtaining the desired goal.

The other function of modern song publishers is copyright administration. That is, the publisher is interested in collecting revenue from all sources to which he is entitled as a copyright owner. There are three primary sources of income that may be derived from a song: licensed performances (chiefly on radio or TV); mechanical reproductions and synchronizations (recordings, motion pictures, videos, and so forth); and print music. (See Figures 2–2 and 2–5.)

The first source is handled by separate agreements which the songwriter and publisher have made individually with one of the performing-rights organizations (see below). The last two sources are managed by the publisher by means of a contract with the songwriter. There are also a few less common sources of income. One is known as "derivative works," an example of which would be a commercial jingle derived from a popular song.

It is easy to see how physically impossible it would be for a songwriter to write new songs and at the same time promote them and manage the income from all sources for all his existing songs. The songwriter and publisher need one another.

The Contract: The Songwriter-Publisher Link —————

A publisher can earn revenue from a song only by owning the copyright t
publisher obtains ownership of a copyright through his contract with
writer. A songwriter's royalty contract is an agreement between the p

the songwriter (here, a collective term for composer and lyricist together). Briefly, the contract provides that the copyright to a song be transferred to the publisher in exchange for a portion of future income from the song. Although the exact terms and other details may vary greatly from contract to contract, there are five main points contained in all songwriter royalty contracts:

1. The songwriter warrants that the song is his own original work and that he has the power to make the contract with no outside claims on the work.

2. The songwriter assigns to the publisher the right to secure a copyright registration of the song.

3. The publisher promises to pay the songwriter a percentage of all his income from mechanical reproduction licenses (records, movie synchronization, videos, and so forth) derived from the song. (This is called the basic "royalty," and the accepted rate is 50 percent.)

4. The publisher also promises to pay a royalty to the songwriter for the sale of printed copies of the song. The percentage will vary and may depend on whether the publisher is also in the print business himself or if the printing is contracted out to a sub-publisher.

5. The publisher promises to pay a royalty (usually 50 percent) on any income from foreign sources (recording licenses, performance licenses, printed music, and so forth).

There may be many other details and limitations covered in a songwriter contract. A provision may appear for making a "demo" recording of the song, if it is necessary and a suitable one does not exist. If more than one songwriter is involved, the contract must specify the percentage of the songwriters' royalties to be paid to each. Certain clauses may be included in some publishers' contracts but not in others. For example, a clause that would favor the songwriter would be one that guaranteed a 50 percent royalty on all sources of income not otherwise specified in the contract. That would cover future forms of recording and alterations in the law that could generate unforeseen payments to the copyright owner.

There is no single standard contract, and the form contract offered initially to a new songwriter is apt to favor the publisher. Experienced songwriters, especially those with a strong reputation (or track record) for writing hits, can usually negotiate better terms than those in the publisher's form contract. There is an organization of songwriters, the Songwriters Guild, which has devised its own songwriter's royalty contract. Naturally, it tends to favor the songwriter in many ways. Some publishers will accept the Songwriters Guild contract only for certain prominent songwriters, and many will not sign it at all.

The publisher has been introduced as a song promoter and an administrator of copyrights. Mention has also been made of the three primary sources of income to which the publisher, as copyright owner, is entitled. The underlying policy which has shaped these sources and determined the direction of music

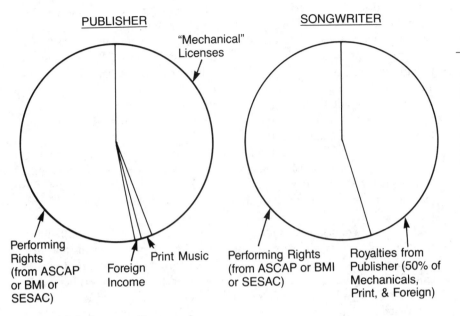

PUBLISHER

SONGWRITER

"Mechanical" Licenses

Performing Rights (from ASCAP or BMI or SESAC)

Foreign Income

Print Music

Performing Rights (from ASCAP or BMI or SESAC)

Royalties from Publisher (50% of Mechanicals, Print, & Foreign)

Figure 2-2. Sources of income from songs.

publishing is the copyright law itself. Since music publishing and recording involve the exercise of the powers of copyright ownership, it will be helpful to devote a section of this chapter to a condensed review of the present copyright law, especially as it applies to songs.

The Copyright Law

The spirit of copyright law is the exclusive right to copy and publish one's own work. That is, the copyright owner has the right to duplicate or authorize the duplication of his property, and to distribute it, whether for profit or not. What follows is the law's elaboration of this idea presented in a shortened, simplified manner. If greater detail is needed, the reader should refer to one of the texts listed at the end of this book or to the Copyright Act itself: Public Law 94–553—October 19, 1976.

History

The first comprehensive U.S. copyright statute was enacted in 1909. It protected musical copyright owners chiefly against unauthorized copying of sheet music. Provisions for licensing "mechanical instruments," such as piano rolls and phonograph recordings, as well as synchronization rights, also appeared in the law. However, there was no protection for the performance of music or for "sound recordings" per se. As a result, the old law could not later be invoked against piracy, the recording industry's worst enemy. Other business laws and court precedents had to be cited, but none very successfully. When jukeboxes became another potential source of income for copyright owners, jukebox operators were untouchable under any existing law. As early as the 1950s, there was serious discussion in Congress and in the music industry about revising the copyright law. However, drafting a new act was extremely problematic due to the conflicting interests of many industries.

In the music business, copyright no longer touched just songwriters and publishers; entirely new industries had been developed. Chief among these were motion pictures, television, and an expanded recording industry. Within the recording industry there were strongly differing points of view concerning licensing rates.

Jukebox operators, who exerted an extremely powerful lobby, were fighting any change in the law which would threaten their freedom from paying royalties. In 1972 Congress passed a law extending copyright protection to performances embodied on "phonorecords" (chiefly records and tapes). This was helpful in combating piracy, but it was not the total answer. An entirely new copyright act was passed in 1976, and it took effect January 1, 1978. This is the current law and the source for the discussion below.

Certain provisions of the 1976 Copyright Law were modelled on the Berne Convention for the Protection of Literary and Artistic Works, a treaty among most nations of the world. The most notable feature was the new duration of copyright (see below). The United States was not a member of the Berne Convention then, but there was a growing concern that intellectual property by U.S. authors was not properly protected on the international level. Thus, our new law paved the way for Berne membership. In 1988, Congress passed an act bringing us into full compliance with Berne, and the United States officially became a member of the Berne Convention in 1989. There have been no dramatic changes in our copyright law as a result. However, we gained reciprocal copyright protection in at least 24 nations with whom we had no previous copyright treaties. In addition, the U.S. creative community gained new prerogatives under the Berne moral rights standard, which provides that an author

> shall have the right to claim authorship of [his or her] work and to object to any distortion, mutilation, or other modification of, or other derogatory action in relation to [his or her] work, which would be prejudicial to [his or her] honor or reputation.

Joining Berne enabled the United States to take a more influential role in drafting the international General Agreement on Tariffs and Trade (GATT), which the United States signed in 1994. This agreement supplements the Berne Convention, enabling us to obtain maximum protection for intellectual property on the international level.

When, in the late 1980s, audio hardware manufacturers prepared to introduce Digital Audio Tape (DAT) recording machines in the United States, a wave of panic overtook the music industry. Songwriters, music publishers, record companies, and the Musicians Union were all deeply concerned that large sales revenues might be lost due to piracy and innocent home audio taping using digital equipment. These interests wished to prevent a recurrence of their losses when home cassette taping became popular. The Audio Recording Coalition and the Copyright Coalition were formed and successfully delayed the U.S. marketing of DAT machines by threat of a class action lawsuit against manufacturers. Ultimately, these coalitions and the Electronics Industries Association arrived at a compromise basis for legislation: a set of hardware safeguards against piracy and a royalty system for the sale of hardware and blank digital audio tape. These provisions became the basis for the Audio Home Recording Act passed by Congress in 1992 (see below).

Digital technology has also brought with it other copyright concerns. One heavily discussed issue is the digital "sampling" of sound recordings. Simple, accessible sampling equipment can lift a chunk of previously recorded material and insert it into a new recording with crystal clarity. This technology has led to some alleged abuses of copyright. One lawsuit involved a 2 Live Crew recording that used digital technology to parody Roy Orbison's recording of "Pretty Woman." This case, Campbell v. Acuff-Rose Music, Inc., reached the Supreme Court in 1994. Unexpectedly, the Court ruled that parody (defined by court precedent) may be a fair use exemption from the copyright law. The ruling specifies that the new recording *must satirize* the original, however, and leaves case-by-case rulings to lower courts.

Another contemporary issue is performing rights for sound recordings. Under the present law, the right of public performance (see below) applies only to musical works, not the sound recordings that embody them. Record companies claim this is a "glitch" in the copyright law. With the onslaught of digital communications technology, these companies fear that future delivery systems will enable consumers to bypass purchasing their products. Thus they advocate performance licensing for individual recordings (in broadcast communications), not just the songs the recordings contain. Although legislation has yet to appear, the position is supported by recording industry unions whose members would benefit from new sources of record company income. Opponents include performing-rights organizations (see below) and music publishers, who feel their rights could be subordinated by such an amendment.

Definitions

There are seven important terms used in portions of the Copyright Act pertaining to music. Since these terms and their definitions are very precise, much of the following is given verbatim from the law itself and related government publications.

1. *Author*—The individual(s) who actually created the work. The term "author" is used collectively to include all contributors—composer(s) and lyricist(s) in the case of songs.

FORM PA
For a Work of the Performing Arts
UNITED STATES COPYRIGHT OFFICE

REGISTRATION NUMBER

PA	PAU

EFFECTIVE DATE OF REGISTRATION

Month	Day	Year

DO NOT WRITE ABOVE THIS LINE. IF YOU NEED MORE SPACE, USE A SEPARATE CONTINUATION SHEET.

1

TITLE OF THIS WORK ▼

Need You So Bad

PREVIOUS OR ALTERNATIVE TITLES ▼

NATURE OF THIS WORK ▼ See instructions

words, music

2 **a**

NAME OF AUTHOR ▼
Mary Jones

DATES OF BIRTH AND DEATH
Year Born ▼ 1972   Year Died ▼

Was this contribution to the work a "work made for hire"?
☐ Yes
☒ No

AUTHOR'S NATIONALITY OR DOMICILE
Name of Country
OR { Citizen of ▶ U.S.A.
Domiciled in ▶

WAS THIS AUTHOR'S CONTRIBUTION TO THE WORK
Anonymous? ☐ Yes ☒ No
Pseudonymous? ☐ Yes ☒ No
If the answer to either of these questions is "Yes," see detailed instructions.

NATURE OF AUTHORSHIP Briefly describe nature of material created by this author in which copyright is claimed. ▼
music

NOTE

b

NAME OF AUTHOR ▼
Joe Smith

DATES OF BIRTH AND DEATH
Year Born ▼ 1974   Year Died ▼

Under the law, the "author" of a "work made for hire" is generally the employer, not the employee (see instructions). For any part of this work that was "made for hire" check "Yes" in the space provided, give the employer (or other person for whom the work was prepared) as "Author" of that part, and leave the space for dates of birth and death blank.

Was this contribution to the work a "work made for hire"?
☐ Yes
☒ No

AUTHOR'S NATIONALITY OR DOMICILE
Name of Country
OR { Citizen of ▶ U.S.A.
Domiciled in ▶

WAS THIS AUTHOR'S CONTRIBUTION TO THE WORK
Anonymous? ☐ Yes ☒ No
Pseudonymous? ☐ Yes ☒ No
If the answer to either of these questions is "Yes," see detailed instructions.

NATURE OF AUTHORSHIP Briefly describe nature of material created by this author in which copyright is claimed. ▼
words

c

NAME OF AUTHOR ▼

DATES OF BIRTH AND DEATH
Year Born ▼   Year Died ▼

Was this contribution to the work a "work made for hire"?
☐ Yes
☐ No

AUTHOR'S NATIONALITY OR DOMICILE
Name of Country
OR { Citizen of ▶
Domiciled in ▶

WAS THIS AUTHOR'S CONTRIBUTION TO THE WORK
Anonymous? ☐ Yes ☐ No
Pseudonymous? ☐ Yes ☐ No
If the answer to either of these questions is "Yes," see detailed instructions.

NATURE OF AUTHORSHIP Briefly describe nature of material created by this author in which copyright is claimed. ▼

3 **a**

YEAR IN WHICH CREATION OF THIS WORK WAS COMPLETED This information must be given
1996 ◀ Year in all cases.

b DATE AND NATION OF FIRST PUBLICATION OF THIS PARTICULAR WORK
Complete this information ONLY if this work has been published.
Month ▶ June   Day ▶ 15   Year ▶ 1996
U.S.A. ◀ Nation

4

See instructions before completing this space.

COPYRIGHT CLAIMANT(S) Name and address must be given even if the claimant is the same as the author given in space 2. ▼
ABC Music Publishing
100 E. Sunset Blvd.
Hollywood, CA 90028

APPLICATION RECEIVED

ONE DEPOSIT RECEIVED

TWO DEPOSITS RECEIVED

FUNDS RECEIVED

DO NOT WRITE HERE OFFICE USE ONLY

TRANSFER If the claimant(s) named here in space 4 is (are) different from the author(s) named in space 2, give a brief statement of how the claimant(s) obtained ownership of the copyright. ▼
Ownership was transferred by agreement with the authors.

MORE ON BACK ▶ • Complete all applicable spaces (numbers 5-9) on the reverse side of this page.
• See detailed instructions. • Sign the form at line 8.

DO NOT WRITE HERE
Page 1 of ____ pages

Figure 2-3. Form PA. Application for copyright registration of a work of the performing arts.

2. *Works* — The basic subject matter of copyright: what the author creates and what copyright protects. The statute draws a sharp distinction between the "work" and "any material object in which the work is embodied." Thus, the work is an abstract entity in itself, distinct from any printed or recorded representation of it. (Form PA is used to register the copyright of a musical work. See Figure 2–3.)

EXAMINED BY		FORM PA
CHECKED BY		
	CORRESPONDENCE ☐ Yes	FOR COPYRIGHT OFFICE USE ONLY

DO NOT WRITE ABOVE THIS LINE. IF YOU NEED MORE SPACE, USE A SEPARATE CONTINUATION SHEET.

PREVIOUS REGISTRATION Has registration for this work, or for an earlier version of this work, already been made in the Copyright Office?

☐ Yes ☐ No If your answer is "Yes," why is another registration being sought? (Check appropriate box) ▼

a. ☐ This is the first published edition of a work previously registered in unpublished form.

b. ☐ This is the first application submitted by this author as copyright claimant.

c. ☐ This is a changed version of the work, as shown by space 6 on this application.

If your answer is "Yes," give: **Previous Registration Number** ▼   **Year of Registration** ▼

5

DERIVATIVE WORK OR COMPILATION Complete both space 6a and 6b for a derivative work; complete only 6b for a compilation.

a. **Preexisting Material** Identify any preexisting work or works that this work is based on or incorporates. ▼

b. **Material Added to This Work** Give a brief, general statement of the material that has been added to this work and in which copyright is claimed. ▼

6

See instructions before completing this space.

DEPOSIT ACCOUNT If the registration fee is to be charged to a Deposit Account established in the Copyright Office, give name and number of Account.

Name ▼   **Account Number** ▼

7

CORRESPONDENCE Give name and address to which correspondence about this application should be sent.   Name/Address/Apt/City/State/ZIP ▼

William Johnson
ABC Music Publishing
100 E. Sunset Blvd.
Hollywood, CA 90028

Area Code and Telephone Number ▶ (213) 555-1000

Be sure to give your daytime phone number ◀

CERTIFICATION* I, the undersigned, hereby certify that I am the

Check only one ▼

☐ author

☐ other copyright claimant

☐ owner of exclusive right(s)

☒ authorized agent of ABC Music Publishing

Name of author or other copyright claimant, or owner of exclusive right(s) ▲

8

of the work identified in this application and that the statements made by me in this application are correct to the best of my knowledge.

Typed or printed name and date ▼ If this application gives a date of publication in space 3, do not sign and submit it before that date.

William Johnson   date ▶ 6-18-96

☞ Handwritten signature (X) ▼   *William Johnson*

MAIL CERTIFI-CATE TO	Name ▼ ABC Music Publishing	YOU MUST: • Complete all necessary spaces • Sign your application in space 8
Certificate will be mailed in window envelope	Number/Street/Apartment Number ▼ 100 E. Sunset Blvd.	SEND ALL 3 ELEMENTS IN THE SAME PACKAGE: 1. Application form 2. Nonrefundable $20 filing fee in check or money order payable to *Register of Copyrights* 3. Deposit material
	City/State/ZIP ▼ Hollywood, CA 90028	MAIL TO: Register of Copyrights Library of Congress Washington, D.C. 20559-6000

9

*17 U.S.C. § 506(e): Any person who knowingly makes a false representation of a material fact in the application for copyright registration provided for by section 409, or in any written statement filed in connection with the application, shall be fined not more than $2,500.

January 1995—400,000 ♻ PRINTED ON RECYCLED PAPER   ☆U.S. GOVERNMENT PRINTING OFFICE: 1995-387-237/33

3. *Ownership*—The ownership of a copyright, or of any of the exclusive rights under a copyright, is distinct from ownership of any material object in which a work is embodied. Although this may seem obvious, the statute indicates that the mere ownership of, let us say, a manuscript copy or a phonorecord does not give a person the copyright to a work.

4. *Copies,* 5. *Phonorecords*—These are the two types of material objects in which "works" are embodied. In general, *copies* are objects from which a

work can be read or visually perceived, directly or with the aid of a machine or device, such as a manuscripts, a book, sheet music, film, or videotape. *Phonorecords* are objects embodying fixations of sounds, such as CDs, cassettes, MDs, DCCs, DATs, and phonograph discs. For example, a song (the "work") can be reproduced in sheet music ("copies") or on records/tapes/compact discs ("phonorecords"), or all of these.

FORM SR

For a Sound Recording
UNITED STATES COPYRIGHT OFFICE

REGISTRATION NUMBER

SR _____ SRU _____
EFFECTIVE DATE OF REGISTRATION

Month _____ Day _____ Year _____

DO NOT WRITE ABOVE THIS LINE. IF YOU NEED MORE SPACE, USE A SEPARATE CONTINUATION SHEET.

1

TITLE OF THIS WORK ▼

Need You So Bad

PREVIOUS OR ALTERNATIVE TITLES ▼

NATURE OF MATERIAL RECORDED ▼ See instructions
☒ Musical ☐ Musical-Dramatic
☐ Dramatic ☐ Literary
☐ Other _____

2 **a**

NAME OF AUTHOR ▼
Melanie Cottrell

DATES OF BIRTH AND DEATH
Year Born ▼ 1976 Year Died ▼

Was this contribution to the work a "work made for hire"?
☐ Yes
☒ No

AUTHOR'S NATIONALITY OR DOMICILE
Name of Country
OR { Citizen of ▶ U.S.A.
{ Domiciled in ▶

WAS THIS AUTHOR'S CONTRIBUTION TO THE WORK
Anonymous? ☐ Yes ☒ No
Pseudonymous? ☐ Yes ☒ No
If the answer to either of these questions is "Yes," see detailed instructions.

NATURE OF AUTHORSHIP Briefly describe nature of material created by this author in which copyright is claimed. ▼
performance

NOTE

Under the law, the "author" of a "work made for hire" is generally the employer, not the employee (see instructions). For any part of this work that was "made for hire," check "Yes" in the space provided, give the employer (or other person for whom the work was prepared) as "Author" of that part, and leave the space for dates of birth and death blank.

b

NAME OF AUTHOR ▼
Duke Hanrahan

DATES OF BIRTH AND DEATH
Year Born ▼ 1951 Year Died ▼

Was this contribution to the work a "work made for hire"?
☐ Yes
☒ No

AUTHOR'S NATIONALITY OR DOMICILE
Name of Country
OR { Citizen of ▶ U.S.A.
{ Domiciled in ▶

WAS THIS AUTHOR'S CONTRIBUTION TO THE WORK
Anonymous? ☐ Yes ☒ No
Pseudonymous? ☐ Yes ☒ No
If the answer to either of these questions is "Yes," see detailed instructions.

NATURE OF AUTHORSHIP Briefly describe nature of material created by this author in which copyright is claimed. ▼
production, creative direction

c

NAME OF AUTHOR ▼

DATES OF BIRTH AND DEATH
Year Born ▼ Year Died ▼

Was this contribution to the work a "work made for hire"?
☐ Yes
☐ No

AUTHOR'S NATIONALITY OR DOMICILE
Name of Country
OR { Citizen of ▶
{ Domiciled in ▶

WAS THIS AUTHOR'S CONTRIBUTION TO THE WORK
Anonymous? ☐ Yes ☐ No
Pseudonymous? ☐ Yes ☐ No
If the answer to either of these questions is "Yes," see detailed instructions.

NATURE OF AUTHORSHIP Briefly describe nature of material created by this author in which copyright is claimed. ▼

3 **a**

YEAR IN WHICH CREATION OF THIS WORK WAS COMPLETED This information must be given in all cases.
1996 ◀ Year

b DATE AND NATION OF FIRST PUBLICATION OF THIS PARTICULAR WORK
Complete this information ONLY if this work has been published.
Month ▶ September Day ▶ 1 Year ▶ 1996
U.S.A. ◀ Nation

4

See instructions before completing this space.

COPYRIGHT CLAIMANT(S) Name and address must be given even if the claimant is the same as the author given in space 2. ▼
X-Y-Z Records, Inc.
200 S. Vine Street
Hollywood, CA 90028

TRANSFER If the claimant(s) named here in space 4 is (are) different from the author(s) named in space 2, give a brief statement of how the claimant(s) obtained ownership of the copyright. ▼
Ownership was tranferred by agreement with the authors.

DO NOT WRITE HERE OFFICE USE ONLY
APPLICATION RECEIVED
ONE DEPOSIT RECEIVED
TWO DEPOSITS RECEIVED
REMITTANCE NUMBER AND DATE

MORE ON BACK ▶ • Complete all applicable spaces (numbers 5-9) on the reverse side of this page.
• See detailed instructions. • Sign the form at line 8.

DO NOT WRITE HERE
Page 1 of _____ pages

Figure 2-4. Form SR. Application for copyright registration for a sound recording.

6. *Sound Recordings*—These are "works," not "copies" or "phonorecords." "Sound recordings" are works that result from the fixation of a series of musical, spoken, or other sounds. Thus, a "sound recording" is a type of "work" distinct from any reproduction of it on tape or disc. (Form SR is used to register the copyright of a sound recording. See Figure 2–4.)

7. *Publication*—Though not a requisite to copyright, publication remains an important concept in copyright law. The Copyright Act defines it in this

EXAMINED BY	FORM SR
CHECKED BY	
☐ CORRESPONDENCE Yes	FOR COPYRIGHT OFFICE USE ONLY

DO NOT WRITE ABOVE THIS LINE. IF YOU NEED MORE SPACE, USE A SEPARATE CONTINUATION SHEET.

PREVIOUS REGISTRATION Has registration for this work, or for an earlier version of this work, already been made in the Copyright Office?
☐ Yes ☐ No If your answer is "Yes," why is another registration being sought? (Check appropriate box) ▼
a. ☐ This is the first published edition of a work previously registered in unpublished form.
b. ☐ This is the first application submitted by this author as copyright claimant.
c. ☐ This is a changed version of the work, as shown by space 6 on this application.
If your answer is "Yes," give: **Previous Registration Number** ▼   **Year of Registration** ▼

5

DERIVATIVE WORK OR COMPILATION Complete both space 6a and 6b for a derivative work; complete only 6b for a compilation.
a. **Preexisting Material** Identify any preexisting work or works that this work is based on or incorporates. ▼

b. **Material Added to This Work** Give a brief, general statement of the material that has been added to this work and in which copyright is claimed. ▼

See instructions before completing this space.

6

DEPOSIT ACCOUNT If the registration fee is to be charged to a Deposit Account established in the Copyright Office, give name and number of Account.
Name ▼   **Account Number** ▼

7

CORRESPONDENCE Give name and address to which correspondence about this application should be sent.   Name/Address/Apt/City/State/ZIP ▼
C.A. Vasquez, X-Y-Z Records, Inc.
200 S. Vine Street
Hollywood, CA 90028

Area Code and Telephone Number ▶ (213) 765-4321

Be sure to give your daytime phone number ◀

CERTIFICATION* I, the undersigned, hereby certify that I am the
Check only one ▼
☐ author
☐ other copyright claimant
☐ owner of exclusive right(s)
☒ authorized agent of X-Y-Z Records, Inc.
Name of author or other copyright claimant, or owner of exclusive right(s) ▲

8

of the work identified in this application and that the statements made by me in this application are correct to the best of my knowledge.

Typed or printed name and date ▼ If this application gives a date of publication in space 3, do not sign and submit it before that date.
Cruz A. Vasquez   date ▶ 9-5-96

☞ Handwritten signature (X) ▼ *Cruz A. Vasquez*

MAIL CERTIFI-CATE TO	Name ▼ X-Y-Z Records, Inc.	YOU MUST: • Complete all necessary spaces • Sign your application in space 8	**9**
	Number/Street/Apartment Number ▼	SEND ALL 3 ELEMENTS IN THE SAME PACKAGE:	
Certificate will be mailed in window envelope	200 S. Vine Stree	1. Application form 2. Nonrefundable $20 filing fee in check or money order payable to *Register of Copyrights* 3. Deposit material	The Copyright Office has the authority to adjust fees at 5-year intervals, based on changes in the Consumer Price Index. The next adjustment is due in 1996.
	City/State/ZIP ▼ Hollywood, CA 90028	MAIL TO: Register of Copyrights Library of Congress Washington, D.C. 20559	Please contact the Copyright Office after July 1995 to determine the actual fee schedule.

*17 U.S.C. § 506(e): Any person who knowingly makes a false representation of a material fact in the application for copyright registration provided for by section 409, or in any written statement filed in connection with the application, shall be fined not more than $2,500.

December 1993—75,000

☆U.S. GOVERNMENT PRINTING OFFICE: 1993-301-241/80,051

way: "'Publication' is the distribution of copies or phonorecords of a work to the public by sale or other transfer of ownership, or by rental, lease, or lending. The offering to distribute copies or phonorecords to a group of persons for purposes of further distribution, public performance, or public display, constitutes publication. A public performance or display of a work does not of itself constitute publication." As a result, performance of a work (live or by broadcast) does not qualify as publication. The work must be made available to the public in some tangible form, or at least an offer must be given to make such tangible forms available.

Upon publication, all "visually perceptible copies" should contain a copyright notice. Usually this is the symbol ©, or the word, Copyright, or abbreviation, "Copr.", together with the year of first publication and the name of the copyright owner. Upon release, all phonorecords should contain a copyright notice. Usually this is the symbol ℗ together with the year of the first release and the name of the sound-recording copyright owner.

Here is an example of the use of these definitions furnished by the Copyright Office: When a record company issues a new release, the release will typically involve two distinct "works": the underlying "musical work" that has been recorded, and the "sound recording" as a separate work in itself. The material objects that the record company sends out are "phonorecords": physical reproductions of both the underlying "musical work" and the "sound recording."

What Is Copyrightable

Copyrightable works are "original works of authorship" including the following: literary works; musical works, including any accompanying words; dramatic works, including any accompanying music; pantomimes and choreographic works; pictorial, graphic, and sculptural works; motion pictures and other audiovisual works; and sound recordings. Since this chapter deals chiefly with songs and their recording, the following discussion stresses the law's application to an individual song, that is, to "musical works" and "sound recordings."

Commencement and Duration of a Copyright

Federal copyright protection of an original work begins as soon as it is "fixed in any tangible medium of expression," such as a manuscript copy or a tape. Copyright continues for the duration of the author's lifetime plus fifty years. For a work created jointly, the term extends for fifty years beyond the death of the last surviving author. After that time the work passes into the public domain and is not copyrightable in its original form. The Copyright Act does not require that a work be registered with the Copyright Office. However, the statute does mention two situations that make registration extremely advisable:

1. In case of infringement, a registration is usually necessary before legal action may be brought. Registration will also establish *prima facie* evidence in court of the validity of the copyright.

2. To be entitled to collect royalties on compulsory licenses for making phonorecords (see below), the owner must be identified in the registration or other public records of the Copyright Office.

Rights Under the Copyright Act

The owner of a copyright has the exclusive right to:

1. Reproduce the copyrighted work in copies or phonorecords. (In the case of songs, these initially take the form of printed music and audio discs and tapes, but may extend to videodiscs and videocassettes as well.)

2. Prepare derivative works based upon the copyrighted work. (Examples of derivative works based on songs are arrangements or adaptations of the music.)

3. Distribute copies or phonorecords of the work to the public by sale or other transfer of ownership, or by rental, lease, or lending. (Although distributing *copies* is usually the business of a publisher or sub-publisher, and distributing *phonorecords* is usually the business of a record company, the right to do these things resides with the current copyright owner. Initially, that is the author, but by agreement these rights may be assigned to another party, such as a publisher.)

4. Perform or display the copyrighted work publicly. (Displaying is more the province of the visual arts. However, the right to perform—or to license performances—is an extremely important one for songwriters and publishers.)

This "bundle of rights" is divisible. That is, any of the above rights may be separated from the rest and transferred or licensed. For example, the right of performance is traditionally separated from the others in songwriter contracts, or omitted entirely. (See the section later in this chapter on Performing Rights Organizations.) Although the life of a copyright is the life of the author plus fifty years, the transfer of any one of the rights may be terminated after thirty-five to forty years under certain circumstances.

Sound Recordings

As stated above, a sound recording is a type of work in itself. Although it is normally based on another work, such as a song, under the Copyright Act a sound recording itself is an entity entirely separate from the musical work it represents. The sound recording of a song is a particular performance version of that song, and as such is fully protected by the statute. In a sound recording there are two elements deemed to be copyrightable:

1. the contributions of the performer(s) whose performance is captured; and

2. the contribution of the record producer who captures and processes the sounds to make the final recording.

Authorship, for the sake of copyright, is given to either the performer(s) or the record producer or both. The Copyright Act itself does not fix authorship and leaves the matter to be worked out between artist and producer. Just as with musical works, ownership of a sound-recording copyright may be transferred to another party. Whereas the author of a song generally transfers ownership to a publisher, the author(s) of a sound recording usually transfer ownership to a record company.

Phonorecords

As indicated above under "Rights Under the Copyright Act," the copyright owner has the right to distribute phonorecords. In practice, this means that the *first* phonorecords may be distributed exclusively (or licensed) under the authority of the copyright owner. For example, the publisher of a song may authorize a particular record company to make and distribute the first recording of that song. After that initial distribution (a form of publication), any other person may obtain a "compulsory license" to make phonorecords of the work and distribute them to the public, but only for the consumer's private use. (This is to protect the original copyright owner's right to offer phonorecords for rent, lease, or loan.) The compulsory license includes the privilege of making a musical arrangement of the work (a derivative work) to the extent necessary to make it conform to the style or manner of interpretation of the performance involved, but the arrangement may not change the basic melody or fundamental character of the work. Obtaining a compulsory license involves merely serving notice on the copyright owner before or within thirty days after making the phonorecords, and before distributing it.

A royalty must be paid on every "embodiment" of the work on a phonorecord. (A separate royalty is paid for each copyrighted song on an album.) The royalty is to be paid on each copy of the phonorecord actually distributed. (In practice, this usually means distributed and paid for.) The Copyright Act stipulates that royalties are to be paid monthly, although it is common practice in the industry to pay quarterly. As of 1992, the rate is 6.2 cents per phonorecord or 1.2 cents per minute of playing time, whichever amount is larger.

To summarize, the copyright owner of the work (a song, for example) may make the first sound recording and distribute phonorecords based on it. After that, anyone may obtain a compulsory license to make his own copyrightable sound recording and to distribute phonorecords based on it, provided that royalties are paid to the original work's copyright owner (generally a publisher).

The Copyright Royalty Tribunal

In drafting the Copyright Act of 1976 the Congress realized that there were several new or rapidly changing issues which were nonexistent at the time the old law was passed. The chief and most controversial issues dealt with copyright licensing and royalties with regard to the industries of cable TV, jukebox operation, public broadcasting, and an expanded recording industry. Realizing that it would be unwise to permanently fix rates and regulations pertaining to these, the Copyright Act makes provision for a five-member Copyright Royalty Tribunal, appointed by the President and subject to the approval of the Senate. The tribunal is empowered to adjust, set, and distribute copyright royalties in certain compulsory license situations:

1. Manufacturing and distributing phonorecords is the oldest application requiring compulsory licensing. The Copyright Royalty Tribunal is responsible "to make determinations as to reasonable terms and rates of royalty payments." The law requires periodic reviews of royalty rates, and the tribunal raises the statutory royalty ceiling on phonorecords every few years. (Although in practice the actual rate paid is often negotiated to a lower amount, the existing statutory royalty rate is important as a standard for negotiation.)

2. Secondary transmission (cable TV) of copyrighted works is subject to compulsory licensing. Royalties are based on gross receipts from subscribers, paid to the Register of Copyrights and later distributed by the Copyright Royalty Tribunal.

3. Public broadcasting is subject to compulsory licensing. The law provides that copyright owners and public broadcasters who cannot reach an agreement on royalties are subject to the terms and rates prescribed by the Copyright Royalty Tribunal.

The royalties in all three of the above situations are usually distributed to copyright owners by an agency, either a mechanical rights licensing agency or one of the performing rights organizations, whichever is appropriate.

In 1993, the President abolished the Copyright Royalty Tribunal and replaced it with the Copyright Arbitration Royalty Panel, which is appointed by the Librarian of Congress. The Panel performs the same essential jobs as Tribunal and also carries out the provisions of the 1992 Audio Home Recording Act. (See below.)

"Fair Use" and Other Exemptions

Although the spirit of copyright law is to ensure certain exclusive rights connected with copyright ownership, the Copyright Act of 1976 includes a body of exemptions and limitations to the statute based on the doctrine of "fair use." These permit the limited use of a copyrighted work for purposes such as criticism, comment, news reporting, research, education, and so forth. According to the wording of the law itself, to determine whether the use of a work is fair use, these factors must be considered:

1. the purpose and character of the use, including whether such use is of a commercial nature or is for nonprofit educational purposes;

2. the nature of the copyrighted work;

3. the amount and substantiality of the portion used in relation to the copyrighted work as a whole; and

4. the effect of the use upon the potential market for or value of the copyrighted work.

In addition to provisions for fair use, libraries and archives may make single copies of copyrighted works under specified guidelines. Certain nonprofit performances of a work may be exempted, including classroom performances, instructional broadcasting, or uses by handicapped persons or other specified groups. Under specific conditions, broadcasting organizations are given a limited privilege to make "ephemeral recordings" for limited, short-term, or archival use.

Home Recording

The most significant amendment to the Copyright Act has been the 1992 Audio Home Recording Act. It decriminalizes consumer home recording for private use. It requires a technological safeguard against using hardware for piracy. And it compensates record companies, publishers, and performers for lost revenue due to home recording. Here is an outline of the act's main provisions.

1. The law applies to all current and future digital audio recording technologies (hardware and software, including DAT, DCC, MD, and CD-ROM). (Home video taping is not addressed.)

2. All consumer-level digital audio recorders used for recording music must contain the Serial Copy Management System (SCMS) to prevent multi-generational digital copying. (This hardware feature safeguards against mass copying connected with piracy.)

3. Importers and domestic manufacturers make royalty payments as follows:

   Digital Recorders - 2 percent of the wholesale price: $1 minimum, $8 maximum; $12 maximum for units with more than one digital recorder. Maximums are to be raised in the future.

   Recording Media (e.g., blank tape) - 3 percent of the wholesale price.

4. The Copyright Office collects royalties, and, on the basis on of record-sales data, they are distributed into two funds. Two-thirds goes to the Sound Recording Fund (for record companies, featured artists, singers, and musicians), and one-third goes to the Musical Works Fund (for songwriters and publishers). The total royalty pool is divided as follows:

   Record Companies 38.41%
   Featured Artists 25.60
   Songwriters 16.66

Music Publishers 16.66
American Federation of Musicians 1.75
American Federation of Television and Radio Artists 0.92

100.00%

5. Consumers receive an exemption from copyright infringement liability for private, non-commercial home digital and analog audio recording.

6. The law provides substantial statutory penalties to ensure full compliance with both the technology and royalty provisions.

Infringement

The Copyright Act contains a few specific legal actions which may be taken by a court in lawsuits involving copyright infringement. Initially, a court may issue an injunction or a restraining order may be issued against a defendant; copies and phonorecords may be impounded or eventually destroyed. Statutory damages may be awarded to the copyright owner up to $20,000 and, in cases of willful infringement, this amount may be increased to $100,000. As an alternative, the plaintiff may sue for *actual* damages. Fines and imprisonment may also be imposed.

Agencies and Subcontracting Organizations

Under the copyright law, there are diversified means of exploiting a song for profit. If one imagines a publisher to own many active copyrights, it becomes clear that keeping up with all possible sources of income would be a real problem. For example, Paul McCartney's song "Yesterday" has been recorded over 1,100 times. The publisher alone could never personally license every recording and each radio or TV performance of that song, as well as collect and audit the royalties from all those sources. The task would be impossibly large and impractical to accomplish in-house.

For that reason, certain agencies and organizations have been formed over the years, specializing in just a few tasks but making their services available to the entire industry. In addition, print music subcontracting businesses aid song publishers in further exploiting their copyrights. There are three main areas with which a song publisher regularly deals: printed music sub-publishers; mechanical rights licensing agencies; and performing rights organizations.

Songs in Print

The Copyright Act empowers a copyright owner to make and distribute copies of a work. Translated, this means that a publisher may publish and sell printed sheet-music copies of any song in his catalog. This is rarely done before the song is recorded, and only the largest publishers, the "majors," print their own music. For the majority of song publishers this is simply not economically feasible, since print-music sales on even the most popular songs are relatively limited in our times. Instead, the print rights to a successful song are licensed out to one or more sub-publishers or selling agents who specialize in printing, packaging, and marketing printed popular music. In return the original publisher is paid a royalty on the wholesale income, often near 20 percent. The end product can take one of two forms:

1. Individual songs: songs from the Top 40, for example, may be printed individually as sheet music.

2. Folios: songs grouped together in some way may be published in what is termed a "folio." Folios are commonly composed of a collection of songs from one album, or written by a particular songwriter, or made popular by a particular artist or group.

Another type of sub-publisher is the educational publishing house. Educational houses are in the business of licensing limited printing rights to hit songs, Broadway shows, and film music. Their products are generally arrangements for school choirs, bands, jazz bands, or orchestras. This type of publishing can be lucrative, but it requires highly specialized marketing techniques. (Educational music is discussed in more depth in Chapter 10.)

Collecting "Mechanical" Royalties

The term "mechanicals," or mechanical royalties, is used to lump together the income derived from phonorecords, motion picture and video synchronization, and other audiovisual or mechanical devices. This also includes the use of music for radio and TV commercials, certain environmental music services, and video-tapes/discs.

Most publishers rely on a licensing agency to write licenses for such rights and to collect the royalties from them. Under instructions from the publisher, the licensing agency negotiates the royalty rate, which may deviate slightly from the statutory royalty rate under the Copyright Act. Once the license is issued, the agency collects royalties from the licensee and, after deducting a small commission (generally 3%), distributes the mechanical royalty to the publisher. This royalty is one of the publisher's main sources of income from a song, 50% of which normally then goes to the songwriter(s).

There are at least four mechanical rights agencies operating in the United States today. However, one of them, the Harry Fox Agency, Inc., dominates this service. The Harry Fox Agency was originated, and is still wholly owned, by the National Music Publishers Association (NMPA). The agency represents over 3,500 publishers, most of whom have no affiliation with NMPA. The Harry Fox Agency conducts periodic audits of record company books, acts as a legislative advocate and, when necessary, institutes litigation on behalf of its clients.

Performing-Rights Organizations: Background ———

Since 1897 U.S. law has granted copyright owners the exclusive right of public performance. No one may publicly perform a musical work for profit without obtaining permission from the owner. However, in the early years of the twentieth century this right was not respected. One could hear the latest songs played in such public facilities as hotels, restaurants, and nightclubs. Yet no royalties of any kind were paid to publishers or songwriters. While European songwriters, "serious" composers, and publishers enjoyed handsome royalties from every form of public performance, there was no American mechanism for the collection of performing-rights royalties. This situation was painfully brought to the attention of American composers, lyricists, and publishers when Giacomo Puccini (composer of *La Bohème* and *Madame Butterfly*) came to the United States in 1910 for the premiere of his new opera, *The Girl of the Golden West*. Puccini was infuriated at learning that public performances of his music in the United States were not being licensed and would yield no income.

Shortly after Puccini's visit, his publisher's U.S. representative began exploring the possibility of starting an American performing-rights organization. He stirred the enthusiasm of several prominent composers of the time, including Victor Herbert and John Philip Sousa, and in 1914 a group of over one hundred persons formed the American Society of Composers, Authors and Publishers (ASCAP). At first, many operators of public facilities resisted paying licensing fees, since there was no established legal ruling in the matter. But soon an ASCAP publisher sued a New York hotel for unlicensed performances of a work by John Philip Sousa. Then in 1915, acting through ASCAP, Victor Herbert sued a New York restaurant for performing his "Sweethearts" waltz without an ASCAP license. Both cases were lost in a circuit court of appeals, but Herbert took his case on to the U.S. Supreme Court. This time ASCAP won, firmly establishing both the licensing of performing rights and ASCAP itself in the music industry.

As new performance media, such as radio broadcasting, developed, ASCAP continued to issue licenses on behalf of its members. Other licensing organizations also developed. In 1931 the Society of European Stage Authors and Composers (SESAC), a small private performing-rights organization, was formed as an agency for the protection of foreign composers. In 1940 Broadcast Music, Inc. (BMI), was founded by radio broadcasters, chiefly in reaction to ASCAP's increasing license fees.

Today's broad variety of contemporary music users (presenters) need to make licensing agreements with ASCAP, BMI, and SESAC in order to have complete coverage. Some users, such as hotels/motels and colleges/universities, negotiate licenses collectively through trade or other organizations, while many other agreements are made individually. The following is a partial but representative list of types of music user licensees:

1. TV networks and local stations
2. Radio networks and local stations

3. Public broadcasting organizations

4. Cable and pay TV companies

5. College and university campuses

6. Hotels and motels

7. Dramatic and movie theaters

8. Concert halls

9. Symphony orchestras

10. Restaurants, nightclubs, and discotheques

11. Certain retail outlets

12. Jukebox operators

13. Stadiums and arenas

14. Amusement parks

15. Business music (background/foreground) services

16. Concert promoters

ASCAP and BMI

ASCAP and BMI are the major performing-rights organizations. While their services to members and functions within the industry are extremely similar, ASCAP boasts the larger gross income and BMI has a considerably larger number of affiliates.

ASCAP is a nonprofit association owned and operated under the direction of its members. Because of ASCAP's extreme power and the grievances filed by some ASCAP members, the U.S. Department of Justice issued a consent decree in 1960. Under the decree, which is still in force, court-appointed "advisors" periodically review several aspects of ASCAP's operation, particularly the formulas used to determine distributions to members.

BMI is a non-dividend-paying corporation originally formed by a group of about six hundred broadcaster-stockholders and presently owned by approximately the same number. The BMI board of directors is made up of principal stockholders. This organization also operates under a consent decree issued in 1966, which is similar to that of ASCAP. Both decrees make provisions for handling grievances.

Membership

Both ASCAP and BMI represent major songwriters, composers, and publishers of all types. Although the benefits to songwriters and song publishers from both

ASCAP office in Nashville, Tennessee. Photo copyright 1986 by Don Putnam.

BMI office in Nashville, Tennessee. Photo by Russell Sanjek, courtesy of BMI.

organizations appear to be nearly alike, there are a few observable demographic differences in membership. For example, songwriters and publishers of Top 40 and rock tend to join BMI, while composers, lyricists, and publishers associated with motion pictures and musical theater favor ASCAP membership.

Each organization offers membership or affiliation to "writers" and publishers. A writer can be a composer or a textual writer, such as a lyricist. The writer(s) and publisher of a song must both belong to the same organization in order for the song to be represented by that organization. Membership or affiliation in more than one organization is not permitted. Each writer and publisher is responsible for keeping his organization up to date on new works.

There are two types of ASCAP membership, full and associate. Full membership is open to qualified publishers and writers (composers, lyricists, and other writers). The chief qualification for full membership is to have at least one original work published, recorded, or performed by an ASCAP licensee. A writer who does not qualify for full membership but has registered the copyright of at least one work may become an associate member.

Due to BMI's corporate structure, its writers and publishers are called "affiliates." Qualifications for affiliation are similar to those for ASCAP membership. However, they are more in the form of liberal guidelines than strict requirements. Factors such as future potential are considered at the time of application.

Licensing

All licenses issued by either organization are blanket agreements. That is, one agreement covers the entire repertoire in the organization's catalog for the length of the agreement. The most important and lucrative licenses are issued to radio and TV networks and stations. Local stations pay ASCAP a fee amounting to 1 percent of the station's gross income. BMI charges stations a similar fee but, because of adjustments, it is believed that BMI favors broadcasters somewhat more than ASCAP does. Networks generally pay a negotiated flat fee of several million dollars. Licensing fees for other users vary widely and are based on one or several applicable factors, including seating capacity, music budget, number of hours music is performed, whether admission is charged, and gross income. ASCAP's current license agreements with colleges and universities are based upon total enrollment alone, or enrollment plus the frequency of paid-admission concerts involving artists who charge $1,300 or more per appearance.

Surveying Performances

In order to determine how to divide revenues among its members, a performing-rights organization must conduct frequent surveys of performances. Two methods are in use today: census and sampling. A census involves reviewing complete lists of performances. ASCAP uses the census method in accounting for TV networks and broadcasted background/foreground music services. Since TV network licenses account for over half of ASCAP's revenue, the organization feels compelled to give a complete and accurate accounting of performances there. Program logs and cue sheets are used primarily, but the information is verified by audio and video taping of network TV programs (around 30,000 hours per year).

ASCAP uses the sampling method for most other types of licensees. The society employs a combination of audio tapes, cue sheets, and *TV Guide* in its sample of local TV stations. ASCAP tapes around 60,000 hours of radio broadcasting per year. The frequency with which a particular station might be included in the sample is determined by such factors as: the amount of the station's current licensing fee compared to other stations; the quota of AM and FM stations for the sample; and random computer selection.

In the past BMI made extensive use of the census method, and for that reason newer publishers and aspiring songwriters have often leaned toward affiliating with BMI. Besides requiring cue sheets from TV networks, BMI now also makes liberal use of the sampling method. During any calendar year each licensed broadcaster is surveyed for a period of three days. Naturally, many stations are surveyed at the same time. BMI applies statistical weighting factors to the current sample to determine its estimate of total performances for a given BMI work.

BMI relies heavily on researching regional editions of *TV Guide* to determine performances on local TV stations. In fact, BMI makes nearly exclusive use of some form of written documentation in making its determinations, and supporters of BMI claim that greater accuracy and more grass-roots representation is achieved through this method. ASCAP's argument is that its audio taping ensures an accurate survey of what was actually broadcast, including the time length and type of credit to assign each performance. The continuing controversy over log (census) surveys versus tape (sampling) surveys is one of the chief philosophical issues that continue to differentiate the services of BMI from those of ASCAP.

Neither organization considers it economically feasible to regularly survey most other types of music users. Instead, income from those sources is distributed on the basis of surveyed radio and TV performances. However, both ASCAP and BMI use the census method for surveying concert/opera performances. Actual concert/opera programs are used to determine performances of "serious" music, since royalty credit for such music is worth several times that of popular styles.

Royalty Distribution

Both ASCAP and BMI use a complex system of weighting to determine how much credit to award a given performance. For example, a network TV performance will be worth many times a performance on a local or syndicated show. Or, a recorded song lasting five minutes will be given greater credit than another on the same station that lasts only three minutes. A distinction is also made between a feature performance and background or dramatic cue music.

Royalties are paid quarterly. Payments are divided equally between a work's publisher and writer. Beyond current performance royalties, affiliates of BMI are

Computerized operations at BMI's New York office. Photo courtesy of BMI.

eligible for bonus payments on works receiving more than 25,000 logged feature performances. Bonuses are computed on a graduated scale of "plateaus" and are for performances other than on network TV or public broadcasting stations.

ASCAP offers its writer members a choice of two methods of royalty distribution: current performances and the four fund system. Newer members and writers of current hits generally favor being paid solely on the basis of current performances. Older, well-established writers often prefer to be paid under the four fund system. The systems work in this way: After all the writers on the current performance system have been paid the remaining money is divided into four groups—the average performance fund (40 percent), the current performance fund (20 percent), the recognized works fund (20 percent), and the continuity of membership fund (20 percent). Each of these has its own criteria and weighting formulas for distribution.

In addition to paying royalties ASCAP has a system of outright awards, for which up to 5 percent of its distributable revenues may be reserved. According to ASCAP, the awards are made to writers whose works "have a unique prestige value and for which adequate compensation would not otherwise be received," or are "performed substantially in media not surveyed by the Society." There are two categories of awards: popular and standard (concert/dramatic).

Foreign Affiliations

Both ASCAP and BMI have reciprocal agreements with performance-licensing organizations throughout the world. Domestic performances of foreign works are accounted along with the regular survey, and our organizations are paid for performances which the foreign agencies survey. ASCAP has more specific procedures than BMI for distributing foreign income. ASCAP members are paid on a current performance basis, and payments from any foreign source exceeding $200,000 are distributed to members in interest, as long as the members and works can be identified. ASCAP endeavors to distribute smaller sums according to the best information available. BMI's standard is to distribute all foreign receipts to its affiliates after deducting 3 percent for administration.

SESAC

SESAC, Inc., is the smallest of the three performing-rights organizations, but its catalog has grown to include Jazz and Contemporary Christian music as well as songs written by notable songwriters such as Bob Dylan and Neil Diamond. Affiliation with SESAC appeals exclusively to writers and publishers of commercially recordable music, since the organization makes no provisions for surveying the works of opera or concert-music composers. Unlike the other organizations, SESAC does not operate under a court-ordered consent decree. Another fundamental difference is that SESAC licenses both dramatic performance rights and mechanical/synchronization rights for its affiliates' works. Performance licenses for SESAC's works are based on a rate card of fixed fees rather than a percentage of the music user's income.

Due to its limited size as a closely-held corporation, SESAC cannot afford the comprehensive survey techniques utilized by its larger competitors. For that reason, SESAC relies heavily on the "charts" published in major trade papers. National network logs and spot checks of local radio and TV programming also come into play. Distributions to writers and publishers are made chiefly on the basis of current chart activity. However, allocations are also affected by other factors: total number of copyrights, their diversity, their growth, seniority within SESAC's catalog, recording and synchronization activity, and promotional efforts on the part of the publisher. Bonus payments are made for various types of chart activity:

1. *longevity*: based on the number of weeks a song has appeared;

2. *crossover*: for appearances on more than one chart; and

3. *carryover*: for particularly successful songs after they have gone off the charts.

In summary, there are three principal services which all performing-rights organizations perform:

1. Making licensing agreements with "music users" that authorize public performances of all the music in the organization's catalog.

2. Monitoring or logging the frequency of users' performances of music from the organization's catalog.

3. Distributing licensing fees (after deducting overhead) to members or affiliates in an equitable manner.

Songs: Songwriting, Publishing, Copyright, and Performing Rights

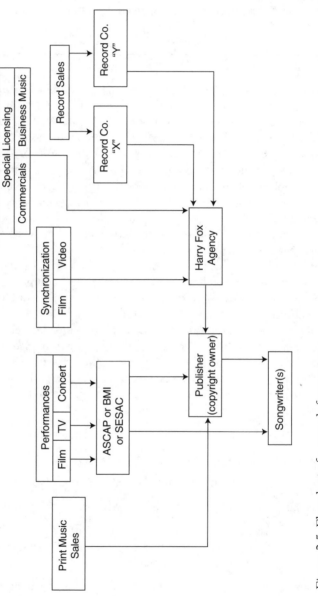

Figure 2-5. Flowchart of proceeds from a song.

This chapter has begun to trace the process of the recording industry, the first two steps of which are songwriting and publishing. The discussion of copyright has been extensive, and some of the information on performing-rights organizations and other subcontracted services may seem to have jumped ahead several links in the chain of events. However, these are all direct concerns of songwriters and publishers, since the source of their livelihood is governed by copyright law and the privileges of copyright ownership. Because the practical application of copyright has determined so much of the structure and operation of the music industry and related fields, mastering these basic concepts will be valuable in gaining the maximum benefit from the chapters ahead.

Review Questions

1. What are the two most basic elements of a song?

2. What are the two main functions of a music publisher?

3. What source produces most income from songs?

4. Discuss the five main points of a songwriter-publisher contract.

5. When did the current copyright law take effect?

6. What is the Berne Convention, and what are the advantages of belonging to it?

7. What developments led up to the Audio Home Recording Act?

8. Discuss one contemporary copyright issue not covered under the present law.

9. What is the difference between a "musical work" and a "sound recording"?

10. How does the copyright law define "publication"?

11. Give some examples of copyrightable works.

12. How long is a copyright in force?

13. Briefly review the four rights applicable to music under the copyright law.

14. What is the difference between a "copy" and a "phonorecord"?

15. Why does the copyright law call for a Copyright Royalty Tribunal?

16. Discuss the spirit of the "fair use" exemption, particularly in educational settings.

17. Name the three main accomplishments in the Audio Home Recording Act.

18. Why is it impractical for music publishers to handle all their own licensing and printing?

19. What does the Harry Fox Agency do?

20. Why did performance licensing come into being in the United States?

21. Name a few types of music users licensed by ASCAP, BMI, and SESAC.

22. What is a blanket license?

23. Describe the two methods ASCAP and BMI use in surveying musical performances. How does SESAC get its performance data?

3

Records: Producing, Recording, Manufacturing, and Marketing

Phonograph records, prerecorded cassette tapes, and compact discs (CDs) are the tangible media, the final results in the chain of the recording industry process. These products are here collectively called "records" and are actually the blend or merger of two distinct musical creations: the song and the recorded production. The song, per se, can be thought of as the original "work." Production has two parts: a performance interpretation of the song and an engineered enhancement of the performance. Ideally, however, both the song and the production should be so closely focused in a single artistic direction that the listener is not conscious of different stages of creation, but only of the final, unified result.

This chapter traces the planning and work behind records and their production, manufacture, and marketing. As in the chapter on songs, the discussion will include aspects of creativity, procedures, and business. The concept of individual functions within the process is also continued here. The first function that must be considered is that of the record producer, who, aside from the artist, is the key creative figure in making recordings.

Record Producers

Before the advent of Rock 'n' Roll and other specialized musical styles, the role of the record producer was of limited importance. He was usually a record company employee who worked in a department known as artists and repertoire (A&R). The main function of A&R was simply to bring together an artist under contract to the company and a song suitable for that artist to record.

Independent record producers emerged along with the new music. They did not work for a record company, but functioned as a contractor to one or more companies. A large percentage of the records released today are still produced by independents. (That is why Figure 2–1 shows pre-production and post-production functions separate from the record company.) There are relatively few staff producers working with popular music recordings.

Record producers come from a variety of backgrounds. Some of them are musicians or former musicians (performers, arrangers, or songwriters) who, having worked in and around recording studios for some time, decide to try producing records. Others are recording engineers, often with little or no training in music, whose talents in recording, mixing, and sound processing qualify them as producers. There is also a trend among some recording artists to produce their own recordings after a few years of experience in the studios. A number of record producers do not fall exclusively into any of the categories mentioned above, and some of the truly phenomenal ones have no credentials at all, other than their track record of hit recordings. A producer may or may not have a sensitive musical ear, or great business abilities, such as that of raising money. He may or may not be wise enough to surround himself with people who have the talents which he does not possess. He may or may not be personally involved in the lives and life-styles of his artists. However, the one thing that all highly successful producers do have in common is an almost unfailing instinct for producing a highly commercial and profitable product that will attract one or more segments of the buying public.

Briefly, a record producer's job is to oversee the making of a master tape from start to finish, including mixing and editing. This can be either a single or an album. However, it is common practice to tape an entire album and then select one or more songs from it to release as singles.

The Producer's Creative Work

Since the producer must work very closely with an artist through the many hours of planning, rehearsing, and recording, it is important for him to have gained the artist's trust and to have a working rapport with the artist. Producer and artist are sometimes friends or associates well before their first recording together. If the artist was discovered by the producer, there is a good chance for agreement in their points of view on artistic matters.

A record producer's ability to make artistic decisions comes into play constantly in the planning stages of recording. Initially, decisions must be made concerning musical material and its treatment. The producer has considerable influence on the choice of songs that will be recorded. Once the "routining" (form) of each song is established, the artist rehearses in collaboration with the producer. For each recording, the producer must either hire an arranger or write the arrangements for the songs himself. An arrangement is a written adaptation or elaboration of the original song that includes the parts for the instruments that will be used to accompany the artist and background vocals. Arranging is sometimes done in two stages: a rhythm arrangement, including the vocal routine and rhythm section (piano, rhythm guitars, drums, and bass); and an instrumental arrangement, including all the other instruments and background vocal parts.

An independent producer will usually have a choice of recording studios and must choose a studio with the right size, "sound," ambience, recording equipment, and engineering personnel for the artist and for the recording's concept. The producer must line up any extra studio musicians needed, and if the artist does not have a self-contained band with recording experience, a complete rhythm section will also be hired.

The Producer's Business Dealings

Agreements with Record Companies

Hiring recording studios and musicians requires both artistic and business judgment on the part of the producer. His relationship with the record company, however, is pure business. Initially, the independent producer will work out a budget for the recording. If he obtains record company support, he will receive an advance payment before the recording is made. This is partly to help defray initial costs and partly a production fee for the producer himself. This and other advances may or may not be recoupable by the record company from royalties, depending upon how valuable (or risky) the producer and his product are to the company. If the independent producer finances his recording from a source other than the record company, an advance against royalties is usually paid upon delivery of the master tape to the company and the signing of a master purchase agreement.

Under a master purchase agreement an independent producer's royalty arrangements can vary widely, depending upon whether the artist is under contract to the producer or to the record company. If the producer holds the artist's recording contract, then the record company will pay a composite royalty to the record producer that includes the artist's portion. This "all-in" royalty is generally at least 10 percent of the retail price of the record (of which the artist's share is usually about half). In this case, the record company normally insists on an option on future recordings by the artist. If the artist is signed directly with the record company, the producer's royalty is much less, usually in the 2–to-5 percent range. Record company staff producers are often paid a salary plus a royalty on the records they produce, often up to 4 percent.

Other Business/Administrative Responsibilities

Outside the exciting aspects of record producing—finding new talent, supervising recording sessions, making business deals—there are several less-glamorous chores. These are necessary parts of the process, and must be mentioned for an understanding of recording and record producing. The record producer and his staff are responsible to:

1. create a budget for the production;

2. apply for compulsory licenses for songs, when necessary;

3. schedule time in the studio;

4. rent extra instruments and equipment;

5. obtain a contractor for extra union musicians, if necessary;

6. complete union and record-company paperwork;

7. maintain accurate records of names, timings, and so forth for label credits, and convey this information to record company;

8. see that all bills are paid in a timely manner; and

9. manage each recording project to ensure that it stays close to its budget.

Recording Studios

Recording studios can be found in every major city of the world and in a surprising number of out-of-the-way places. Occasionally, major recordings are made in unusual places (for example, Jamaica, South Africa, or rural Louisiana) because of the availability of specialized local musicians. Some record producers work regularly outside the principal recording centers and, technically, a major label's master tape can be created anywhere in the world. However, the vast majority of commercial recording takes place in New York, Los Angeles, and Nashville.

The large record companies own their own recording facilities, but a great deal of recording activity in the industry takes place in independent studios. Since multitrack recording is now employed universally for commercial music, a recording facility is usually described by how many tracks, or independent channels, its largest recording machine is capable of carrying. Most facilities seriously engaged in commercial recording contain eight-, sixteen-, or twenty-four-track recorders—and frequently, several of each. A recording studio's prices are based primarily on the size and type (analog or digital) of recording machine to be used. Other factors that determine price are which recording engineer is used, which studio or "room" in the facility is used, and what time of day the studio is used (nighttime is prime time for performers).

The physical layout of a recording studio consists of two main chambers: the studio proper and the control booth. The larger of the two is the studio proper, where the musical performances take place. Microphones, mike booms, acoustic baffles, and often instruments are standard equipment in the studio, and there may be a small, isolated singer's booth attached to it. A soundproof window and door separate the studio from the control booth. The most impressive item in the

(a)

(b)

Recording studio control booths:
(a) classic 24-track analog system: Capitol Records Studio "C" (Photo by Charles Comelli, courtesy of Capitol Records, Inc.).
(b) compact 24-track digital system with modular recorders (Photo courtesy of Trusty Tuneshop Recording Studios, Nebo, KY).

booth is the large mixing console, located directly in front of the window. Other equipment includes the recording machine(s), monitor speakers, and "outboard" devices, such as patching panels, equalizers, echo/reverberation/delay units, compressors, filters, and other sound-processing devices. Electronic keyboards may also be set up in the control booth for recording.

During recording sessions the engineer and producer will generally sit together at the console, while a third person, the recordist, operates the recording machine and keeps a running log of the various "takes." People in the studio and control booth can hear one another (and themselves) through the studio's microphones and a P.A. system called a "talkback."

Making a Master Recording

One essential key to good multitrack recording is the concept of *isolation*. Isolation attempts to eliminate the leakage of sound from one track to another in both the studio and on the tape. Multitrack recording offers great flexibility to the producer, allowing experimentation through adding and deleting tracks, and trying different versions of the main vocal line and backup vocals. Without virtual isolation of the various tracks, this flexibility would not be possible.

Isolation is made possible partially by the capabilities of the recording machine, with its extremely low level of "crosstalk" between tracks. Also, acoustic baffles placed between instruments performing together in the studio and proper microphone placement greatly reduce sound leakage to other microphones. Isolation is also enhanced by recording each song in stages, rather than having all the performers in the studio at once. As a result of isolation techniques, all the performers must use headphones to listen to one another and to previously recorded tracks.

Basic Tracks

The first stage in recording a song is to record what are known as the basic tracks. These generally consist of little more than the rhythm instruments, each on a different track: background keyboards, rhythm guitar(s), bass, and drums. Many producers use up to eight microphones running to six tracks for the drums, and some use two microphones for a piano. While the rhythm section records the basic tracks, the artist may sing along on a reference track to help the musicians gain a better feeling for the song as it progresses. Subsequently, the reference vocal track will be discarded. Obtaining good basic tracks may require many "takes." Sometimes a single good take cannot be obtained, and the producer may decide to have the engineer splice together segments from two or more takes.

Background Vocals and Instrumental "Sweeteners"

Once the basic tracks are satisfactory, the later stages can proceed. The process of adding new tracks to previously recorded ones is known as "overdubbing." Often, the first overdub to be recorded is the background vocal. Generally, the background group consists of two or three singers, either all-female or a male-female mix. (If the artist is an experienced background vocalist, or if some special effect is desired, the artist may perform the background vocals.)

The next stage consists of adding tracks containing extra instruments. These are often referred to as "sweeteners," because their purpose is to enhance and enrich the main vocal track. The most common type of sweetener consists of string instruments, such as violins, violas, and cellos. Often these instruments will be recorded on one series of tracks and then be overdubbed again, playing the same material on another series of tracks. That way, a small group of string musicians can be used to simulate the sound of a much larger string section.

The next few tracks may be devoted to woodwind and brass instruments, collectively called the "horns." The final instrumental tracks are reserved for featured instruments, such as lead guitar, synthesizer and other keyboards, and additional percussion instruments.

The Main Vocal Track

Some artists record the main vocal track as the second stage in the recording process, immediately following completion of the basic tracks. Many others prefer to wait until all the other material has been recorded before performing the main vocal. This usually takes place at a different time from the other recording sessions. During the vocal track recording, a producer's ability to work with his artist is most critically tested. In this stage of recording the producer's function could be compared to that of an athletic coach. He must be capable of instant decisions, such as:

1. when to push the artist harder for an effect and when to release pressure;

2. whether to stop a take because of one bad note, or to rerecord that section of the track later;

3. when microphones need adjusting for better results;

4. when a general break in the session should be called; and

5. when time should be spent playing back a take.

The main vocal track on a finished recording may have been achieved in one successful take, or it may be an edited composite of different trials. A bad note or phrase here and there may be corrected by "punching in." That is, the artist listens to the tape up to the phrase where the mistake was made, at which point the engineer punches the record button on the main vocal track and the artist sings just that one phrase. Then the engineer immediately "punches out" of the record mode.

The availability of a few extra tracks on the master tape can allow the artist to record more than one version of the main vocal track. That way the producer has a choice of performances, and sometimes individual phrases from two or more versions will be combined to achieve the end result during the final mixdown.

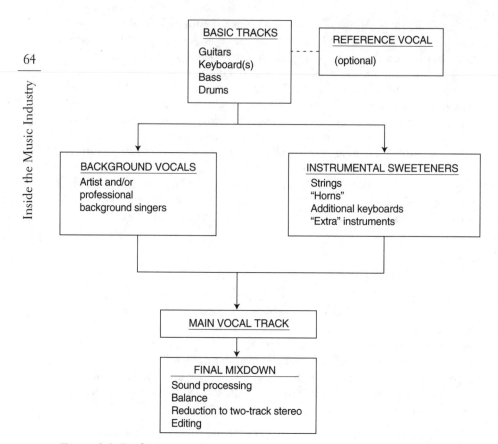

Figure 3-1. Producing a master tape.

Digital Recording

Conventional (nondigital, analog) tape recorders store sound on tape by making magnetic patterns that are analogous to the patterns of sound waves picked up by microphones. Such analog recordings can be quite fine, but they can be easily marred by technical defects. Tape hiss is the most common of these. As a result, most analog tape recorders have an unavoidable fault of limited high-frequency response, even when operated at high speeds. To get rid of hiss, it must be processed or encoded out of the tape by using a noise reduction system (for example, Dolby or dbx). One mechanical problem can be wow and flutter, caused by inconstant speed in a recorder's drive motor. Another problem can crop up when an especially loud moment in the music occurs, causing distortion on the tape. This is common on classical records and necessitates a recording process called "compression."

Advances in electronic miniaturization and computer technology have benefited the field of recording in several ways, the most visible of which is the development of the digital audio recorder. While an open-reel digital recorder physically resembles an analog machine, its method of recording sound is entirely different. Digital recording equipment takes samples of sound—47,000 samples per second—and translates each sample into a sequence of numerical information. This code is recorded onto magnetic tape for storage. When played back, the equipment reconstructs the sequence of samples into an extremely accurate image of the original patterns of sound.

Digital tapes can be edited and mixed down with the same flexibility as analog tapes, but the technical character, and therefore the sound quality, of a digital master tape is considered to be vastly superior to that of an analog master tape in several respects. Frequency response is widened and is "flatter" throughout the sound spectrum. Since there is virtually no tape hiss or other extraneous noise on a digital tape, the signal-to-noise ratio of the recording is greatly enhanced. The result is a dynamic range increase from around 60 dB to greater than 90 dB. Since a digital recorder can handle such range with ease, louder moments in the music are recorded without audible distortion and with no need for compression. A digital master tape is impervious to small amounts of mechanical wow and flutter in the recording machine, and there is no measurable effect during playback. In mixing down or copying from one digital machine to another, there is no degeneration of sound quality, such as there always is in analog recording technology.

A newer alternative to the open-reel digital recorder is the modular multitrack digital recorder. Recording on video cassette media (either Super-VHS or High-8), one of these machines can hold eight tracks for up to 150 minutes of sound. Two or more such modules can be synchronized for multitrack recording that affords great flexibility.

Mixdown

After all the material on the multitrack tape has been recorded to the producer's and artist's satisfaction, it is time to mix it down to a two-track stereo master tape. Normally, a producer will not do this immediately, but will wait a few days in order to gain a fresher, more objective point of view. Major record companies and some studios have special mixing rooms, but often the mixdown is done using the same console and booth where the multitrack tape was made. During mixdown the producer and engineer (and often also the artist) listen to each track, and decisions are made concerning such problems as the proper equalization and use of filters (sophisticated tone controls); when to use echo, reverberation, delay, or other electronic processing; and where to place each track in the field of stereo sound.

Tracks are played back individually, in groups, and all together to achieve balance and perspective. Sophisticated mixdowns also require considerable outboard electronic equipment for sound processing. The final mix is recorded on a two-track master tape (analog or DAT). Many studio consoles are equipped with computerized mixdown software that memorizes each programmed setting and recalls it at the exact moment required during the mixdown.

Post-Production

Once the stereo master tape is finished and delivered to the record company, the producer must still do a great deal of post-production work to help the recording to become a salable product. If the recording is an album, the producer, often in collaboration with the artist, must choose an order for the songs and select songs to be featured on single record releases. When the reference master disc is cut, it must be quality-checked by the producer and record company staff before manufacturing can proceed. The design and artwork for the CD/cassette printed insert often incorporate suggestions from the producer or the recording artist. Marketing campaigns and strategies are often discussed in collaboration with the record producer, who may have valuable marketing ideas or personal contacts in the field who can be called upon for promotion. Music videos, a vital promotional tool in the industry, can also closely involve the record producer and his ideas.

Manufacturing CDs and Prerecorded Cassette Tapes

Compact Discs

Digital disc reproduction technology has been hailed as an advance in recording as significant as the LP record and stereophonic sound were in their day. The standard format is the Sony/Philips compact disc, whose playback systems take full advantage of digital technology and make possible fully digital sound in the home.

Each compact disc (CD) is only about 4 ¾" diameter, but is capable of storing over seventy-two minutes of music. A CD has circular tracks containing billions of tiny "pits" only 1/10,000 mm deep. The CD's tracks are protectively sandwiched between layers of resin. During playback, a closely focused laser-optical assembly illuminates and "reads" the pits in the CD as it spins. Circuitry inside the player decodes the pit information, filters it, and reconstructs it as an audio signal by means of digital-to-analog conversion. This signal is then playable through any ordinary home stereo system. Random access features and CD changers allow the listener to program a particular playing order for a series of songs; or, an exact point on a CD can be located and played time and again with extreme accuracy.

CD Manufacturing

When a new digital master tape arrives at a CD pressing plant, it is first subjected to some last-minute editing needed to produce the final product. While the tape plays, a glass master disc is created by burning the tiny pits with a laser beam under computer control. The glass master then goes through a series of electro-

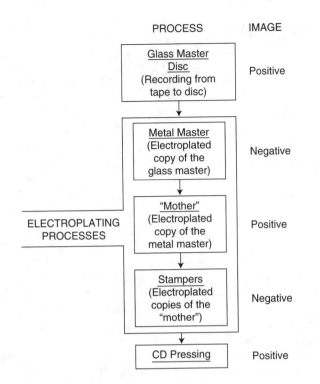

PROCESS   IMAGE

Process	Image
Glass Master Disc (Recording from tape to disc)	Positive
Metal Master (Electroplated copy of the glass master)	Negative
"Mother" (Electroplated copy of the metal master)	Positive
Stampers (Electroplated copies of the "mother")	Negative
CD Pressing	Positive

ELECTROPLATING PROCESSES

Figure 3-2. Manufacturing a CD from a master tape.

plating processes which yield a *metal master,* a *mother,* and ultimately a *stamper.* The stamper is mounted inside an injection molding machine, where a transparent image is made with plastic or high-grade polycarbonate resin. Over this inner transparent disc a very thin coating of aluminum is spread. (The shiny aluminum will reflect the CD player's beam so that the pits can be "read.") A protective layer of ultraviolet curing resin seals the inner disc. Finally, the "label" is silkscreened onto the non-playing side of the disc, and it is assembled into its plastic "jewel case" and outer packaging.

Tape Duplication

Prerecorded cassette tapes are mass-produced in duplicating plants. A special tape is prepared from the original stereo master tape. The order of songs on the copy may be slightly different than on the CD in order to equalize the length of the sides or programs on the final tape. The duplicating machine consists of a deck for playing the master tape and a group of "slave" recording machines on which blank tape is recorded. For increased productivity, duplicating machines are made to operate at high speeds, 60 or 120 inches per second. Normally, all four tracks of the finished tape are recorded simultaneously. During duplication, the tape is wound on a small hub and later loaded into its plastic cassette.

CD/Cassette Packaging

Record companies often expend great amounts of money and effort on the covers of CD/cassette printed inserts, because the point-of-purchase impact of a provocative cover has an undeniable influence on "impulse" buying. An insert may be thought of as a merchandising tool for the recording, and each design should be visually arresting and competitive when on display in a retail store.

Graphics on the cover of a CD/cassette (single or album) require careful planning. The first step is to decide on the total concept. Once the concept is clear, graphic artists prepare a general layout, showing the graphic design and the placement of words. At this point approvals are sought from record company officials. If the recording artist's or record producer's contract includes the right of consent for artwork, that approval is also obtained. From that point the insert's production proceeds more mechanically. Graphics are completed and sent to the printer, who manufactures the inserts, then sends them to the CD pressing and tape duplication plants. After CDs are placed in their "jewel boxes" and cassettes are put into their boxes, the insert completes the assembly.

It is usual for the title, artist, and catalog number to appear on the cover and side of the packaging. Another important part of the layout of an insert is the "copy" printed on the back and inside. The copy usually includes both technical and artistic credits, information on the songs, and often all the song lyrics. Technical credits commonly contain the names of the producer, engineer, recording studio, mastering lab, and insert designer. Artistic credits, besides the feature artist, may include group members, background singers, studio musicians, and arranger. Information on the songs may be divided between the insert and the CD/cassette label. For each song there will generally appear the name(s) of songwriter(s), the publisher, the performing-rights organization, and the timing of the performance. The phonorecord copyright logo for the CD/cassette's sound recording (Ⓟ, date, and copyright owner) should also appear on either the label or the insert.

Marketing and Merchandising Recorded Audio Products

The entire process of bringing a product "to market" and persuading consumers to buy it is called "marketing." Most of today's manufacturers of consumer goods depend heavily upon a marketing division, which can influence a great deal of the company's style of operation—and sometimes the nature of the product itself. The record business is no exception. A record company generally operates from a very lean upper administration which often consists of only three principal divisions: business/finance, artists & repertoire (A&R), and marketing. The vice president for marketing may oversee a number of departments, such as sales, promotion, publicity, and advertising. In some companies the marketing division

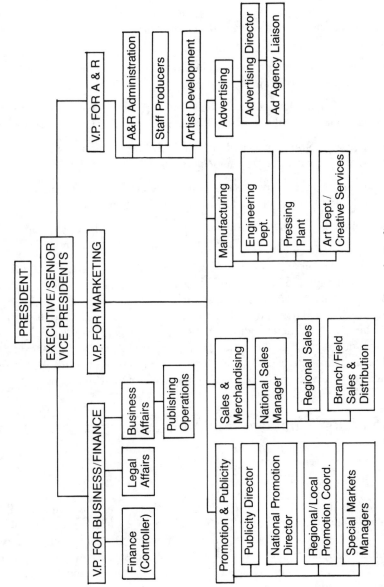

Figure 3-3. Organizational chart: a record company (hypothetical).

PRESIDENT

EXECUTIVE/SENIOR VICE PRESIDENTS

V.P. FOR BUSINESS/FINANCE
- Finance (Controller)
- Legal Affairs
- Business Affairs
- Publishing Operations

V.P. FOR MARKETING

Promotion & Publicity
- Publicity Director
- National Promotion Director
- Regional/Local Promotion Coord.
- Special Markets Managers

Sales & Merchandising
- National Sales Manager
- Regional Sales
- Branch/Field Sales & Distribution

Manufacturing
- Engineering Dept.
- Pressing Plant
- Art Dept./ Creative Services

V.P. FOR A & R
- A&R Administration
- Staff Producers
- Artist Development

Advertising
- Advertising Director
- Ad Agency Liaison

also includes manufacturing (record pressing and packaging) and an artist development department. The latter is concerned with the overall career growth of artists under contract to the company and coordinating promotional activities such as concert tours.

Together, staff members from various departments under the record company's marketing umbrella work out a marketing strategy for each new record. For releases by a major artist, this can be quite elaborate. Beginning with the development of an overall marketing concept, the strategy will often go on to include such tasks as:

1. planning in which markets and in which cities or regions the recording will first "break" on the air;

2. planning an extensive promotional campaign which could involve participation by the artist and as much coverage as possible by the news media;

3. designing promotional materials and advertisements, and planning how, when, and where they are to be used;

4. designing merchandising aids, such as point-of-purchase displays or give-away items, and planning for their most effective use; and

5. coordinating with the artist's personal manager and talent agent concerning possible engagements or a tour timed with the recording's release.

As a marketing strategy is carried out, the success of the campaign is watched closely. Although product sales are of paramount importance, the success of a marketing strategy is also measured by such signs as radio and national TV exposure, international demand, and new performance opportunities for the artist.

Marketing and merchandising represent the strategic "big picture." However, in order to carry out the strategy, marketing experts rely to a great extent on the tactical functions of promotion, publicity, and advertising. The following section explores the recording industry's applications of these functions.

Promotion, Publicity, and Advertising

Record Promotion

(For simplicity and adherence to industry tradition, any recorded product will be referred to here as a "record.") The immediate targets of record promotion are radio broadcasters and broadcast programming services. Record companies consider radio airplay to be the most direct way of exposing a record to the buying public. The main tools are special promotional copies of the record, called "promo" records, which are placed in the hands of broadcasters and programming consultants.

Record promotion is carried out in two ways, by mail and by record promoters. Since there are several thousand music-formatted radio stations in the United States, personal contact by a record company representative with all of them is impossible. Most promo records are mailed to stations together with suggestions for which song(s) to play, if the product is an album. Follow-up telephone calls to station music directors or program directors are standard procedure. Through these contacts a company representative can be sure the material arrived, hear the broadcasters' reactions to it, and convey significant information about how the record is performing in other cities.

Record promoters can be on the staff of a major record company's promotion department or work independently, usually for a combination of smaller and larger companies. Their job is to persuade broadcasters and programming consultants to schedule their company's newest releases for playing on the air. If the new record is by one of the superstars, little or no persuasion may be necessary. However, promoting new or rising artists is a fiercely competitive business, since many stations broadcast, in rotation, a weekly playlist of only thirty or less current releases. When compared with the several hundred new singles and albums released each week, these limited playlists are a valid illustration of the great risks involved in every area of the record business.

Astute record promoters concentrate their major efforts on what are termed "reporting stations." These are the 200–300 radio stations whose playlists Broadcast Data Systems tracks weekly to help make up the "charts" of top records. Promoters call regularly on station music directors and program directors, and on programming consultants. The promoter plays new releases, tries to develop an atmosphere of trust and rapport, and learns the personal tastes of these decision-makers. A record promoter's credibility rests chiefly on the quality of information he conveys about his products.

The record promoter may be empowered to offer promotional give-away merchandise to a station in return for airplay and announcements. Common giveaways include albums, T-shirts, and tickets to a local concert by the artist. Personal favors to station personnel, such as invitations to press parties, are also acceptable. On the other hand, commercial bribery, called "payola," is forbidden by federal law. (See Chapter 6 for more information on broadcast operations and personnel.)

Publicity and Advertising

The main function of publicity is to bring an artist and his newest release to the attention of the press and other media so that the public may be informed. A large record company will usually have in-house publicity staff, while smaller companies depend on outside public relations (PR) firms. In either case, the most elaborate publicity campaigns are developed around newly "breaking" artists or artists whose early records have not received the attention the company believes they should. The pattern of a publicity campaign consists of three phases: planning, execution, and follow-up.

In the planning phase all the tactics of the campaign are worked out and printed materials are prepared. Publicists hold meetings with the artist and his personal manager to obtain the artist's biography, photographs, and an impression of his personality. From these meetings and other research a formal "bio" is written and an "ideal image" for the artist is developed. Publicity people may work with the artist to prepare him for future interviews. Press releases are worked out using "angles" on the record, the music, the image, and the artist's career to date. A publicity plan is developed which details, step by step, how the execution phase will be carried out.

Executing the publicity campaign is complex, and its success often depends on precise timing. The media are given press kits containing photographs, a biography, press releases, and other pertinent information. Videotapes or review copies of the new record are given to reviewers. Many times these activities must be carried out in person by the publicity staff, and follow-up contacts are usually also necessary. Later stages of the campaign may include lining up stories and interviews for popular magazines.

Often the artist performs several engagements or an entire tour, partially for earning income and partially for exposure that will publicize a new record. When performances are scheduled, a local campaign must be executed in each concert location, including press, radio and TV, and possibly appearances by the artist in local record stores and on the broadcast media. Publicity people must maintain close coordination with the artist's staff as well as with promotion and publicity contacts in each location.

The follow-up phase of a publicity campaign is relatively simple. The staff makes sure that the press and media have been saturated as much as possible with publicity material. Efforts are made to build on the exposure already gained: obtaining stories, interviews, and other forms of publicity in prestigious and influential publications. Continued publicity for the artist is especially important between record releases. Public visibility is considered essential both to an artist's career development and to the sales of his records.

The advertising of records can be considered an adjunct to publicity. Often very large budgets are devoted to it, but just as often the record company will promote more than one release in the same ad. Print advertising is common, particularly in trade papers and in magazines whose audience is likely to buy records. Local newspaper advertising is sometimes purchased by local retailers, but more often it is paid for partially or totally out of advertising allowances offered to the retailer from a record company's distributor. Radio and TV spot advertisements are also traditional, but are a less-consistently-used method. Radio airplay is still considered to be the best and most credible form of sales promotion for a record.

Music video broadcasting is the TV counterpart to radio airplay. Tapes originally conceived as promotional aids are played almost continuously by MTV, VH-1, and other national cable TV broadcasters. Music video, an established area of the recording industry, has grown to become the most powerful form of indirect record advertising. (See Chapter 6 for more information on music video.)

Distribution and Sales

Direct Mail

Since the mid-1950s, when Columbia Records pioneered the idea of record clubs, mail has been one of the major channels of record and prerecorded tape distribution. Columbia and BMG (RCA and other labels) are still the major sponsors of record, CD, and tape clubs, although several independent distributors and small specialty record companies offer their merchandise exclusively through mail order. For example, the Musical Heritage Society releases five or six new classical recordings per month and mails out a small magazine to announce new offerings and advertise older releases from its catalog of several thousand albums.

Another type of direct mail distributor is called a TV merchandiser or TV packager. Such companies license past hit singles, often from a variety of artists and companies. The recordings are recombined, remastered, and repackaged as a new album or album set. Local TV advertising is used to sell the recordings, which are ordered by mail or phone. TV merchandisers can often attract sufficient public attention to be able to sell some of their products through retailers and rack jobbers (see below).

Major Label Branch Distributors

Only the largest record manufacturers can afford to maintain their own branch offices. Currently, these include companies such as Sony Music Entertainment (including Columbia, Epic, etc.), Polygram (including A&M, etc.), EMI Music (including Capitol, etc.), BMG (including RCA, Arista, etc.), Warner Music Group (including Asylum, Elektra, etc.), and MCA/Geffen/GRP. Each company may support up to twenty offices nationally and a number of branches abroad. The staff of a branch office is divided roughly into two categories: promotion and distribution. Promotion personnel include record promoters, advertising specialists, and market coordinators. Distribution personnel include a sales manager, members of the sales force, field merchandisers, and inventory specialists. The operating procedures of branch distribution generally follow this pattern:

1. Salespersons visit each dealer account to show new catalogs, convey relevant information on current releases, and offer purchasing incentives.

2. Dealer orders are taken for merchandise and processed through the branch office.

3. The company's pressing plant or warehousing facility ships the merchandise to the dealer.

4. Dealer accounts are billed.

5. Field merchandisers call on dealers to help with displays and other point-of-purchase tools.

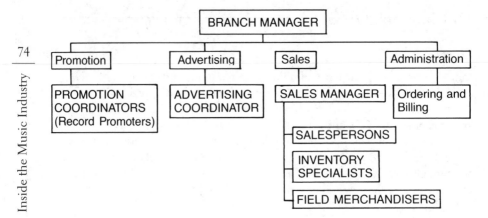

Figure 3-4. Organizational chart: major label branch office (hypothetical).

6. Inventory specialists regularly visit dealers to determine how well the company's products are selling and to offer advice on reordering.

The chief products which a branch office distributes are recordings produced under the manufacturer's own labels. However, frequently major record companies have distribution or manufacturing/distribution agreements with independent record companies. Naturally, the branch office must give prime attention to its own company's releases, but the affiliated small independent label shares the reputation of the major company and acquires a measure of its power in the marketplace.

Independent Distributors

Another distribution route for independent record companies is through independent distributors. These are regional operations which are either individually owned or part of a national distribution chain. An independent record company often employs a network of independent distributors in order to achieve adequate national coverage. Also, major labels sometimes contract with independent distributors in geographical areas not covered by one of their branch offices. The operating procedures of independent distributors follow the same general pattern as those of the branch office distributor outlined above, but the independents must usually accomplish their work with fewer personnel.

One-Stop Distributors

A type of subdistributor is called the "one-stop." One-stops originated as suppliers to jukebox operators, but the number and variety of their customers has expanded greatly over the years. One-stop distributors buy moderate quantities of recordings from various branch offices and independent distributors, mark up the merchandise slightly, and resell it to customers who carry inventories too small to be regular distributor accounts. Merchandise related to records generally represents a significant portion of a one-stop's business. This includes items like blank cassette tape, audio accessories, CD and tape care products, and books. One-stop customers vary from schools and libraries to bookshops, variety stores, gas stations, and neighborhood convenience stores.

Rack Jobbers

Today, concession and consignment marketing plays a significant role in retail business. Portions of department stores and even some entire retail outlets are made up of varied concessionaires and consignment centers. In the record business there has developed a type of concessionaire/consigner called the rack jobber. Racks of records and tapes from these merchants appear in a wide assortment of establishments, such as department stores, supermarkets, drugstores, variety stores, and discount houses. Although major retailers (e.g., Wal-Mart and Kmart) deal directly with distributors, a respectable amount of retail record sales are credited to rack jobbers.

The business of rack jobbing is a hybrid of sub-distribution and retailing. Due to the large number of display racks he must service, the rack jobber can buy from regular distributors at special discounts, or may even become large enough to be considered the functional equivalent of a distributor. The rack jobber does not wholesale his products, as the conventional distributor does, but sells directly to the public using a retail store's display space. The rack jobber and retailer usually agree upon one of the following basic business arrangements:

1. *Concession Arrangement:* The jobber rents or leases floor space for an agreed amount and is paid 100 percent of all sales of his merchandise.

2. *Consignment Arrangement:* There is no rental fee, but the jobber and retailer share the income from sales.

3. *Modified Concession Arrangement:* A minimum lease fee is paid, and the retailer retains either a percentage or a dollar amount when sales exceed a certain figure.

The rack jobber "services" each store by removing unsalable merchandise and restocking the racks with fresh products. Payments are calculated by means of bar-code data on goods sold. Rack jobbing appeals to retailers because their only investment is display space. Retailers are relieved of taking financial risks on inventory, and they do not need to use their own staff for buying, inventory control, or merchandising.

Record Retailers

At one time most music listeners visited independent neighborhood record stores or music dealers to shop for records. Today, record retailing is dominated by regional and national chains of large stores placed in shopping malls and other commercially strategic locations. Examples are Blockbuster Music, The Where-house, and Tower Records. There are still some smaller "mom and pop" record stores, but because musical styles have proliferated and the size of record company catalogs has grown so enormously, these independent stores must carry a limited, specialized stock and must be located in an optimal place to sell that stock. One typical location might be in an inner-city black neighborhood. Another might be near a college campus, where both rock and classical music are appreciated. Foreign imports and ethnic records can also be sold successfully in the proper surroundings.

The big advantage retail record chains have is buying power. Due to the large inventories they maintain, chains generally order and warehouse goods centrally, rather than individually by store. The net result is that they receive better treatment from record distributors than do smaller accounts. Chains receive larger discounts because of their sizable orders. In addition, they may be given preference for free promotional merchandise, sales gimmicks, and publicity events, such as in-store visits by recording artists.

There is also the matter of return privileges. Most manufacturers allow up to 100 percent of goods ordered to be returned for credit if unsold within a specific time frame. Chains with a large amount of buying power can obtain higher return authorizations and reduce the risk of having to keep unsalable merchandise.

The added financial leverage and other considerations which retail record chains derive from their size allows them more operating flexibility, particularly in the area of pricing. The retail record business is extremely competitive, and a small difference in the price of a current release can mean a great difference in attracting clientele and in dollar volume. Distributors are inclined to favor large accounts like chains when offering any special prices and advertising allowances they are authorized to give.

The idea of multimedia home-entertainment centers has grown in recent years to include TV, video cassette recorders (VCRs), CD players, audio cassette machines, and even multimedia personal computers (e.g., Best Buy and Circuit City). To accommodate this trend, larger record retailers have expanded their operations to become audio/video entertainment stores (e.g., Blockbuster). Besides CD and audio cassette departments, such a store contains a sizable video department including a substantial supply of music videos. The format for these may be limited to VCR cassettes or could include laser discs. One retail chain has even test-marketed CD-ROM software, a crossover into the computer market.

Cut-Out Vendors

When a release no longer sells at an acceptable level, the manufacturer drops the title from its catalog. Records and tapes that have been "cut out" of a catalog can still be sold, but not at previous prices. This overstock of semi-obsolete merchandise is generally sold to a type of distributor known as a cut-out vendor. The price of each unit is extremely low, sometimes below the manufacturer's cost. The vendor, in turn, offers to sell the products to retailers and rack jobbers, again at extremely low prices. The bargain retail price of these items is expected to be attractive to consumers who are budget-minded but are prone to impulse buying. Stores and rack jobbers frequently display cut-outs prominently to attract attention and sometimes even advertise them. Cut-out records are sometimes the work of artists with a large following, and such merchandise is known to sell particularly well.

Used CD Stores

The marvelous durability of CDs has given rise to a new type of record retailer: the used CD store. Such businesses normally buy CDs from their customers at about one-third the retail price and re-sell the merchandise at about two-thirds the retail price. Although a few regular record outlets carry used CDs, it is more usual to find independent used CD stores.

Recording Industry Awards

Just as motion pictures, television, and theater have their achievement awards, so does recorded music. However, since records involve both creative effort and the sale of a product, there are two classifications of awards: the Grammy for creative contributions and the Gold or Platinum record for high sales figures.

Grammy Awards

Each year the National Academy of Recording Arts and Sciences® (NARAS®) honors outstanding creative achievements in recording by granting a group of awards called "Grammys." Nominations for Grammy Awards are made by voting members of NARAS®, and results of the final vote of that membership are revealed during a nationally televised ceremony. The principal categories of awards are record of the year, album of the year, song of the year, and best new artist. There are also awards in special fields of performance, such as Pop, Rock, Country, Jazz, Rhythm and Blues, Rap, Classical, and others. Grammys are also awarded for work behind the scenes, such as producing, engineering, arranging, and CD/cassette packaging.

Gold and Platinum Records

The Recording Industry Association of America (RIAA) sponsors an ongoing Gold Record Award program in recognition of outstanding domestic sales of individual records and albums. Criteria for the award have varied over the years in consideration of price increases and market expansion. Any recording (single- or album-length) is eligible for a Gold Record Award when 500,000 units have

Grammy Award® logo. By permission of the National Academy of Recording Arts & Sciences®.

been sold (all formats combined). Platinum Record Awards are given for the sale of one million units. "Multi-Platinum" Awards are given for each 1 million unit-sales increment beyond that. Music videos on VCR cassette and laser disc are also eligible for Gold and Platinum Awards (single: every 25,000 units sold; long form: every 50,000 units sold). RIAA certifies Gold and Platinum Record Awards through sales figure audits conducted by an independent auditing firm.

The business of making and selling records represents a clear illustration of one of the balancing principles in business: potential profit versus potential risk. In the recording industry there are huge profits to be made in all three phases: creating, manufacturing, and marketing. At the same time, there are attendant risks at every step, which could be costly or even disastrous to the success of the recording project. For example, if the work of an artist or producer does not come up to expectations, the master tape will be unusable. If quality control is not maintained in mastering and pressing, great amounts of time and money may be lost in recutting, replating, and repressing. If mistakes in judgment are made regarding publicity, or if record promoters fail to obtain airplay, the sales of the record may never get off the ground. Any of these critical links in the chain may be the weak one. On the other hand, if all goes at least reasonably well, and there is adequate financing behind a project, the ingredients for success will be present. Once the producer, artist, record company, radio stations, and retailers have done their work, it is then left to the listening public to determine whether a record will be a hit, and thus a financial success.

Review Questions

1. Briefly, what is the record producer's job?

2. Discuss a few tasks that are part of a record producer's creative work.

3. Describe the independent record producer's relationship with the record company.

4. Briefly describe the two main chambers in a recording studio. What does each typically contain? What is the function of each?

5. Why is isolation important in multi-track recording?

6. Define each of the stages of making a master recording: basic tracks, background vocals/instrumental sweeteners, and the main vocal track.

7. Describe two or three advantages digital recording has over analog recording.

8. Briefly describe what happens in a mixdown.

9. Why are the graphic covers on CD/cassette inserts important?

10. In the insert copy, what are some of the technical credits? Some of the artistic credits? The song information?

11. What are a record company's three principal divisions?

12. What is the job of a record promoter? How can he carry out that job?

13. Describe a few ways new recordings are publicized and advertised.

14. What is the connection between the functions of radio airplay and music video broadcasting?

15. Describe a few of the functions of a major label branch office.

16. What is an independent record distributor? A one-stop distributor? A rack jobber? A cut-out vendor?

17. What are some advantages that big retail record chains have over smaller independent retailers?

18. What are the four principal categories of Grammy® Awards, and how are winners chosen?

19. What are the criteria for receiving Gold and Platinum Record Awards?

4

The Recording Artist's World

Thus far, this book has concentrated on the larger, general aspects of the recording industry without treating any one activity or person in great depth. The discussion has also focused primarily on people and equipment functioning *behind* the scenes. On the other hand, most of us are better acquainted with what is happening *before* the scenes—who the leading recording artists are and what are their top songs.

The term "artist," as it appears in this book, is used to indicate any artistic entity and thus can mean any "act" from a solo singer to a complete band. The present chapter delves into the world of the musical recording artist. Much of it deals with the business side of an artist's activities, and the reader will get a glimpse of what it takes—outside of talent—for an artist to conduct a successful career in the music business. This chapter deals with *people* and their activities in association with musical artists. After introducing the typical recording artist's long-term and short-term associates, the business of obtaining a first recording contract will be explored. Finally, the entire range of personal appearances will be discussed, from showcases and one-night club engagements to TV appearances and entire tours.

Long-Term Associates

The types of business associate with which a musical artist may surround himself can be quite varied and depend solely on the needs of that particular artist. In fact, it is not absolutely essential that an artist have any associates at all. For example, if you walk into the lounge of a modest hotel and hear someone playing at a piano bar or a soloist singing to his own guitar accompaniment, the chances are that such an artist has no need for a staff or management of any kind. The artist has developed his "act" to a limited professional level by himself. He may have "booked" himself into the lounge engagement simply by applying to the management or through some union announcement. He has probably negotiated all the main contractual arrangements himself: length of the engagement, payment, hours, conditions, and so forth. He collects his fee and manages his finances by himself. These activities can also be carried out with the aid of professional associates. However, this particular artist is able to make his way at his present career level without any help—as long as matters are kept simple: an uncomplicated solo act playing or planning one engagement at a time, fulfilling just one contract at a time, and being paid a modest wage with little attention to career development or long-range planning.

At what point does it become necessary for an artist to seek professional assistance, and what type is called for initially? David Baskerville suggests that the need arises about the time that the artist begins to command a fee higher than the union minimum wage, known as "scale." This is a good rule of thumb, but another might be: when the artist's career becomes too complicated to manage along with performing. The problem could be a lack of time or expertise or both. The type of help an artist in this situation feels he must obtain is some form of management. There are two main management areas: personal and business. If the two areas are combined, it is sometimes called "total management." An artist generally first seeks a *personal manager*, since that individual must be the most versatile associate and must work extremely closely with the artist.

The Personal Manager

It is a sad fact that many personal managers have little or no professional experience at all in the music industry. Sometimes a personal manager is a relative or friend of the artist who has been "promoted" to managerial status simply because the artist feels he can trust that individual. The matters of trust and a mutual belief in the abilities of one another cannot be treated too lightly; they can form the cornerstone of the entire relationship between artist and manager.

Like songwriters and the publishers who represent them, artists and their personal managers need each other. Young, aggressive managers will often scout undiscovered, talented artists and will approach them with offers of management. Likewise, an aspiring artist needing managerial help, or simply believing that having a personal manager will improve his career, will seek a manager. Once the initial contact has been made, a period of getting acquainted generally follows before a contract is negotiated. The manager will watch and listen to the artist perform, and there will often be lengthy meetings between artist and prospective manager. Such discussions will explore the strengths (and limitations) of both parties. Some of these areas might be:

Artist

1. present status of development and experience (reputation, performance level, songwriting, recording experience);

2. future possibilities of career development (image, performing, recording, songwriting); and

3. present status of the artist's management (existing contracts, financial records, assets, and liabilities).

Personal Manager

1. sincerity, honesty, and credibility;

2. "track record" with other artists; and

3. industry contacts.

Some of the important things that both parties are asking themselves during these discussions are: Do we share the same view of how this artistic career should develop? Can the other party deliver what he promises? Can I take advantage of the other party's strengths and also tolerate his weaknesses? Can we get along personally during a long-term relationship? Once these concerns are laid to rest, a management contract can be negotiated. At this point the uninitiated artist may be concerned only with the question "What is this relationship going to cost me?" However, there are many other issues that must be treated in any artist-manager agreement. The following is a brief outline of eight main points.

1. *Appointment.* Indicates the type of management (personal, business, total); outlines manager's duties; gives manager limited power of attorney to carry out those duties; usually disclaims any obligation to actually obtain ("book") employment for the artist. (See section Talent Agent below.)

2. *Compensation.* Establishes what percentage of artist's income is the personal manager's commission; whether based on gross or net earnings; whether calculated on all sources of income (performances, recording royalties, songwriter's royalties, performing rights income, endorsements, and so forth) or on only some of them. The commission usually ranges from 15 to 25 percent of the artist's gross earnings.

3. *Reimbursement.* Allows for approved manager's expenses in connection with the artist to be reimbursed.

4. *Artist Warranties.* States exactly what existing active contracts the artist is party to which could affect the present management contract. May also concern ownership of artist's professional name.

5. *Exclusivity.* Generally calls for artist to grant manager the exclusive right of representation, but manager can also represent other artist-clients.

6. *Term.* Length of initial contract (usually one to three years) and option term

(usually several one-year periods). Exercising an option is usually the prerogative of the manager but can provide a degree of protection for the artist as well.

7. *Accounting.* Gives artist the right to obtain an audit of manager's books. May include a trust provision applying to money received by either party.

8. *Grievances.* Provides for arbitration in the event of a dispute.

A few comments about artist-manager agreements should be added. First, some personal managers assume control of the artistic, business, and even personal affairs of an artist to an extreme extent. This has led to a common misconception that an artist works for his manager. However, exactly the opposite is true. The manager is employed by his client, the artist, who pays him a commission for his services. In many contracts the percentage starts low and escalates as the artist becomes more successful and earns larger sums. In addition, almost every contract includes a provision for commissions to continue after the end of the term or if it is broken off for other reasons. Here is an example. An artist first signed with Manager A, who obtained a recording contract for him on Label Z. At the end of the contract's term the artist decides to sign with Manager B. Manager A is still entitled to a commission on the artist's subsequent record royalties from Label Z. The original management contract could provide that commissions from this source of revenue (and others in which Manager A helped to secure) will taper off over a period of time following the termination of the contract.

What does a personal manager actually do? What are his duties and obligations to his artist-client? His is a complicated and diverse job for which there is room here to give only a capsule description. A major test of the personal manager handling a new artist is his ability to function as a business manager until the artist's income can justify engaging business assistance. Not all personal managers have this capability. Therefore, one of the duties is to engage the help of a business manager/accountant and other individuals as needed. Some of these may become long-term associates of the artist, but many of them are brought in for short-term employment. The most important of these are discussed in more detail further along in this chapter.

A personal manager may need or wish to act as business manager for the purpose of decision-making. However, accounting and other routine functions are generally delegated. Also, it is difficult for a personal manager to be the artist's booking agent as well. In the states of California and New York, where most booking is done, strict licensing laws make it impossible for booking and personal management to be performed by the same person. Therefore, a personal manager will usually seek a good talent agent for his artist. An attorney is needed whenever contracts need review and advice prior to the artist signing them. As the artist's reputation grows, it may become necessary for the personal manager to hire a public relations firm or a press agency to maintain the proper image before the public. If concerts or tours are planned, various crews and promotional staff will need to be lined up. The manager also has a hand in hiring any musicians or other supporting artists who perform and record with the main artist either regularly or on an as-needed basis.

The personal manager is the chief negotiator for all the artist's contracts. This may begin with talent agency agreements and extend through a recording contract, product endorsements, publishing, and nearly all other business arrangements connected with the artist's career. Probably the single most important of these is the recording contract, and many artist-manager agreements specify that the personal manager will do everything possible to obtain a recording contract for the artist, if one is not already in effect.

The personal manager must be highly attuned to the style and artistic potential of the artist. Part of the manager's job in this connection is to attend rehearsals and performances and to work with the artist on polishing the presentation style, song routining and programming, and other aspects of performance. The choice of material is also crucial. If the artist performs "outside" material, that is, songs which he has not composed himself, then the personal manager has a responsibility to screen or help to screen new material.

A manager's screening chores extend beyond artistic material, however. He saves the artist immense amounts of time by screening all offers of business deals, requests for appearances, and other personal encounters which could be either potential opportunities or nuisances. At the same time, the personal manager must maintain a constant liaison with the contacts who are important to his client. He must get to know people in various departments of the record company his artist is signed with, and he must often maintain pressure on certain of these individuals to promote his artist's records. A constant dialogue must be conducted between the manager and the talent agent so that continuity of performance bookings (and, therefore, cash flow) is maintained. Other long-term and short-term associates must be dealt with on a day-to-day basis. In addition, there are always union matters concerning the artist himself and the supporting artists. If the artist is also a songwriter, the personal manager may have regular dealings with song publishers and the artist's performing-rights organization.

Even if the artist has a separate business manager, the job of the personal manager somewhat overlaps that function. It is often the personal manager's duty to make sure that payments due to the artist are paid. Somewhere in most artist-manager contracts this responsibility is spelled out.

Another responsibility often called for in artist-manager contracts requires the personal manager "to be available at reasonable times and places to confer with the artist on all matters concerning his artistic career." This phraseology points to the one function of the personal manager that is most important and most crucial to his relationship with the artist: *advisement*. In the best of artist-manager relationships all decisions carried out by the personal manager are with the approval of the artist. So, theoretically, the manager is there to advise the artist and to carry out the artist's decisions. The function of advisement is so important that the musician's union, the American Federation of Musicians, has outlined five areas where advice and counsel should be given:

1. selecting material (literary, artistic, and musical);

2. matters relating to publicity, public relations, and advertising;

3. proper format for the best presentation of the artist's talents;

4. selecting a talent agent to procure maximum employment for the artist; and

5. types of employment the artist should accept for maximum benefit to his career.

In summary, an artist's personal manager is there to handle the day-to-day matters of administration and to offer guidance on career development, including the planning of long-range goals and strategies. The personal manager is generally the single most important individual in the artist's world, for he is responsible for building, maintaining, and sustaining the artist's career.

Talent Agent

The job of a talent agent or agency is to obtain employment for the artist. In popular entertainment the two activities, artist management and "booking" talent, are clearly divided. The global term "talent agent" has come into currency relatively recently. Older terms, such as "booking agent" or "theatrical agent," are still around, but the preferred expression today is "talent agent," mainly because it is more general. There are successful talent agents who work independently, but usually an established artist will be signed with one of the large agencies and his account will be assigned to one or more agents in the firm. The larger agencies have offices located in major entertainment centers in the United States as well as internationally. Some of these are the William Morris Agency, Agency for the Performing Arts, International Creative Management, Associated Booking Corporation, and Premier Talent Associates (strictly for rock artists).

There are several areas of entertainment in which a talent agent might obtain work for a musical artist: live performances (clubs or concerts), TV and radio appearances, stage productions (musicals), motion pictures, recordings, and advertising spots. Employment in each of these fields is closely regulated by one or more unions. Many agencies, especially the larger ones, are "franchised" by the various unions. However, all agents are subject to union regulations concerning artist-agent contracts.

When an agency takes on a particular artist as a client, there may be several contracts to be signed. Each contract covers a different field of entertainment and satisfies the requirements of the regulating union in that field. Before actually working in a particular field, the artist will need to become a member of its union. The following are the principal artists' unions: American Federation of Musicians (AFM), American Guild of Variety Arts (AGVA), American Federation of Television and Radio Artists (AFTRA), American Guild of Musical Artists (AGMA), and Screen Actors Guild (SAG).

Although an agency may try to secure the representation of an artist in all fields, artists and managers sometimes prefer to engage several talent agents who are specialists in just one or two fields. Artist-agent contracts will often be written for three years, unless union regulations call for a one-year term. However, in the contract there is usually an escape clause stating that if the talent agent fails to obtain work for the artist within a given period — say, four months — the artist may give notice of termination and then seek another agent.

A talent agent is paid a commission based on his client's earnings from any work in a field the agent has under contract. The exact percentage varies—10, 15, or 20 percent—depending upon the type of employment (that is, which union is involved) and the length of the employment.

An aggressive talent agent actively markets the talent of his clients. He locates people and organizations who need the talent he represents, then finds out what they can pay and when the artist will be needed. He makes an offer to book one of his clients for the job. If the prospective employer wishes one of the more popular artists but cannot really afford him, the agent generally tries to book a less well-known artist who performs in a similar style. Once an agent has lined up employment, the artist's manager is contacted. At that point the artist, through his manager, may accept or decline the offer. Some reasons for declining could be:

1. The pay is insufficient.

2. The artist has a conflicting engagement during the requested time.

3. The artist and manager feel that taking that particular engagement is not a good career move.

Either of the first two points could be further negotiated, or the booking might be offered to a different artist. However, if an artist refuses too many offers procured by the talent agent, he may run the risk of being ignored by the agent in the future.

Artists and talent agents come together in a number of ways. Less-experienced artists may simply go knocking on doors until they find representation. Good personal managers generally have contacts in several agencies which could represent their clients. The record company with which an artist signs may also have recommendations. It is important that there be an amicable relationship between personal manager, talent agent, and record company because of the need to coordinate closely the timing of record releases with that of publicity, promotion, and live performances. In fact, the connection between record companies and talent agencies is so close that an agency sometimes actually obtains the artist's record contract for him. When this happens, the agency assumes all the responsibilities which a business manager normally would with regard to that contract. The agency collects all record royalties and pays them to the artist after taking its commission. The agency also makes sure that the record company's computation of the artist's royalties is in order.

There is one large exception to the structure and function of talent booking as discussed above: classical music. There, the artist's own manager usually handles the details for all aspects of the artist's work, including recording, booking concerts and opera, motion pictures, and broadcast media. Classical recital work is regulated under the rules of the American Guild of Musical Artists. Some of the larger cooperating "total management" agencies that represent this type of talent are Columbia Artists Management, Hurok Attractions, the William Morris Agency, and Shaw Concerts. In classical talent management the composite commission runs fairly consistently at 20 percent.

Business Manager/Accountant

As an artist's career develops and his work becomes more complicated and lucrative, his personal manager reaches a point where he can no longer oversee the business affairs of the artist. He must obtain the long-term services of one more associate: a business manager, or accountant, or some combination of these two functions.

The business manager handles all the financial affairs of the artist. Briefly, he collects income; prepares budgets, financial reports, and tax returns; pays bills and tax obligations; and consults with the artist and personal manager on tax matters, business negotiations, and financial planning.

Collecting monies due the artist can be time-consuming and sometimes troublesome. For example, it may be necessary for the business manager or his representative to accompany the artist on tours, since the potential income from these can be quite substantial, and the artist needs to be sure he is receiving his rightful share of the proceeds from each concert. Also, some record companies have a reputation for miscalculating their artists' royalties. The special auditing expertise of a business manager or accountant may be needed to ensure that an artist's proper royalty is paid.

All aspects of an artist's financial administration are supervised by the business manager. It is not unusual to find a business manager helping to prepare budgets for recording sessions, concerts, and tours. Also, the artist and personal manager will periodically wish to review the current financial status of the artist and his various enterprises, and this will necessitate preparing financial statements, balance sheets, and so forth. Once an artist is earning a level of income calling for a business manager, he also needs good tax advice. An important function of the business manager is to give his client information and counsel on tax alternatives and ways to minimize taxes during the high earning years. Long-term financial planning is tied closely to this service. The business manager may be qualified to offer such advice, or he may call in a specialist in investing and estate planning.

Business managers are generally paid a percentage of the artist's income, as are personal managers. The typical commission for a business manager is 5 to 10 percent of the client's gross income; however, a limit may be imposed when the artist's income becomes exceptionally large. It is also possible to hire a business manager on a flat monthly or yearly retainer, which is considered advisable when the artist's income is high.

Some artists do not need a real business manager but do need help with routine financial matters. In this case hiring an accountant usually suffices. A qualified accountant can keep track of income, conduct audits if necessary, pay bills, give some tax advice, prepare tax returns, and prepare various financial reports. An accountant is usually paid an hourly or monthly fee.

Music Industry Attorney

The field of music and entertainment law is a specialty unto itself requiring a thorough knowledge of the mechanics of the industry. Such lawyers are also expected to have expert knowledge in several areas of law, including contracts, copyrights, business/corporate law, libel/slander, tax law, and trademarks. Music industry attorneys generally represent clients from either the area of talent/creativity (artists, record producers, and so forth) or the area of business interests (record companies, unions, and the like). Since technology, popular trends, and the laws governing the music industry are evolving relatively quickly, these attorneys must constantly reeducate themselves. Legal issues involving new art forms (such as music videos) and copyright law, among others, are surfacing daily, and a good music industry attorney must keep abreast of all new developments.

The most important services that an attorney can perform for an artist are connected with the numerous contracts the artist is constantly asked to sign. One service is drawing up whatever contracts the artist or personal manager needs to issue. However, the attorney usually spends far more time reviewing incoming contracts and advising his client on the legal and business implications of these, along with any available alternatives.

In the course of such counsel the attorney often becomes one of the negotiators of a contract. Ideally, his function in such matters is to negotiate only the *legal* aspects of the agreement. However, in many cases the attorney is either asked to become the artist's chief negotiator or simply takes the task upon himself. At this point the attorney's function begins to overlap those of personal manager, business manager, and talent agent. In fact, there are attorneys who actually do serve their clients simultaneously as attorney and personal manager. This encroachment has been frowned upon by the Conference of Personal Managers and others because of the temptation to breach the attorney's responsibilities as a "fiduciary" (representative) of the artist. (A fiduciary cannot seize opportunities for himself that would otherwise belong to the party he represents, and personal management could be viewed as such an opportunity in certain cases.)

Attorneys may be paid by one of several arrangements. Probably most common is the hourly fee, where the attorney is paid strictly for the time devoted to his client's work. There is also the possibility of a flat rate for each piece of work without regard to time. Most successful artists pay the attorney a monthly fee, called a "retainer," which covers routine services. Extra services, such as time in court, are generally billed to the client in addition to the retainer.

The least desirable method of payment, from the artist's point of view, is for the attorney to receive some percentage (usually at least 10 percent) of revenues generated by the contracts he negotiates. Singing entertainer John Davidson advises artists never to pay an attorney on a percentage basis. This and the warnings of others go on to point out that, by awarding the attorney a commission, the artist has involved him in the future day-to-day running of the artist's career. Another danger is conflict of interest. For example, the attorney might negotiate a recording contract for the artist with Label X, and subsequently the attorney is hired by Label X as its chief legal counsel. Although the attorney will probably be required to disclose this conflict of interest, it will eventually work to the artist's disadvantage.

Supporting Artists

Many rock bands and other acts are self-contained and need no other musical artists when performing or recording. However, numerous other artists will need a group of supporting artists for some particular event or series of events. Recording sessions, TV specials, concerts, and tours can mean hiring anything up to an entire orchestra with arrangers, a conductor, background vocalists, and even dancers. It would be impractical to keep all these people hired on a continuing basis. Therefore, they are issued a contract for the particular job only. Supporting artists working under such an arrangement are good examples of short-term associates of the artist. In the course of his career the artist will experience many different types of short-term relationships.

Coaches, Choreographers, and Costume Designers

When a young artist first becomes associated with a personal manager, his talent may be somewhat raw and undeveloped. For some types of music a lack of polish may be desirable. However, for most artists on their way to the top the personal manager will insist that the artist have some contact with a professional vocal coach or other entertainment expert who can help groom the artist and his act. This type of attention can be likened to packaging a product so that it can be merchandised more effectively.

Vocal teachers and coaches specializing in contemporary styles can be found in the major recording centers (Los Angeles, New York, and Nashville). A drama coach may also be used, either to work with a musical artist's own act or to help him prepare for some particular TV, film, or live appearance as an actor. If movement is part of the artist's act, a choreographer is often brought in to polish the existing movement and to help create movement and staging to go with new material. Since the artist's visual appearance must be closely associated with his musical style, it is common for the personal manager to hire costume experts to design and make a wardrobe specifically for that artist. Even if the artist's costume is supposed to resemble common street clothes, it is considered important that this wear be tailored to exactly fit that artist's body. A professional hairstyle will usually complete the artist's stage image.

PR Firms and Press Kits

One of the first things a personal manager must do for a new artist-client is to have a press kit (or "promo" kit) prepared. This is generally an elaborate-looking folder containing publicity photographs of the artist, a résumé or short biography, reviews and information about recent performances and recordings, and other promotional materials. Finer press kits are usually created and assembled by public relations (PR) firms, which may be called upon to update the kit peri-

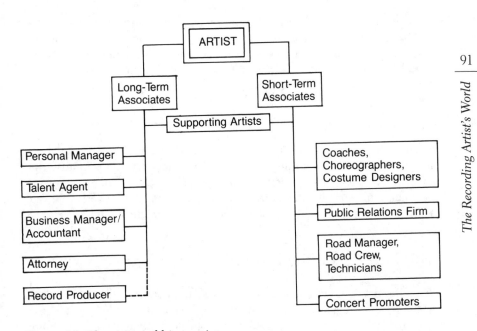

Figure 4-1. The artist and his associates.

odically. Sometimes a distinctive logo is created as well, and this may be used on subsequent concert publicity and record jackets. The rock band Chicago has just such an identifying logo. For a lesser known artist a press kit usually also includes a sample CD or cassette.

The press kit is a sign of professionality, and it is necessary to have even before approaching a talent agent. Many copies of the kit are generally made, because it can be used in a number of ways. The personal manager uses the kit in nearly all his dealings on behalf of the artist. The PR firm itself may be instructed by the personal manager to send out copies of the kit to the media and elsewhere in connection with various events. The talent agent sends or shows the kit to prospective employers and concert promoters. The advertising department of the artist's record company will use the kit in connection with campaigns to sell the artist's records and to promote his concert tours. An artist's press kit is updated constantly as his career develops.

Road Manager, Road Crew, and Technicians

For complex concert tours, or even just for individual appearances, a number of behind-the-scenes personnel are needed. It is the job of the road manager to oversee all logistical operations: the transfer of equipment, accessories, and wardrobe. A road crew is hired to help him, and they will generally arrive several hours before a performance to set up and test all the equipment. The lighting and sound technicians who will work during the performance are usually part of these operations. All such personnel are generally hired for particular events and are generally not retained in between engagements or tours. (The road manager and his responsibilities are treated in more detail in the section "Personal Appearances," later in this chapter.)

Concert Promoters

A concert promoter is a local marketer of talent. His main duty is either to book an artist with a local employing organization or to create a booking by arranging for the place and time of a performance. Beyond that the concert promoter's work falls into two main areas: organizing and financing the concert event, and acting as liaison between the artist, the local media, and the public.

The First Recording Contract

Obtaining a recording contract is a major goal for most new artists. The belief is that from recordings all else flows: international recognition, artist royalties, promotional concerts and tours, publisher/songwriter royalties, and performing rights fees (from ASCAP, BMI, or SESAC). Under the best and most successful conditions it works just that way. For this reason the recording contract is such a major issue when a new artist and a personal manager consider an association together.

Referring back to the exploratory artist-manager talks, we might imagine a smart artist asking himself, "Has this manager obtained good recording contracts for other clients? Or, if not, does he have the right sort of contacts in the industry to obtain one for me?" The answers to these questions can usually be discovered with a little investigation. At the same time the manager may have been pondering. "Is this a 'hit' artist? Can I convince a record company to sign him and commit a large budget to him?" Answers to the manager's concerns are somewhat elusive and rest more in the realm of creativity. However, the issue of a recording contract is usually so fundamental in the minds of both individuals, that signing an artist-manager agreement is sometimes made contingent upon obtaining a recording contract beforehand.

The "Demo" Recording

At some point the artist must make a demonstration ("demo") recording for audition purposes and consideration for a professional recording contract. Often an artist may make a high-quality studio demo recording before encountering a potential personal manager, and such a recording may become a factor in initial artist-manager relations. It is also common for musical groups today to own sophisticated electronic gear, including portable mixing boards, four-track tape recorders, and processing equipment. Recording and mixing down a multitrack demo tape at home is a relatively easy task for such artists.

Some artists without personal managers attempt to market their demos themselves either directly to record companies or through indirect grass-roots efforts. For example, an artist may make a studio recording of four to eight songs and then have a limited run of CDs or cassettes pressed on a private label. The artist (or one of his friends) then visits radio program directors and disk jockeys in the local area, plays the music for them, and tries to convince them to give it some airplay. The hope is that a local hit will be created, leading to regional attention to the record. Armed with this brief marketing history, the artist hopes to approach a record company, offering the potential of a national hit record in return for a good recording contract. This plan sounds good in theory, and it sometimes leads to a career boost. However, it is expensive and very risky. The artist stands a better chance of success by allowing a personal manager or other associate to represent him when seeking a recording contract.

If the artist does not have a good, up-to-date demo recording at the time of signing with a personal manager, a new demo is made. An audio demo (CD or cassette) often consists of four songs which show different facets of the artist's talent and his potential for making single and album hit recordings. Frequently, a fast, bright number is chosen as the opener, the first thirty seconds of which are crucial for capturing the auditioner's attention. Usually the song arrangements are kept to about three minutes.

The manager and artist generally try to hold down the expenses of the demo recording. One way of doing this is to use a smaller two-, four-, or eight-track studio instead of a twenty-four track facility. Another way is to hire a minimum of supporting artists (players and singers) or none at all. The idea of the recording is to present an audition that focuses strictly on the featured artist. In recent years it has become common for a record producer or even a record company to advance the cost of a demo recording ($500–$5,000 typically) to a promising artist. In return, the artist signs an agreement giving the producer or company first refusal on a subsequent recording contract.

"Selling" the Artist

Once a professional demo recording has been made, it is up to one of the artist's long-term associates to use it to obtain a recording contract for the artist. It is important that one of these associates do the actual "selling," because each has a vested interest in the artist's future. Getting a label interested in an artist can be a drawn-out, energy-consuming process, and it is only logical that those who stand to benefit from a recording contract should be the ones to sacrifice the time and effort. Usually the artist's personal manager does the legwork, but an attorney or talent agent has been known to line up a contract. It largely depends on which of them has the most influence with the leaders and power brokers of the industry, and how well that influence can work to the benefit of the artist.

There are many common strategies for placing an artist with a record company. Here are three that are used separately or in combination:

1. The manager approaches a record company directly, armed with demo recording and press kit. He may try to work directly with one of the top executives, or he may attempt to enlist the help of someone in middle management who wishes to curry favor by bringing hot new recording talent to the company. If the manager knows a staff producer with the company, he may first try to interest that individual.

2. The manager approaches an independent record producer who has worked with artists similar to his own client and has been successful at selling masters to labels. If the producer becomes interested in the artist, it could lead to a recording contract, either with a label or with the producer.

3. The manager works through third parties (for example, a publisher or talent agent). If the artist is also a published songwriter, chances are that his publisher will be interested in exerting influence on label executives and record producers, since he has a vested interest. In addition, the manager plays the demo recording for as many other industry people as possible or brings them to live performances, trying to impress them with the artist's talent and potential. The idea is to give the artist and his work a great deal of word-of-mouth publicity, which will ultimately reach the ear of an important record executive.

If the artist has sufficient talent, and if the manager does everything in his power to procure a recording contract, then the results should be satisfactory. Ideally, the manager's campaign should be so successful that more than one record company is bidding to sign the artist. Whenever this is the case, the artist and manager must choose one company, and the decision could rest on such factors as how much money it is willing to commit to promotion, the provisions of the contract it offers, and the company's prestige.

The Recording Contract Itself

In a record contract both the artist and the record company promise to make an investment and to assume a certain degree of risk. The artist's main investments are his preparation time, talent, and artistic effort. At risk are the artist's potential earnings from recordings. The artist also risks career development by placing himself in the hands of the record company for the period of the contract. On the record company's side the investment and the risk are calculated monetarily. The costs of recording, manufacturing, marketing, and promoting the work of a new artist are tremendous. For most CD/cassette releases, sales of over 250,000 units (all audio formats) are required for a record company to recoup its investment. Yet, over 80 percent of new releases never even reach the break-even point. Generally, a new artist needs a few years of exposure and more than one CD/cassette release for his recordings to begin to sell satisfactorily. These facts sharply illustrate the risks taken by a record company with each new artist's contract.

Naturally, both the artist and the record company wish to reduce the risk and improve the chance for success. However, each party also attempts to favor his own side by influencing the content and wording of the contract. The chief negotiator for the artist is generally his personal manager, aided by an attorney. Larger record companies maintain attorneys on their staff and one of these, along with a company management representative, will normally negotiate for the company. The usual procedure is that the company first offers its standard contract, and then the artist's side negotiates changes in the document in the artist's best interests.

A recording contract can be one of the most complicated documents the artist will ever sign. However, for study purposes it is possible to reduce a typical document to its main points. The following is a summary of the essentials found in most recording contracts.

Term of Contract and Recording Commitment

Normally the term is a one-year initial period with several one-year options, exercisable only by the record company. The artist's recording commitment is the minimum number of masters he will make during each period. In the initial term this could be as few as four (equivalent to one CD/cassette single) or as many as twelve (a CD/cassette album) or more. For each option period the number of required masters may increase. A "pay or play" clause may be included, whereby the company is released from its commitment to record the artist by paying him a nominal sum (often union scale for the required masters).

Master Recording

The record company schedules all recording sessions and pays for recording expenses. Matters of artistic control, such as the choice of songs, studio, supporting artists, and so forth, are negotiable. The contract may call for artistic decisions to be made by mutual consent, but the company usually reserves the right of final approval on each master.

Ownership of Master and Sound Recording

The company owns each master tape as well as the "sound recording" embodied on it (for copyright purposes). The artist is one of the "authors" but grants power of attorney to the company for each sound recording. Some artists negotiate for obtaining ownership after some period of time (for example, following the last option period, or after ten years).

Publishing

Whenever the artist is a songwriter, the company may attempt to co-own the publishing rights to songs written and recorded during the contract term. At the least the company will insist on discounted mechanical licenses for these "controlled compositions," typically 75 percent of the statutory rate.

Exclusivity

The artist is prohibited from recording as a *featured* performer for any other company during the contract term. This provision may extend beyond the contract's term for songs recorded under the contract.

Name and Likeness

The company may use the artist's name, biographical material, and likeness (in photos or artwork) to advertise and promote his records. This privilege can sometimes extend to merchandising projects outside the recording industry.

Assignment of Contract

The company is allowed to assign the artist's contract to another company at a later date. The artist will usually negotiate for the right to approve the assignee.

Group Clauses

If the artist is a group (or duet), further provisions are usually made:

1. The company claims the exclusive right to use the group's name on records.

2. Royalties to the group may be higher than for individual artists on the company's roster.

3. If a member leaves the group, he might still be under contract to the company. The company may claim the right to approve his replacement in the group.

Default

This provision generally favors the company. If the artist does not meet his contractual obligations, the company can suspend the artist. If the artist then makes records for a new company while the contract is in effect, the old company can obtain an injunction on the sale of the new records and sue for damages. If the company defaults by not paying royalties or by refusing to be audited, the artist must sue. The artist usually tries to insert a termination clause into the contract to avoid court actions on either side.

Royalty Provisions

Since royalties are among the most negotiable points of a recording contract, many record companies do not attempt to spell out the conditions in the main document. Instead, a "Royalty Provisions" rider is attached. The following summarizes the main points regarding artist royalties.

Recording Fund

The budget for each recording project in a contract is structured as a "fund." Normally a budget minimum and maximum for the project will be stipulated. Any positive difference between the maximum and the actual cost of completing the recording project goes to the artist as cash compensation.

Royalty Rates

Royalties are usually based on the suggested retail price of each release on units distributed domestically through normal retail channels. The royalty percentage paid on cassettes is the "basic" rate. For new artists the royalty range is 9 to 13 percent. Better known artists may earn 14–16 percent, and superstars command 16 to 20 percent. Royalties may be graduated with increases occurring at the 200,000– and 400,000–unit plateaus.

Royalties are less for digital formats such as CD, MD, and DCC, ostensibly because of higher manufacturing costs. Typically, record companies pay 85 percent of the "basic" rate for sales in these formats. (Other discounted royalties apply to foreign sales and any type of direct marketing, such as record clubs.)

Joint Recordings

One type of joint recording is a collaboration between two artists on the same song (for example, Mariah Carey and Boyz II Men on "One Sweet Day"). The other type is an LP compilation including one or more songs recorded by one artist coupled with songs recorded by others. In either case the royalty paid to each artist is prorated according to his contribution to the entire product.

Packaging Charges

The record company normally deducts a percentage of the artist's royalty to cover the expenses of packaging the product (for example, plastic cassette cases and CD "jewel cases") and for preparing and printing insert material. For cassettes the deduction is 20 percent, and for CDs it is 25 percent.

Other Recoupable Company Expenses

The company deducts from the artist's royalties all actual production costs connected with the artist's recording sessions, including union wages to supporting artists, equipment rental, arranging and copying, blank tape, and studio rental. This clause is standard and normally nonnegotiable. "Cross-collateralization" clauses are also common. Such provisions can require that the company recoup expenses from all previous recordings by the artist before any new royalties are paid.

Reserves

Up to 40 percent of an artist's royalties may be withheld, sometimes for as long as two years, as the company's financial cushion against records distributed but subsequently returned by dealers.

Nonroyalty Records

Royalties are not paid on copies of a recording which are not intended to be sold. These include the following:

1. *"Freebies"*: The company pays no royalty on promotional records given away to company sales and promotion personnel, radio and TV stations, movie studios, and so forth.

2. *"Cut-outs"*: No royalty is paid on records deleted from the company's catalog and sold to cut-out vendors for 50 percent or less of the wholesale price.

Flat Fee Income

The company may license a master to a third party (for example, for use in a TV show, movie, or business music service) or may sell it outright. The fee for any of these will be a one-time flat amount, not a percentage. The artist receives a share of this fee, usually around 50 percent.

Music Video

Record companies include music video provisions in recording contracts because such productions involve high expense (often over $75,000) and little hope of profit-making. The usual video royalty is 50 percent of income from all sources (broadcast licensing, VCR cassette and laser disc sales, foreign income, etc.).

The record company advances the production costs up to a certain budget. The music video provisions usually state that the first 50 percent of those costs are recoupable from the artist's audio royalties and the remaining 50 percent from his video royalties. The cost of making a music video is rarely recouped entirely.

If the song involved in a music video is a "controlled composition" (written by the artist), fees for synchronization and distribution rights (see Chapter 6) are normally waived. The company and the artist usually collaborate on selecting a producer, director, and story idea for the video.

Statements

The artist's royalties are normally paid every six months. If the artist believes the statement (and payment) to be incorrect, he has a stipulated period (which can range from six months to two years) to register a written objection.

Amounts designated as royalty advances and budgets for production and promotion are measures of the faith a company has in the potential success of an artist. The larger the financial commitment, the greater will be the company's effort to do everything in its power to recoup its investment. However, from the artist's viewpoint, creative control is usually a major consideration. The choice of songs, the producer, the arranger, the supporting artists, the studio, and the recording dates—all are matters of great personal concern to most artists. In many cases creative concessions can be negotiated in return for financial considerations which the company deems important.

It is the opinion of several prominent music industry attorneys that the various discounts and deductions mentioned above, which many record companies are accustomed to taking from the royalties of their recording artists, are indefensible and unfair. On the other hand, record companies must pay a great deal up front for recording funds, production and manufacturing costs, and promotion. Since most records released fail to recoup the money the company has invested, it could be argued that the artist should share the financial burden by accepting royalty deductions and discounts. However, if production expenses are recouped from monies due the artist, then should not ownership of the master tape and its copyright likewise be shared with the artist?

Fortunately, most recording artists do not depend upon record royalties as a sole means of support. If an artist is a songwriter, there will be income from his performing rights organization and from publishing. Over and above such sources related directly to recording, most artists earn the majority of their income from doing what they have always loved doing: *performing*.

Personal Appearances

From the time a musically inclined person first plays or sings in front of others to the time when he can look back on a successful career as a recording artist, one activity remains constant: live performance. A very young artist may first perform for his friends. Later, when his act is a little more developed, he may be able to obtain one-night engagements, usually paying below union scale. After some years of work it may become necessary for the artist to join a union in order to obtain some particular engagement. This is a major move, which places him in a higher professional class. From that point there is no looking back, and the artist who can continue to develop artistically and command increasingly bigger fees will be eligible to follow the path to a recording career outlined previously.

For each personal appearance an artist must prepare extensively. The long hours of work an artist must spend in order to learn new material and polish his act are difficult for many nonmusicians to understand. Practicing an instrument or singing for hours or even days on end is a familiar task to any artist, but one hidden from the audience during what the artist tries to make a fresh-sounding performance.

Personal appearances can take place either in a live environment or on TV. The latter will be discussed farther along. There are two basic types of live environments:

club dates—including hotel dining rooms and lounges, ballrooms, discotheques, restaurants, cabarets, and theme park stages; and concerts—including educational and community concert halls, indoor and outdoor theaters, auditoriums, convention centers, sports arenas, stadiums, gymnasiums, and racetracks.

Club Appearances

Showcases

Young artists often get their start on a professional level by performing at clubs. One way that clubs have of hiring new, inexpensive talent is by sponsoring showcase evenings. These are similar to old-fashioned variety shows, since no one artist dominates the evening. A showcase appearance can be as brief as one song. However, it is more usual to allow each artist to perform one entire "set," a block of time usually lasting about forty-five minutes. A showcase performance gives the artist an opportunity to test his material before a live, paying audience, and it is also a chance for important people—such as potential managers, talent agents, and record executives—to see him perform his act.

A showcase can also lead to further engagements. If the audience likes the artist, the club owner (or manager) may invite him back to perform for an entire evening. The showcase, if done in a reputable club, can be an important "credit" to add to the artist's press kit when he seeks employment at other clubs.

One-nighters

A one-nighter, or one-night stand, in club work is the next step up from a showcase. It is an engagement to perform several sets lasting an entire evening. Artists at all levels play one-nighters. Even a long-established artist may accept a few one-nighters to test new material in his act or if the one-nighter happens to fall conveniently between more important engagements.

Extended Engagements

The most desirable type of club employment is an extended engagement. This can be any engagement lasting longer than one evening, but it usually extends over several weeks. Any artist who has shown a club owner that audiences there appreciate his work becomes a draw for that club, and the owner will frequently ask the artist to appear several nights per week over some period of weeks.

Many established recording artists, especially in the Country or Adult Contemporary styles, find that extended engagements in theme parks and prestigious clubs are not only good income but also one of the best ways to make contact with (and expand) their own special audiences. Clubs in Las Vegas, Reno, Atlantic City, and Miami have multiweek contracts with prominent artists who perform there year after year. The acts of the biggest artists playing in the main dining rooms may earn large salaries for performing the same material in the same way two shows each evening, six evenings per week. A sizable number of somewhat lesser artists earn good salaries by performing nightly in the lounges of these establishments.

Concents

A concert, put simply, is just another type of one-nighter. The basic differences between concerts and club dates are the place, the size of the audience, and the basis for payment to the artist. Concerts bring artists and their fans together. For artist and audience alike, there is probably nothing to compare with the frenzied excitement of a big, successful concert. A concert, or better, a series of concerts in different locales (a tour) is also a stimulus to the artist's career. The advertising, promotion, and publicity connected with a concert can draw special attention to the artist, increasing his potential audience and also his record sales. There is big money in concerts. Besides the main artist, others who can benefit include supporting artists, concert promoter, talent agent, personal manager, and road crew. Such services as public relations firms, advertising agencies, news media, technicians, and concessionaires also stand to profit from concert events.

The Opening Act

It is unusual for one artist (the "headliner") to appear alone on a concert bill, even if the artist is a self-contained band. Usually, there is a featured supporting artist appearing as the opening act. The opening act is paid either a flat fee or a small percentage of the ticket revenue (the "gate").

It is not always easy to perform at the beginning of the concert. Some of the audience is still entering during this performance or simply milling around. The audience is usually impatient for the artist they paid to hear, and they can be rude or abusive toward the opening act. Once the headliner comes on stage, the opening act may be forgotten, unless it is also the accompanying band for the headliner.

Why do artists perform as opening acts under such adverse conditions? Opening acts are often relatively unknown artists just getting a foothold in the industry. There are two main advantages for these artists:

1. It is good experience and employment that often pays better than club work.

2. It is exposure for the artist who may be trying to attract the attention of a talent agent or a recording company.

During the remainder of this chapter the term "artist" will refer only to the headliner.

Concert Promotion and Preparations

The local concert promoter, briefly introduced earlier, acts as liaison between the artist's management associates (personal manager and talent agent), the local media, and the local public. His most crucial job is to market the artist and the performance event extensively through publicity and advertising. Naturally, copies of the press kit are important to this function, but the concert promoter often needs to develop some original advertising and publicity material.

The promoter makes all the local arrangements and finances all expenses connected with the concert. First he must line up a place for the event, known in the industry as the "venue." He must pay such expenses as rental of the venue, printing, transportation, personnel, and security. The promoter obtains any permits or licenses required to hold the event, sometimes including performing-rights licenses (ASCAP, BMI, and SESAC). All such costs are reimbursed to him out of the gross receipts from the concert. A contract will have been signed between the promoter and the artist to divide the remaining gross receipts, with the larger portion always going to the artist. The division can vary widely, depending upon the popularity of the artist, the city, and the size of the hall. The artist's share ranges from 60 to 90 percent. The initial contract with a concert promoter generally covers just one event. However, if the artist is well received, the promoter will often try to negotiate an exclusive contract with the artist for future appearances in that particular city.

Prior to the actual concert the artist is generally involved in several forms of preparation. For a particularly big event the artist tries to arrive in town a little ahead of time. The concert promoter or record company often sets up a number of preconcert activities to publicize the event and create public excitement about it. These may include a radio interview with a local disc jockey (perhaps at a shopping mall), a record-signing session at a local record retailer, and other brief appearances. For major artists, press parties will be held before or after the event. Technical preparations generally take place at the venue just a few hours before the concert. Checks of the lights, sound, and the artist's own equipment must be made, and a little rehearsing may be done to get the "feel" of the venue.

College Campus Concerts

One source of concerts that attracts artists in many different styles of music is the college campus. Some universities budget substantial amounts of money for concert series, and within a college or university there may be student organizations willing to underwrite concerts by artists who are particularly popular among those students. Instead of using a professional concert promoter, a campus concert manager or student may function as promoter by doing the bookings, arranging advertising, making local arrangements, and dealing with the artist and his associates. College representatives, agents, personal managers, and artists meet regularly through national or regional conventions of the National Entertainment and Campus Activities Association (NECAA). Showcase performances by new and established artists are a regular feature of those meetings.

Contracts and Riders

A new artist may agree to play a one-shot showcase for very little or no money at all, simply for the exposure. However, for a one-nighter, a concert appearance, or an extended engagement, not only must payment be negotiated, but several other conditions as well. One-nighters in clubs are sometimes contracted on a handshake. However, reputable clubs and nearly all concert venues are unionized, requiring certain written conditions for any engagement of union members. The unions involved are AFM for instrumentalists and AGVA for singers and other entertainers. It is considered the best policy to have a written contract between artist and club owner for *any* engagement. Club and concert contracts are quite similar. The following are the main points of a typical engagement contract, and what is called a "personal rider," which gives all of the artist's special requirements. Provisions applying strictly to concert contracts are marked with an asterisk (*).

General Terms:

1. *Time and place of the performance.*

2. *Duration of the performance.* The number of hours; number and length of breaks (if any).

3. *Manner and amount of compensation.* Normally, one half upon signing the contract; the remainder on the date of the performance. When the artist's payment is a percentage of gross receipts, a guaranteed minimum is sometimes negotiated.

4. *Seating capacity of the venue.**

5. *Provisions for breach of contract and force majeure.** Anything beyond the control of the parties involved and their associates which prevents an event from taking place.

Personal Rider:

1. *Ancillary rights.** Rights to make and release audio recordings, videotapes and videodiscs, and films derived from a concert performance. Normally, these belong to the artist or to his record company.

2. *Billing.* The precise manner in which the artist's name is to appear in advertising, displays, programs, publicity, and on marquees. Includes placement of the name and percentage of space relative to other artists and information.

3. *Ticket manifest.** A notarized printer's accounting of all tickets by number, color, and price. The promoter normally assumes liability for any counterfeit tickets.

4. *Stage manager, stagehands, and electricians.* These are normally hired by the club owner or concert promoter to assist the artist's technicians.

5. *Security.* This sometimes specifies the type and number of security officers backstage, outside, and in the hall or club.

6. *Dressing rooms.* Adequate, private dressing rooms are required for the artist and his supporting artists. Security is normally provided.

7. *Refreshments.* Clubs may have a house policy on free drinks and food for entertainers. Anything over and above this is generally at the artist's expense. Obtaining refreshments may be the responsibility of the concert promoter.*

8. *Transportation.** The concert promoter lines up a limousine for the artist.

9. *Rehearsals.* Specified reasonable times for rehearsing is guaranteed to the artist.

10. *Accompanying musicians and sound technicians.* If the artist is bringing only key assisting artists and little or no crew, the club owner or concert promoter is responsible for hiring the extra needed musicians.

11. *Return options.** Concert promoters will try for exclusive rights to book and promote a good artist in that city. Attached to this may be a restriction on the artist from making other appearances in the same locale.

Touring

A tour is really nothing but a series of concerts, or one-nighters, held in different places along a planned tour route. Some tours are limited, but most are on a national scale. Others can be international or world tours.

Normally, a tour is scheduled to coincide with the release of a new album by the artist. In some cases a record company will help financially with the tour by making up any deficits, or will at least support it with publicity releases and other marketing assistance. (A company for which the artist is a spokesperson will often help sponsor the tour.) The purpose of any tour is, therefore, twofold. It earns income for the artist, and it is a way of promoting the artist's records, especially the latest ones.

Touring is a grueling affair. The constant pressure of performing and rushed travel between engagements takes its toll in stress upon the artist, in fact upon all personnel on the tour. Some artists enjoy being on the road, while others consider it a necessary evil.

Keeping a Tour on Track

All arrangements, including bookings, lodgings, equipment purchase, and transportation, must be back-scheduled from the starting date of the tour. The planning stages of a tour involve the artist, personal manager, the talent agent, various concert promoters, and a salaried employee of the artist known as the road manager. Once the tour begins, it is the duty of the road manager to be sure that the logistics work as planned and that everything else runs as smoothly as possible. For each individual engagement along the tour itinerary the road manager has prescribed duties. The following are some of them.

Two to ten days before the concert:

1. Coordinate with local promoter on all arrangements made by him.
2. Schedule sound and light checks.
3. Schedule rehearsal (if any).
4. Plan stage and equipment setup.
5. Make a list of local technicians for backup.

One day before the concert:

1. Be sure that any contracted advances have been received.
2. Coordinate again with local promoter.
3. Check lodgings and local transportation.
4. Make sure all personnel understand time schedule.

On arrival at the venue:

1. Contact promoter for ticket manifest and other details.
2. Check hall, stage, and dressing rooms.
3. Direct road crew ("roadies") in setting up equipment.
4. Direct sound and light check.
5. Coordinate with security officers and determine artist's route of entrance and exit.

During the concert:

1. Spot-check empty seats in the hall against leftover tickets as insurance against counterfeiting.
2. Be available to artist and promoter in case of unforeseen difficulties.

After the concert:

1. Obtain from promoter signed manifest, box office statement, and payment.
2. Monitor road crew repacking equipment.
3. Handle lodging checkout and other bills.
4. Make sure schedule is met to allow group to arrive on time at next stop.

TV Appearances

Like concerts and tours, live TV promotional appearances are a way for artists to increase their audiences and promote their current activities. Most TV appearances

Day	Performance Location	Day	Performance Location
1	San Diego, CA	35	New Orleans, LA
3	Los Angeles, CA	38	Miami, FL
6	San Francisco, CA	39	Jacksonville, FL
9	Portland, OR	41	Atlanta, GA
11	Seattle, WA	43	Greensboro, NC
14	Minneapolis, MN	45	Norfolk, VA
16	Iowa City, IA	48	Washington, DC
18	Madison, WI	51	Philadelphia, PA
19	Detroit, MI	53	Pittsburgh, PA
21	Chicago, IL	55	Cincinnati, OH
22	Indianapolis, IN	57	Buffalo, NY
24	Cleveland, OH	60	Boston, MA
27	Kansas City, MO	62	New Haven, CT
29	Oklahoma City, OK	65	New York, NY
31	Dallas, TX		
32	Austin, TX		
33	Houston, TX		

Figure 4-2. U.S. concert tour itinerary (hypothetical).

are scheduled during the artist's nontour periods or between extended club engagements. However, a concert series in New York or Los Angeles may be heralded with a TV appearance by the artist a day or two before the opening. Talk shows (for example, David Letterman or music video channel interviews) are prime vehicles for personal appearances. The artist might perform as part of the promotion. The one consistent feature of such appearances is that the artist's new album, engagement opening, motion picture, or other activity will be "plugged" and discussed.

At one time musical TV specials were common, with several new ones appearing each month of the regular season. In recent years, with the growth of music video, interest in producing and viewing conventional musical TV specials has nearly disappeared. Today, it is more usual to see videotaped concerts. Cable networks and pay-per-view channels are particularly strong programmers of taped concerts. The premiere transmission of a particular concert is sometimes scheduled to coincide with the release of the concert on commercial video software.

Developing a successful career as a recording artist is generally a long, arduous undertaking requiring grit, patience and, naturally, great talent coupled with a charismatic presence before audiences. Successful promotion and marketing of the artist's talent are also prime factors.

An artist may begin performing in unpretentious surroundings, such as informal high school or college gatherings. After more experience he may move on to local club work or move to one of the major talent centers to seek work and career advancement. Choosing a personal manager may well be the most crucial decision

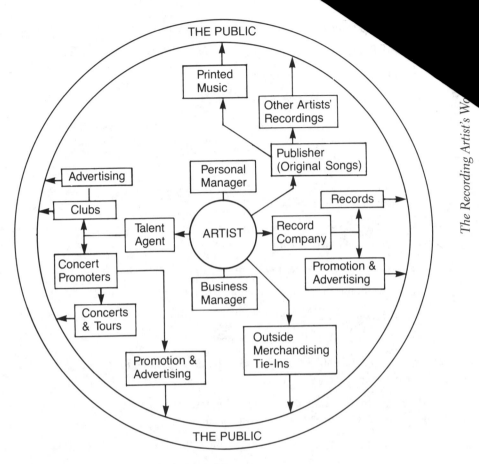

Figure 4-3. The recording artist's world.

the artist will make. From the artist's association with his personal manager and other long-term associates (that is, talent agent and business manager), numerous opportunities may come. Paramount among these is the first recording contract, a sign of professional arrival that can open many other doors. Increased opportunities to perform for increased fees often follow the signing of a lucrative contract with a good, supportive record company. Making music videos, concert work, and touring normally parallels successful recording activity. Finally, cable TV appearances, and motion pictures are the ultimate extensions of the work of especially versatile artists.

Review Questions

1. At what point will an artist need help in managing his career?

2. What will a personal manager seek in a prospective artist-client? What will an artist seek in a prospective personal manager?

nore important points in an artist-manager agreement.

ie duties of a personal manager and discuss a few of them.

s of a talent agent.

erence between a business manager and an accountant?

is the most important part of a music industry attorney's job.
discuss a few other areas with which he must be familiar.

ht be included in a press (or "promo") kit?

9. artists' "demo" recordings. What goes on one? What can be done with one? Who pays for it?

10. Outline three approaches a personal manager might take in placing an artist with a record company or a producer.

11. Can new artists make a lot of money from recording? Why or why not?

12. How long is the term of a recording contract?

13. Who owns each "sound recording" the artist makes?

14. What is a "controlled composition"?

15. Are artist royalties and packaging charges the same for CDs and cassettes? Explain.

16. Can record companies recoup the costs of making a recording? A music video? Discuss the business side of each.

17. Discuss the three types of appearances for which a club might engage an artist.

18. What is an opening act? Why do artists take this kind of work?

19. Discuss the jobs of the concert promoters and the road manager.
    Discuss how they interact during a tour.

20. Name a few provisions of a typical personal rider to a club or concert contract.

21. Why do artists appear on TV talk shows?

Part 2

Music and Media

5

Radio: History and Musical Trends

The connection between music and broadcasting has always been an intimate one. Throughout the history of radio, music programming has been a constant stabilizing factor. Records and radio have sometimes been competitors, as in the 1920s, and sometimes close partners, as in the age of the disc jockey since the late 1940s. Musical shows have had their heydays in TV as well. There have been periods when musical variety shows "ruled the waves" and catapulted singers into superstardom. More recently, the music video has created an entirely new trend in TV broadcasting, akin to the disc jockey format but containing elements of theater as well. Music and broadcasting continue to work hand in hand as they have for years. Music is one of the chief materials for broadcast programming, while broadcast media provide a form of promotion for popular music.

First Steps

Radio was originally developed as a step beyond the telegraph and the telephone. In the late 1890s Guglielmo Marconi experimented with transmitting dot-dash messages, received a British patent for his wireless telegraph, and by 1901 was able to transmit across the Atlantic Ocean. Wireless voice communication was made possible with the epochal invention of the oscillating "audion" radio tube

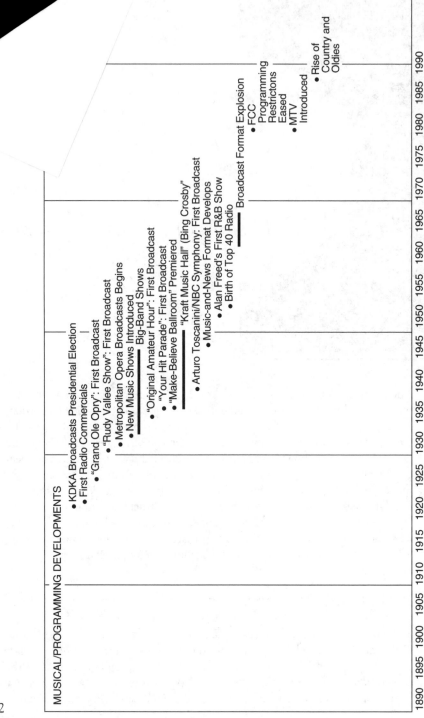

MUSICAL/PROGRAMMING DEVELOPMENTS

1890 1895 1900 1905 1910 1915 1920 1925 1930 1935 1940 1945 1950 1955 1960 1965 1970 1975 1980 1985 1990

- KDKA Broadcasts Presidential Election
- First Radio Commercials
- "Grand Ole Opry": First Broadcast
- "Rudy Vallee Show": First Broadcast
- Metropolitan Opera Broadcasts Begins
- New Music Shows Introduced
- Big-Band Shows
- "Original Amateur Hour": First Broadcast
- "Your Hit Parade": First Broadcast
- "Make-Believe Ballroom" Premiered
- "Kraft Music Hall" (Bing Crosby)
- Arturo Toscanini/NBC Symphony: First Broadcast
- Music-and-News Format Develops
- Alan Freed's First R&B Show
- Birth of Top 40 Radio
- Broadcast Format Explosion
- FCC Programming Restrictions Eased
- MTV Introduced
- Rise of Country and Oldies

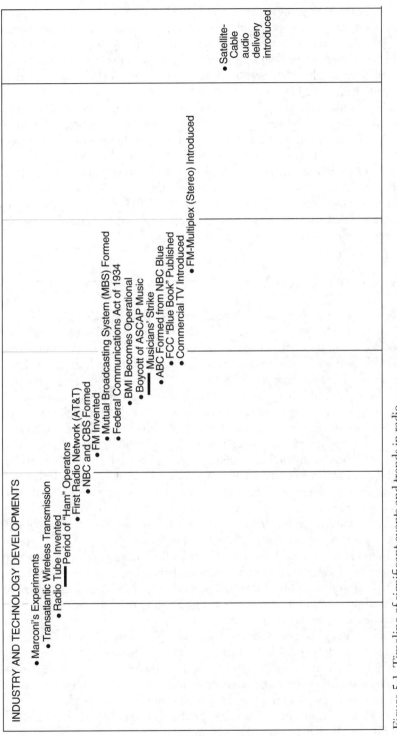

Figure 5-1. Timeline of significant events and trends in radio.

INDUSTRY AND TECHNOLOGY DEVELOPMENTS

- Marconi's Experiments
- Transatlantic Wireless Transmission
- Radio Tube Invented
- Period of "Ham" Operators
- First Radio Network (AT&T)
- NBC and CBS Formed
- FM Invented
- Mutual Broadcasting System (MBS) Formed
- Federal Communications Act of 1934
- BMI Becomes Operational
- Boycott of ASCAP Music
- Musicians' Strike
- ABC Formed from NBC Blue
- FCC "Blue Book" Published
- Commercial TV Introduced
- FM-Multiplex (Stereo) Introduced
- Satellite-Cable audio delivery introduced

in 1906 by the American "father of radio," Lee DeForest. From about 1910 until the United States' entry into World War I (1917) radio was in the hands of amateur broadcasters, "ham" operators who would talk to one another through the night over their homemade transmitters. However, with the U.S. involvement in the war came a federal takeover of all radio operations, and the medium had to wait until nearly 1920 to develop further.

Once public radio operations were allowed to resume, radio did not develop into a mass medium right away. People thought of radio as a wireless telephone, and it took time for the person behind the microphone to become adept at communicating with large audiences rather than one-on-one. Another problem was society's orientation to the print media for communicating information. In 1920 there were fewer than one thousand radio sets in the United States and only three licensed stations. Nevertheless, radio station KDKA in Pittsburgh bravely broadcast the presidential election returns that year (with interspersed recorded music) and gave birth to regular radio programming.

The First "Golden Years"

Radio, the new *free* information-entertainment medium, took off almost immediately. By 1922 nearly seven hundred stations had been licensed, and they broadcasted music, sports, drama, vaudeville, and political news events. That year, with more and more families owning radios, the first broadcast commercials were heard. The following year The American Telephone and Telegraph Company (AT&T) established the first radio network with the idea of providing expanded programming services to its affiliates. Although AT&T felt compelled to withdraw from network radio in 1926, RCA immediately picked up the idea and formed the National Broadcasting Company (NBC). The idea was also adopted by the Columbia Broadcasting System (CBS), and within two years the 16 affiliates of CBS were in heavy competition with NBC's Red and Blue networks, which encompassed forty-eight stations. Ultimately, in 1934 a fourth network came into the picture: the Mutual Broadcasting System. MBS gained sixty affiliate stations within a year with which it competed with the three other networks, each with eighty to one hundred twenty affiliates.

Almost at the outset of the network battles the federal government realized the need for updated laws and increased regulation. Congress passed the Radio Act of 1927 and the Federal Communications Act of 1934, settling numerous technical problems and setting criteria for directing radio towards the public's necessities, interests, and convenience.

Programming patterns developed early in radio's history, and music played an extremely important role in it. In fact, one possible reason for radio's early popularity was its audible superiority to the acoustical phonograph in reproducing music. Entire radio programs were devoted to live and recorded music, and if a nonmusical program ran short, the time could be filled by playing music. Early statistics on radio programming show that during radio's first decade more than 60 percent of all broadcasting was music.

Although the 1920s were the Jazz Age and radio was quickly becoming a mass medium, a strong trend in broadcasting was classical and light classical styles of music. Music was also regularly combined with comedy, drama, and vaudeville. Variety shows, such as "The Eveready Hour," presented a broad choice of entertainment, ranging from minstrelsy to classical virtuosos. Nashville's "Grand Ole Opry" was first heard in 1925. One of the biggest radio spectacles of the time was NBC's 1926 inaugural broadcast, which included performances by such names as the New York Philharmonic Orchestra and soprano Mary Garden, as well as music by four dance bands and the humor of Will Rogers.

The first musical variety show on radio to feature strictly popular music was "The Rudy Vallee Show," which premiered on NBC in the fall of 1929. This was also the first of many shows to revolve around a single star, with guest personalities or world celebrities for supplemental contrast. When Vallee came to radio he already had a national identity as a collegiate-looking crooner who was known as the "vagabond lover." Through radio he became the heartthrob of millions of young ladies.

The Great Depression

The immense success of Vallee's show led network programmers to revise their thinking concerning who their audiences really were. This led to major changes that determined network radio personalities and program formats over the next two decades. "The Eddie Cantor Show" was the follow-up hit after Rudy Vallee, incorporating music and comedy into a vigorous format. This combination of popular music and comedy must have been perfect for those audiences in the early years of the Great Depression, and by 1932 the way seemed clear to broadcasters. In the fall of that year a more impressive array of talent was unleashed than radio audiences had heard up to that time. Comedians Jack Benny, George Jessel, Fred Allen, Burns and Allen, and the Marx Brothers were introduced. Many new programs that season centered around singers, such as Bing Crosby, Paul Robeson, Jane Froman, and Al Jolson.

Another major trend in Depression radio shows that countered the slick professionalism of those new shows was the rise of amateurism and audience participation. The appearance of Major Bowes' "Original Amateur Hour" in 1934 heralded a craze which led to numerous imitations over the next two years. Few contestants on these programs ever went on to successful careers in entertainment (Frank Sinatra being a conspicuous exception), but the spirit of competition and the desire for achievement was evidently overwhelming to contestants and audiences alike in those mid-Depression years. Quiz shows were likewise a fast-growing fad. Comedy and music figured into these as well. There were a few antiquiz parodies, such as "It Pays to Be Ignorant," and later some musical quiz shows, such as "Cab Calloway's Quizzicale." The most successful combination of music and comedy was "Kay Kyser's Kollege of Musical Knowledge," in which contestants had to give the *wrong* answer to musical questions.

A "Make-Believe Ballroom"

By 1935 a new type of music was sweeping the nation, a music for the young which lifted the spirits and symbolized the country's struggle to overcome the Depression. This music was big-band "swing." Network radio did its part to popularize big bands and their new sounds. Every evening at 10 or 11 P.M. the networks began a four-hour series of "remote" broadcasts from the great ballrooms and nightclubs of New York, Chicago, and Los Angeles. Every half hour listeners could hear a different band. Soon, several of the nation's leading bands had their own regular network series, the most famous of which was Benny Goodman's "Let's Dance." The sweet and swing sounds of Goodman, Tommy Dorsey, Duke Ellington, Glenn Miller, and others were brought regularly into the living rooms of millions of Americans as they listened or jitterbugged to the latest songs and instrumental riff tunes.

One of the longest-running musical shows in radio, "Camel Caravan," began as a big band show. Starting in 1933, the Casa Loma band was featured in a mix of up-tempo tunes and romantic ballads. Then, in 1936 Benny Goodman's band replaced Casa Loma, and the show began to be targeted to a younger market. "Camel Caravan" lasted into the early 1950s, featuring various musical stars, the last of whom was singer Vaughan Monroe.

In contrast to big-band swing, Bing Crosby's crooning voice had been captivating American audiences since 1932. Beginning in 1935, Crosby began an eleven-year run as the star of "Kraft Music Hall." This show boasted a large roster of guest artists, but Crosby always managed to sing approximately ten songs on each program. Bing Crosby, along with other vocalists, helped to offset the big-band craze and to make song lyrics more essential.

The shows of the 1930s mentioned thus far were normally formatted to thirty or sixty minutes. However, an important component in the history of radio music was the fifteen-minute musical show. Several of the popular bandleaders and vocal artists of the time gained significant reputations in America's heartland through daily, fifteen-minute network shows. One of the earliest of these was Paul Whiteman, who performed a series of "Old Gold Specials" beginning in 1929. Fred Waring's classy stylings were heard from the mid-1930s until he moved into television. The "Chesterfield Show" was initiated in late 1939, featuring Glenn Miller for three years. This show eventually became the "Chesterfield Supper Club," whose later singing stars included Perry Como, Frank Sinatra, and Dorothy Kirsten between 1933 and 1950.

Riding the early crest of popular music broadcasting, a new type of network musical program was introduced by NBC in 1935: "Your Hit Parade." Each week the ten most popular song hits were presented in ascending order, number one always coming last. The songs were performed live (by staff singers, not by the original recording artists), and when one song remained at number one for several weeks, it would be rearranged in new ways to keep it sounding fresh. Lucky Strike Cigarettes was the sponsor, and in order to fill time a "Lucky Strike Extra" (an older song) would be performed. The early staff band for the show was Orin

Tucker's, and one of the staff singers was a very young Frank Sinatra. "Your Hit Parade" had a tremendous influence on the music-listening public and was a potent force in broadcasting and the record industry. The show was one of the important forerunners of the Top 40 broadcast format.

Local (nonnetwork) radio also contributed significantly to history by spawning the "disc jockey." Recorded music shows had been a part of commercial radio from its very start. However, with the great surge of audience interest in music shows occurring in the mid-1930s, recorded music programming got a new lease on life which has survived and flourished to this day. A few early disc jockeys, such as Martin Block, even earned national reputations. Block's show, "Make-Believe Ballroom," which started in 1935 over WNEW (New York), was reviewed by *New Yorker* magazine as "gaily creating the illusion that the country's foremost dance bands are performing on four large stands in a glittering, crystal-chandeliered ballroom." Block's idea was taken from Al Jarvis, whose show of the same name was heard over KFWB (Los Angeles), and the same format was imitated in hundreds of stations in the late 1930s and 1940s. A spin-off of the "Make-Believe Ballroom" concept was the daily fifteen-minute "Bing Crosby Show," consisting entirely of records by the famous crooner.

Classical Music and Opera

As mentioned above, classical and light classical music played an important role in radio programming during the 1920s. A classical music "hour" format was born when WEAF (New York) premiered the "The Victor Hour"—later, "The RCA Victor Hour"—in 1925. This program had its own staff orchestra and regularly featured the finest concert and operatic artists of the time, such as John McCormack of the New York Metropolitan Opera. The popularity of this series soon led to similar programs with a variety of sponsors interested in projecting a dignified image. One offshoot of this type of program was "The RCA Educational Hour," begun in 1928. This program, which became "The NBC Music Appreciation Hour," ran under the direction of Walter Damrosch until 1942.

The New York Philharmonic Sunday afternoon broadcasts, heard over CBS, became a staple of radio's "golden years." In addition, several influential conductors believed in the power of radio to disseminate concert music, particularly Leopold Stokowski, who began broadcasting in 1930. The most notable radio conductor, however, was Arturo Toscanini. The NBC Symphony Orchestra was created exclusively for him, and he conducted it from 1937 to 1954.

Opera has had the longest broadcast history of any type of music. As early as 1910, Enrico Caruso was heard over the air when *Cavalleria rusticana* and *I Pagliacci* were broadcast experimentally from the Metropolitan Opera. While NBC's first network broadcast was a variety show (including orchestral and choral forces), CBS chose to inaugurate its network in 1927 with an operatic work. Deems Taylor's *The King's Henchman* (libretto by Edna St. Vincent Millay), which had become a success at the Metropolitan Opera, was broadcast in its entirety. The longest-running classical series in radio is the Saturday afternoon series of Metropolitan Opera broadcasts. This program began in 1931 as a network presentation and continues today in syndication. There are a number of all-classical music stations in the United States, the most notable of which are WQXR (New York), WFMT (Chicago), and KFAC (Los Angeles).

Broadcasters vs. ASCAP

Since the inception of commercial radio the performing rights to most copyright music had been under the control of the American Society of Composers, Authors and Publishers (ASCAP). Radio networks operated under blanket licenses from ASCAP, which allowed them unlimited use of the ASCAP catalog in return for a percentage of gross income from advertising sales. During 1935–1939 the tariff was 2⅛ percent, amounting to about $6 million annually. When, in 1937, ASCAP began talking of increasing the percentage after 1939, the National Association of Broadcasters (NAB)—long a foe of ASCAP—had good reason to plan for a battle. In late summer of 1939 powers within NAB unveiled the blueprint for a new music licensing organization: Broadcast Music, Inc. (BMI). This alternative to ASCAP, to be owned by broadcasters, hoped to earn a place in the music industry by righting some of the wrongs in the ASCAP organization:

1. Fewer than 150 music publishers and hardly more than 1,000 songwriters shared the fees collected by ASCAP.

2. Only the networks were licensed; independent stations were treated in a laissez-faire manner.

3. Only "live" performances of music, or those on electrically transcribed programs, were surveyed.

BMI, which went into operation in 1940, sought to attract smaller publishers and newer songwriters by making membership less exclusive than ASCAP. It broadened both its licensee roster and its survey to include independent stations and commercially recorded music. The more than six hundred founders of BMI financed the venture by purchasing stock ($300,000) and paying initial licensing fees totalling $1,200,000. The corporation was intended to make no profit and pay no dividends.

BMI's drive for recognition was given a boost during its first year of operation, when the controversial issue of licensing phonograph records for use on the air was decided. In a 1940 lawsuit involving Paul Whiteman's records the court ruled that, having purchased a record, a broadcaster was free to use it on the air without obligation to the artist or record company. This freed radio to unleash its emerging breed of disc jockeys and their long programs of recorded music. BMI seemed all the more attractive to songwriters and publishers because it considered the playing of a record to be a "performance" and paid its members accordingly.

For some time before the establishment of BMI, ASCAP's monopoly in the field of music licensing had been a controversial issue. However, BMI was considered by some observers as an even more threatening concentration, being an organization of powerful broadcast interests potentially in control of an important area of copyright. Consequently, in 1941 the Justice Department, in a move to try to limit competitive practices of both BMI and ASCAP, signed consent decrees with both organizations.

But the battle had not ended. The dispute between broadcasters and ASCAP over licensing fees reached a point in 1941 where ASCAP music was boycotted for a time. For its music programming, network radio had to depend on its budding catalog of BMI songs and on music in the public domain. That meant playing a great deal of established classical music at times when popular styles might be expected. Listeners were also treated to endless hearings of Stephen Foster's immortal "Jeannie with the Light Brown Hair."

The Musicians' Strike

Matters were made worse when the American Federation of Musicians (AFM), under the leadership of its new president, James C. Petrillo, threatened to strike against the record industry. In 1942 the AFM carried out its threat. Although the strike was nominally against record companies, the real target of the strike was the broadcasting industry, in which the employment of instrumentalists had been eroding for some time. The first phase of this trouble involved the increased use of electronic organ in place of an ensemble of players; the second involved the growing amount of recorded music programming since the 1940 court decision. The AFM's demands called for a welfare fund for unemployed musicians to be maintained by payments from the record companies (two of which— Columbia and RCA—also owned major networks: CBS and NBC, respectively). It has been estimated that in 1942 music accounted for 75 percent of broadcast programming, and the AFM hoped that its strike would hit radio and the recording industry hard.

However, both broadcasters and record manufacturers could see the strike coming for some time. Broadcasters were able to stockpile large libraries of records before the strike began. Record companies responded with conservatism. One situation that made this possible was that the war effort had created a shortage in virgin shellac needed to produce high-quality phonograph records. In addition, the major labels had vaults full of unreleased masters into which they could dip whenever necessary. Furthermore, musicians were allowed to play on recordings made for the U.S. government (in support of the war effort), and many of these could be used for commercial purposes, including radio broadcasting. Musical "electrical transcription" programs, a steady source of programming, were also unaffected by the AFM's ban.

One *musical* side effect of the musician's strike was an increase of the importance of vocalists in popular music. (AFM membership included only instrumentalists, not singers.) In the past the big swing bands had somewhat subordinated the role of singers and vocal groups attached to them. However, now that recorded bands were in short supply, vocal soloists and groups—some of them coached to sound like instruments—began to reenter the spotlight.

Ultimately, Petrillo and the AFM prevailed. In the course of 1943 and 1944 all major record labels negotiated agreements with the AFM to contribute to the musicians' fund. However, the union's goals were only partially achieved. Although the new welfare fund did benefit union members, the original idea to force radio to hire and maintain more staff musicians was thwarted by the changing trend in radio away from live music in favor of disc jockey record shows and special transcriptions. After the war live music in dramatic radio shows declined sharply and finally disappeared completely as the entire face of radio programming changed drastically.

The end of the war also brought a change in network structure. Federal investigations of possible or potential network monopolistic practices had begun as early as 1940. An early report recommended divorcement between NBC's red and blue networks. Finally, in 1943 NBC Blue was sold to Edward Noble, president of the Lifesaver Candy Company, for $8 million. The three stations owned by that network together with its nearly two hundred affiliates formed the new American Broadcasting Company (ABC). Unlike other networks, ABC was owned by neither music industry interests nor by newspapers. By war's end in 1945 there were four clearly differentiated major radio networks operating nationally: the Columbia Broadcasting System (CBS), the National Broadcasting Company (NBC—old NBC Red), the American Broadcasting Company (ABC), and the Mutual Broadcasting System (MBS).

The Rise of Music-and-News

Radio was undergoing a facelift as it emerged from World War II, and radio manufacturers were again in full swing. Beginning in 1946, local stations started to attract more attention, and the networks began to lose a tremendous amount of their audience plus a significant amount of advertising revenue. One reason was that the leading network shows had not kept pace with changing audience tastes. Many radio artists, such as Bing Crosby or Fibber McGee and Molly, had been on the radio almost from the beginning of network radio itself. The results were that local stations began gaining larger market shares of listeners and network affiliates began to change their style of programming for certain times of the day to compete with local stations.

The new, successful style of local programming involved recorded music, hourly news updates, and numerous "spot" announcements, which were prerecorded, or live commercials squeezed in between the playing of records. Announcers for such shows were called disc jockeys (later, "DJs"). The DJ programming format had proven itself a decade earlier with recorded music shows such as the "Make-Believe Ballroom" and "Milkman's Matinee" (an all-night show). Now the popularity of music broadcasting was increasing at a phenomenal rate. Radio, rather than restricted to home listening, was becoming a portable, mobile form of entertainment. The public wanted to listen in their cars, at recreation spots (such as the beach), and at work. Disc jockey programming filled those bills exactly.

Advertising dollars followed close behind. The DJ format of music-and-news began to attract such a large number of sponsors that soon the spot announcement time began to rival the amount of time devoted to records. The Federal Communications Commission (FCC) viewed this situation with alarm. In 1946 the FCC issued a report, *Public Service Responsibility of Broadcast Licensees,* called "The Blue Book," in which guidelines for the length and frequency of commercial spots were given. The report also documented the commercial abuse case histories of several stations. The worst case of programming abuse was a station where 2,215 commercial spots were broadcast in one sample week, an average of 16.7 commercials per hour.

The handwriting was on the wall for network radio. During 1947 the post-World War II cold war and anticommunist national climate brought about a series of investigations of entertainment media by the House Committee on Un-American Activities. One unfortunate result of these protracted witch-hunts was the radio (and TV) industry's self-regulatory practice of blacklisting its associates who had been accused or slurred by the committee. This resulted in the loss of a considerable amount of writing and acting talent. In their panic the networks often behaved brutally. One example was the pirating of shows from one network to another. MCA, at that time a giant agency which handled many radio artists, engineered several such moves, usually involving a show going from NBC to CBS. The rivalry between RCA/NBC and Columbia/CBS during the 1940s was not restricted to radio. During 1946 NBC and CBS each made an unsuccessful bid to the FCC asking for adoption of its particular method of color TV. Then, in 1948–1949 there was the record industry's "war of the speeds" between Columbia's LP and RCA's 45–rpm record.

Affiliate stations on all four networks, with their need to survive, began to pre-empt large segments of their "sustaining" network shows. With dwindling revenues and fewer major sponsors at the network level, these one-time monoliths of the industry were forced to turn over larger and larger blocks of air time to their affiliates for local programming, which usually meant DJ shows. In the course of the 1950s network radio declined to a mere skeleton of what it once had been. Even its daytime soap operas eventually could not hold their audiences, since they had to compete with DJs and a growing number of daytime television shows. Eventually, networks merely provided their affiliates with a minimum of "services": hourly news, special events coverage, and short features which might appear scattered through the broadcast day.

The Impact of TV

The introduction of commercial television had a significant impact on radio as early as the postwar years. TV had been in an experimental stage all through the 1930s, and the war effort had temporarily suspended the development of video technology. However, immediately following the end of World War II the development of TV was resumed full force. This helped to satisfy American consumers' pent-up desires to buy and to be entertained. In 1946 TV sets became readily available, and transmitters began to appear in the nation's major cities. Heeding the comments of media observers that TV would become "radio's Frankenstein" and that it would "do to radio what the Sioux did to Custer," the networks quickly got involved. Early network TV shows were mostly adaptations of the radio series that had been popular in prior years. The novelty of TV was irresistible, and by 1950 it was reported that in the larger metropolitan cities (such as Los Angeles, New York, Philadelphia, Baltimore, and Chicago) more people watched TV than listened to the radio.

Fortunately for the future of radio, there was a four-year respite from the "cancerous" growth of TV stations. In 1948 the FCC called a halt to issuing new TV station licenses, ostensibly to study issues in television, AM radio, and FM radio concerning frequency assignments. The beginning of the Korean War in 1950 provided an excuse to prolong these investigations, which stretched out until 1952. However, during the "freeze," network and local television programming continued to develop. Audiences also grew, but not to the full potential of the TV medium, since only the largest cities had more than one station. The years of the freeze gave AM radio the time it needed to establish new programming patterns, especially the music-and-news format. By the time the FCC again began issuing TV station licenses and television resumed its boom, a solid, continuing place for radio had also been ensured.

Top 40 Radio

Although a general music-and-news format for radio had become the rule in the early 1950s, it was not yet refined. Independent stations were extremely diversified in the types of regionally popular music they might broadcast, but the choice of particular records to be played was generally left to the individual DJ. A station would often concentrate on one style within a gamut that ran from Country and Western (C&W) to Rhythm and Blues (R&B), with intermediate shades of popular, "Sweet" (Easy Listening), and the new Rock 'n' Roll. The earliest Rock 'n' Roll DJ was Alan Freed, who did his first R&B show for WJW in Cleveland in 1952. From record lyrics Freed drew the name "Moon Dog" for himself and the term "Rock 'n' Roll" to identify the music. His show was so successful that he became involved in promoting huge Rock 'n' Roll events, such as the "Moon Dog Coronation Ball." In 1954 Freed was hired by WINS in New York and became one of the first nationally known DJ "personalities" of the new era.

The ultimate extension of music-and-news formatting was the Top 40 concept, designed to attract wider audiences and greater advertising revenues. (The idea of programming around top hit songs was not new. "Your Hit Parade," for years a successful program in radio, had been adapted for TV in 1950.) In Top 40 programming the unique feature was the rotation formula, the repetitive play-

ing of the top ten or fifteen hits throughout the broadcast day, v
playing of other songs from the Top 40 list. A weekly "Top 10 /
became a common feature. What was once the idea behind a /
had now become a daily programming concept.

Top 40 radio was pioneered by Todd Storz, owner of a ch/
South and Central United States. Storz began putting the /
1953, first at KOWH (Omaha) and his newly acquired W
Soon the Top 40 concept took on other features which have becu..
from it: brief hourly news; numerous "canned" ads and jingles; an "upbeat ʒⱱⱼ
of delivery by the DJ; station promotions, contests, and gimmicks; and a generally tight format, allowing no dead air time between each small event. No longer
would the selection of records be based on a DJ's preference or reports from local
record dealers. Stations now began employing a "playlist" culled from national
newsletters and from "charts" published in national trade publications. The style
of music might cross over occasionally into Rock 'n' Roll, country, and so forth,
but only if one of the records that had made the Top 40 that week was in that style.

With the sensationally quick spread of Top 40 radio in the mid-1950s stations
became willing promoters of records. Naturally, the broader the exposure a
record company could obtain for its latest product over radio, the greater were its
chances of becoming a hit. This situation predictably led to bribery and other
unethical forms of promotion, collectively known as "payola." Although the
enforcement of a prescribed playlist by a Top 40 station's management often
shielded DJs from payola conditions, the abuse existed nonetheless. The payola
system involving local stations was stumbled upon by a congressional subcom-
mittee during its 1959–1960 investigations into rigged quiz shows. Alan Freed
and Dick Clark (host of TV's "American Bandstand" show) were among the
more notable witnesses called to testify in these and later hearings. Freed stated
that he sometimes accepted payment *after* he had promoted a record he liked,
but that he was in constant control of his program. Clark, aided by ABC network
support, was totally vindicated but had to divest himself of a number of record
and publishing interests in order to avoid possible future conflicts of interest.

The Age of FM and Stereo

One problem which had plagued AM (amplitude modulation) radio reception
since its beginning was audio static—the hissing, popping, and crackling noises
especially abhorrent to music listeners. In 1933 Edwin Howard Armstrong, a
Columbia University physics professor, patented the major elements of a new
method of broadcasting based upon frequency modulation (FM). Although FM
broadcasting could carry only over a line-of-sight radius, much shorter than AM
under good conditions, an FM signal was not subject to static interference. It also
offered the possibility of other high-fidelity advantages as well, such as an
increased music frequency range up to 15,000 Hz (compared with AM's 9,000
Hz). Armstrong immediately began working with RCA to develop his invention;

ever, RCA's administration soon decided to pursue television research full .ne. It also viewed FM as threatening to the status quo of its interests in network broadcasting. Armstrong proceeded to campaign for FM on his own by convincing the FCC to allocate a few experimental channels to it and by working with progressive-minded broadcasters willing to set up new stations. By early 1940 there were twenty-two FM stations authorized by the FCC and limited manufacture of FM receivers had begun. However, U.S. entry into World War II halted the development in this as in all areas of broadcasting.

At war's end, with 430 new FM station applications awaiting approval, the FCC realized that more broadcast space would be needed to accommodate FM channels. In 1945, over the objections of Armstrong and other researchers, the FCC decided to relocate the FM band by "kicking it upstairs" to its present range of 88–108 MHz. Although this move made existing receivers and transmitters obsolete, a successful period of adjustment followed, and by 1947 the transition was complete. During that period another important trend in FM broadcasting began. In 1946 FM stations which had sister AM stations began to simultaneously broadcast programs going out over AM. This practice of "simulcasting" continued to dominate FM broadcasting for the next twenty years and became one of the factors which ensured FM's economic survival during some extremely difficult times.

By 1950 the full impact of TV began affecting the growth of FM in much the same way that it had hit conventional AM radio a few years before. From 1949 to 1959 almost the only FM stations that could avoid closing down were either affiliated with an AM station or were dependent for part of their income on selling music services to retail stores in competition with Muzak® (see Chapter 9). However, in the late 1950s the future began looking brighter. As the AM band grew more and more crowded, the growth potential of FM began to be more appealing to broadcasters. The new interest in high fidelity, spawned by the development of the LP and 45–rpm record, also created renewed interest in FM's more refined sound. Finally, there was the possibility of multiplex stereophonic broadcasting.

Stereo FM became a practical reality in 1961, when the FCC began permitting multiplex broadcasting. The idea took off immediately, and by the mid-1960s more than 50 percent of FM stations were broadcasting in stereo. At about the same time the FCC ruled that no more than 50 percent of an AM station's programming could be simulcast over its FM affiliate. Rather than restricting FM stations, the "50–50 ruling" had the effect of opening up new, more closely targeted markets. Stereo broadcasting was now free to flourish. In addition, a low-overhead FM station could afford to seek a specialized market. Progressive rock, jazz-only, all-talk, or all-news stations were (and still are) not unusual. Noncommercial college stations also spread quickly. There was a virtual explosion of new broadcast formats, and FM radio began growing at a phenomenal rate.

By the mid-1970s there were approximately 3,500 FM stations nationwide, compared with about 4,400 AM stations. By 1980 FM audiences exceeded those for AM in several of the larger markets, such as New York, Los Angeles, Chicago, Dallas-Ft. Worth, and Washington, DC. During the 1970s FM continued its commitment to "beautiful" music (or easy listening). However, in complete contrast with such stations, the FM band also offered album-oriented rock (AOR) stations. At the same time the AM band developed middle-of-the-road (MOR), or adult contemporary, format. The AM and FM domains have shared several musical style formats, including Country, Black (Urban Contemporary), Spanish, and Top 40.

The 1980s and early 1990s saw developments in radio's regulatory standards, musical style trends, and technology. The FCC loosened many of its former restrictions on broadcasting, especially concerning program content. It lifted requirements to broadcast news and public affairs, and it eliminated restrictions on the length and frequency of commercials. The diversity of broadcast formats that had sprung up in the 1960s became less polarized in the 1980s. Blending of broadcast formats complemented the trend toward crossover musical styles in recording. In the same decade, the baby boomers' demand for "their" music spawned many "Golden Oldies" and "Classic Rock" stations. In a move to revitalize interest in Top 40 this format renamed itself Contemporary Hit Radio (CHR). The Country Music explosion in recordings around 1989 (see Chapter 1) resounded in radio with an unprecedented growth in the Country format. By the end of 1994 there were more Country stations in the United States than any other format.

In technology, cable TV broadcasters of the early 1990s developed systems for delivering digital-quality audio to homes. One example is DMX (Digital Music Express), which offers more than 30 channels of music in all styles (even separating classical music from opera). A "black box" in the home decodes the signal into commercial-free, digital-quality stereo sound, and a LCD display on the hand-held controller shows title and artist information for each selection. Broadcasting, be it AM-FM or satellite-cable, is taking its place at the vanguard of the information superhighway.

Review Questions

1. Before public radio operations, what were some uses of radio?

2. What types of radio programming could listeners expect in the early 1920s?

3. Name and discuss a few popular musical radio shows of the 1920s and 1930s.

4. How did radio help to promote the "Swing" era?

5. What were the chief differences between "Your Hit Parade" and the "Make-Believe Ballroom"?

6. Which style of music has the longest broadcast history?

7. Discuss the broadcasters' 1939 boycott against ASCAP and its results.

8. Discuss the Musician's strike against the record industry and its impact on radio.

9. How did the DJ trend begin, and what was the result?

10. Did early TV kill radio? Explain.

11. What were the chief features of Top 40 radio in the 1950s?

12. When did FM come fully into its own? What were some of the reasons?

13. Name one musical trend and one technological trend of the early 1990s.

6

Music in Broadcasting: Radio and Video

Today's commercial radio stations are generally run according to firmly established business practices. The station's format is chosen and retained as long as surveys demonstrate that the market for it has not been glutted and as long as advertising clients continue buying air time. When the business of broadcasting begins to run rough, station management may bring in a consultant to fix the flaws, reprogram the station, or even create an entirely new format for it. Some broadcasters retain a consulting or programming service on a permanent basis in the belief that a consultant's continuing research is more tried and true and more cost-effective than research which the individual station could carry out. This chapter will explore several facets of radio broadcasting. At the conclusion there is a section on music video, its development, and nature.

Station Organization and Operations

The organization of a radio station may vary according to its size, type of programming, size of market, and competition. Larger stations have more full-time personnel than smaller operations, but a ratio of three or four full-time employees to one part-time employee is common in the industry. At larger stations the work is divided between many specialists, while at the smallest stations the staff

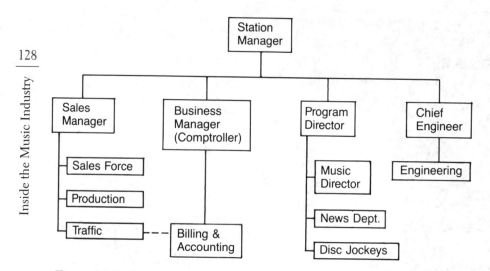

Figure 6-1. Radio station organization—small/medium market (hypothetical).

may have to do more than one job. Figure 6–1 shows a hypothetical organization of key positions and operations for a radio station in a small-to-medium market.

Station Manager

The individual responsible for overall operation of a station is the station manager. He is the ultimate decision- and policy-maker, and is usually the key figure in planning station promotions, format adjustments, and so forth. The station manager is also the liaison between the station and its owner, be that an individual or the front office of a chain. The main department heads working under the station manager include the sales manager, program director, chief engineer, and business manager/comptroller.

Sales Manager

A commercial radio station's sole source of income is its sale of advertising air time. The higher a station's ratings, the greater is its potential for selling air time and charging higher rates for that time. The sales manager's job is to establish and maintain a clientele of advertisers for the station. Larger stations may have a sales force of five to ten people; at smaller stations the sales manager may work by himself. The sales department normally takes charge of producing commercials for local advertisers. This may entail writing ad copy and making recordings at the station or coordinating with advertising agencies. The "traffic" function often comes under the sales manager. Traffic involves making up the daily schedule of commercial spots and then logging what was actually broadcast for billing purposes.

Business Manager/Comptroller

The day-to-day financial functions of a larger radio station are handled by the business manager's office. Routine functions, such as billing and payroll, are accomplished by the staff much the same as in any business. Business planning for the station is generally carried out between the business manager/comptroller and the station manager. In smaller stations all of the business responsibilities may be assumed by the station manager.

Program Director

Everything that goes out over the airwaves from a radio station is ultimately the responsibility of the program director. That includes music, news, commercials, promotions, and public service announcements. The program director is constantly concerned with the details of programming content and scheduling, including what records to play; what tempo(s) of music to use; what types of commercials work best at particular times; how many commercials to use each hour; how much time to devote to news, weather, traffic reports, and so forth; and how to make the most effective use of public service announcements. This array of concerns explains why the program director has such a variety of staff under him, including the station's music director, news department, and announcers/disc jockeys.

Music Director

The program director's assistant is the music director, sometimes called the "music librarian." This person performs several duties which aid the program director in deciding which records will appear on the station's weekly playlist. Many records must be auditioned each week, some of which are brought to the station by record promoters. The music director meets with promoters and screens their information and products. Research must be conducted each week (see below) to determine what records are likely to be enjoyed by the station's listeners. The music director performs this research, and either he or his staff maintains files on the popularity of individual records for future use in programming.

News Department

The size of a station's news department is a clear reflection of the size of the station itself. Smaller stations may have no news department at all, making them dependent on "tear-and-read" stories that come in over one of the national news wire services. At the other end of the spectrum the news department of a large station in a large market may have an entire staff, consisting of copywriters, announcers, reporters, and even helicopter crews.

Disc Jockeys (DJs)

The personality behind the microphone is probably the most crucial factor in determining a radio station's public appeal, particularly if its programming is aimed at the youth or young adult market. Although announcing record titles and artists is the chief excuse for a DJ's patter on the air, there is a vast array of other announcements which he must impart within the short spaces of time between records and taped commercials. These may include advertisements, promotional announcements, time and weather reports, and announcements about local events. A DJ must be informative, yet entertaining, and he must find the proper balance between talk and music for his particular format and audience. A station's programming schedule is usually divided into six "dayparts," each served by a different DJ shift:

Morning Drive	(6 A.M.–10 A.M.)
Midday	(10 A.M.–3 P.M.)
Afternoon Drive	(3 P.M.–7 P.M.)
(Early) Evening	(7 P.M.–10 P.M.)
(Late) Night	(10 P.M.–2 A.M.)
Overnight	(2 A.M.-6 A.M.)

The most desirable shifts on an AM station are the Morning and Afternoon drives, since that is the time most people are listening. However, a DJ's particular radio personality is also a factor in scheduling his shift within the total schedule. In smaller stations a DJ may be required to be a licensed engineer.

Chief Engineer

A large radio station may have a sizable staff of engineers who are supervised by the chief engineer. Radio engineering is composed of several duties. The engineer must monitor the quality and volume level of the sound being transmitted. He also performs routine maintenance on the station's broadcast equipment. Transcribing commercial spots to tape cartridges, or "carts," is another necessary chore, since each spot is usually broadcast by using a cart rather than a record. Broadcasting music from CDs is now the rule, and some engineering departments can make their own with a CD "burner."

Broadcast Formats

Radio's format explosion of the 1960s and subsequent market research has revealed that there is not just one radio audience but many. In any single radio "market," or geographical broadcast area, there are usually two large principal target markets: youth and adult. Within each of these there can be many differences in listener taste, and these varying preferences are served by the various broadcast formats.

The main component in the format of most commercial stations (other than news/talk/information stations) is the general style of music which is broadcasted. Some of these, such as Country or Rock are composite, single-style designations used by the recording industry as well. Other formats, such as middle-of-the-road (MOR) or album-oriented-rock (AOR), are more generalized, taking in a broader cross section of musical styles (including some Country and R&B).

It has been suggested that asking a station to describe its format is somewhat like asking someone for his or her name. The possibilities for individualism can be infinite. Nevertheless, certain generic labels have surfaced over the years, partially through the efforts of overseers and observers of the radio industry. Arbitron, a major broadcasting rating service of the American Bureau of Research—similar to A. C. Nielsen—identifies as many as sixteen distinct music formats, while surveys published in the *Broadcasting & Cable Yearbook* discuss more than twenty. In order of station numbers, the following lists the twenty most popular music formats with non-music formats interspersed.

1. Country

2. Adult Contemporary

3. Religious

4. Oldies

   News/Talk

5. Contemporary Hit Radio (CHR)/Top 40 News

6. Rock/AOR

7. Variety/Diverse

   Talk

8. Classical

9. Middle-of-the-Road (MOR)

10. Classic Rock

11. Jazz

12. Spanish

13. Gospel

14. Progressive

    Sports

15. Urban Contemporary

16. Beautiful Music

    Educational

17. Black

18. Big Band

Agriculture and Farm

19. Nostalgia

20. New Age

The following are brief introductions to the most popular music formats. Text in *italics* quotes the definition given in *Broadcasting & Cable Yearbook* (1994).

Country

Country music, ranging from older traditional country and western to today's "Hit Country" sounds. The amount of news and talk on country stations varies widely from station to station. Originally, this musical style was called Country and Western (C&W). There is not much truly "Western" music left, and the designation has been shortened to "Country." The growth of stations in this format has been phenomenal from the 1970s through the 1990s. Currently, country stations are the most numerous. There are country stations in all the major radio markets as well as great numbers of them in smaller towns and rural areas.

Technically, the modern Country format is quite similar to MOR, with station ID jingles, DJ voice segues over the beginning and ending of records, hourly news and weather, frequent commercial spots, and a tight continuity of sound. The chief differences are the styles of music played.

Country audiences include a wide span of ages, from fifteen to sixty-five, centering on the twenty- to thirty-five-year-old group. Partly for that reason and partly because of the modernization of country music, there is noticeable variety in the musical styles heard on many country stations. The artists may range from old-time Country to Country-Rock, Pop, contemporary, and occasionally even soul.

The proliferation of Country music stations is intimately related to the development of the "Nashville Sound" and "Young Country" (see Chapter 1). These styles are perhaps more universal than any other contemporary musical style, and that accounts largely for the broad appeal of Country music radio. Moreover, recordings by many of these artists have become crossover hits, played with great frequency on MOR and CHR stations, and numerous Country-style songs have been adapted for Beautiful Music listening.

Adult Contemporary and MOR

Adult contemporary—*Recent popular songs, with a few oldies. The songs tend to be upbeat and soft. News and talk segments are prominent during rush hour "drive times." Also known as "Lite."* **MOR (Middle-of-the-Road)**—*Traditional AM format featuring a balanced mix of music, news, and talk. Songs are usually popular standards. Announcers are often personalities who try to keep the listener interest-*

ed and informed. News, both local and national, plays an important role at most MOR stations; coverage of sporting events and other features of interest to the community is common. At one time a single format, these two are still closely related. They reflect traditional versus progressive tastes. The styles and personalities of DJs in these formats are similar and just as important as those on modern Country and CHR stations. The DJ may be a slick, glib, "show biz" type, sweeping the audience along and driving the show forward. However, the target audience for Adult Contemporary/MOR is post-CHR, people in their late twenties or thirties.

Religious and Gospel

Religious—*Inspirational/spiritual talk and music. Most religious stations air Christian sermons or songs.* During the 1980s one of the fastest-growing radio formats was "Christian" music. At this point Religious stations have become the third most popular. Sponsorship of these stations may be non-commercial or partially commercial. Apart from sermons the broadcast style of Religious stations is usually relaxed, even serene. Listeners tune in for inspiration rather than emotional stimulation. Although the age demographic among listeners is broad, the target audience is post-thirty. **Gospel**—*Especially popular in the South, evangelical music is programmed on many Religious format stations.*

Oldies, Classic Rock, Big Band, and Nostalgia

Oldies—*Hit songs from the fifties, sixties, and seventies. Usually played by upbeat DJs, with news, talk, and special features (chart countdowns, trivia contests, etc.) playing an important role.* **Classic Rock**—*Popular rock music of the seventies and eighties. Also see* **Rock/AOR**. **Big Band**—*Popular music from the thirties and forties. Primarily instrumental works by bands such as Glen Miller's Orchestra and Tommy Dorsey.* **Nostalgia**—*Popular tunes from the thirties, forties, and fifties. Nostalgia stations often feature on-air personalities, and usually have heavy news and information coverage.* The pastime of listening to the big hits of yesteryear developed in the 1970s and 1980s alongside the public's increasing love of nostalgia. As the decades in the definitions suggest, each variant format appeals to a different age demographic. Oldies and Classic Rock are particularly interesting, since they respond to market demand from "Baby Boomers" (people born between 1946 and 1964).

CHR/Top 40

Current hot selling records. Usually a playlist of 20 to 40 songs continuously played throughout the day. DJs are often upbeat "personalities." News and information are given light coverage. In the "classic" CHR/Top 40 format the continuity is tighter and the programming is more closely structured than in any other radio format. For example, it is common to hear a song's introduction begin before a high-powered DJ finishes announcing the record, and the DJ will usu-

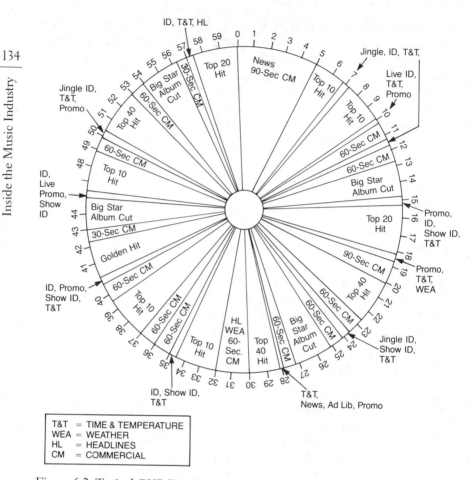

Figure 6-2. Typical CHR/Top 40 clock hour.

T&T = TIME & TEMPERATURE
WEA = WEATHER
HL = HEADLINES
CM = COMMERCIAL

ally segue back into his line of chatter before a record has completely ended. There is no "dead" air time on a CHR station. The energy and forward thrust of the programming is intended to appeal to a teenage target market.

The program structure of CHR has typical and predictable elements which are planned in the form of a clock (see Figure 6–2). This ensures that in any given hour all the features of the format will appear with calculated frequency and emphasis.

Music research and classification are essential in this format. Not only are the Top 40 songs subdivided by tens for rotation, but many popular recordings not currently in the Top 40 are scheduled with less frequency than the central rotation. Some possible categories are records just entering or exiting the central rotation (sometimes subclassified by tempo/mood); records not on the current survey but requested frequently by listeners; hits within the last nine months;

"Solid Gold" hits of the past three to five years; album cuts from Top 10 albums (in local sales); and classic Rock or Pop played for nostalgia value.

The classic CHR format has been loosened in recent years, and strict clock scheduling has been modified. There is a tendency to blend the "now" sound of Top 40 with the flexibility of looser formats, which may cluster commercials together in order to present longer "sweeps" of uninterrupted music.

Rock/AOR

Rock music from the sixties to the present. Album-oriented-rock features music "sweeps" or uninterrupted sets. News plays a secondary role. Also see **Classic Rock.** Album-oriented Rock evolved from the "underground" and "progressive" Rock stations of the 1960s and early 1970s. Many AOR stations can still boast the most extreme of Rock styles heard on radio. (However, the Progressive format now claims this as its territory. See **Progressive** below.) Many artists heard on AOR stations record only album-length CD/cassettes or only rarely have a single release. Yet there is a diversity of Rock styles heard on these stations, much of which stations in other formats will never touch. Stylistically, one Rock/AOR station may wish to give the laid-back impression of completely unstructured programming, while another may project the high-energy of a CHR or MOR station. In either case Rock/AOR is aimed at teen and young adult audiences.

Variety/Diverse

A station listing four or more formats. Typical of noncommercial stations. To a limited degree many commercial stations engage in variety programming. For example, during evening or late-night hours, a Rock or CHR station may soften its format to include more older music or quasi-MOR artists. Or, on weekends, an Adult Contemporary station may run a syndicated Jazz show for a few hours. College radio stations, other than those in the Progressive/Alternative domain, often employ a Variety format. A split between Classical and Jazz is common, and additional musical styles vary from station to station.

Classical

Classical music, often long pieces played without interruption. Announcers provide extended commentary and criticism on the pieces. Special features, such as live concerts, are common. Primarily a noncommercial FM format. Classical stations appeal mostly to a post-thirty-five-year-old audience.

Black and Urban Contemporary

Black—*Music, talk, and news targeted at black listeners. Music at these stations is similar to Urban Contemporary stations, but this format caters more directly to the interest and tastes of black audiences.* **Urban Contemporary**—*Dance music,* often from a variety of genres (i.e., rhythm & blues, Rap). Most Urban Contemporary stations emphasize music by black artists. News and public service announcements often focus on the local area, lending the station's image an aura of community involvement. The target age group for Black and Urban Contemporary is eighteen to twenty-four. However, demographic studies reveal that these audiences are a mix of black and white. Among the factors accounting for this are diversified audience tastes and crossover musical styles such as Rap and R&B.

Other Formats

Jazz—Primarily a noncommercial FM format. Some Classical stations program jazz music features. Like the Classical format, Jazz appeals mainly to a post-thirty-five-year-old audience. **Spanish**—The significant demographic here is, of course, culture rather than age. The particular style or mix of styles a Spanish-language station emphasizes will determine the age demographic of its target audience. Florida, New York, the Southwest, and California are the chief areas for Spanish-language stations. However, they thrive in every urban center where there is a substantial Hispanic population. **Beautiful Music**—Uninterrupted instrumental soft music. There is usually very little talk and few commercials. Also known as "Easy Listening." The basic song material on these recordings comes from a vast range of traditions, spanning Tin Pan Alley, the Broadway stage, Top 40 pop songs of the past, and even certain Rock classics. The target market for Beautiful Music is adults, mostly over thirty-five years old, who wish to have unobtrusive music playing while they go about their business. For that reason Beautiful Music is sometimes described as "background" music and is compared with Environmental Music by Muzak® (see Chapter 9). Although some Beautiful Music stations use a live announcer for record identification and news, the majority are partially or completely automated (see below), and announcements may be "canned." **Progressive**—Progressive stations play many types of music, often including avant-garde music not played on conventional stations. Primarily a noncommercial format, common among college radio stations. Also known as "alternative."

A significant trend in radio since the 1960s has been noncommercial "public" broadcasting. Stations of this type are nonprofit and are licensed by the FCC "for the advancement of an educational program." Public radio stations are assigned to the lower end of the FM band. Most of these facilities are located on college campuses and are student-operated to benefit degree programs in communications, theater, and music. Other stations operate in the public sector, many of them labeling themselves "alternative" or "community access" radio. Typically, the format of a public radio station is either all of one type, such as classical music, or is in blocks on a program-by-program basis. Music, public affairs, cultural information, religion, and instructional programs are some of the areas employed in block formats. Musical styles most frequently heard on noncommercial stations include Classical, Jazz, and Folk.

Over two hundred public stations have qualified for funding assistance from the Corporation for Public Broadcasting and are affiliates of National Public Radio, the counterpart of TV's Public Broadcasting System. Such stations must meet minimum criteria in power, staffing, hours of operation, studio facilities and equipment, and a programming thrust toward a general audience. Affiliates may receive service and development grants and are given access to the special syndicated programs produced for NPR by its larger affiliates and other sources.

Research and Music Programming

In commercial radio, research is considered to be the keystone of success. There are two types of research in radio that are conducted on a regular, cyclic basis. One is audience research, in which Arbitron, Pulse, and other firms conduct semiannual surveys ("sweeps") to determine the popularity ranking, or "ratings," of stations in a particular market. The other type of research is conducted weekly (or more often) by a station or programming service to determine which records should be played and with what frequency—the station's "playlist."

The Playlist

In reality a radio station's playlist can be several ranked lists, each covering one part of the rotation of recordings, symbolized here:

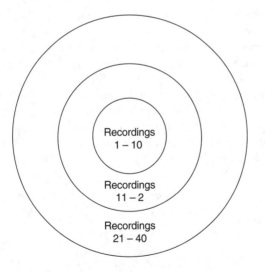

Usually, there are different playlists for singles and albums. Making up the playlist is the responsibility of the music director and/or the program director, sometimes called the "gatekeepers" of the station's programming. Some independent stations rely on a programming service for their playlists (see below). If a station is part of a chain, such as RKO, a large part of the research is carried out by staff in the chain's front office. In that case, stations will be regularly supplied with a partial or total playlist.

The playlist functions within a station mainly as a programming guideline supplied by management to aid, protect, and (to a degree) control a DJ's choice of records. However, a station's playlist is normally available also to the public and may even be printed and distributed professionally. The list may be useful to local record stores and record distributors, and also to radio stations operating in other markets. In determining their own weekly playlists, local stations typically utilize record charts, information from record promoters and tip sheets, local record sales, other stations' playlists, and internal data.

Charts

Rankings of the most popular records are published in several weekly trade journals, notably *Billboard* and *Radio and Records*. The data that determine chart positions are sales figures from retail sources and frequency of airplay in selected geographical areas. SoundScan point-of-sale scanning determines chart sales data. This system sends bar-code data from the cash registers of selected record retailers to a central computer, which compiles comprehensive retail sales data. Broadcast Data Systems tracks the playlists of reporting stations and compiles the data by computer.

Billboard's "Hot 100," the most famous chart, is a ranking of single records and the document most widely consulted by music directors and program directors as well as record industry managers. For each record title on the Hot 100 complete information is given concerning artist(s), producer, songwriter, label, and catalog number. The chart shows the record's position during the current and previous two weeks (1—100), the number of weeks the record has been on the chart, and the "peak" position attained by the record during its chart life. For records "demonstrating the greatest airplay and sales gains" during the current week, the position number is enhanced with a distinguishing mark called a "bullet." The Hot 100 chart is of greatest use to Top 40 and MOR programmers. A chart showing the 200 top albums follows a similar format, *Billboard* also serves areas of the record and radio industry by publishing a series of more specialized charts:

Top Albums	Hot Singles	Top Videos
Blues	Adult Contemporary	Top Video Sales
Top Classical	Country	Laserdiscs
Top Classical Crossover	Dance/Club Play	Music Video
Contemporary Christian	Dance/Maxi-Singles Sales	Rentals
Country	Latin	
Gospel	R&B	
Heatseekers	Hot R&B Airplay	
Jazz	Hot R&B Singles Sales	

Top Albums *(continued)* **Hot Singles** *(continued)*

Jazz/Contemporary   Rap
The Billboard Latin 50   Rock/Album Rock Tracks
Kid Audio   Rock/Modern Rock Tracks
New Age   Hot 100 Airplay
Pop Catalog   Hot 100 Singles
R&B
Reggae
World Music

Record Promoters and Tipsheets

As pointed out in Chapter 3, a good record promoter, far from being a nuisance, can perform a valuable service to broadcasters by providing information. He can do this by drawing the programmer's attention to such research data as recent chart activity involving his products, trade paper reviews and "picks," data on airplay from stations in other areas; the frequency of a record's airplay on competitive stations in the local area, reports on the demographic appeal of a record as shown in sales and airplay, and sales figures on his company's newest singles and albums.

Other sources which radio programmers read regularly are industry tip sheets. These newsletters print "inside" information on what records are breaking out and where, and they generally contain charts. Typical radio tip sheets are the *Bill Gavin Report* and the *Monday Morning Quarterback*.

Local Record Sales

Although some sales information is available from record promoters, a station's music director will normally phone a few local record retailers and wholesalers (distributors, one-stops, and so forth) on a weekly basis. Data on local sales is considered extremely important in fine tuning a playlist to include local and regional hits which may not be ranked very high in the national charts.

Other Playlists

Since playlists are normally distributed openly, it is not unusual for radio stations in different locales to exchange them (by fax machine) occasionally or regularly. Programmers consider it valuable to find out what records are being programmed on stations in other markets. Such arrangements are normally carried out between stations with similar formats located in markets with comparable demographic qualities, such as population and ethnic mix. In addition, trade periodicals publish playlists from large and influential stations.

Billboard® HOT 100® SINGLES™

FOR WEEK ENDING JAN. 20, 1996

COMPILED FROM A NATIONAL SAMPLE OF TOP 40 RADIO AIRPLAY MONITORED BY BROADCAST DATA SYSTEMS, TOP 40 RADIO PLAYLISTS, AND RETAIL AND RACK SINGLES SALES COLLECTED, COMPILED, AND PROVIDED BY SoundScan®

THIS WEEK	LAST WEEK	2 WKS AGO	WKS. ON CHART	TITLE PRODUCER (SONGWRITER)	ARTIST LABEL & NUMBER/DISTRIBUTING LABEL	PEAK POSITION
				★ ★ ★ No. 1 ★ ★ ★		
1	1	1	8	ONE SWEET DAY ▲ 8 weeks at No. 1 W.AFANASIEFF,M.CAREY (M.CAREY,M.MCCARY,N.MORRIS,W.MORRIS,S.STOCKMAN,W.AFANASIEFF)	◆ MARIAH CAREY & BOYZ II MEN (C) (D) (M) (T) (V) (X) COLUMBIA 78074	1
2	2	2	9	EXHALE (SHOOP SHOOP) (FROM "WAITING TO EXHALE") ▲ BABYFACE (BABYFACE)	◆ WHITNEY HOUSTON (C) (D) (M) (T) (V) (X) ARISTA 1-2885	1
3	3	3	10	HEY LOVER ▲ RED HOT LOVER TONE (R.TEMPERTON,LL COOL J)	◆ LL COOL J (C) (D) (M) (T) (V) DEF JAM/RAL 577494/ISLAND	3
4	10	11	24	MISSING B.WATT,T.THORN,J.COXON (T.THORN,B.WATT)	◆ EVERYTHING BUT THE GIRL (C) (T) (X) ATLANTIC 87124	4
5	6	7	23	BREAKFAST AT TIFFANY'S D.CASTELL (T.PIPES)	◆ DEEP BLUE SOMETHING (C) RAINMAKER 98138/INTERSCOPE	5
6	9	10	15	NAME L.GIORDANO (J.RZEZNIK)	◆ GOO GOO DOLLS (C) METAL BLADE 17758/WARNER BROS.	6
7	5	5	10	DIGGIN' ON YOU ● BABYFACE (BABYFACE)	◆ TLC (C) (D) (M) (T) (X) LAFACE 2-4119/ARISTA	5
8	12	13	7	ONE OF US R.CHERTOFF (E.BAZILIAN)	◆ JOAN OSBORNE (C) (D) BLUE GORILLA 852368/MERCURY	8
9	4	4	23	GANGSTA'S PARADISE (FROM "DANGEROUS MINDS") ▲2 D.RASHEED (A.IVEY,JR.,L.SANDERS,D.RASHEED,S.WONDER)	◆ COOLIO FEATURING L.V. (C) (D) MCA SOUNDTRACKS 55104/MCA	1
10	11	12	7	YOU'LL SEE MADONNA,D.FOSTER (MADONNA,D.FOSTER)	◆ MADONNA (C) (D) (V) MAVERICK 17719/WARNER BROS.	6
11	8	9	14	BEFORE YOU WALK OUT OF MY LIFE/LIKE THIS AND LIKE THAT SOULSHOCK,KARLIN,D.AUSTIN,C.WOLFE (A.MARTIN,C.SCHACK,K.KARLIN,D.AUSTIN,C.WOLFE)	◆ MONICA (C) (D) (M) (T) (X) ROWDY 3-5052/ARISTA	7
12	7	8	17	FANTASY ▲2 M.CAREY,D.HALL (M.CAREY,C.FRANTZ,T.WEYMOUTH,D.HALL,A.BELEW,S.STANLEY)	◆ MARIAH CAREY (C) (D) (M) (T) (V) (X) COLUMBIA 78043	1
13	18	18	22	TELL ME ● B.P.WILSON (B.WILSON,A.LARRIEUX,D.BROWN)	◆ GROOVE THEORY (C) (D) (T) (X) EPIC 77961	5
14	13	16	19	RUNAWAY ● J.JAM,T.LEWIS,J.JACKSON (J.JACKSON,J.HARRIS III,T.LEWIS)	◆ JANET JACKSON (C) (D) (M) (T) (V) (X) A&M 581194	3
15	27	27	11	TIME D.GEHMAN (M.BRYAN,D.FELBER,D.RUCKER,J.SONEFELD)	◆ HOOTIE & THE BLOWFISH (C) (V) (X) ATLANTIC 87095	15
16	25	26	11	BE MY LOVER A.BRENNER,G.A.SARAF (G.A.SARAF,A.BRENNER,M.THORNTON,L.MCCRAY)	◆ LA BOUCHE (C) (D) (T) (X) RCA 64446	16
17	17	17	11	BEAUTIFUL LIFE D.POP,M.MARTIN,JOKER (JOKER,J.BALLARD)	◆ ACE OF BASE (C) (D) (M) (T) (V) (X) ARISTA 1-2889	15
18	19	19	7	TONITE'S THA NIGHT J.DUPRI (J.DUPRI,R.PARKER,K.HARRISON,T.CRUM,R.AIKENS,R.NEAL,C.SATCHELL)	◆ KRIS KROSS (C) (D) (M) (T) RUFFHOUSE 78092/COLUMBIA	18
19	20	20	16	ANYTHING 3T (T.JACKSON,T.JACKSON,T.JACKSON)	◆ 3T (C) (D) (T) MJJ 77913/550 MUSIC	19
20	26	25	34	AS I LAY ME DOWN S.LIPSON (S.B.HAWKINS)	◆ SOPHIE B. HAWKINS (C) (D) COLUMBIA 77801	6
21	22	23	24	BACK FOR GOOD C.PORTER,G.BARLOW (G.BARLOW)	◆ TAKE THAT (C) (D) (V) ARISTA 1-2848	7
				★ ★ ★ GREATEST GAINER/SALES ★ ★ ★		
22	38	47	6	NOBODY KNOWS T.RICH (J.RICH,D.DUBOSE)	◆ THE TONY RICH PROJECT (C) (D) (M) (T) LAFACE 2-4115/ARISTA	22
23	14	15	10	YOU REMIND ME OF SOMETHING ● R.KELLY (R.KELLY)	◆ R. KELLY (C) (D) JIVE 42344	4
24	23	28	25	ONLY WANNA BE WITH YOU D.GEHMAN (M.BRYAN,D.FELBER,D.RUCKER,J.SONEFELD)	◆ HOOTIE & THE BLOWFISH (C) (V) ATLANTIC 87132	6
25	16	14	5	I GOT ID/LONG ROAD B.O'BRIEN (E.VEDDER)	PEARL JAM (D) (V) EPIC 78199*	7
				★ ★ ★ GREATEST GAINER/AIRPLAY ★ ★ ★		
26	32	34	4	SITTIN' UP IN MY ROOM (FROM "WAITING TO EXHALE") BABYFACE (BABYFACE)	◆ BRANDY (C) (D) ARISTA 1-2929	26
27	30	33	14	SET U FREE G.ACOSTA (G.ACOSTA,N.RENEE)	PLANET SOUL (C) (T) (X) STRICTLY RHYTHM 12362	27
28	34	36	29	ROLL TO ME A.CLAY (J.CURRIE)	◆ DEL AMITRI (C) (X) A&M 581114	10
29	29	30	31	KISS FROM A ROSE (FROM "BATMAN FOREVER") ● T.HORN (SEAL)	◆ SEAL (C) (D) (V) ZTT/SIRE 17896/WARNER BROS.	1
30	33	35	25	CARNIVAL N.MERCHANT (N.MERCHANT)	◆ NATALIE MERCHANT (C) (D) ELEKTRA 64413/EEG	10
31	39	40	10	THE WORLD I KNOW E.ROLAND,M.SERLETIC (E.ROLAND)	◆ COLLECTIVE SOUL (C) (D) (V) ATLANTIC 87088	31
32	15	6	4	FREE AS A BIRD J.LENNON,P.MCCARTNEY,G.HARRISON,R.STARR (J.LENNON,P.MCCARTNEY,G.HARRISON,R.STARR)	◆ THE BEATLES (C) (V) (X) APPLE 58497/CAPITOL	6
33	21	21	7	SOON AS I GET HOME C.THOMPSON,S.COMBS (F.EVANS,C.THOMPSON,S.COMBS)	◆ FAITH EVANS (C) (D) (M) (T) (X) BAD BOY 7-9040/ARISTA	21
34	41	41	7	WONDER N.MERCHANT (N.MERCHANT)	◆ NATALIE MERCHANT (C) (D) ELEKTRA 64376/EEG	34
35	35	32	13	DREAMING OF YOU G.ROCHE (F.GOLDE,T.SNOW)	SELENA (C) (V) EMI LATIN 58490/EMI	22
36	28	22	11	BULLET WITH BUTTERFLY WINGS FLOOD,A.MOULDER,B.CORGAN (B.CORGAN)	◆ SMASHING PUMPKINS (C) (D) VIRGIN 38522	22
37	37	37	6	NO ONE ELSE J.OLIVIER,S.COMBS (J.C.OLIVIER,S.COMBS,T.ROBINSON,DA BRAT)	◆ TOTAL (C) (D) (M) (T) BAD BOY 7-9042/ARISTA	37
38	43	39	16	HOOK S.THOMPSON,M.BARBIERO (J.POPPER)	◆ BLUES TRAVELER (C) (V) (X) A&M 581176	38
39	40	42	7	NATURAL ONE (FROM "KIDS") W.GAGEL (L.BARLOW,J.DAVIS,W.GAGEL)	◆ FOLK IMPLOSION (C) (D) LONDON 850430/ISLAND	39
40	42	43	44	RUN-AROUND S.THOMPSON,M.BARBIERO (J.POPPER)	◆ BLUES TRAVELER (C) (V) (X) A&M 580982	8
41	31	31	12	LOVE U 4 LIFE D.SWING (DEVANTE 4HISDAMNSELF)	◆ JODECI (C) (D) (T) UPTOWN 55133/MCA	31
42	44	38	12	BLESSED G.PENNY,E.JOHN (E.JOHN,B.TAUPIN)	◆ ELTON JOHN (C) (D) (V) ROCKET 852394/ISLAND	34
43	36	29	15	WHO CAN I RUN TO ● J.DUPRI (ROEBUCK,SIMMONS,ALSTIN,JR.)	◆ XSCAPE (C) (D) SO SO DEF 78056/COLUMBIA	8
44	48	49	37	DECEMBER E.ROLAND,M.SERLETIC (E.ROLAND)	◆ COLLECTIVE SOUL (C) (V) ATLANTIC 87157	20
45	50	50	6	GET TOGETHER A.ZIGMAN (C.POWERS)	BIG MOUNTAIN (C) (D) GIANT 17750	45
46	24	24	7	TOO HOT B.DOBBS (A.IVEY,B.DOBBS,G.BROWN)	◆ COOLIO (C) (D) (T) TOMMY BOY 7718	24
47	51	63	3	LET'S PLAY HOUSE DAT NIGGA DAZ (MICHEL'LE,SNOOP DOGGY DOGG,KURUPT,DAT NIGGA DAZ,NATE DOGG)	◆ THA DOGG POUND FEATURING MICHEL'LE (C) (D) DEATH ROW/INTERSCOPE 53230/PRIORITY	47
48	49	48	33	WATERFALLS ▲ ORGANIZED NOIZE (ORGANIZED NOIZE,M.ETHERIDGE,L.LOPES)	◆ TLC (C) (D) (M) (T) (V) LAFACE 2-4107/ARISTA	1
49	55	59	10	RIDIN' LOW R.PREUSS (R."RIKKO"PREUSS,D.WILSON)	◆ L.A.D. FEATURING DARVY TRAYLOR (C) (D) (T) HOLLYWOOD 64004	49
50	47	44	14	I'D LIE FOR YOU (AND THAT'S THE TRUTH) ● R.NEVISON (D.WARREN)	◆ MEAT LOAF (C) (D) (X) MCA 55134	13
51	52	52	7	WE GOT IT C.STOKES,S.MATHER (C.STOKES,S.MATHER,J.CARTER,A.TOUSSAINT)	◆ IMMATURE (FEATURING SMOOTH) (C) (D) (T) MCA 55148	51
52	56	62	17	I'LL BE THERE FOR YOU/THIS HOUSE IS NOT A HOME G.MACKILLOP,D.WILDE,P.SOLEM (D.CRANE,M.KAUFFMAN,A.WILLIS,P.SOLEM,D.WILDE,M.SKLOFF)	◆ THE REMBRANDTS (C) (D) EASTWEST 64384/EEG	17
53	45	45	5	JUST TAH LET U KNOW E.WRIGHT (E.WRIGHT,A.TROTTER IV,R.PACE)	◆ EAZY-E (C) (D) (T) RUTHLESS 5532/RELATIVITY	45
54	46	46	8	I REMEMBER TIM & BOB (N.MORRIS,W.MORRIS,S.STOCKMAN,T.KELLY,B.ROBINSON)	BOYZ II MEN (C) (D) (T) MOTOWN 860480	46
55	54	51	15	CELL THERAPY ORGANIZED NOIZE (ORGANIZED NOIZE,R.BARNETT,T.BURTON,C.GIPP,W.KNIGHTON)	◆ GOODIE MOB (C) (D) (M) (T) LAFACE 2-4113/ARISTA	39
56	67	70	13	I MISS YOU (COME BACK HOME) (FROM "NEW YORK UNDERCOVER") HEAVY D (HEAVY D,T.ROBINSON)	◆ MONIFAH (C) (M) (T) (X) UPTOWN 55107/MCA	56
57	70	—	2	VISIONS OF A SUNSET (FROM "MR. HOLLAND'S OPUS") S.STOCKMAN (S.STOCKMAN)	◆ SHAWN STOCKMAN (C) (D) (X) POLYDOR 580962	57
58	64	67	8	WHEN LOVE & HATE COLLIDE P.WOODROFFE,DEF LEPPARD (J.ELLIOTT,R.SAVAGE)	◆ DEF LEPPARD (C) (D) (V) MERCURY 852424	58
				★ ★ ★ HOT SHOT DEBUT ★ ★ ★		
59	NEW ▶		1	CUMBERSOME J.ROSS,J.POLLOCK,T.MORRIS (J.ROSS,J.POLLOCK)	◆ SEVEN MARY THREE (C) (D) MAMMOTH 98111/ATLANTIC	59
60	57	54	16	DANGER P.F.CUTTIN,OUTLOUD (OUTLOUD,P.F.CUTTIN)	◆ BLAHZAY BLAHZAY (C) (T) (X) FADER 127049/MERCURY	46
61	73	78	6	JUST A GIRL M.WILDER (G.STEFANI,T.DUMONT)	◆ NO DOUBT (C) TRAUMA 98116/INTERSCOPE	61
62	53	53	12	CRUISIN' D'ANGELO (W.ROBINSON,M.TAPLIN)	◆ D'ANGELO (C) (D) (T) (X) EMI 58468	53
63	65	58	12	WHERE EVER YOU ARE DENZIL FOSTER,T.MCELROY (DENZIL FOSTER,T.MCELROY)	◆ TERRY ELLIS (C) (D) (X) EASTWEST 64361/EEG	52
64	66	68	19	COME WITH ME SHAI (SHAI)	◆ SHAI (C) (D) (M) (X) GASOLINE ALLEY 55081/MCA	43
65	68	66	11	I WILL REMEMBER YOU (FROM "THE BROTHERS MCMULLEN") P.MARCHAND (S.MCLACHLAN,S.EGAN,D.MERENDA)	◆ SARAH MCLACHLAN (C) (D) (X) ARISTA 1-2893	65
66	76	71	12	SEXUAL HEALING 20 FINGERS (M.GAYE,O.BROWN,D.RITZ)	MAX-A-MILLION (C) (D) S.O.S. 14248/ZOO	60
67	63	65	18	DO YOU SLEEP? J.PATINO,L.LOEB (L.LOEB)	◆ LISA LOEB & NINE STORIES (C) (D) (V) GEFFEN 19388	18
68	69	72	10	THROW YOUR HANDS UP/GANGSTA'S PARADISE M.THOMPSON,J.WILLIAMS,D.RASHEED (M.THOMPSON,J.WILLIAMS,K.BLUE,A.EDWARDS,A.CRISS,L.SANDERS,S.WONDER)	◆ L.V. (C) (T) (X) TOMMY BOY 7699	65
69	72	73	12	HOOKED ON YOU SOULSHOCK,KARLIN (SOULSHOCK,K.KARLIN,A.MARTIN,K.JONES)	◆ SILK (C) (D) (T) (X) ELEKTRA 64359/EEG	54
70	NEW ▶		1	CAUGHT A LITE SNEEZE T.AMOS (T.AMOS)	◆ TORI AMOS (C) (X) ATLANTIC 87081	70
71	78	76	15	INCARCERATED SCARFACES/ICE CREAM RZA (R.DIGGS,C.WOODS)	◆ CHEF RAEKWON (C) (D) (T) LOUD 64426/RCA	37
72	85	87	4	FU-GEE-LA S.REMI (N.JEAN,S.MICHEL,L.HILL,A.MCGRIER,T.MARIE)	◆ FUGEES (M) (T) (X) RUFFHOUSE 78194*/COLUMBIA	72
73	84	86	3	WHERE DO U WANT ME TO PUT IT J.JAM,T.LEWIS (J.HARRIS III,T.LEWIS,M.HORTON)	◆ SOLO (C) (D) (T) (V) (X) PERSPECTIVE 587512	73
74	61	61	20	BROKENHEARTED ● K.CROUCH,K.JONES (K.CROUCH,K.JONES)	◆ BRANDY (C) (T) (X) ATLANTIC 87150	9
75	82	83	9	ROSEALIA D.ROTHCHILD (K.GRIFFIN)	BETTER THAN EZRA (C) (D) (X) ELEKTRA 64352/EEG	71
76	86	93	6	BEWARE OF MY CREW (FROM "A THIN LINE BETWEEN LOVE AND HATE") SNOOP DOGGY DOGG,LT HUTTON (R.GILLION,J.STAMPS,T.DAVIS,S.CONERLY,D.WILLIAMS,LT HUTTON,C.BROADUS,L.TROUTMAN)	◆ L.B.C. CREW FEAT. TRAY D & SOUTH SENTRELL (C) (D) (T) JAC-MAC 17722/WARNER BROS.	76
77	75	75	11	HURRICANE STUDIO TON (M.WHITEMON,E.STEVENS,B.JONES,D.STEVENS,T.STEVENS)	◆ THE CLICK (C) (T) (X) SICK WID' IT 42335/JIVE	63
78	74	74	12	(IF YOU'RE NOT IN IT FOR LOVE) I'M OUTTA HERE!/THE WOMAN IN ME R.J.LANGE (S.TWAIN,R.J.LANGE)	◆ SHANIA TWAIN (C) (D) MERCURY NASHVILLE 852206	74
79	92	89	16	SOLITUDE P.FOX (E.MCCAIN)	◆ EDWIN MCCAIN (C) (D) (V) LAVA 98141/ATLANTIC	72
80	83	82	15	MAGIC CARPET RIDE PIZZAMAN (N.COOK)	◆ THE MIGHTY DUB KATS (C) (T) (X) SM:)E 9014/PROFILE	58
81	62	64	7	EAST 1999 D.J.U-NEEK (BONE,D.J.U-NEEK,TONY C)	◆ BONE THUGS-N-HARMONY (C) (D) (T) RUTHLESS 6332/RELATIVITY	62
82	95	84	8	FAST LIFE BUCKWILD (N.WILSON,A.BEST,N.JONES)	◆ KOOL G RAP (C) (T) COLD CHILLIN'/EPIC STREET 78081/EPIC	74
83	90	91	13	WE'VE GOT IT GOIN' ON D.POP,M.MARTIN (D.POP,M.MARTIN,H.CRICHLOW)	◆ BACKSTREET BOYS (C) (D) (T) JIVE 42329	69
84	89	92	14	AUTOMATIC LOVER (CALL FOR LOVE) J.WIND,QUICKMIX,O.JEGLITZA,THE BERMAN BROTHERS (J.WIND,QUICKMIX,O.JEGLITZA)	◆ REAL MCCOY (C) (D) (M) (T) ARISTA 1-2876	52
85	88	81	17	BOOM BOOM BOOM THE OUTHERE BROTHERS (HULA,K.MAYBERRY)	◆ THE OUTHERE BROTHERS (C) (T) (X) AUREUS 1100	65
86	80	79	14	RUNNIN' J.DEE (T.HARDSON,E.WILCOX,J.YANCY,D.STEWART)	◆ THE PHARCYDE (C) (T) (X) DELICIOUS VINYL 58483/CAPITOL	55
87	77	77	5	IT MATTERS TO ME S.HENDRICKS (M.D. SANDERS,E.HILL)	◆ FAITH HILL (C) (V) WARNER BROS. 17718	77
88	79	80	14	AIN'T NUTHIN' BUT A SHE THING C.JAMES (C.JAMES)	◆ SALT-N-PEPA (C) (D) (T) (V) LONDON 850346/ISLAND	38
89	94	88	17	A MOVER LA COLITA DJ JUANITO (DJ JUANITO)	ARTIE THE 1 MAN PARTY (C) (D) (T) GROOVE NATION 78048/SCOTTI BROS.	65
90	NEW ▶		1	STAYIN' ALIVE K.O'TOOLE,D.LONGWORTH (R.GIBB,B.GIBB,M.GIBB)	◆ N-TRANCE (C) (T) (X) RADIKAL 15562/AVEX-CRITIQUE	90
91	NEW ▶		1	ALL CRIED OUT A.MARANO (FULL FORCE)	DENINE WITH COLLAGE'S ADAM MARANO (C) (X) VIPER 0201/METROPOLITAN	91
92	NEW ▶		1	ENERGY P.LORIMER,R. "HUMPTY" VISSION (DEVONE',R. "HUMPTY" VISSION,P.LORIMER,AMANDA C.)	DEVONE (C) (D) (T) WING/AQUA BOOGIE 852636/MERCURY	92
93	81	85	15	THROW YOUR SET IN THE AIR MUGGS (L.MUGGERUD,S.FREESE)	◆ CYPRESS HILL (C) (M) (T) (X) RUFFHOUSE 78042/COLUMBIA	45
94	91	90	20	SENTIMENTAL D.AUSTIN (D.AUSTIN,C.WOLFE,D.COX)	◆ DEBORAH COX (C) (D) (M) (T) (X) ARISTA 1-2852	27
95	96	99	12	EAST SIDE RENDEZVOUS M.CARLO (A.L.T.,O.G.ENIUS,FROST,ZANELLA,SCOZZESE)	◆ FROST (C) (T) RUTHLESS 1534/RELATIVITY	73
96	87	94	3	CAN'T BE REALLY GONE J.STROUD,B.GALLIMORE (G.BURR)	◆ TIM MCGRAW (C) (D) (V) CURB 76971	87
97	99	—	2	CELEBRATION/TAKE YOUR CHANCE BASE B. (ARIS,KESSELBAUER,COTTURA,HARDISON)	◆ FUN FACTORY (C) (T) (X) CURB EDEL 76972/CURB	97
98	97	95	5	SOMETIMES I MISS YOU SO MUCH (DEDICATED TO THE CHRIST CONSCIOUSNESS) P.M.DAWN (A.CORDES,K.WEST,A.BROWN)	◆ P.M. DAWN (C) (D) (T) (V) GEE STREET 854476/ISLAND	95
99	93	96	11	THE RIDDLER (FROM "BATMAN FOREVER") PRINCE RAKEEM (C.SMITH,R.DIGGS,N.HEFTI)	◆ METHOD MAN (C) (D) (T) ATLANTIC 87100	56
100	98	98	4	YOU PUT A MOVE ON MY HEART QUINCY JONES (R.TEMPERTON)	◆ QUINCY JONES INTRODUCING TAMIA (C) (D) (V) QWEST 17751/WARNER BROS.	98

◯ Records with the greatest airplay and sales gains this week. ◆ Videoclip availability. ● Recording Industry Assn. Of America (RIAA) certification for sales of 500,000 units. ▲ RIAA certification for sales of 1 million units, with additional million indicated by a numeral following the symbol. Catalog number is for cassette single. *Asterisk indicates catalog number is for cassette maxi-single; regular cassette single unavailable. (C) Cassette single availability. (D) CD single availability. (M) Cassette maxi-single availability. (T) Vinyl maxi-single availability. (V) Vinyl single availability. (X) CD maxi-single availability. © 1996, Billboard/BPI Communications.

86 BILLBOARD JANUARY 20, 1996

Figure 6-3. A *Billboard* "Hot 100" chart of single records. Copyright © 1996 BPI Communications, Inc. Used with permission from Billboard, Soundscan, Inc./Broadcast Data Systems, Inc.

Internal Data

In smaller stations, especially those without a music director, the DJs either make up their own playlists or contribute a great deal of input to the station's playlist. In all but the most tightly programmed stations a DJ is given some airtime in which to play records of his own choice. Often, these are new releases, perhaps by new artists in whom the DJ has particular confidence. If one of the records becomes a hit, the DJ will enjoy some credit for having "discovered" the act in his market. In addition, it is standard procedure for all stations to maintain a file on records that have been requested by listeners over the phone. This gives the station yet another pipeline to local and regional preferences which could result in gaining a larger audience market share.

Consultants and Programming Services

Competition among local radio stations is always keen. Each station tries to gain a larger and larger audience, primarily because that is the key to attracting and holding advertisers. Whenever a station begins to lose some of its audience and its ratings suffer, the station's management seeks the answer to its problems through research. Sometimes the research is conducted by internal staff, but more often outside consultants are brought in to conduct research and make recommendations, particularly concerning format, scheduling, and promotion. By the same token, a station which is at the top of the ratings wants to remain there. That station manager may use consultants from time to time to polish and refine the station's format, scheduling, and promotion.

A consultant brought in to improve a station's programming or fix its format is sometimes called a "radio doctor." His initial job is to thoroughly study the programming (and often the operation) of the station, perform audience research in the local market, and provide data on similar stations in similar markets. Finally, the consultant submits a report to the station manager with recommendations that may range from simple scheduling changes to a complete overhaul of the station's format and promotional policies.

Various research methods are employed by consultants. One general approach is through interviewing. "Call-out" research entails telephoning hundreds of people and testing their reactions to part of a record played over the phone. Carefully selected discussion groups is another approach. To discover who buys what records, consulting firms often work through retailers to urge customers to fill out questionnaires. Similar techniques are used in obtaining information from people who call requesting that a certain record be played.

A key area of a radio consultant's research is finding out *exactly who* make up the station's actual and potential audience. The most important demographics are considered to be age, sex, and income bracket. Once those parameters have been established, the consultant can more accurately recommend ideas for station promotion, general format, scheduling, and advertising policies.

Sometimes a station will change its entire format either by itself or on the recommendation of a consultant. In the late 1970s, when the popularity of Disco music died almost overnight, many stations shifted subtly to Rock or MOR formats. However, the most dramatic format shift in the industry occurred in 1980, when KHJ (Los Angeles), seemingly the nation's premiere Top 40 ("Boss Radio") station, abruptly and unexpectedly switched to a Country format. Since 1981 radio stations have been free to change formats at will without FCC involvement.

An extension of the radio consultancy field is the programming service.

Organizations providing programming service do the same job as a local program director or music director, but they do it on a national level. That means that their programming research reflects the habits of a large number of stations sharing a similar format in a wide variety of markets as well as up-to-the-minute data on national record sales. The larger programming services have client stations in several different formats. All stations in the same format subscribing to a programming service receive the same weekly playlist, which the station may modify or use verbatim. Many station managers consider playlists provided by a service to be more reliable and cost-effective than those which could be generated within the station itself.

Syndication and Automation

An elaboration of the programming service concept is the practice of syndication. Simple examples of radio syndication are the regular newscasts and special sports events carried by affiliates of a network. In music programming there is a long history of prerecorded syndicated shows, such as "American Top 40," tapes of which are leased by stations for local broadcasting. Traditionally, syndicated music shows and pop music specials have been associated with programming consultancy firms, many of which are the producers of syndicated products. While some stations may carry only a few syndicated music features or none at all, the programming of many stations is 100 percent syndicated. This means that all the music has been pretaped ("canned") by the syndication service, and most of the station's broadcast material consists of those tapes. Between tapes a live announcer may provide news, weather, station IDs, promotions, and so forth, but much of that material, along with commercial spots, may be prerecorded as well. Leading syndication services offer subscribers a variety of formats: Beautiful Music, traditional Country, modern Country, MOR, CHR, and AOR. The content of tapes is customized according to the intended time of day. Normally, a station is provided an initial library of tapes, and the service guarantees a number of updates throughout the year. There is no need for such a station to maintain playlists.

Syndicated stations operate using automated equipment, and many are *totally automated*. Computer-controlled tape consoles coordinate the programming by bringing in spot announcements in exactly the right place between blocks of uninterrupted music. Because automation lends itself best to such long musical interludes, it is used most widely for the programming of Beautiful Music stations.

A totally automated station can operate with a minimum of personnel, and the resultant savings in overhead is the main attraction of the automated method. On the other hand, rigid scheduling patterns and the lack of personal, spontaneous contact with a live announcer can be perceived by some listeners, who may tune out the station as a result.

Cable radio, a recent development in automated broadcasting, bypasses radio stations entirely. Using satellite technology, two companies—Digital

Automated broadcast equipment. Photo courtesy of Broadcast Programming.

Music Express (DMX) and Digital Cable Radio (DCR)—each broadcast up to thirty-odd stereo channels of music in all styles to homes and businesses. The music is free of commercials and DJ talk, and the sound is digital (CD) quality. A cable-radio subscriber must have a cable TV connection and use the cable company's digital decoding box to unscramble the broadcast. The music plays through any stereo set, and the user selects a channel with a hand-held controller that also displays information about the currently heard selection. Information can include title, artist, label, chart position, etc.

Advertising Music

To any regular radio listener, one familiar sound is the tight-knit vocal group crooning something like "Double-U Jay Jay Jay-ay-ay-ay. . . ." That would be the station's "ID," or logo. It is probably the briefest form of musical advertising in the broadcast industry, and nearly every station with a popular-type format squeezes in its ID as often as possible. Far more airtime, however, is devoted to the station's bread and butter: paid commercial spots. Some prerecorded spots in radio and TV may contain no music at all. But the use of music in broadcast advertising is so universal that a decision *not* to use music of some sort in a commercial is usually made very deliberately.

Commercials without music are generally intended to appeal strictly to the listener's *conscious* intellect and reasoning powers. This can be done through dramatization or by talking directly to the audience. In the latter case the sponsor (and his ad agency) may feel that the product is one that will sell best if a direct, sincere pitch is made. Investment brokers and pharmaceutical manufacturers are examples of such sponsors.

Music, on the other hand, has the power to affect the *unconscious* emotions, and the emotional appeal strategy is extremely prevalent in broadcast advertising. A good jingle or musical underscoring can work hand in hand with the words of the advertising copy to emphasize the positive aspects of a product or service while it mellows the emotionally negative side of it. For example, an ad for an airline may be designed to play up the excitement of going on vacation while attempting to allay the fear of flying. The character of the music in such a commercial can easily paint the fun of a trip and also project a comforting, personal image of the airline's personal services.

There are four especially powerful functions which music can perform in commercials. Initially, the music of a commercial can *arrest the audience's attention* and do it without interrupting the flow of entertainment. In musically formatted radio, as well as TV with its incessant musical segues in and out of program segments, there is so much musical sound surrounding the commercial spots that continuity of programming is actually enhanced by the insertion of musical spots. It then remains for the individuality of the commercial's content, including its music, to hold the attention of the audience.

Many commercial spots aim to *create a mood* by underscoring it with "mood" music. Spots produced for cosmetic and beauty products may have a sensuous, sexy atmosphere, while automobile ads may vary in character from excitement to snobbish prestige. Music is essential in creating such "environments."

Another commercial attribute found in advertising music is the *cohesiveness* it can lend. A powerful jingle can certainly unify a single commercial, but if a group of spots is produced using the jingle in a variety of musical styles (for example, contemporary, country, black, and so forth), the music can virtually be the catalyst of an entire advertising campaign.

Music's *memorability* is generally considered to be its most important attribute in advertising. A clever original jingle or the adaptation of a song already known to the audience can become inseparably attached to a product through repeated hearings. Studies have shown that once the public has learned a jingle, the music and the type of product associated with it will be remembered for a very long time, even though the particular brand name associated with it may grow somewhat obscure. The two most important virtues of a memorable jingle are thought to be simplicity and repetition. An uncomplicated melody with lots of musical repetition and repeated mentions of the product (or some attribute of it) seem to make up the formula.

On the other hand, no one has yet proven a correlation between the memorability of a jingle and its ability to actually sell. Ad agencies operate on the long-standing premise that the simpler a jingle is, the more likely the consumer will remember it and hum it; and the more often it is hummed, the more likely the consumer is to buy the product. One study and many anecdotal reports show that (1) people recall and recognize familiar jingles outside their original advertising context; (2) people remember the *type* of product associated with the jingle (e.g., detergents, beer, automobiles); but (3) without words many people do not readily recall the *exact* product named in the jingle.

Although the actual effectiveness of commercial jingles cannot be measured accurately, the power of music in advertising, as described above, is undeniable. Now that several of the attributes of that power have been introduced, we shall explore the process of musical commercials—how they are conceived, created, and contracted for the broadcast media.

The Sponsor and the Advertising Agency

Businesses that wish to advertise normally rely on ad agencies to help them, and larger sponsors retain their agencies on a continuing basis. Any broadcast advertising project, from a single commercial spot to an entire national media campaign, normally begins as a collaboration between sponsor and ad agency. Among the first matters discussed are the nature of the product, the budget for the advertising project, and the scope of the project (geographic extent, which media to use, and so forth). The agency then works up a general "concept" for the project, including suggestions for music and its treatment in the commercial spots.

Most ad agencies have a limited number of creative personnel on their staffs. These people may include copywriters but rarely composers. The copywriters are mainly employed to provide the spoken part of a commercial, but they may also create the lyrics (or the general idea) for a jingle. The "copy" written by these individuals always contains "logo lines," which are the central focus of a commercial and may be required to be included in any jingle connected to it.

Sometimes a sponsor decides to license a preexisting song which has been popular, rather than commissioning new, original music. The idea is to seize the audience's attention with a familiar sound and transfer to the product the good feelings associated with the song. Sometimes the words of the song are altered by the ad agency to fit the product more closely. Examples of songs from the past successfully transferred to commercial spots include "Good Vibrations" (The Beach Boys—adapted for a Sunkist soft drink) and "Anticipation" (Carly Simon—adapted for Heinz ketchup).

The Jingle Writer and the Music Production Company

Since an ad agency seldom employs a musical staff, it must subcontract all musical services. Some spots consist chiefly of the announcer's voice speaking over an unobtrusive musical background. The agency will normally choose the music for such a commercial from a tape library service rather than commissioning new music. Libraries have a wide variety of generic music recorded in timed segments that correspond to a number of applications, especially commercial spots. The library normally charges a reasonable one-time fee for the unlimited advertising use of one musical segment (or "needle drop"). Library music is employed most frequently in low-budget local radio and TV advertising.

A sponsor wishing some specific musical identity for its product will require the ad agency to obtain the services of either a free-lance individual songwriter specializing in jingles (a jingle writer) or a music production company.

Jingle writers generally get their start as free agents. However, once successful, many writers find it more practical to form a production company. A music production company devoted to creating commercial spots is sometimes called a "music house," or "jingle house." Often these are built around two or three jingle writers plus a small administrative staff. Most jingle houses are found in the major recording centers (New York, Los Angeles, and Nashville) and in other cities where the advertising industry flourishes, notably Chicago, Atlanta, and Dallas.

Normally, the ad agency will have worked with a few particular music jingle writers or production companies, and will ask each of them for a musical demo together with a bid on the music. The bid can be for just composing the jingle (a "creative fee"), but more often the agency prefers a package that includes all production costs and ends with the delivery of a finished audio tape. At briefings with potential bidders the ad agency provides advertising copy and information on the product, the target market, the type of music desired, and how it will be used (radio, TV, or both).

Another important matter considered during the briefing is the overall *form* of the sound track. There are many different formal variants in musical spots, normally determined by the placement of music and the announcer's voice in relation to one another. A commercial may be spoken all the way through, with only a musical "tag" at the end for the product's logo. But more often music will be heard throughout the spot. Possibly, the sound track for the entire commercial will consist solely of the vocal/instrumental jingle. Or, the focus of the spot might be the announcer's "voice over" the music, which in turn simply provides a background, or "bed," for the voice from beginning to end. The classic form for commercial spots is the "doughnut," which is a three-part form:

1. *The Front*: Music comes up full with the entire vocal jingle.

2. *The Bed* (or "doughnut"): Music comes down and is given a light, unobtrusive treatment while announcer "pitches" the product.

3. *The Tag*: Music comes back up with a brief reminiscence of the jingle, generally its "hook" line or logo line.

On the basis of information gleaned at the briefings, the bidders proceed to generate one or more sample jingles. They make demo recordings of these and submit them to the agency. After reviewing the bids and demos, the agency and sponsor make their selection. Contracts are then signed and production can begin.

Musical Production

The production of the finished music track is quite similar to that of a record or (if film synchronization is necessary) a movie sound track—but on a smaller

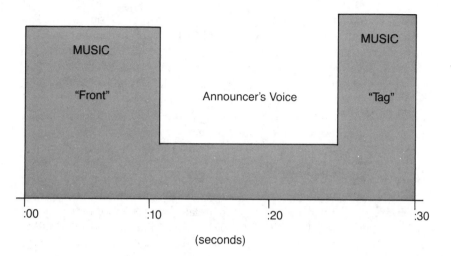

Figure 6-4. Commercial spot in "doughnut" form.

scale. Initially, the jingle must be scored (arranged) for singers and instruments, parts copied, singers and instrumentalists hired, and studio time booked. The process of taping a jingle is likewise similar to making the master tape of a record (see Chapter 3), but often more compressed or reduced. For example, the vocal tracks may be recorded along with the basic tracks, or all tracks for the recording may be done simultaneously. Such simplified procedures are followed because the finished product will normally be a compatible stereo/monaural tape and because every effort is made to save money in the studio. Another method of saving money is to use electronic music synthesizers in place of groups of musicians. Automated drum machines and synthesizer keyboards played by one musician (often the jingle writer) are sometimes all that are necessary to produce a full-sounding background for a musical commercial.

Strict adherence to a prescribed time length is crucial in recording commercial spots. The most common time lengths for a commercial are fifteen or thirty seconds, but any timing between fifteen and sixty seconds is possible. More than one time version may be recorded, or a basic long version may be recorded initially, with carefully placed editing points so that it can be cut down for shorter versions (or "lifts").

Jingles for large national campaigns are usually recorded several times, each in a different musical style. The first version may be in a contemporary Pop style aimed at network TV or MOR radio, but other master tapes may be recorded using Country and R&B styles, so that those markets can be addressed comfortably.

Payments, Copyrights, and Commissions

Music in commercial advertising generates income for the many individuals and firms involved in its production. The most obvious of these are the musical performers. Payment rates for performers are controlled by the various unions. Payments to singers are set by the American Federation of Television and Radio Artists for radio and the Screen Actors Guild for television. Instrumentalists and musicians involved in music preparation (arranging and copying) are paid according to American Federation of Musicians scales. Union contracts for all of these organizations require that the initial payment for services covers a thirteen-week period of advertising usage of the recording. If the commercial is used beyond that time, reuse payments must be made to the performers.

Freelance jingle writers are paid what is called a "creative fee." The contract for this fee may work one of two ways. The first (and oldest) method is for the agency or sponsor to pay the jingle writer for complete ownership of the music and words. Thus, the jingle would be a "work made for hire" under the copyright law, and the writer would have no further claim on it except through his performing rights organization (ASCAP or BMI). The second method is that the jingle writer (or jingle house) is paid a smaller fee but retains ownership of the music's copyright. This means that the writer or jingle house becomes the publisher of the music, which can be quite advantageous. Not only will the performing rights royalties double, but the writer-publisher is now free to exploit the music as a popular song, building on its exposure as a jingle. This procedure has advanced the careers of several songwriters, notably Barry Manilow.

When a commercial spot uses a preexisting song, a license must be negotiated with the owner of its copyright. A publisher's fee for the exclusive advertising use of a song over a specified time period can be quite high. Reportedly, some songs have been licensed for over $100,000. Most sponsors with budgets that high are aiming at network TV, so the negotiated rights include a synchronization license (discussed in Chapter 7).

The advertising agency, which spends the sponsor's money to cover all aspects of production, is paid last. As part of the advertising strategy the agency purchases air time for the sponsor's commercial spots. The sponsor then pays the agency for the air time, and the agency pays the broadcasters—but only after deducting a 15 percent commission.

Music Video

To most TV viewers and certainly to any whose set is connected to a cable system, music video is a standard part of today's broadcast programming. With their novel optical effects and contemporary sound, music videos may appear to have been invented along with the wonders of the modern digital electronic revolution. Yet the roots of visual clips coupled with music go back in the history of commercial television almost to the beginning.

Background

The earliest forerunners of the music video were TV variety shows and the TV version of "Your Hit Parade" in the 1950s. These shows were often broadcast live, and the songs were usually enhanced with stage settings and sometimes even an elementary story line. There were also syndicated TV shows in the 1950s made up of film clips by popular MOR artists of the day, such as Peggy Lee or the Les Brown Band. In 1967 the Beatles introduced a new song, "Strawberry Fields Forever," with what was probably the first modern music video. The clip made liberal use of editing techniques and humorous optical tricks for which the Beatles' films had become famous, but "Strawberry Fields Forever" projected a distinctive image, a unique mood that perfectly complimented the psychedelic nature of the song. Not only was this clip aesthetically akin to modern music video, but it served the same purpose. It was a promotional tool for stimulating interest in a new record.

During the late 1960s and 1970s promotional clips for individual records were rather sporadic. It was more usual to see full, feature-length documentary films, such as *Woodstock*, *The Complete Beatles*, and *Girl Groups*. Around 1978, during a period when record sales began declining sharply, record companies began to curtail promotional funds for tours and to seek an alternative, low-budget method of promoting their new artists. Thus, the modern music video clip was born. At first music videos were circulated mainly among nightclubs and discos. This exposure uncovered the fact that the video was a means of placing new talent before the public in a manner as effective as the live concert.

Enter MTV

The biggest single move in music video's history occurred in August 1981, when Warner Amex Cable Communications launched MTV (Music Television), a rock-formatted cable TV operation catering to a youth and young-adult audience. The popularity of MTV, replete with "VJ" (video jockey) shows, immediately skyrocketed. One of the services provided by MTV in its first years was the introduction of new, unknown artists into the living rooms of millions of music listeners. The most phenomenal example was the obscure British group Duran Duran, who became inseparably connected with the medium of music video. MTV's programming has become more restrictive and playlist-oriented in recent years (partially for economic reasons) and it is more difficult now for new mainstream artists to be seen and heard there.

MTV has led the way for other broadcasters in this bonanza. During music video's first years the clips were considered strictly promotional and could be offered free to TV broadcasters in the same way that promotional copies of records were given to radio stations. Consumer demand shown in the meteoric success of MTV, coupled with tapes that were free for the asking, caused TV network affiliates and independent stations alike to clamor for the new "visual radio." Even later, when record companies had to begin charging for the use of their music videos, the tide could not be stopped.

An Expanding Market

In early 1985 MTV Networks, Inc., inaugurated a new venture, VH-1 (Video Hits-1), which featured "personality" VJs and a MOR format aimed at an older audience than MTV. This news was hardly shocking, since artists outside the realm of Rock had been making music videos for some time. Originally programming only 30 percent current videos, VH-1 now targets the twenty-five to thirty-five-year-old market with 70 percent current videos.

From the start MTV had had a competitor in the Video Music Channel. Later, Country Music TV and the Nashville Network, both new cable broadcasters, began regularly carrying periods of music videos, and other cable broadcasters use music video clips in several musical styles as fillers between their scheduled programs. The networks also became involved, notably NBC with its show, "Friday Night Videos."

The record business has reached a point where every new record/tape release with aspirations to be a hit must have a music video clip to accompany it. Much of this necessity has arisen out of video nightclub exposure, which is vital in areas where cable is not received. Club video play is also the main type of exposure for independent labels whose inexpensively produced clips are unlikely to be programmed nationally. Many video clubs are considered to be in the vanguard of new artist discovery, and radio disc jockeys can be seen there catching reactions to the latest Rock videos.

The future of music video also looks bright outside of TV and video clubs. The industry is campaigning to place more and more music-related video products in the home on videocassette. These range from albums of individual clips by popular artists to documentaries to feature-length movies centering on music and dance.

There is also the question of whether the music video will eventually replace the strictly audio entertainment media: radio, records, and tapes. This seems unlikely because of people's diverse listening habits. Those habits seem to be polarized in two directions: *home* listening and *mobile* listening. Home listening habits are gravitating more toward music video, but audio tapes, CDs, and radio appear to be the favored media for music listeners on the move.

The "Forms" of Music Video

The music industry defines two principal classifications of music video, both of which are based on length:

1. *Clip:* A three- to five-minute video based on a single recorded song and often built around a dramatic or video "concept."

2. *Long Form:* A video lasting longer than a clip, even if based on a single song. This form includes the taped concert, video album (one or more artists), documentary, and feature-length film.

Visual Aspects

The music video has established a new synthesis of components, both audio and visual. The audio component of a clip-length video is usually a studio-produced recording (which is simultaneously released as a record). This recording becomes the entire sound track for the video. The visual side of music video allows for much more variety, since four distinct components can come into play in any combination. Not every video makes use of all four, but here is a description of each:

1. *On-Screen Musical Performance.* Some videos are strictly "performance videos," that is, nothing but clips from movies made of concert performances. However, most videos incorporate on-screen performance along with one or more of the other components. In that case, the artist is usually videotaped using specially designed sets and props. The artist mouths the words (in "lip sync") along with the recording or pantomimes playing an instrument associated with it.

2. *Movement and Dance.* Whenever a video features an on-screen performance, the artist usually moves in some way with the music. With certain artists, notably Michael Jackson and Madonna, dance movements are an integral part of the total performance. Many videos use dance to help enact a story line, and these may employ professional dancers as a main visual attraction. Some videos based on actual dance music resemble large theatrical "production numbers."

3. *Story/Pantomime.* The lyrics of many popular songs invite enactment, and dramatic vignettes have become a standard component of the music video. Even when the lyrics are not narrative or when the music has no lyrics, the creators of the video will often make up pantomime sequences that they feel can be associated with the song or will make an impact on the viewer. Thus, many videos, with their underlying plots enacted in dramatic sequences, are really concept "mini-films."

4. *Special Optical Effects.* Some of the most striking features of music videos, especially rock videos, are the spectacular optical effects and graphics. The music video has become a mass outlet for special effects which were previously found mainly in the domain of avant-garde filmmakers. Some of these effects are created through editing, but most employ some form of computer generation or electronic processing developed for the TV medium. Paradoxically, the special effects in music videos can be the most artistic qualities about them and at the same time their most commercially compelling features.

If ever the TV medium could be called a "dream machine," that expression would best be illustrated by the music video. Partially through special optical effects, music videos have developed a tremendous power to evoke the feeling of dreams and fantasy. Such surreal imagery is aided in many cases by lyrics which are about dreams or which purposely obscure the distinction between conscious and unconscious perceptions. The stories and images in music videos often involve popular fantasies, sexual and otherwise. Any particular music video might even be thought of as a suggested fantasy for the record it is based on.

Some of the optical effects in music videos—for example, rapid montage sequences—were derived from TV commercial spot techniques. In fact, several directors of TV commercials, notably Bob Giraldi, have become among the most sought-after music video directors. From the viewpoint of record companies, music videos are actually commercials for records. We are also reminded of a music video's commercial purpose when we view the name of the artist, song, album, and record company at the beginning and end of the video, like the "front" and "tag" of a commercial spot in doughnut form.

The spectacular visual effects seen in music videos have also had an impact on artists developing their in-person concert image. Many touring artists feel they must now match on stage the visual extravagance of their own music videos.

Awards

MTV began making its own award presentations in 1984, but the field for those awards is somewhat restrictive, since a video must have been shown on MTV in order to qualify. The year 1984 also saw the initiation of "Gold Awards" and "Platinum Awards" for music videos, given by the Recording Industry Association of America and similar to the awards given for audio-recording sales. Music video categories now figure prominently in the Grammys® and other artistic awards.

Costs, Contracts, Licenses

There are an estimated fifty to one hundred music video clips released each week. With an average production cost of greater than $75,000, the business of music video has become a large and powerful force in its own right.

Music videos, be they clips or long forms, are designated as distinct audiovisual works under the copyright law. As such, each video has the potential of earning income from various sources, but its copyright owner also has contractual and licensing obligations similar to those in motion pictures. The remainder of this discussion will center chiefly on clips of individual songs.

The copyright of a music video is normally owned by the company releasing the record associated with it. The record company makes flat payments for all production costs connected with making the video at rates set or negotiated through union agreements. This includes paying the recording artist for his appearance in the video. Thus, the video itself is a "work made for hire" in which the record company is the "author" for all practical purposes. The artist's recording contract normally contains a music video rider, and under its provisions a percentage of production costs may be deducted from the artist's video and record royalties. The record company hopes to recoup the rest of its costs through income from exploiting the video. The artist's contract provides for a royalty share of this income.

Since the music video involves the use of previously copyrighted material, namely the song, the record company must obtain a synchronization/performance license (see Chapter 7) from the publisher of the song. This will allow the use of the music in conjunction with visual images and the performance of the completed video over broadcast media and in clubs. In some cases the license might be granted for only a token payment or may be free in consideration of the video's promotional value to the song. A separate agreement between record company and publisher may be executed to cover possible income from consumer sales/rentals (videocassettes and videodiscs).

In the early years of music video, record companies provided the clips to broadcasters and clubs free of charge, just for the promotional value that could be derived. (Broadcasters of music videos and clubs have always paid for performance licenses from ASCAP and BMI to cover the *songs* on the clips.) Because of rising video production costs and the need for synchronization/performance licenses, major record companies now charge for the use of music videos. For television the fee varies according to the use. On the low end of the scale a one-time performance over a TV network might cost about $1,000, while on the high end the exclusive right to broadcast a choice video for a given time period could be in excess of $250,000. Another source of income for record companies is nightclubs. There are now video library agencies, such as Rockamerica, which service these clubs by leasing videos from record companies. Video cassette releases of long forms and collections of clips now comprise complete "Music Video" departments in retail entertainment stores (see chapter 3), and account for significant figures in sales and rentals.

We have observed that music and broadcasting have been partners almost from the very beginning of radio. At several junctures recorded music has affected some entirely new trend in radio broadcasting, such as the rise of the disc jockey. Another sign of the partnership was the proliferation of broadcast formats, reflecting the rich diversity of product offerings from the record industry.

Broadcasting has also had a significant impact on the record industry, especially on its methods of promoting recorded products. With the rise of music-formatted radio, broadcasters became willing promoters of new and established recording artists, because records provided program material that was in demand. A similar fortuitous arrangement for TV and cable broadcasters came into being when the popularity of music video exploded. Video exposure is now a prime consideration for record companies signing and promoting both new and established artists.

Despite the firm establishment of music video, the field of radio steadily continues to thrive. The public seems to have established a firm place and fixed functions for both radio and video performances in all commercial musical styles. Radio is not likely to be superseded by TV in the near future, and satellite/cable delivery of music promises to be an exciting development.

Review Questions

1. Discuss some ways in which a radio station's Program Director and Music Director work together.

2. Why might a "drive time" disc jockey receive a higher salary than a disc jockey working another daypart?

3. Choose three radio music formats and listen to each for thirty minutes. Discuss similarities and differences in the formats you heard.

4. What is a playlist and why is it important to the popularity of a radio station?

5. What is a chart and how is it made up?

6. Aside from the "Hot 100" and "Top 200 Albums," name two or three other *Billboard* charts.

7. In addition to charts, what are the usual influences on a radio station's playlist?

8. What are some reasons a radio station might call in a consultant?

9. Discuss similarities and differences between syndication, automation, and cable radio.

10. There are four power functions of music in commercials. Discuss two or three of them.

11. Do people usually remember a particular product when they recognize a jingle? Explain.

12. Outline the process of producing commercial spot music from the sponsor's preferences to the recording sessions.

13. What is a "doughnut" form?

14. What are the two ways a jingle writer may contract for the ownership of a newly created jingle?

15. Before MTV, was there any music video? Explain.

16. What is the difference between MTV and VH-1?

17. Explain the difference between a "clip" and a "long form" music video.

18. What are some of the visual aspects of music videos?

19. What does a music video cost to make and who owns it?

20. Do broadcasters have to pay for the use of music videos? Explain.

7

Dramatic Music: Films and Television

Music for motion pictures and dramatic TV shows is both an art and a craft. The very best scores have been able to stand on their own as art, and sound track music on records has sometimes been more successful than the movie from which it came. At the same time film music is a dramatic craft, meshing with the action, dialogue, and underlying ideas of the film. As a craft, a film score is a piece of art made to order. The challenges to the film composer are to write music that is of high artistic quality, fits the feeling and style of each scene in the film, and can be synchronized precisely with the visual details, dialogue, and additional sound track sources.

There can be no doubt that the musical score of a film influences our general impressions of the film and our perceptions of the film's value and meaning. Most great films also contain great film scores. Conversely, a poor score can devalue an otherwise good motion picture.

The field of film music has a tradition of artistic and technological growth. This chapter will explore the history of that tradition, the functions of music in motion pictures, the process of creation and synchronization, and business aspects of film music.

Films: History and Musical Trends ───────────

Inside the Music Industry

From almost the day of their introduction to the general public, films have sought to combine sight and sound in a meaningful way. Sound was a big problem at first. Edison and others working with film around the turn of the twentieth century experimented with combining phonograph recordings of voice with motion picture images. The results were acceptable from the standpoint of synchronization but impractical for audiences of more than one person. The sound was so faint, because of the strictly acoustical means of reproduction, that even two or three phonographs playing at the same time were not adequate for a small auditorium. Recorded sound tracks would have to wait until the development of electroacoustical recording technology in the 1920s before becoming a reality. (See Chapter 1 and below.) Thus, a period of silent films lasting nearly thirty years was ushered in.

Silent Films

The use of music to accompany silent films was at first a necessity rather than an aesthetic enhancement. In early movie houses the noisy projector was located within the auditorium itself rather than inside a booth. Movie exhibitors would hire pianists to play merely to cover the noise of the projector. The music varied according to the whims and abilities of the player. Popular songs of the day, classical pieces, and improvisations were the usual fare. During the second decade of the century movie pianists tended to *accompany* the films more closely, providing reinforcement for emotions and action displayed on the screen. As this trend became widespread and more refined, libraries of generic musical cues were published for sale or made available on rental.

The larger movie palaces maintained an orchestra or had an organ ("The Mighty Wurlitzer") to simulate an orchestra. In the case of a few early films the studio provided a custom-written orchestral score. D. W. Griffith's *The Birth of a Nation* (1915) had a score composed by Griffith himself in collaboration with Carl Briel. In Europe Sergei Eisenstein's *Potemkin* (1925) boasted a masterful score by Edmund Meisel which audiences found "overwhelming."

Development of Hollywood Studios

In the early days of silent movies the films were made exclusively in the New York area because that was the center for actors and the technical talent of show business. As movies became more sophisticated, requiring more space for sound stages and a variety of landscapes for exterior shots, a new locale for moviemaking became necessary. Southern California had all the necessary requirements plus a pleasant climate year round, and Hollywood (near Los Angeles) became the new center of activity. By 1916 about half the motion pictures released were made in Hollywood, and by the early 1920s that figure had increased to over 90 percent.

Many studios prospered during the "Roaring Twenties," but in the course of that decade there was a general shakeout of smaller studios in favor of a few giants which emerged to control the film industry. The largest of these included Universal, Fox (later, Twentieth-Century Fox), and Metro (later, Metro-Goldwyn-Mayer). The power of these leviathans also extended beyond the production of films, since they owned chains of theaters or controlled distribution to blocks of theaters.

With the development of major studios came the inevitable star system. This idea was derived from the stage stars of Broadway and vaudeville, but the appeal of screen stars was geared to the mass audiences of films. Dashing Douglas Fairbanks, Sr., and innocent Mary Pickford, together with comics such as Charlie Chaplin and Harold Lloyd, were examples of the new breed of stars. Hollywood quickly learned that it is far easier and more durable to market a movie star than a story.

Early "Talkies"

Music as an adjunct to films had become an established practice. The need for synchronizing music with film was clear, but there was no ready solution to the problem. Experimental methods of various types were tried, including filming conductor's cues along the bottom of the picture and having the film control an organlike musical device. But none of these attempts was capable of reproducing a full sound track: voice, music, and sound effects. For this, recording technology had to become involved. Techniques borrowed from phonograph recordings and radio transcriptions were used to make the sound track of the first sound films, which were brought out by Warner Bros. beginning in 1926. These were only short films featuring vaudeville singers, but they served to whet the public's appetite for sound movies.

The first full-length sound film was *The Jazz Singer* (1927), released by Warner Bros. and starring Al Jolson. Its sound track consisted mostly of songs with very limited dialogue. The sound for this and other early sound films was made using the Vitaphone method, developed by Bell Laboratories. The sound was recorded first on sixteen-inch wax transcription discs spinning at 33 1/3 rpm (rather than the standard 78 rpm of the day). These were then mastered, and copies were pressed for distribution with the film. The discs were played on a turntable which was synchronized with the projector. Warner Bros.' pioneering work in the distribution of sound films temporarily gave that studio the inside track in the industry and made it one of the giants by 1930.

Sound Develops

Only the early sound films used disc recordings for their sound tracks. Soon an entirely new technology of "photographed sound" appeared, based on earlier experiments by Lee De Forest. This optical method became the industry standard and, with a few refinements, has remained so ever since. With this method the sound track was recorded directly onto film, with the track running alongside the frames. The track could not be seen on the screen, but a photoelectric sys-

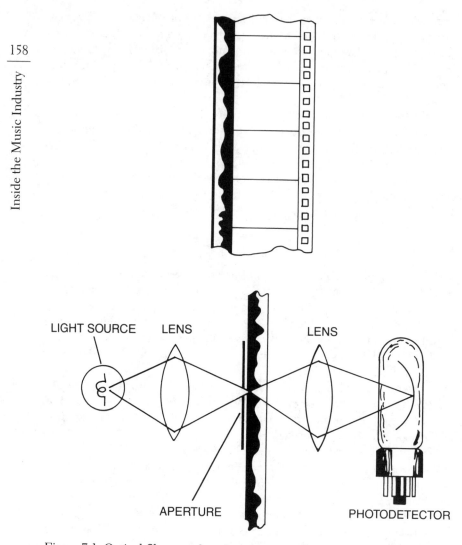

Figure 7-1. Optical film sound track system.

tem would translate the patterns on the strip into electronic impulses which could be amplified and heard as sound. During the early years the sound track was recorded entirely as the movie was being shot. That meant that the orchestra had to be present either on the set itself or somewhere nearby on the same sound stage. Naturally, little editing of the sound track was possible.

Producers had differing views concerning the place of music in early sound films. Some movies were literally "talkies," in which music was left out of dialogue scenes or the film had no music at all. Other films made use of music as a catalyst to give the film coherence and continuity—a holdover from silent-movie days. Still others felt that music required some visual justification and that the *source* of the music had to appear on the screen at least once. A distant shepherd's pipe could be the background for a pastoral love scene, or a street musician could be playing during a city street scene. This type of music usage became known as "source music."

The most natural type of film for these literalists was the movie musical. Following *The Jazz Singer*, Hollywood inundated the public with countless musicals until a temporary saturation was reached in the early 1930s. Nightclub and theater scenes, with their visible "live" orchestras, dominated many of the sketchy screenplays written for musical films. Inevitably, the movie *theme song* trend emerged and had its first wave of popularity during the 1930s. To be effective, the theme song of a film was generally heard in its entirety at least once, often delaying the progress of the story to do so. (Today, this situation is usually avoided by presenting the song during the opening or end credits.)

Film Music Matures

In spite of certain technical recording problems, the 1930s brought forth several symphonic film scores with musical significance. Notable among Hollywood composers was Max Steiner, who composed scores for *Of Human Bondage* (1934), *Dark Victory* (1939), and *Gone with the Wind* (1939), and whose career continued well into the 1960s. In Europe three film scores of the 1930s were especially outstanding: Sergei Prokofiev's *Lt. Kije* (1933) and *Alexander Nevsky* (1938), and Arthur Bliss' *Things to Come* (1935).

Two major trends developed in American film music during the late 1930s. One, inherited from silent movie days, was a tendency to illustrate visual details in the music. This was especially effective in comedies, where every humorous facial expression and sight gag might be accompanied by some effect in the music, much in the manner of a cartoon. (The tendency became known as "Mickey Mouse" music.) However, such literalism was heard in serious films as well. For example, the score might make use of a music box when an "innocent" child appeared, or distant drums might be heard at the mere mention of Indians in the dialogue.

The other trend was an increase in the dimensions of the typical film score: Larger orchestras were often employed for major films, but even more noticeable was the sheer amount of music heard during films of that era. Wall-to-wall scoring under virtually every scene tended to heighten the sentimental, "schmaltzy" qualities of the screenplay and production style of such films. Although the intention of ever-present music was that it should act as a dramatic catalyst, the practice was self-defeating, since the potential power of the score was lost in its overabundance.

Composers of the period noted for their heavy scoring included Max Steiner, Alfred Newman, and Erich Korngold. In an attempt to bind together such extensive scores and give them a unified direction, composers in the 1940s began to employ a system of leitmotivs in each film. The leitmotiv, originally developed

(a)

Score to main title of Gone with the Wind, *music by Max Steiner. Photo courtesy of the David O. Selznick Archives, Theater Arts Library, Harry Ransom Humanities Research Center, The University of Texas at Austin.*

in operas of the nineteenth century by Richard Wagner and others, is a short musical phrase which is identified with some particular character, object, idea, or emotion. Its purpose is to subliminally remind the audience of the connection each time the leitmotiv is heard.

(b)

Two motion picture scores of the 1940s were famous for their use of leitmotivs to create dramatic effects and symphonic unity. Bernard Herrmann's music for the Orson Welles film *Citizen Kane* (1941) was as inventive as the film itself. Herrmann, who came from radio along with Welles, brought new dimensions of realism to the screen through his music. Hugo Friedhofer's score to *The Best Years of Our Lives* (1946) won an Academy Award. For this film Friedhofer composed an array of themes representing characters and their relationships to one another. The themes were combinable and so organic to the film that the score helped significantly to draw the audience into the story and involve it with the characters.

Miklos Rozsa brought a new sound to film music in his score to an early Alfred Hitchcock psychological thriller, *Spellbound* (1945). It was the sound of the theremin, an electronic forerunner to the modern synthesizer, which gave the eerie effect of gliding from note to note. Rozsa used the theremin to represent the warped personality of the picture's main character. He also used it effectively in *The Lost Weekend*, released the same year. Both scores were so successful and widely imitated that the theremin's sound soon became a cliché.

During the 1940s several films were produced which dealt with the lives of historical composers or fictional musicians. The life of George Gershwin was portrayed in *Rhapsody in Blue* (1945). Classical music was integrated into such films as *A Song to Remember* (1945), based on the life of Frédéric Chopin, and *Song of Love* (1947), which dealt with Robert and Clara Schumann. These films were somewhat fictionalized. *Humoresque* (1947) was the entirely fictional story of a concert violinist in which Isaac Stern's playing was used on the sound track.

The work of a noted concert-music composer was also heard in films during this period. Aaron Copland (1900–1990), famous for his ballets on American subjects, wrote several distinguished film scores, including *Of Mice and Men* (1939), *Our Town* (1940), and *The Red Pony* (1949). The peak of Copland's film efforts was the music to *The Heiress* (1949). The dramatic impact of this motion picture relied heavily upon its score, which won an Academy Award.

Originally composed movie theme songs by no means disappeared during this period. David Raksin's score for *Laura* (1944), a tough-guy detective story, was based exclusively on its famous theme song. When this beautiful but complex tune reached number one on the Hit Parade, it was a surprise to everyone. Another theme-song movie was the international intrigue film *The Third Man* (1950). Its haunting theme song, played on a zither, also became a hit.

Upheaval and New Directions

Around 1950 a combination of developments nearly devastated the movie industry. In 1949 the Justice Department won an antitrust ruling in the United States Supreme Court against studios which also owned theaters. The immediate result was that the studios had to divest themselves of their theater holdings. The long-range impact was economically grim. It meant that movies would have to compete in the open market for bookings. That signaled the end of "B" movies. Studios also could no longer afford exclusive contracts with actors, studio orchestra musicians, and various other production staff. These problems caused a restructuring of the industry in which many services were simply subcontracted for an individual studio picture, and "package" deals with independent movie producers became more and more attractive. The production of new movies was slowed tremendously, and every new release had to be a "feature." Eventually, studio operation became financially impractical for many of the majors, and gradually they became absorbed by large conglomerate corporations such as

Gulf and Western (Paramount), Kinney (Warner Bros.), TransAmerica (United Artists), and MCA (Universal).

The 1947–1952 hearings of the House Committee on Un-American Activities accounted for the loss of a tremendous amount of creative talent during those years and later. The committee ostensibly was investigating Communist infiltration into the motion picture industry. Anyone who had had anything whatever to do with the Communist Party during the desperate years of the Great Depression was asked (under oath) to admit it and to give the names of others so involved. The result in Hollywood was the destructive blacklisting of all "suspects." Careers were ruined and Hollywood was deprived of the talents of numerous fine writers, directors, producers, and the like.

The greatest threat of all to the future of Hollywood was the rise of television as a mass medium. Since 1947 TV receivers had become generally available, and in the larger cities TV was becoming the dominant form of entertainment. Then, in 1952 TV stations began proliferating at a tremendous rate, and people everywhere were staying home to view a variety of entertainment, including movies and movielike TV dramas. Previously, family entertainment had been the domain of motion pictures. Now television had conquered that domain, and the movie industry had to offer new and special attractions in order to lure audiences back into movie theaters. These attractions came in the form of technical improvements in sight and sound and new production styles geared to specialized audiences.

Technical Enhancements

At that time the most obvious difference between movies and TV was the size of the screen. Early TV screens measured only nine to twelve inches, while movie screens were bigger than life. Hollywood made viewing even more spectacular by introducing 3–D and Cinerama, both of which were intended to give audiences the impression of real three-dimensional depth. These were moderately successful. A third technique, Cinemascope, which was a wide-screen format, finally emerged as the popular standard. The absence of color was another of TV's faults that Hollywood capitalized on (until the mid-1960s), and motion pictures in color soon became the norm.

Sound in motion pictures was also enhanced significantly. The first and most important development was stereophonic sound, introduced in *Julius Caesar* (1952). Not only was the sound track to this film given extra dimension through stereo, but in some places the musical score by Miklos Rozsa utilized the separation of channels to present contrasting musical ideas. The stereo idea was eventually extended to six channels through a new technology developed by the Dolby laboratories. The largest-grossing pictures from the mid-1950s through the 1970s all made use of the most advanced sound techniques.

Quest for New Audiences

Movies had been forced out of mass entertainment and into special entertainment. One method Hollywood used to seek specialized audiences was the introduction of new social themes in its films. A popular theme was "rebellious youth," seen in *The Wild One* (1953), starring Marlon Brando, and *Rebel Without a Cause* (1955), starring James Dean. Later, the heart of the youth market itself was discovered through such films as *The Endless Summer* (1966), *Easy Rider* (1969), and the long list of Elvis Presley films. With the gradual loosening of censorship between 1953 and about 1968, motion pictures were freer than before to seek adult audiences. One sign of this was the trend toward adapting novels and plays to the movie medium. *East of Eden* (1955, music by Leonard Rosenmann) is a good example. Another sign was the use of a new type of realism, influenced partly by the importation of foreign films and partly by the new vogue of "method" acting that had developed in the Actor's Studio in New York. One of the most significant films of this type was *On the Waterfront* (1954), which contained a unique score composed by Leonard Bernstein.

Another important trend in motion pictures from this period is a penchant for the psychological. Alfred Hitchcock was the master of the thriller with a psychological twist, and the 1950s were the heyday of the Alfred Hitchcock thriller, culminating with *Psycho* (1960). The bleakness of the story and setting of *Psycho* was underlined by having it filmed in black and white. The film's musical score by Bernard Herrmann was also purposely monochromatic, using only a string orchestra. Portions of this score clearly illustrate psychological tendencies in film scoring that had begun in the 1950s. Whereas music for films in "The Golden Age" (ca. 1935–ca. 1945) tended to illustrate only what could be seen on the screen, later film scores often reveal the unseen to the audience. For example, in *Psycho* the scene of Janet Leigh taking a shower appears innocent and carefree at first. However, the music "plays against the scene," giving the audience a foreboding of the terrifying murder about to take place. This technique was later used extremely successfully in *Jaws* (1975), where people are shown romping on the beach and in the surf while John Williams' music imparts to the audience the hideous danger that lurks in the depths.

Jazz, Epics, and Theme Songs

Another new direction explored in films of the 1950s and 1960s was the scoring of jazz to project a special atmosphere. The pioneering steps in this direction were taken by Alex North in his music for *A Streetcar Named Desire* (1951). This score used stylized jazz themes to illustrate the story's characters and squalid New Orleans setting. Leith Stevens' score for *The Wild One* (1953) was genuine jazz in the West Coast cool style, including improvised solos. However, the most celebrated film score of this type was Elmer Bernstein's music for *The Man with the Golden Arm* (1955), which was arranged and performed by West Coast jazz musicians. The story of this film dealt with a jazz musician (played by Frank Sinatra). Although Bernstein denied that the music was genuine jazz (since it lacked improvisation), this score (and its subsequent success as a sound track record) made it the single most important influence on future jazz-oriented movie and TV scores. Otto Preminger, who produced this film, went on to engage Duke Ellington to compose the music for *Anatomy of a Murder* (1959).

Another trend in motion pictures which emerged forcefully during the 1950s was the epic film, especially the biblical epic. Beginning with a forerunner, *Samson and Delilah* (1949, music by Victor Young), the splendor of each of these was augmented by a luxuriant score. *Quo Vadis?* (1951) is probably the classic of this genre. Its music by Miklos Rozsa attempted to evoke the atmosphere of Rome at the time of Nero, with some themes based on authentic ancient musical fragments. Later biblical epics include *The Robe* (1952, score by Alfred Newman), *The Ten Commandments* (1956, score by Elmer Bernstein), *Ben-Hur* (1959, score by Miklos Rozsa), and *King of Kings* (1961, score by Miklos Rozsa).

As mentioned above, the trend toward movie theme songs has resurfaced regularly in the history of sound films. During the 1950s the "theme song film" reemerged, and with it came what has been termed the "pop song concept" of film scoring. Dimitri Tiomkin was at first the undisputed master of this technique. His music for *High Noon* (1952), the first "adult" western, was centered on a tune heard time and again throughout the film, "Do Not Forsake Me, Oh My Darlin'." This song became an immediate pop hit and led the way for later hit theme songs of the decade, notably Tiomkin's *The High and the Mighty* (1954) and Alfred Newman's *Love Is a Many-Splendored Thing* (1955). Henry Mancini built a good deal of his well-earned reputation by writing film scores around theme songs, notably "Moon River" (from *Breakfast at Tiffany's*, 1961) and *Days of Wine and Roses* (1962). Several instrumental themes have also become hits, notably from the films *Dr. Zhivago* (1965, Maurice Jarre), *The Pink Panther* (1964, Henry Mancini), *Romeo and Juliet* (1968, Nino Rota), and *Love Story* (1970, Francis Lai).

Later, theme song film scores began to be based on music written by actual pop song writers. "Mrs. Robinson," written for *The Graduate* (1967) by Paul Simon and performed by Simon and Garfunkel, is a good example. The idea of basing sound tracks on pop songs was taken to its extreme in The Beatles' first film, *A Hard Day's Night* (1964). The trend toward pop song scores grew so widespread during the 1960s that it became distressing to many serious film composers. Bernard Herrmann even left Hollywood to compose music for British films.

The success of movie theme songs and sound tracks sold on records had been a financial balm to the industry in the 1950s. Moviemakers also realized the valuable promotion a film could gain from the popularity of its theme song. Rather than assigning the publishing rights of film music to established publishers, as had been done in the past, studios began to retain these for exploitation. Some studios, notably MGM, even started their own record companies.

Musicals

Although the trend toward musical films was short-lived during the early years of talkies, the idea never really disappeared. During the 1950s spectacular movie musicals were part of Hollywood's strategy to regain its audiences. Following the lead of the Fred Astaire-Ginger Rogers films of the 1930s and 1940s, movie musicals after 1950 typically contained a great deal of dance. The bright, new star of most of these was dancer/choreographer Gene Kelly. Kelly appeared in two original movie musicals which must be considered classics of the genre: *An American in Paris* (1951) and *Singin' in the Rain* (1952). Other musical successes of the decade include *High Society* (1956) and *Funny Face* (1957) (both prominently featuring Fred Astaire's dancing), and *Seven Brides for Seven Brothers* (1954).

Following up on Hollywood musicals and the trend toward adapting plays into film scripts, Hollywood filmmakers (notably, MGM, the leader in spectacular films) began optioning Broadway musical shows for film adaptation. Although the musical *On the Town* (1944, music by Leonard Bernstein) had been made into a film in 1949, the main thrust of the Broadway musical-film began in 1955. From that point to 1972, nearly every year brought forth at least one adaptation of a Broadway musical. A list of the Academy Awards for "Scoring of a Musical Picture" illustrate the depth of this trend:

1955	*Oklahoma!*
1956	*The King and I*
1958	*Gigi*
1959	*Porgy and Bess*
1961	*West Side Story*
1962	*The Music Man*
1964	*My Fair Lady*
1965	*The Sound of Music*
1966	*A Funny Thing Happened on the Way to the Forum*
1967	*Camelot*
1968	*Oliver!*
1969	*Hello, Dolly!*
1971	*Fiddler on the Roof*
1972	*Cabaret*

The New American Cinema

From the mid-1960s through the 1970s there were two opposing trends in filmmaking. One trend was toward "little films," not extravagant in any way, but intended to be significant and meaningful. Films featuring Jack Nicholson typify this category: *Easy Rider* (1969), *Five Easy Pieces* (1970), and *One Flew Over the Cuckoo's Nest* (1975). In contrast to these was the opposite trend, toward blockbusters, which were heavily budgeted and were counted on to be high-grossing films. Examples of this type of film include *Patton* (1970), *The Godfather* [I and II] (1972, 1975), and *Star Wars* (1977). During the 1970s and 1980s the success of one blockbuster film often led to a series, such as the *Star Wars* trilogy.

Musicals, the traditional mainstay of extravagant film production, have become rare and sporadic for economic reasons. Musical play adaptations from Broadway are relatively modest productions, such as *The Wiz* (1978) and *A Little Night Music* (1978). Newer movie musicals tend to focus on stars rather than spectacle. A prime example is *Grease* (1978), featuring John Travolta and Olivia Newton-John. Barbra Streisand's *Yentl* (1984) was not strictly a musical, although it did include several fine songs.

Musical sound tracks have become more important than ever in the New American Cinema. No longer is music a mere accompaniment to the action and scenery of films. Lengthy portions of the score are now brought to the foreground. This has been particularly true of scores and songs written in one of the contemporary popular styles. Quincy Jones' jazz/soul score to *Shaft* (1971) broke new ground for the use of black music in films. Country and western and bluegrass styles had been used for source music previously but not as the chief style of the sound track. However, these became the main ingredient in the sound tracks of *Bonnie and Clyde* (1967), *Deliverance* (1972), *Urban Cowboy* (1980), and *Places in the Heart* (1984).

Rock styles have earned their own place in specialized films from late 1960s to the present. *Blackboard Jungle* (1955), featuring Bill Haley, was an early forerunner of this trend. Rock songs of the past were used effectively to create a nostalgic atmosphere in *American Graffiti* (1973), *The Big Chill* (1983), and *Forrest Gump* (1994). Newer films normally have used songs performed by contemporary rock groups, either previously recorded or written specifically for the film. *Easy Rider* pioneered the trend. However, the tremendous success of *Saturday Night Fever* (1977) led to a string of youth and dance films in the 1980s which feature "song scores." A representative list includes *Fame* (1980), *Footloose* (1984), and *Dirty Dancing* (1987). In the 1990s, an example is *Waiting to Exhale* (1995).

Classical music has also found its way into the foreground of film music during this period. Two of Stanley Kubrick's films, *2001: A Space Odyssey* (1968) and *A Clockwork Orange* (1972), made prominent use of masterpieces by Richard Strauss, Beethoven, and other composers. *Kramer vs. Kramer* (1979) featured portions of *The Four Seasons* by Vivaldi, and the sound track of *Ordinary People* (1980) was characterized by repeated hearings of Johann Pachelbel's Canon in D. *Amadeus* (1984), based on the later life and music of Mozart, is surely the pinnacle of films dealing with composers.

Two film composers rose to particular prominence during the 1970s: Jerry Goldsmith and John Williams. The careers of both extended back to about 1960. Part of Goldsmith's lengthy list of credits includes: the *Planet of the Apes* series of films, *The Sand Pebbles* (1966), *Chinatown* (1974), *Star Trek: The Motion Picture* (1979), *Star Trek V: The Final Frontier* (1989), and *Malice* (1993). John Williams is famous for large symphonic scores written for films that feature adventure and excitement. A partial list of his achievements since 1975 includes:

> *Jaws* (1975)
> *Star Wars* trilogy (1977, 1980, 1983)
> *Close Encounters of the Third Kind* (1977)
> *Superman* (1978)
> *Indiana Jones* trilogy (1981, 1984, 1989)
> *E.T.—The Extra-Terrestrial* (1982)
> *Jurassic Park* (1993)
> *Schindler's List* (1993)

In the late 1970s a significant improvement in motion picture sound was developed by the Dolby laboratories. The new technology incorporated the Dolby noise reduction system (see Chapter 3) along with multichannel sound track recording. Dolby Stereo® sound is recorded on a split optical sound track. This is coded so that theaters equipped with six-speaker Dolby Stereo® in the auditorium can take full advantage of the multiple tracks, while theaters with only two-speaker stereo (or monaural sound) can exhibit the same picture with satisfactory results. Dolby Stereo® has also succeeded in extending the upper range of movie sound tracks, previously limited to 7,500 Hz.

New electronic technology also found its way into film scores themselves during the 1970s. Music synthesizers and processors were originally used in varying degrees alongside traditional acoustic instruments. In 1981 the British film *Chariots of Fire* utilized an all-electronic score composed and performed by Vangelis.

Production in the motion picture industry of the 1970s resembled that of the 1920s in several ways. Numerous films were made in New York (or in European countries) rather than in Hollywood. Film producers and directors once again held the spotlight, and some of them were clear counterparts to big names of the 1920s. The work of Woody Allen occupies a position similar to that of Mack Sennett, and George Lucas is comparable to Samuel Goldwyn.

During the first half of the 1980s the industry also began to thrive much as it had during the 1920s. Each year the number of films released was on the increase due to the new demands of a new market: the *home* market. Cable TV systems grew significantly during this time, and four distinct national cable movie broadcasters had come into being by 1984. Parallel to this development, sales of videocassette players mushroomed in the early 1980s. This created an entirely new type of distribution for movies of recent and past vintage: videocassette sales and rentals.

During the same period Hollywood experienced a renaissance in quality film making accompanied by equally distinguished musical scores. Notable among those films were *On Golden Pond* (1981, score by Dave Grusin), *Gandhi* (1982, score by George Fenton and Ravi Shankar), *Amadeus* (1984, score by W. A. Mozart), *Out of Africa* (1985, score by John Barry), and *The Color Purple* (1985, score by Quincy Jones, *et al.*).

The 1990s have seen a revival of the musical film. These were made not in the traditional manner but as Disney animated musicals. With Oscar-winning scores and songs by Alan Menken, four of these were *The Little Mermaid* (1989), *Beauty and the Beast* (1991), *Aladdin* (1992), and Pocahontas (1995). *The Lion King* (1994) contained an Oscar-winning song by Elton John and Tim Rice, and in home video release this film became the biggest selling video cassette of all time.

Today, despite home video, people still enjoy the magic of seeing a new film in a darkened theater in the midst of a large audience, the screen bigger than life and the digitally recorded "surround sound" seemingly infinite in dimension. Hollywood is still chalking up occasional blockbusters, but there is also a fast and steady turnover of less-pretentious films destined for their secondary market of cable TV and videocassette viewers.

Functions of Music in Films

If you were to ask three different film composers what they consider the function of music in films to be, you would probably receive three differing opinions. Further, if you ask one composer about the function of his score in three different movies, he would probably be inclined to point out the differences between them. However, despite divergences in philosophy, a few composers have been able to synthesize and to communicate some general principles about film music. One of the most articulate was Aaron Copland, author of five books and numerous articles on music. In 1949, the year in which he composed his Academy Award-winning score to *The Heiress*, Copland wrote an article on film music for the *New York Times* in which he outlined five major functions of music in a dramatic film score. Since these are as valid and comprehensive today as they were at that time, the remainder of this discussion is based on them. Here, quoted, are Copland's "ways in which music serves the screen":

1. It creates a more convincing atmosphere of time and place.

2. It underlines psychological refinements—the unspoken thoughts of a character or the unseen implications of a situation.

3. It serves as a kind of neutral background filler.

4. It builds a sense of continuity.

5. It underpins the theatrical buildup of a scene, and rounds it off with a sense of finality.

Atmosphere: Time and Place

When writing a score the composer must always consider the style of the film itself: its own way of treating time and place. If the film has a historical setting that attempts authenticity, the composer will be free to employ historical elements in the music also. If the style of the film is historical fantasy (for example, King Arthur), exoticism may be the element to play up. In other films ethnic elements (ethnicity) are the key style features involving characters and locale. Science fiction films present a very special problem, since no one knows how the music of the future will sound. Again, the style of the film itself can guide the composer into playing up an atmosphere of adventure, heroism, mysticism, or whatever the film demands.

Source music can aid a film in projecting time and place. This could be in the form of the film's theme song sung or played on screen as source music. Another, more contemporary method is the use of *implied* source music, where source recordings are woven into the sound track for the purpose of creating atmosphere. This technique has proven effective in numerous nonmusical films with scores involving Rock styles. One of the most successful was *American Graffiti*. The "song scores" of many youth films of the 1980s were assembled to exploit the power of implied source music.

The Psychological — Unspoken, Unseen

Composer Earle Hagen has stated that "The selected, deliberate, psychological usage of music is the principal burden of the picture composer." The power of this aspect of a film score is that it can control the audience's perception of what it sees on the screen. For example, a perfectly innocent-looking scene can be filled with sinister foreboding, or an otherwise tragic occurrence can be made into a comic gag— all through the power of the music. The composer's control over emotion can extend over the entire film, and it is possible to speak of creating a psychological "climate" in which an audience can become absorbed. Composer Quincy Jones has referred to a musical score's responsibility to create an "emotional fabric" for the film.

Neutral Background, Filler

Many people think that a film score is not supposed to be noticed. This is neither entirely true nor entirely false. Nearly any film with an instrumental score contains scenes in which the music's sole duty is to provide a subliminal enhancement to the visual and dramatic action. Without music such scenes would no doubt seem dry and lifeless. Dialogue scenes can be done with or without music. If music is used, the composer has the challenge of making the music enhance the scene without being noticed. Hagen has commented that there are two methods of approaching music under dialogue: Pay little attention to the dialogue and depend on a low volume level when the music is dubbed into the scene; or compose the music as a counterpoint to the dialogue. The latter will require close attention to the spoken details of the scene: its pacing, rhythm, pauses, and pattern of ideas. Any composer dealing with music under dialogue must also consider the pitch range of the actors' voices. For a clear, clean sound track, the music must avoid those ranges as much as possible. A solo instrument, such as a clarinet, works well, since its range is uniform and controllable.

Continuity

Film historians have written that the nature of the film medium is jumpy and choppy, constantly in danger of falling apart. Animated cartoons are the clearest example, and their ever-present musical sound tracks maintain the necessary continuity while enhancing the visual comic effects. Rapid montage scenes in feature films are another good example, where the score acts as a catalyst, holding visual images together with its unifying musical ideas. Sometimes music must be left out of some particular scene to keep it from becoming too melodramatic or maudlin. However, on a large scale a good musical score can succeed in lending an extremely powerful unifying element to the film.

Building Dramatic Climaxes

Music can sneak into a scene as a sort of emotional cushion and prepare the audience for something about to happen. As the scene builds in intensity the music builds with it, supporting the drama with an emotional foundation that matches the pacing and intensity of the scene. "Effective music heightens the emotional stakes," says Hagen.

The Process of Film Music

The composer of a film score is normally hired when the film goes into production, but there are many cases of his being brought in at the last minute. Knowledgeable directors realize that the longer the composer is exposed to the film and the longer he has to put his ideas together, the better the score will be. If there are songs or dance numbers performed on screen, the composer must write and record these before the scenes for them are shot.

After the film has been shot and when it is near its final "cut," there is a screening of the film to determine where the music will go. The film's composer, director, producer, and music cutter (editor) should all attend this screening. As the film is shown, the viewers "spot" where music should start and stop. The producer, director, and composer exchange ideas about the type of music for each cue or sequence.

At the screening the music cutter takes notes on the place of every musical cue, and then he and the composer review each spotted scene for details. They run these on a professional type of movie viewer called a moviola, which has a footage/frame counter. Then the music cutter converts the footage/frame readings to timings and makes a detailed breakdown sheet (cue sheet) for every musical cue. (See Figures 7–2 and 7–3.) Each sheet provides timing information that the composer will need in writing and synchronizing his music for the scene, such as important lines of dialogue, action, pauses in the action, and entrances and exits of characters. The types of camera shots (cut, fade, and dissolve) are also shown. Timings are given to the nearest 1/3 second, since generally that is the closest necessary to synchronize music with the film.

For a feature film a composer usually has four to six weeks to complete and record the musical score. He works through the score one cue at a time, aided by a videocassette copy of the film, chronograph (or stopwatch) and a digital metronome (click generator). A cue may be only a few seconds long or it may last several minutes. In scenes requiring lengthy periods of music, a "sequence" of cues is composed. The cues of the sequence are designed to overlap precisely after they are recorded. This will be the job of the music mixer during dubbing.

Because of the shortage of time, the composer normally neither orchestrates nor copies orchestra parts for his score. Although this practice has been criticized by concert music composers, it should be understood that most film composers hand their orchestrators a very detailed short score or sketch which leaves little to the imagination. AFM union rules call for a separate scale for music copying, and this is normally built into the music budget. One must bear in mind that every aspect of filmmaking is a collaborative effort.

The composer normally is the producer of the recording session. He may hire

Feet	Seconds	Feet	Seconds	Feet	Seconds	Feet	Seconds
1	2/3"	21	14"	41	27 1/3"	61	40 2/3"
2	1 1/3"	22	14 2/3"	42	28"	62	41 1/3"
3	2"	23	15 1/3"	43	28 2/3"	63	42"
4	2 2/3"	24	16"	44	29 1/3"	64	42 2/3"
5	3 1/3"	25	16 2/3"	45	30"	65	43 1/3"
6	4"	26	17 1/3"	46	30 2/3"	65	44"
7	4 2/3"	27	18"	47	31 1/3"	66	44 2/3"
8	5 1/3"	28	18 2/3"	48	32"	68	45 1/3"
9	6"	29	19 1/3"	49	32 2/3"	69	46"
10	6 2/3"	30	20"	50	33 1/3"	70	46 2/3"
11	7 1/3"	31	20 2/3"	51	34"	71	47 1/3"
12	8"	32	21 1/3"	52	34 2/3"	72	48"
13	8 2/3"	33	22"	53	35 1/3"	73	48 2/3"
14	9 1/3"	34	22 2/3"	54	36"	74	49 1/3"
15	10"	35	23 1/3"	55	36 2/3"	75	50"
16	10 2/3"	36	24"	56	37 1/3"	76	50 2/3"
17	11 1/3"	37	24 2/3"	57	38"	77	51 1/3"
18	12"	38	25 1/3"	58	38 2/3"	78	52"
19	12 2/3"	39	26"	59	39 1/3"	79	52 2/3"
20	13 1/3"	40	26 2/3"	60	40"	80	53 1/3"

Figure 7-2. Footage/timing conversion table (35-mm film).

the musicians himself, but more usually he turns this over to a contractor, who may also play in the recording session. The recording studio and engineers will have been scheduled far in advance in accordance with the film's deadlines. The recording session usually starts with cues requiring the largest orchestra, and often the first recording is the film's main title music. The recording session may be broken up into cues recorded "to picture," to a click track, to free timing, and "wild" (see below). Additional tracks, such as musical overlays and sweeteners, are recorded last.

After the music cutter has done any necessary intercutting from different takes and has made a master of all cues, the next step in the process is dubbing. Dubbing is nothing more than the final sound mixdown for the film, including voice, sound effects, and music. A normal feature film in stereo may require a week to dub, but six-track Dolby Stereo® sound tracks can take considerably longer. The composer is normally present during dubbing. Some directors do not like inexperienced composers to attend dubbing sessions, because they complain about the volume level of their music suffering in the final mix. However, many composers can be of great help during a dubbing session.

	:00	Camera pans over faces in the room.
	:01½	John: "You, too."
	:02⅓	CUT to Sylvia.
⊕	:03	Camera starts to zoom in.
	:04½	—Holds on MCU⁽ᐧ⁾
	:06⅔	Begin DISSOLVE to flashback.
	:07½	DISSOLVE finishes. Picnic scene. Young Sylvia hands young John a napkin.
	:09⅓	SOS⁽ᐧ⁾ John smiling.
	:10⅔	CUT to Sylvia saying "Hungry?"
	:11½	Begin pause.
⊕	:12½	
	:14⅓	John: "Only for you."
	:15½	ECU⁽ᐧ⁾ Sylvia's face.
⊕	:16½	They kiss.
	:19⅔	Begin DISSOLVE.

ECU = Extra Close-Up
MCU = Medium Close-Up
SOS = Shot Over Shoulder

Figure 7-3. Hypothetical breakdown sheet—composer's picture cue marks added.

The dubbing room is equipped with projection equipment, a dubbing console, and several "dummy" machines (dubbers), which play back sound in synchronization with the projector. Two or three engineers operate the console, which controls and mixes dummy sources of dialogue, sound effects, and music. The process is similar to mixing down musical recordings (see Chapter 3), except that long periods of sound may be recorded on each take. The engineers work through each reel of the film using the projected picture, a footage counter, and mixing cue sheets with information on all sources of sound.

All sound recording up to and including the final mix is done on magnetic tape. The final step in sound processing, and indeed the final step in the film's production, is to transfer the sound to the optical sound track on the final print of the film itself. This last step will make it possible for the theater projector to play back the sound track as the picture is exhibited on the screen. (See Figure 7–1).

Recording Techniques

One of the chief differences between film music and that written for the concert or theatrical stage is the need to synchronize the music exactly to action, dialogue, and effects which photography has fixed permanently on film. There are various inherent problems connected with music synchronization. Some of these concern the length of a musical cue which must, for some reason, be recorded in one take rather than as a sequence. Others concern maintaining precise musical synchronization with visual details in a scene. Still others concern budget. Over the years several solutions to the problems of synchronized music recording have been sought. The four techniques described below represent the best methods that have been found.

Free Timing

The technique of composing and recording to the stop-watch only is called "free timing." It is the most common means of synchronizing music and film. On the written score the composer places frequent timing references taken from the breakdown sheet. These are for the benefit of the conductor (often the composer himself) at the recording session. At the moment the conductor starts the cue, either he or the music cutter punches a button which starts the large studio stop-watch or chronograph (called the "clock"), which is in the conductor's view. As the cue is rehearsed, the conductor checks each timing reference to be sure the music is at the right place in time. Small variations in the speed of the music may be made for the sake of synchronizing with the clock. The scores to many low-budget films have been recorded entirely in free timing.

Picture Cueing

The technique of picture cueing, or recording "to picture," is another form of timed recording, but one which requires a higher music budget (for film, equipment usage, and technicians). On the written score appear frequent timing references just as in free timing. However, additional symbols are also shown for synchronization devices known as "streamers" and "punches" (Figure 7–4a). A streamer is a diagonal line scribed on the film's emulsion over a length of three to five feet (2 2/3 seconds to 4 seconds). The frame at the very end of the stream-

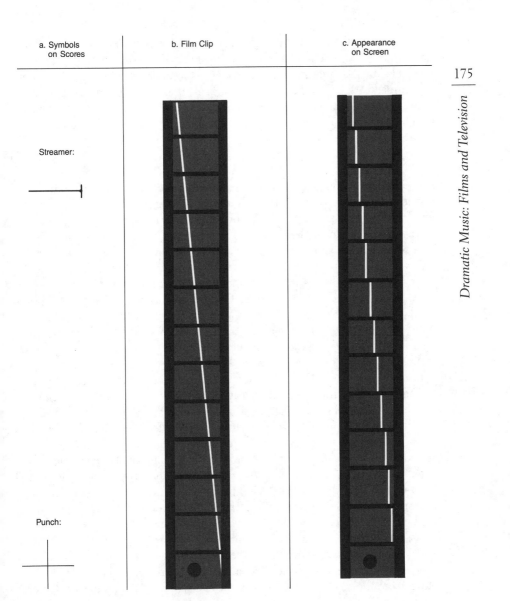

a. Symbols on Scores	b. Film Clip	c. Appearance on Screen

Streamer:

Punch:

Figure 7-4. Streamer and punch.

er contains a punch, which is a hole punched out of the center of the frame (Figure 7–4b). On the screen a streamer will look like a vertical white line moving across from left to right (Figure 7–4c). When the line reaches the right edge, the punch causes a burst of light on the screen.

These marks are made on a black-and-white work copy of the film (or electronically on video tape) by the music cutter prior to the recording session. During recording the conductor views the film (without sound). Streamer and punch marks appear at the very start of the cue and at important timing points along the way. Punches may occur occasionally during the cue to assist in timing. Normally, the clock is also running during recording for the conductor's reference between screen markings. When the cue is played back, it can be synchronized with the projector. This convenience not only shows whether the cue is in synchronization with the picture, but it can also convey some of the overall effect of the music.

Click Track

A click track is nothing more than a digital metronome calibrated to film frames instead of beats per minute. Since film moves through the projector at twenty-four frames per second, a wide variety of musical tempos (speeds) can be derived by causing a click to occur at exact frame intervals. Originally, a click track was created by making a mark at the top of a frame of a piece of sound film. Then a loop was made using that frame plus the desired number of blank frames. When played back through a dummy machine, the looping film would provide a precise clicking sound at exact intervals. Greater refinements in tempo could be achieved by aligning the click with one of the four sprocket holes next to the frame. The digital metronome/click generator now simulates film loops.

Figure 7–5 shows the correspondence between timing, click numbers (beats), and footage for a ten-frame click track. The clicks of this relatively quick tempo also provide for closer synchronization with picture details compared with free timing. While free timing is somewhat accurate—depending on the conductor—to 1/3 second (eight frames), each individual beat of this particular click track is automatically and precisely synchronized with every tenth frame (5/12 of a second). Further, the composer can write in musical details *between* clicks, and the conductor can bring these out in recording. Every half-beat of a ten-frame click track corresponds to an interval of five frames—less than 1/4 second. The composer will decide on the exact click tempo for a cue based upon both the dramatic tempo of the scene and the timings of important events within the scene.

In recording a cue to a click track the conductor, and often also the musicians, wear headphones through which the clicks are heard. The music cutter starts the click track, and after a few "free" clicks for the conductor and musicians to get used to the tempo, the conductor starts the musicians and conducts to the pulse of the clicks. The cue may end in the click tempo, or it may move into free timing (the clock having been running during the click portion).

Click tracks are most useful in scenes where the musical tempo needs to be even and/or fast. The classic click-track cue is for a chase scene, where a quick tempo must be maintained over a long period, and precise reference points, such as gunshots or photographic effects, must be considered. Music for fast-moving comedy scenes also is often recorded to a click track, and animated cartoons make use of click-track recording more than any other type of film.

Recording "Wild"

Some musical cues require only approximate timings or none at all. A short cue, such as a segue that ends on a long-held note, is one example. Others include

Click No.	Timing	Footage
1	:00	00' 01 frame
2	:00 5/12	00' 11 fr.
3	:00 5/6	01' 05 fr.
4	:01 7/24	01' 15 fr.
5	:01 17/24	02' 09 fr.
6	:02 1/12	03' 03 fr.
7	:02 13/24	03' 13 fr.
8	:02 23/24	04' 07 fr.
9	:03 3/8	05' 01 fr.
10	:03 19/24	05' 11 fr.
11	:04 5/24	06' 05 fr.
12	:04 15/24	06' 15 fr.
13	:05	07' 09 fr.
14	:05 11/24	08' 03 fr.
15	:05 7/8	08' 13 fr.
16	:06 7/24	09' 07 fr.
17	:06 17/24	10' 01 fr.
18	:07 1/12	10' 11 fr.
19	:07 13/24	11' 05 fr.
20	:07 23/24	11' 15 fr.
21	:08 3/8	12' 09 fr.
22	:08 19/24	13' 03 fr.
23	:09 1/6	13' 13 fr.
24	:09 15/24	14' 07 fr.

Figure 7-5. Ten-frame click chart (144 beats/minute).

generic "canned" music cues found in rental libraries. Such cues are generally recorded "wild," that is, with no reference to a clock, a picture, or a click track. Obviously, this is the simplest type of film music recording. Most feature films contain very few cues recorded in this way, although source music and other cues which must be done before the film is shot are normally recorded wild.

Television Scores

Most of the dramatic shows, situation comedies, and motion pictures made for television are scored, recorded, and dubbed in exactly the same manner as distributed feature films. In fact, most of those types of shows are originally filmed rather than recorded on videotape. A made-for-TV film is put together exactly like a feature film, except for periodic breaks for commercials. For each of these breaks the composer provides a short musical segue cue (a "commercial bumper") in addition to the normal scenic cues. The scores for segments of dramatic and comedy series are made up of a combination of custom music for the segment and stock bumpers and other cues recorded ahead of the season, to be used as needed. The presence of stock cues is especially obvious in daytime dramas.

TV shows of the above types which are videotaped (rather than filmed) use similar procedures for composing and recording musical scores, but the method of dubbing is different. Whereas film uses footage/frames as its basic timing reference, professional videotape provides a channel for time code pulses. The industry standard for this is the SMPTE (Society of Motion Picture and Television Engineers) Time Code.

Business Aspects of Film Music

As with any industry that deals in copyright material, the film industry operates through contracts, licenses, and other legal agreements. In film music the main legal instruments are the composer-producer contract for the score and the synchronization and performance licenses for using preexisting musical material. Licensing must be also secured for broadcasting a movie and for distributing video tape/disc versions of a film.

Composer's Contracts

When a composer is hired to write the score to a motion picture, he and the film's producer sign a contract for the work. In the case of well-established composers, the fee involved is for composing and orchestrating only. Other expenses involving music copying and hiring musicians for the recording session are budgeted separately. However, a newer composer just breaking into the industry will often sign a package agreement. In that case the fee covers more than just composing and could include all expenses involved in the scoring and recording of the music.

Since the producer has paid the composer an outright creative fee, the composer-producer contract treats the film score as a "work made for hire" for the purpose of copyright. (See Chapter 2.) This means that the producer owns all the rights to the music that the copyright law grants to the composer in other cases. Film score contracts work similar to songwriter contracts, but the producer generally assigns the publishing rights to a music publisher (often his own). These include the rights of recording, performance, and printing. As in a songwriter-publisher contract, the film composer is normally entitled to future royalties from his music, including a share of mechanical fees from recordings and royalties from printed music and home video distribution.

A "performance" of a film score technically takes place every time the film is shown in a theater or over TV. However, since 1950, performance fees cannot be collected from movie theaters in the United States. Nevertheless, performing rights organizations in foreign countries, particularly England, France, and Italy, continue to be particularly strong in the area of movie theater licensing. Therefore, composers and publishers of film music still benefit from ASCAP and BMI income from films which go into foreign distribution. The music in films broadcast on TV qualifies for credit with performing rights organizations in a similar manner to other broadcast music.

Synchronization and Performance Licensing

The presence of songs and entire song scores in many of today's films brings with it a different set of business arrangements than with "original" scores. A theme song written by the film's composer specifically for that film may be contracted as part of the score. However, utilizing the talents of pop songwriters in films has become extremely prevalent. Whether a song is already in existence or has been written specially for a picture, outside interests are usually involved in the copyright ownership. The song may already have a publisher, or a prestigious songwriter may insist on retaining rights to his work. If the producer wishes to use an existing recording of the song, the matter will also involve the record company and artist. In order to incorporate the song in a film the producer must obtain licenses covering three rights: synchronization, public performance, and making copies for distribution.

The synchronization right allows the filmmaker to record music in synchronization with the visual portion of a film. The performance right allows the filmmaker to exhibit the film publicly in theaters and elsewhere. The third right grants the filmmaker the authority to make copies of the film containing the song, and to distribute them to the public by sale or rental. Naturally, licenses for synchronization and performance are also written between record companies and song publishers in the production of music video clips and long forms. (See Chapter 5.) This last right, sometimes called "software rights," is crucial to the manufacture of home videocassettes and videodiscs, whether they contain film or music video material.

The Harry Fox Agency (see Chapter 2) normally researches song and recording copyright owners for film producers and acts as mediator in license negotiations. Licensing fees are not fixed and depend on the current market value of the song or recording.

Sound Track Albums

As mentioned above, the score and songs from the sound track of a film can become important commercial entities in themselves when released on records. Not only can the recordings make money for the composer, producer, and others involved with the film, but a hit song or sound track album serves to promote the film as long as the music is heard on the air and the records are stocked in stores. At one time most major studios had their own record label subsidiaries. This is no longer the case, and most film sound tracks are released through major record companies. Even when a studio is affiliated with a record company, the sound track album may be assigned to an unaffiliated label because of preexisting contractual arrangements between the label and the composer. Songs heard on a sound track album are normally taken directly from the recording made for the film. However, instrumental score music may be rearranged before being recorded, both because a new arrangement may make isolated cues into more interesting listening and because hiring a smaller orchestra to rerecord may be more economical for the studio than paying union reuse fees to the members of the original large recording orchestra.

In the course of this chapter the history, functions, creation and production process, and business aspects of film music have been examined. Like popular songwriting, film music is both a business and an art. However, only in recent years has the artistic side of film music come to be recognized. While much has been written about the origins and evolution of various styles of popular music, accessible books and articles about film scores have been sparse and uneven. Perhaps this is because film music is an adjunct and an enhancement to another art, the film. But the best film scores, like the best ballet scores, can stand on their own as music only.

The broadest possible spectrum of musical styles can be heard in film music, ranging from the "classical" styles of the past to modern pop songs to the most avant-garde experiments in New Music. The strange and almost unexplainable thing about film music is that, through the magic of the film medium, an audience willingly accepts any style of music, as long as it is right for the movie. The same audience would surely reject many of those scores in a concert setting. The conclusion which can be drawn from this is that the connection between drama and music is a very ancient, perhaps even primeval, one. But judging by the vigor of the film and video media, this is a connection that will be with us for some time to come.

Review Questions

1. Why was sound impractical in early films?

2. About how long did the age of silent films last?

3. Name one silent film for which an orchestral score was written.

4. What was the title and year of the first "talking" motion picture?

5. Compare the Vitaphone method of sound track recording with the optical photo-electric method.

6. When did the "Mickey Mouse" music and "wall-to-wall" scoring tendencies flourish? Who were some composers of that era?

7. What were some of the events that led film makers to take new directions around 1950? What were some of those directions.

8. Identify some examples of jazz or rock music used as the basis of a film score.

9. Name two or three Broadway musicals that have been adapted for film and a Disney musical film of recent years.

10. What are a few accomplishments of composer John Williams?

11. Identify and describe two or three of Copland's "ways in which music serves the screen."

12. How does a composer know which scenes of a film require music?

13. What is a music "cutter"?

14. Describe what happens in recording to "free timing," to "picture," and to "click track."

15. Does music for TV differ greatly from that for movies? What might be different?

16. If a film score is a "work made for hire," is the composer paid just once for *everything?* Explain.

17. If a producer wants to use an existing song in a film, what licensing must be obtained?

18. Are sound track album recordings always taken directly from the film? Explain.

8

Music Criticism and Journalism

In our age of information and communication it is only natural that the print medium should occupy an important role in connection with music in contemporary life. On a daily basis music critics document performances, premieres, and revivals in the various repertoires of American music. Weekly, many of these critics write longer, more reflective articles about past and coming events and make observations about the changing musical scene. Weekly and monthly periodicals serve music professionals, semiprofessional performers, and the general public with news and reviews on a wide variety of musical topics. Music journalism is the key information and communication tool both within the world of music and between the musical world and the interested public.

This chapter divides the field of the written word into two major areas: music criticism in the daily press, and journalism in periodicals other than daily papers. A brief history of music criticism is followed by a profile of music criticism in today's world. The latter part of the chapter surveys the spectrum of music-related periodicals by presenting brief descriptions of representative publications.

Music Criticism: Historical Perspective

The Eighteenth Century

The "Age of Reason," which flowered in the eighteenth century, was supported by a spirit of criticism. Baroque ideals and artistic forms were being rebuilt into rational, "natural" phenomena, and the earliest of modern music criticism was a part of this movement. Early music critics were influenced heavily by the writings and critical spirit of French thinkers and encyclopedists, although most musical writers were English and German. In 1711–1712 Joseph Addison wrote a set of critical essays about Italian opera for London's *Spectator* magazine. In Hamburg theorist-critic Johann Mattheson not only emulated Addison but also established the world's first music periodical, *Musica critica* (1722–1725). Mattheson and later German critics (notably, J. A. Scheibe) upheld the torch of progressivism, downgrading Baroque extravagance and contrapuntal complexities in favor of the newer, simpler rococo melody-centered style associated with the Age of Reason.

Many readers of general and music periodicals at the time were members of the rising middle classes. A successful Leipzig magazine aimed at middle-class devotees of German *Singspiel* was J. A. Hiller's *Wöchentliche Nachrichten und Anmerkungen, die Music betreffend,* begun in 1766.

In France music criticism was carried on chiefly by philosophers and aestheticians. Most of it, published in general periodicals, consisted of operatic controversies centered on French versus Italian tastes. In England no music periodicals existed at this time, but valuable essays were published. The most important English essayist was the worldly, well-traveled Charles Burney, who wrote an "Essay on Musical Criticism" as a preface to one part of his *General History of Music* (1776–1789).

Around the turn of the nineteenth century daily papers frequently printed notices concerning musical premieres, but these were usually quite brief. For more expanded reviews, composers and the public looked to the new and influential musical magazines which were cropping up, especially in Germany. In magazines such as J. F. Rochlitz's *Allgemeine musikalische Zeitung,* begun in 1798, reviews of the works of Haydn, Mozart, Beethoven, and Schubert could be read. E. T. A. Hoffmann, Beethoven's passionate literary admirer, wrote for that journal beginning in 1809.

The Early Romantic Age

Hoffmann and numerous other critics of his time displayed the roots of three tendencies which successfully dismissed rationalism and set the tone for romantic music criticism: passionate subjectivism, exaggeration for effect, and cultist propaganda. Theirs was an era when musical events were just beginning to become a part of public life, and most readers were likely to be uneducated in music. Thus, the early decades of the nineteenth century saw the main arena of music criticism move from specialized journals to the daily and weekly periodicals aimed chiefly at middle-class audiences. Johann Rellstab wrote for Berlin's oldest daily paper, the *Vossische Zeitung,* beginning in the first decade of the century, and he maintained his reputation as a leading music critic until his death in 1860. In France during 1827 François-Joseph Fétis initiated the famous *Revue musicale,* a periodical which survived until 1880 and was revived during the

writer-composers, notably Hector Berlioz. The *Gazette musicale de Paris*, an
even more progressive journal, was begun in 1834 as a forum for composers, one
of the most outspoken of whom was Franz Liszt.

Weber and Schumann

During the romantic age many composers found themselves on both the serving
and receiving ends of music criticism. They were usually also deeply interested in
literature, and one of the earliest of these was Carl Maria von Weber, the noted
composer of *Der Freischütz*. His critical writing began in 1801 at the age of fourteen, when he wrote a retort to a newspaper critic's review of an early opera of his.
Subsequently, Weber wrote for several magazines and newspapers, including the
Allgemeine musikalische Zeitung. Among his contributions was the development
of the preview article, which served to prepare the audience for a musical event.

Subjectivity and intuition as tools of romantic criticism were epitomized in
the writings of Robert Schumann. His work as a critic and essayist began in 1831
with a rave review of an early Chopin work, typical of the support and encouragement he continually gave to young, promising composers. In 1834 he initiated his own periodical, the *Neue Zeitschrift für Musik*, which he continued to edit
for ten years. Schumann did not always write his criticism in the first person. Typically, he would speak through the fanciful "League of David," who were constantly joined in battle against the "Philistines" of shallow invention and glib
virtuosity. The league consisted of three imaginary characters, two of whom were
based on facets of Schumann's own bipolar personality: Florestan, the fiery revolutionary, and Eusebius, the romantic dreamer. The third member of the
league was Master Raro, the wise mediator between the other two. (Raro may
have symbolized the steadying influence of Clara Wieck Schumann.)

Toward Modern Music Criticism

The German language continued to be the dominant one in the field of music
criticism during the romantic age. The leading music critic throughout the second half of the nineteenth century was Eduard Hanslick, who wrote for Viennese newspapers from 1855 until his death in 1904. Hanslick, vehemently
opposed to the music of Liszt and Wagner, was a propagandistic supporter of
music that agreed with Viennese tastes of the time, particularly Brahms and
Johann Strauss. His reviews and essays were witty and pointed, and they were
perused with interest by even the most unmusical readers. One reason for his
popularity was that his reviews reflected audience reactions. In opposition to
Hanslick, a prominent pro-Wagner (anti-Brahms) critic in Vienna during the
1880s was the perceptive and sensitive composer Hugo Wolf.

Bernard Shaw is not usually thought of as a music critic, yet he wrote on music
from the time of his arrival in London in 1876 until his death in 1950. From 1888
until 1894 music criticism provided the chief source of income for Shaw, writing

for the London *Star*—part of the time under the pseudonym "Corno di Bassetto" (Bassett Horn)—and later for *The World*. Shaw was extremely knowledgeable about music, and many of his reviews were genuine learning experiences for the reader. In an article which began as a mere performance review, Shaw would often make a smooth transition into a clear and persuasive discussion of the aesthetics of the works performed, leaving the reader with far more to ponder than the original event would have suggested. Several anthologies of Shaw's criticism have been published, and the editor of one of them asserts that "Shaw wrote what is perhaps the most lively and brilliant musical journalism ever penned." There is no doubt that he was the father of modern music criticism in the English language.

The Early Twentieth Century

A lengthy progression of nineteenth-century composer-critics was brought to a close with Claude Debussy, who contributed articles to various periodicals from 1901 to 1918. Most of these were written as conversations with a fictitious alter ego, "Mssr. Croche, the Dilettante-Hater." In his typically impressionistic, antiacademic fashion Debussy expressed his philosophy of music criticism tersely: "To render one's impressions is better than to criticize, and all technical analysis is doomed to futility."

In England music criticism had begun to come into its own with the writings of Bernard Shaw. Fortunately, Ernest Newman, a critic of immense wit and broad knowledge, was there to carry on the tradition beginning in 1905. Newman became a great Wagner expert, and he helped England to appreciate not only Wagner but also Richard Strauss and Hugo Wolf, who were two of Wagner's musical heirs. In the hands of Newman, music criticism in England became almost a branch of literature.

The finest music criticism written in Germany during the first half of the twentieth century was the work of Alfred Einstein. Writing at first in his native Munich and later for the *Berliner Tageblatt* (Berlin Daily Paper) (1927–1933), Einstein's reviews and essays were springboards for deeper reflections concerning style and aesthetics. Unfortunately, the rise of Nazism forced Einstein to leave Germany. In the late 1930s he wrote a few pieces for British publications before moving on to the United States for his final years as a teaching scholar.

One problem facing all music critics in the twentieth century has been modern (new) music. Since Beethoven there has been an ever-widening gap of understanding between composer and audience. This chasm extended naturally to the music critic, who, in a way, has been an extension of audiences through the years. In print this problem has often taken the form of an attack on the music (and sometimes even the personal appearance and life) of a composer misunderstood in his time. Nicolas Slonimsky attributed such invective to an attitude of "non-acceptance of the unfamiliar" but suggested that at times such writings may have been merely to make a readable newspaper story. In the course of the twentieth century this tendency has been tempered and counterbalanced by the rise of libel laws and the tendency of composers and performers to use them to redress damaging reviews.

Music Criticism in the United States

American music criticism got started considerably later than Europe beginnings. *Dwight's Journal*, introduced in Boston in 1852, was the first channel for a rather dogmatic brand of criticism. John Dwight's enterprise lasted until 1881, and in that year William Apthorp began to write criticism for the *Boston Evening Transcript*, using an altogether different method. Employing a somewhat French style which anticipated Debussy's approach, he continued writing for that paper until 1903. After Apthorp, Philip Hale maintained the high standards of music criticism in Boston.

Meanwhile, in New York brilliant music journalism flowed from what has been called the "Great Five" critics. James Huneker, known today chiefly as a Chopin authority, wrote for various New York papers. William Henderson was the *New York Times* music critic from 1887 until 1902, and worked for the *Sun* from that year until 1937. Richard Aldrich, a charming, aristocratic writer, followed Henderson on the *Times* and remained there until 1923. Henry T. Finck was music critic for the *New York Evening Post* from 1881 until 1924. Henry Krehbiel, a prolific writer on music, was music critic for the *New York Herald Tribune* for forty years until his death in 1923.

Lawrence Gilman followed Krehbiel at the *Tribune* (1923–1939) and contributed to several prominent magazines. A significant step in American music journalism during this early period was the introduction of *The Musical Quarterly* in 1915. Although this journal has leaned heavily toward musicology, its "Current Chronicle" section has presented critical reviews.

A second "Golden Age" of New York music criticism extended from the late 1930s to the mid-1950s. Olin Downes had become chief music critic for the *New York Times* in 1923, when Aldrich retired to consultant status. Five years later Oscar Thompson joined the *New York Sun* (succeeding Henderson), but moved to the *New York Evening Post* in 1937. In 1940 Virgil Thomson was appointed music critic for the *New York Herald Tribune*. During the war years music criticism in New York was dominated by these three distinguished writers. Oscar Thompson died in 1945, but a healthy rivalry continued between Downes and Virgil Thomson for nearly ten more years. In 1954 Thomson left music criticism to pursue composition more actively, and Downes died the following year. The job of music editor at the *Times* was filled for five years by Howard Taubman, and then by one of the most brilliant American musical journalists of this century, Harold Schonberg. Schonberg continued as senior critic with the *Times* until his retirement in 1980.

One unique trend in American music criticism has been an effort on the part of music critics to prepare writers newly entering the field. In 1928 Oscar Thompson established the first college course in music criticism in the United States. He followed this in 1934 with his handbook, *Practical Musical Criticism*. In the early 1950s a series of annual workshops in music criticism was initiated, largely through the efforts of Olin Downes and Virgil Thomson. These workshops led to the formal organization in 1958 of the Music Critics Association

(MCA). During the same period, Raymond Kendall at the University of Southern California established a degree program in music criticism, which for a time was replete with an internship and placement service cosponsored by the MCA. More recently, Peabody Conservatory has established a master's degree program in history and criticism, and the MCA has expanded its annual workshop into a weeklong Institute for Music Critics and Editors.

Newspaper Criticism Today

On the staff of a modern newspaper there are three jobs connected with music criticism: editor, music critic, and stringer.

The editor, usually an arts editor or arts/culture editor, may supervise several critics who review artistic and cultural events. The editor generally does some writing and is responsible for putting together the arts page of the daily paper as well as the entire arts section or supplement to the Sunday edition.

Regular music critics are salaried employees of the paper whose job consists principally of attending concerts and other musical events, and then writing reviews for the next day's paper. In the case of a morning paper this can be problematic, since the final deadline usually falls sometime around 11:00 P.M. Occasionally, the critic can solve the problem by leaving the event early. If a review cannot be completed quickly enough, an alternative solution is for the editor to place the review in the following day's paper. Music critics on papers of all sizes may occasionally be asked to review plays and art events when necessary. Larger papers may have a chief (or senior) music critic plus other critical staff.

A stringer is a writer who works free lance for a paper on a nonregular basis. In music criticism a stringer may be called in when two or more important musical events occur at the same time or overlap, and the paper's regular staff cannot handle them all. This problem crops up during music festivals. Stringers are also employed to review specialized musical events for which a regular music critic does not feel qualified.

Qualifications for Music Criticism

There are two schools of thought concerning a music critic's basic qualifications. One point of view is that the critic should first be a good journalist and secondarily know something about music. This is a commercially oriented opinion, which values a writer's ability to present an interesting story over his ability to convey informed, meaningful criticism.

The other, more widespread view is that the critic should have a musical background, perhaps in performance or composition, but preferably have a formal education in music history and literature, including training in analysis. The ability to read an unfamiliar score, for example, will give the critic an edge where new music is concerned. The critic who reads a score can prepare ahead for a premiere instead of depending solely on impressions of the work during the performance. A critic's first impressions of the sound of a work are also less likely to be prejudiced by the quality of the performance itself if he is following a score. Experiences in performance, which a formal musical education normally entails, give the critic insights useful in reviewing performance and interpretation.

This is not to downgrade the importance of good journalism. It is generally agreed that music critics should not only take courses in journalism but should gain as much early experience as possible writing for school papers and smaller local papers before applying for positions on metropolitan dailies. The career profiles of most successful American music critics show a dedicated beginning on the staff of a paper (or magazine) with a small circulation, then gradual upward mobility through positions of increasing importance and influence.

What a Music Critic Does

Nightly Performance Reviews

There are three large categories of newspaper criticism: nightly performance reviews, Sunday pieces, and record reviews. The most common and best-known of these is the nightly performance review. In the case of classical music, a critic may be reviewing the debut of a new artist, a performance by an artist of some reputation (ranging from local to international), an orchestral concert, an opera or other musical show, a composer's showcase concert, or any one of a number of hybrid presentations. With such a wide variety of talent to consider, the classical critic is constantly faced with problems of scope and aesthetic standards. An amateur or semiprofessional group cannot be judged by the same measures placed on a world-touring act; a college orchestra cannot be criticized for not sounding like a major symphony orchestra. Many critics must walk a narrow line between maintaining high aesthetic standards and what they feel to be a duty to encourage the development of the arts within the community.

Reviewing pop and rock concerts, jazz, nightclub acts, and ethnic performances has its own special problems. While classical music has a standard, predictable repertoire of music for the most part, other styles of music often have specialized, quickly changing repertoires. A critic or stringer who is about to review a performance by a Rock band will need to be knowledgeable about the group's past albums, its current songs, and other background aspects. All this is necessary if the critic is to make intelligent comments on the group's current development and stylistic direction.

Sunday Pieces

The Sunday piece written by a music critic is generally more literary than the nightly review. A critic may take time to reflect on the events of the current season. Or, more usually, the Sunday piece will give the writer an opportunity to preview coming musical events. At the opening of the fall season this might be very general. On the other hand, a preview piece for a Sunday during the season would more likely be a "news peg" or "lead" article on some particular event in the coming week. The music critic needs time in preparing a Sunday piece, both because it is longer than a nightly review and because research may be necessary. For example, if a new or long-forgotten work is to be performed, the critic will need to become familiar with it (through a score and/or recording) in order to prepare the audience for what to expect. Likewise, if an entirely new production of a well-known opera is to be given, the critic may wish to research material concerning previous productions of the work by the same company.

Record Reviews

Although record reviews are normally considered to be the province of magazines, in recent years they have gained wide acceptance as short features in daily newspapers. These reviews are generally written by the paper's regular critics and arts editor. They may be a regular part of the Sunday arts section, or they may appear irregularly when space needs to be filled in daily editions.

Survey of Music Periodicals

Newspaper music criticism is by no means the only form of music journalism. At one time there were three major U.S. classical music magazines: *The Etude*, *Musical America*, and *The Musical Courier*, all very general in nature. Today, there is a variety of periodicals which deal with some aspect of music, and most of these are aimed at a specific group of readers. The following survey does not attempt to mention all periodicals with music coverage, but merely reviews a representative sampling. Each periodical in the survey has a professional editorial/writing staff.

Trade Journals

The best known periodical in the music and entertainment industry is *Billboard*. Its central features are the "Hot 100" singles chart, the "Top 200 LPs" chart, and an array of smaller specialty charts. (See Chapter 6.) *Billboard* is published weekly and is packed with news stories and regular columns covering various facets of the industry, which has now expanded to include videocassette sales/rental and music video. Regular record reviews and "pick lists" are features of particular interest. Frequently, a multipage center section is devoted to promoting some musical style or phase of the industry. *Radio & Records* is a weekly that also publishes charts, but these reflect only airplay and not retail sales. Articles and published playlists in this periodical reflect its narrow but numerous audience of broadcasters.

The weekly tabloid *Variety* is also of some interest to those in the music industry. However, the chief focus of the paper is show business, including filmmaking, drama, radio and TV broadcasting, club work, and even the classical concert stage. Abbreviated record charts appear in each issue.

The Music Trades is a monthly publication targeted to music retailers, particularly the instrument trade. Besides major articles each regular issue is taken up mostly with sections called "Industry Forefront" and "Retailer Update." These are series of half-page stories on industry news concerning manufacturers, distribution deals, clinics, and so forth. There are also several half-page editorials and copious news briefs on people and products. Special issues of *The Music Trades* cover the annual International Music Market and NAMM Summer Session shows, both sponsored by the National Association of Music Merchants. A similar publication is *Musical Merchandise Review.*

Professional Periodicals

There is a group of periodicals read chiefly by professional musicians, songwriters, publishers, and the like. Some are the publications of professional organizations, such as *International Musician*, the organ of the American Federation of Musicians—the musicians' union.

The noncommercial, public relations magazine is another type of professional periodical. One example is *Grammy Pulse*, published by the National Academy of Recording Arts and Sciences (NARAS®). This quarterly magazine contains feature articles, news briefs, and interviews focusing primarily on performers. The Annual Awards Issue is of special interest, since it not only features Grammy® Award winners but also presents interesting material about the ceremony.

ASCAP and BMI (see Chapter 2) publish their own quarterly public relations periodicals. ASCAP *Playback* includes news briefs and medium-sized articles about members, but focuses its feature articles on new developments of interest to both publishers and writers—for example, technology, legal developments affecting the society, and the funding of special projects. *BMI Music World* spotlights BMI's performer-writers and presents news of the organization. One issue per year focuses on country music.

Two prominent commercial magazines in the professional category are *Musician* and *Jazziz*. Both of these monthlies are aimed at the contemporary and jazz instrumentalist and lean heavily toward feature articles about performers. Both magazines contain news briefs and record reviews but also have some distinctive features. *Musician* runs moderate-size articles on "scenes" such as Nashville. *Jazziz* reviews audio products and important performing engagements.

"Semipro" Magazines

There is a body of periodicals targeted to professional musicians as well as aspiring players who do not depend on music for a living. Three monthly magazines are representative of this classification: *Keyboard*, *Guitar Player*, and *Electronic*

Musician. Keyboard focuses on people and equipment. It contains interviews with prominent players, columns by experts, articles on new technology, and news stories on new equipment—both electronic and acoustic. *Guitar Player* focuses on contemporary players and their styles. Each issue contains more than ten "Workshop" columns written by well-known performers and other individuals in the guitar world. There are feature articles on players and on equipment, besides brief new-product profiles. *Electronic Musician* focuses most closely on digital, MIDI-related topics: new equipment, interfacing MIDI equipment, sequencing and recording, and multi-media. This magazine's readership consists chiefly of keyboardists and guitarists.

Educational Journals

Music Educators Journal is the monthly organ of the Music Educators National Conference (MENC), an organization consisting primarily of music teachers in the nation's public schools. Each issue is closely formatted to contain up to ten feature articles and several "departments." The latter include "All the Best" (editorial), "For Your Library" (reviews), "MENC Today," "Idea Bank" (forum on current topics), "Video Views" (educational video reviews), and "Current Reading" (periodical article summaries).

The Piano Quarterly is read chiefly by classical pianists and piano teachers. Writings by and about major concert artists appear alongside articles on interpretation and teaching techniques. Reviews of newly published music (mostly pedagogical) are featured, but book and record reviews are also printed. News briefs focus on awards and professional appointments.

Popular (Consumer) Magazines

One entire area of music journalism has been called the "Rock press." Periodicals covering Rock music and its artists have been popular since the 1960s, and *Rolling Stone* is the most successful survivor of that era. This biweekly slick tabloid has always been directed at an audience of young adults and adolescents. Music was chosen as its chief focus because, in the words of *Rolling Stone's* original editor, "Music is the greatest definable part of the youth culture." The full coverage today takes in what could be termed the "youth entertainment culture," whose principal media are records and TV. Feature stories on rock and entertainment personalities are prominent. *Rolling Stone* prints brief record charts (mostly drawn from other publications) and one unique page, "On the Road," which displays the current tour schedules of prominent performers. *Rolling Stone* has been widely imitated both in the United States and in other English-speaking countries. Probably the most successful challenger is the youth culture monthly, *Spin*.

Another major area of consumer music journalism might be called the "audio press." Probably the most prototypical monthly audio magazine is *Stereo Review*. Nearly every issue has a theme, going into depth on a single area of equipment (speakers, car stereo, Japanese technology, and so forth). Feature articles on the special topic are prominent, but there are also pieces on music, generally referenced to some part of the recorded repertoire. Record reviews constitute the largest part of each issue. Other leading audio monthlies are *High Fidelity, Audio,* and *CD Review.* The last-mentioned is unique for its coverage of digital only equipment and recordings.

Music criticism has evolved through one century of rationalism and another of subjective opinion. Twentieth-century criticism has become a blend of those extremes tempered by scholarship. Today's critics are far better prepared for their job than were those of previous eras. They view their role and responsibilities to artist, composer, and audience more seriously now than ever before. Though occasionally misunderstood or underrated, the field of music criticism continues to thrive and make its mark on the musical world and on public life.

With the growth of music as an industry, our times have seen a proliferation of music journalism far broader in scope than the few music magazines around the turn of the century would have suggested. In some of these newer periodicals—those that contain reviews of records, books, print music, or music videos—a form of music criticism also comes into play. However, articles about artists, musicians, musical products, repertoire, interpretation, and audio topics must also be considered legitimate music journalism in today's world. The sheer volume of information published regularly about these matters attests to their importance and reflects the deep interest which readers take in this very lively aspect of music in contemporary life.

Review Questions

1. Which country was the leader in music criticism during the 18th and 19th centuries?

2. What were the accomplishments of composer-critic Robert Schumann?

3. What was Bernard Shaw's contribution to music criticism?

4. Who were the early Boston music critics?

5. What was the period of the "Great Five"? Can you name two or three of these critics?

6. Describe the music criticism scene in New York from the 1930s to the mid-1950s.

7. What has been done in the United States to define and elevate the level of music criticism?

8. What is the difference between a regular music critic and a stringer?

9. What does a newspaper typically look for in a music critic?

10. What is the difference between a nightly review and a Sunday piece.

11. For each of the following categories of music periodicals, name one representative publication and tell a little about it:

a. Trade Journals

b. Professional Periodicals

c. "Semipro" Magazines

d. Educational Journals

e. Popular (Consumer) Magazines

Part 3

Music in Business Settings

Business Music

"Background music, "mood music," "elevator music," "airline music," "wallpaper music," "canned music," "Muzak®." All these terms (and more) have been used to describe a type of music which seems to be ever-present as we go about our daily lives. We hear it in the bank, the supermarket, the doctor's office, the airport, the restaurant, on the phone when we are put on hold, and perhaps in our own workplace.

What is the reason for this outpouring of musical sound? What do the people who pay for a background music service hope to accomplish? One answer is that they hope to run a smoother operation, have fewer problems to deal with, and increase profits. This proceeds from a premise, which has been partially proven through controlled experiments, that music can perform certain psychological or therapeutic functions—that music can have an effect on human behavior.

Studies described later in this chapter point to a number of positive results from the presence of background music. One of these is increased office productivity. Another is an enhanced buying mood resulting from the music's ability to relax customers and induce them to remain in a store for longer periods. Yet another positive application of background music is in places associated with potential stress. Office workplaces are one example, but hospitals, airports, and medical/dental facilities are others.

Background music is the most familiar type of business music. However, another trend is "foreground" music, which has different uses also discussed in this chapter. The musical repertoire used in foreground music is similar to that heard on the radio. In fact, whenever people use radio music to accompany work or pleasure, they are employing music (with interruptions from disc jockeys and commercial spots) in a foreground function.

Foundations of Background Music

Rhythm seems to be a natural biological function in humans, and a rhythmic accompaniment to work appears to be a very ancient practice. Often rhythm is necessary to keep some difficult physical team effort together. There are vast collections of work songs, sea chanteys, and the like, which show music's usefulness for this purpose. These types of songs also support the theory that music has been used to improve morale in the workplace for a very long time. The advice, given by Snow White's dwarfs, to "whistle while you work" has a strong foundation in human tradition.

Functional mood music first came into being in the church environment. During the seventeenth century Italian cathedrals utilized instrumental sonatas and concertos to enhance the Mass. Improvised organ music for this purpose had probably been going on for centuries before, but the use of composed sonatas was the first step in formalizing mood music. This music was used to maintain mood and concentration during inaudible portions of the service taking place at the altar and during quiet segments such as communion.

In the course of the seventeenth and eighteenth centuries, it became customary among the aristocracy to have music playing during the evening meal, particularly if it were a banquet gathering. During Mozart's time in the late eighteenth century, garden parties, birthdays, and other celebrations were generally accompanied by music. Often a new serenade or divertimento would be commissioned for the occasion. Some of this music is interesting to listen to directly, but the vast majority of it is definitely background music intended to blend in with the general ambience of the event.

The industrial revolution of the nineteenth century brought public middle-class restaurants whose customers wished to imitate the habits of the upper classes. Live background music became common in many of the better eating places of Europe and later in the United States. In the twentieth century, live music in restaurants has largely been replaced by recorded music, but a few cafés catering to culture consumers or the wealthy still hire musicians to entertain. Lounges in hotels and elsewhere carry on the tradition by presenting a piano player or guitarist as part of their ambience.

The idea of recorded background music has been credited to Major-General George O. Squire. In 1922 Squire conceived the notion of piping recorded music into people's homes as an alternative to radio, which itself was fairly new at the time. A company in Cleveland, Ohio, carried out Squire's idea using direct wire lines. But there were only a few subscribers, and eventually the service was abandoned. The idea was picked up again in 1934 at the height of the Depression. A company in New Jersey called Wired Radio, Inc., began to provide hotels and restaurants with "wired" music throughout the day chiefly as an enhancement to mealtimes. The success of catchy-titled firms such as Kodak led to renaming the company "Muzak." Senator William Benton soon bought the company, and in 1935 it began to build its own unique library of recordings.

Industrial applications of background music were introduced in England during World War II. There, music was played in defense plants in an effort to reduce fatigue. Later, a study sponsored by the British government demonstrated the advantages of a constantly ascending stimulus progression (see below) in the programming of utilitarian music. Subsequent studies by Muzak confirmed and refined this principle into the formula which became the cornerstone of Muzak programming.

Muzak and Its Philosophy

The term "Muzak," like "Kleenex" or "Xerox," in everyday speech has come to be used as the generic equivalent of an entire type of product—in this case, background music. However Muzak® is the registered trademark of Muzak Limited Partnership, (hereafter called Muzak) the leading distributor of environmental music with 34 branch offices and nearly 200 franchised dealers worldwide. Through 200,000 subscriber accounts in the United States and an additional 25,000 in other locations, it is estimated that Muzak's service reaches over 80 million people daily. The company terms its main background music service "Environmental Music by Muzak®."

Muzak takes the point of view that "music" is something to be listened to directly and for its artistic value. Environmental music by Muzak®, on the other hand, is functional and to be heard, but it is not supposed to be listened to directly. As one franchised Muzak dealer puts it, "Music is art. Environmental Music by Muzak® is science." It is the science of a sound environment that is unobtrusive in nature, purposely nonentertaining and nondistracting. It functions as an integrated physical and psychological part of the overall work environment. In an office or factory the idea is to fill empty silences, soften or mask the sounds of machines and outside conversations, relieve the tedium of monotonous, repetitious tasks, and reduce stress and fatigue.

Environmental Music by Muzak's Exclusive Library of Recordings

Over the years, Environmental Music by Muzak® has been criticized for its blandness, yet that is precisely what makes it function so predictably. Instead of using commercial recordings, which may contain such distractions as climactic moments, unpredictable changes in instrumentation, and uncontrollable emotional content, the company has chosen to record its own exclusive music library. Each new song added to the library has a special arrangement and is recorded by professional musicians in a commercial studio. Research has determined that vocal music is distracting and, therefore, not suitable to this type of programming. So, the entire repertoire consists strictly of instrumentals.

In the past the Muzak library stressed old standards. However, the emphasis now is on staying contemporary. Every year about 1,000 selections from the master catalog are deleted to make room for new recordings. The *current* library is confined to 5,000 selections, which are constantly being updated. Muzak makes its new selections mainly on the basis of recent chart activity. It requires only about six weeks between a song's establishment on the charts and its placement in the library.

Programming for Environmental Music by Muzak® ——

As soon as a new Environmental Music by Muzak® recording is made, it is analyzed for its "stimulus value." This is based on a set of numerical values derived from such variables as tempo, rhythm, instrumentation, and size of orchestra. A stimulus value is assigned to the recording for computerized programming purposes.

Muzak divides the program day into fifteen-minute segments. During each of these segments five or six recordings are played. The selection and order of recordings is made largely on the basis of a predetermined pattern of stimulus values called the Stimulus Progression®. The first selection is moderately low in stimulus value. Selections after that grow progressively higher in stimulus value until the end of the fifteen-minute segment. (See Figure 9–1.) The earliest research to establish and verify the technique of Stimulus Progression® was conducted in the 1950s.

The same basic lifting curve is used for each segment. However, the range of values for every segment is not the same throughout the day. Muzak recognizes what is called the "standard efficiency curve," the highs and lows of worker efficiency during normal work shifts. During a daytime shift low points usually occur between 10 and 11 A.M., and between 3 and 4 P.M. Coffee breaks are the usual compensation for these dips in efficiency. Environmental Music by Muzak® programming further compensates by mirroring the curve with an increased heightening of stimulus values. (See Figure 9–2.) During low periods, the range of values for each fifteen-minute segment gradually rises. Following the low period the range settles back to normal. In order for subscribers in the four time zones of the continental United States to obtain the benefit of efficiency curve compensation, Muzak sends out two musical programs simultaneously — one for Eastern-Central and one for Rocky Mountain-Pacific. Programming is done in the Muzak home office largely by computer and is delivered twenty-four hours a day.

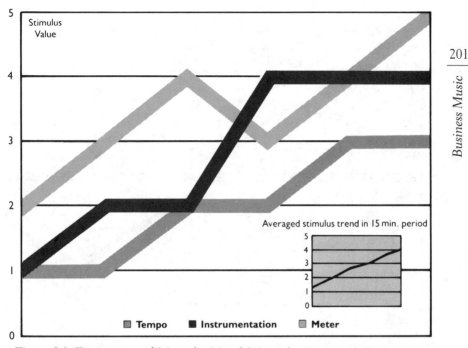

Figure 9-1. Environmental Music by Muzak® Stimulus Progression® in a typical fifteen-minute segment of programming. Courtesy of Muzak Limited Partnership.

Research Studies

Despite Muzak's sixty-year reputation for improving conditions the workplace, there will always be skeptics. For that reason the company periodically publishes "Research Reviews" to show the effects of Environmental Music by Muzak® programming. The following texts have been drawn verbatim from the Muzak research report, "Business Music: A Performance Tool for the Office/Workplace."

Error Reduction

A study was conducted by Muzak® in conjunction with researchers from the University of Washington to investigate the effectiveness of Environmental Music by Muzak® with Stimulus Progression® in the office/workplace. The study resulted in statistically significant increases in the accuracy rate for the group that worked with Muzak's music in their work environment.

Ninety people were recruited and randomly assigned, in three groups of thirty, to three separate work settings. Each work station represented a different audio environment: (1) Environmental Music by Muzak® with Stimulus Progression®, (2) a radio format frequently found in the office/workplace, and (3) silence, as a

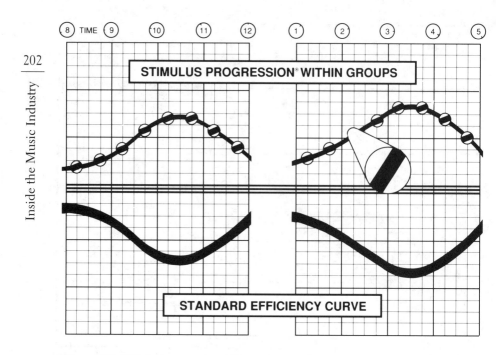

Figure 9-2. Efficiency curve and Environmental Music by Muzak® programming curve. Courtesy of Muzak Limited Partnership.

control measure. Each group was required to perform the same variety of tasks designed specifically to resemble the office environment. The three measures tested over the course of an eight-hour day included:

1. Editing a manuscript

2. Two cognitive tests, and

3. A series of satisfaction surveys.

The editing task was measured two ways: throughout a single session which spanned 90 minutes and across two sessions totaling approximately a half day. In both the short-term and long-term measurements the results showed a statistically significant improvement in the accuracy rate for the group in the Muzak Environmental Music condition.

The shorter session resulted in a 21.3 percent increase in accuracy for the Muzak group, whereas the radio group improved only 2.4 percent throughout the session, and the silence group decreased in their editing performance by -8.3 percent.

The longer measure, spanning a half day, demonstrated even more striking improvements. The test subjects listening to Muzak's Environmental Music improved 25.8 percent, while the radio group participants improved only 2.3 percent, and the subjects in the silence condition decreased in their accuracy rate by -4.4 percent. (See Figure 9–3a.)

Two separate cognitive tests, or standard psychological tests that measure a person's problem solving abilities, were also submitted to each test participant three times throughout the day. The average test scores for each group were measured according to the percent they improved throughout the day.

The simpler of the two tests (called the Differential Aptitude Test) showed a substan-

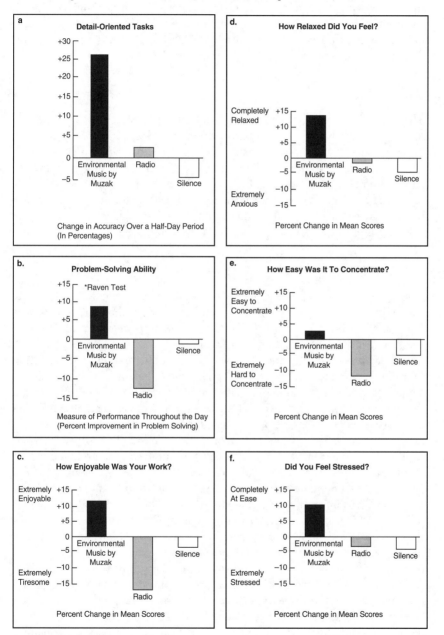

Figure 9-3. Results of Environmental Music by Muzak® study. Courtesy of Muzak Limited Partnership.

tial difference between the three groups and their performance. Those in the Muzak Environmental Music group increased in their performance by 20.9 percent over the course of the day, while the people working while listening to the radio only improved 4.1 percent and the silence group improved 11.9 percent.

The more demanding of the two cognitive skill tests (called the Raven) showed even more dramatic results. The subjects working while listening to Environmental Music by Muzak® improved their accuracy by 13 percent over time while the radio group's accuracy rate actually dropped by -12.2 percent, and those in the silent condition by -0.5 percent. (See Figure 9–3b.)

Productivity

There was an abundance of research conducted during the 1950s, '60s, and '70s that supports the benefits of business music in the office work environment. . . . Among those earlier studies, Equitable Life Insurance Society found that the work output of a test group of transcribers increased 17 percent during the six weeks after the introduction of music in their office. Mississippi Power & Light Co. tested music in their billing department and realized an 18.6 percent increase in their productivity after nine months. Additionally, the average decrease in errors per 1,000 cards processed was 37 percent during the same period. . . .

Stress Reduction

One of the most widespread concerns about employee health and productivity centers on the role of stress in the workplace. According to the "Mitchum Report On Stress in The 90s," "Fifty percent (50 percent) of Americans report more stress in their daily lives today than five years ago."

Research & Forecasts, Inc., the N.Y. based public opinion and marketing research corporation, conducted a national public opinion poll on the subject. When asked about the source or causes of daily stress, over one third of the respondents (36 percent) cited their work situation. Work was the response that far outweighed any other factor mentioned. Money was reported as the second ranking stressor by 22 percent of those surveyed. Seventy five percent (75 percent) of those questioned said that listening to music was the preferred way of alleviating the pressure of their daily stress. . . .

Chronic migraine headaches are believed to be symptomatic of higher levels of stress for some individuals. A study conducted by Janet E. Lapp at California State University shows significant improvement for combating migraines using music. Three groups of ten people were formed: a biofeedback group, a music-placebo group, and a non-treatment control group. The study spanned one year and involved thirty people whose mean age was thirty-five-years-old. Results were apparent after 10 sessions, which was a brief intervention period designed for monitoring the groups' progress. The music group had achieved superior results to the other two conditions in terms of reported decreases in severity, intensity, and duration of headaches. Data gathered during a one-year follow-up indicated that while both the biofeedback and music group maintained the positive change, only the music group participants showed a continued marked improvement in decreasing the frequency of the headaches.

Other well-accepted physiological indicators of stress include blood pressure and respiration rate. At Creighton University's St. Joseph Hospital, Muzak's music was tested in the day surgery preoperative holding area. Environmental Music by Muzak® was installed, and patients were split into two groups: one that heard Muzak's music and a control group that did not. One hundred and eighty six (186) people were evaluated in the study for changing physiological measurements as well as observed behavioral indicators of their emotional state. The experiment continued for several months with patient evaluations occurring at three points in time: upon arrival, immediately before surgery, and just after surgery. Results showed that Muzak's Environmental Music reduced patient stress as indicated by reduced blood pressure, lowered pulse rate, reduced respiration rate, reduced anxious behavior such as fidgeting and depression, increased calmness, and the patients' reported lower anxiety levels. . . .

Sound Masking

The *Journal of the Acoustical Society of America* published an article by Van-Summers, Pisoni, Bernacki, Pedlow, and Stokes in May 1988 that discussed consistent results from two experiments they conducted. They investigated and found a greater intelligibility of the human voice while listeners simultaneously heard masked noise than when silence existed behind the speaking voice. Dreher and O'Neill (1957) reported that speech produced by an individual with noise in the environment is more intelligible than speech produced in a quiet environment.

The first journal article cited above was an attempt at replicating earlier research. Forty-one (41) students participated in one study, thirty-nine (39) subjects in the other. The pattern of the results are nearly identical for the two studies. Speech produced with masked noise was more accurately identified than the same speech uttered in silence. Apparently, given several studies which produced consistent results, certain acoustic characteristics of speech produced in masked noise, above and beyond changes in amplitude, make it more intelligible in a noisy environment than in a quiet atmosphere.

One of the benefits of Muzak's business music is the ability to mask surrounding office noise. The benefits include additional privacy and clarity that would be provided to conversations in the office environment. In a business where discussions center around personal and sensitive information for an individual or a family, conversations may be afforded extra care concerning the confidential nature of the business. For example, insurance, billing, banking, or doctor's offices and hospitals are just a few environments where additional privacy and speech clarity to employee/client relationships could be perceived as a valuable business tool. . . .

Personal Responses

A study discussed previously that was conducted by researchers at the University of Washington using Muzak's Environmental Music, radio, and silence included submitting a series of surveys to the ninety (90) test participants. A general measure of satisfaction was derived through a factor analysis and showed the Muzak group reported an average increase of 9.3 percent while the radio group reported a decrease in satisfaction at -7.6 percent, and the silence group, also dissatisfied, reported an average -4.4 percent measure of satisfaction. The following questions were asked:

How enjoyable was your work?

How relaxed did you feel?

How easy was it to concentrate?

Did you feel stressed?

The results of the survey questions show a statistically significant positive response from the Muzak group relative to the radio and silence groups. (See Figure 9–3, c-f.)

Other Background Music

The chief unique properties of Environmental Music by Muzak® are (1) its unique library containing purposely bland instrumental recordings of popular music and (2) its programming according to the Stimulus Progression® principle. Instrumental music is the rule for a background-music situation, since vocals might be distracting. However, Stimulus Progression® is not necessary in every place where background music might be useful or appropriate. Thus, many types of light, unobtrusive instrumental music could be appropriately used as background music where productivity, stress reduction, and sound masking are not important.

Figure 9–4 shows a variety of light, unobtrusive instrumental music offered by the leading business music services via satellite and on-site tape or CD player. (Delivery systems are discussed below.) Not all the styles shown would be appropriate in a commercial setting such as an office. However, many restaurants, hotels, etc. can make good use of an all-instrumental type of environmental music that enhances the particular ambiance of the establishment. Thus, the figure represents a broad choice of background styles.

Delivery Systems

As Figure 9–4 shows, most business music today is delivered to the user through two systems: Direct Broadcast Satellite (DBS) and user-controlled tape or CD machines. DBS now serves most business music users, although there are still many who prefer the on-site control that tape or CD provides.

Satellite (DBS) Services			On-Site Services	
Muzak®	3M	DMX	Muzak Tones® (tape)	AEI Music (tape or CD)
Environmental Music by Muzak®	Ambiance	Beautiful Instrumentals	Contemporary Background	Background Instrumentals
Light Classical	Class Act	Lite Classical	Light Symphony	
			Featured Instrument & Composer	
		Chamber Music	Chamber & Baroque	
Contemporary Instrumentals		Contemporary Instrumentals	Light Instrumental	Contemporary Instrumentals
Contemporary Jazz Flavors	Smooth Jazz	Lite Jazz		Electric Blends
		New Age	New Age Instrumental	
		Classical Guitar		
		Piano	Contemporary Piano	
		Environmental Sounds		

Figure 9-4. Instrumental Background Music.

Muzak Satellite uplink. Photo courtesy of Muzak Limited Partnership.

Satellite

A DBS system such as Muzak, 3M, or DMX uplinks all of its channels simultaneously to a satellite. Earth reception is through the user's satellite dish, and each user has a unique code or "address" that controls which channel(s) will be received (and when, if dayparting is employed). One advantages of DBS is ease of operation. Another is sound quality, since all DBS music services use chiefly CDs in their broadcast operation. Digital Music Express (DMX) excels in sound. It broadcasts digitally, and the receiver at the user's end decodes the signal so it can be amplified and heard.

All DBS (satellite) services offer programming from the "head end," that is, from the uplink site. For any user, a single channel can run constantly or different channels in dayparts. That is, during one segment of the day, the downlink

DBS antenna on roof of a subscriber (Taco Bell). Photo courtesy of Muzak Limited Partnership.

site will receive one channel, but during another period it could choose to receive a different channel. For example, a restaurant may wish upbeat music for the lunch hour, while it may prefer soft, relaxing music during the dinner hour. (Within a single service, all channels may be interchanged.) DMX's receiver may be operated with a hand-held remote controller, allowing daypart programming from inside the store itself. Thus, for example, during preparation and cleanup times, the staff of a restaurant might choose to listen to Rap, a style that may be inappropriate there during regular business hours.

Tape/CD Services

If a music user cannot have a satellite dish for any reason, there are two alternatives. One is Muzak's relay system by which the Muzak franchiser receives all DBS channels, then relays one of them to the user's receiver via an FM subcarrier frequency. The other alternative is an on-site tape or CD player that can run for long periods of time. Both Muzak Tones and AEI Music offer a tape system.

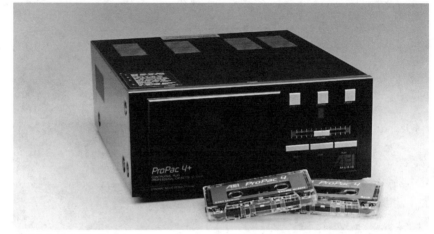

AEI Music's ProPac 4 cassette player and ProDisc CD player. Photos courtesy of AEI Music Network, Inc.

The player is either a single or dual-cassette unit that automatically plays each cassette front and back, then repeats the process. Thus, a machine can run for several hours without repeating any music. AEI Music offers a four-hour continuous-play changer for its programmed CDs. The machine chooses the starting track at random, then continues playing from that point in numerical order.

Each new user receives a tape or CD player and a beginning library of cassettes or CDs. Customers may exchange these on a 30-, 60-, or 90-day basis or may have unlimited exchanges. Each service maintains a large master catalog of available tapes/CDs. These are updated constantly as new recordings are licensed by the services. Each company publishes a monthly or bimonthly newsletter describing newly catalogued tapes/CDs and giving information on current artists as well as any promotional campaigns the service may be running in conjunction with record companies.

AEI Music's ProDisc CD player

Foreground Music

As stated above, the function of background music is to provide unobtrusive musical sound which is not intended to be noticed. However, another type of business music has just the opposite function. Foreground music is business music programmed to be noticed. Originally introduced in restaurants, it is designed for places of leisure, atmosphere or intense style identity, where the presence of a recognizable recording might be an enhancement rather than a distraction. The philosophy of foreground music holds that the right music supports the image — or fantasy — of the surroundings. Thus, it is not unusual to hear Top 40 hits played continuously in the young adult fashion section of a department store. Nor is it out of place to hear Adult Contemporary and Rock in "concept" restaurants and lounges catering to a crowd in their twenties and thirties. Likewise, one would not be surprised to hear a long series of Country vocals in a western clothing store or a barbecue restaurant.

The main feature that typifies foreground music is the use of commercial recorded releases by "original" artists, usually vocal. Another important feature is the consistency of programming in any style. Thus, foreground music can be a merchandising tool useful to a number of public places with a musical style targeted to their particular clientele.

Some retailers and restaurateurs use a CD changer or merely tune a radio to a station playing a particular style of music. This sound, commercial spots and all, is played throughout the establishment. This rather cheap practice, if not properly licensed, can be dangerous (see below). The more generally accepted means of delivering foreground music to customers is through either satellite transmission or a special tape or CD machine on the site.

Styles and Channels

Figure 9–5 represents all foreground music styles of the chief music services. Clearly DMX is the leader in this area in terms of variety. In addition to its nine programs of background music, DMX offers 67 foreground channels. (DMX also transmits 30 of the 76 channels via TV cable for home or business use. See also chapter 6.) The key is variety and programming flexibility — the power to fine-tune the style of the foreground music to the style, purpose, and clientele of the establishment. Just as in radio programming, foreground music programming relies on knowledge of demographic profiles. However, in this case, what matters is the "market segment identity" of a single restaurant or retail outlet.

Programming Strategy

Foreground music services offer on-site consultation and printed guidelines concerning programming. Muzak's strategy for arriving at the optimum music style(s) for a particular foreground music setting is a process called "Quantum Modulation[SM]." This is a multi-step procedure divided into two main components: selection and assembly. The goals of Quantum Modulation[SM] are (1) to

Satellite (DBS) Services			On-Site Services	
Muzak®	3M	DMX	Muzak Tones® (tape)	AEI Music (tape or CD)
Hitline	Best of the Charts	Hottest Hits	Hitline Contemporary Pop	Pop Styles
		Power Hits Album Rock Folk Rock Heavy Metal Alternative Rock New Music		Alternative Styles
Jukebox Gold	Classic Rock	Classic Rock 50's Oldies 60's Oldies 70's Oldies	American Graffiti Classic Pop	Timeless Pop Oldies Rock
'70s Songbook Foreground Music One Hot FM		Adult Contemporary New Adult Contemporary Great Singers Show Tunes Movie Sound Tracks	Mature Vocals Broadway Classics	Adult Alternatives
Expressions	Lite FM	Soft Hits Love Songs	Contemporary Jazz Instrumentals	Jazz-Contemporary

Figure 9-5. Foreground Music Styles.

Classic Jazz

	Instrumentals	Nostalgia
	Stardust Memories	Vocals with Jazz
	Traditional & Dixieland	
	Jazz with Vocals	
Big Band/Swing		
Dixieland		
Jazz/Vocal Blends		
Traditional Blues		
Contemporary Blues		
Traditional Country	Country Classics	Country-Classic
Modern Country	Country Hitline	Country-Contemporary
Bluegrass		
Rap		
Hot Country		
Country Currents		
Urban Adult Contemporary		Urban Contemporary
Motor City Sound		R&B
R&B/Rap Hits	Dance Music	
Dance	Specialty Rock & Pop	
Urban Beat		
Reggae		
Polka		
Beach Party		
Ranchera/Tejano		
Salsa	Latino	Salsa
Latin Contemporary	Latin Instrumentals & Pop Vocals	Latin Blends
Latin Styles		American/Español
Fiesta Mexicana		
Mariachi		Mariachi
Brazilian Music		
Flamenco Music		
Gospel		
Christian Inspirational		
Contemporary Christian		
Opera		

Figure 9-5. Foreground Music Styles, continued.

Muzak®	3M	DMX	Muzak Tones® (tape)	AEI Music (tape or CD)
		Symphonic		Classical
		Hawaiian Music	Hawaiian	Hawaiian
		Cajun		
		Folk Music		
		U.K. Hits		
Eurostyle		Euro Hits		Euro Blends
		Euro Oldies		
		French Hits	French	French
		Italian Hits	Italian	Italian
		Dutch Hits		
		German Oldies/Schlager		
		German Rock Music		
		Flemish Music		
		World Beat		Global Imports
				Tropical Blends
		Traditional South African Music		
		Greek Music		
		Oriental/Eastern		Irish
		Mediterranean		Chinese
		Norwegian Music		
		Danish Music		
		Indian Music		
		Holiday Music		
		Children's		
Holiday			Seasonal & Specialty	Special Occasion
				Children's/Family

214

DMX for Business' 120-channel DBS receiver. Photo courtesy of DMX, Inc.

positively affect customers' mood and emotion and (2) to manage the flow of programming from song to song and throughout the day. Figure 9–6 shows Muzak's Quantum Modulation^{SM}.

DMX publishes a much simpler "Music Application Chart," a matrix table. One dimension represents the energy level of the desired music. The other shows the image an establishment might wish to project. Within each cell are sub-cells for various age demographics. Figure 9–7 shows the DMX guide.

Ancillary Services via DBS

In the pre-satellite days of business music, only a few ancillary services were available through on-site receivers and tape systems. These were and still are important parts of the audio environment of a store or office. One of the older services is **Music on Hold,** by which telephone callers receive a music program while they are on hold. This lets callers know that they are still on line and may keep them from becoming irritated while they wait. Some businesses insert advertising or product news into the music program ("messages on hold"). Another older service is the **Paging/Intercom** feature. Supermarket shoppers have all heard a voice paging employees or addressing customers about some in-store promotion.

Zoning

An advantage of being able to receive several channels of music from one DBS service is "zoning." This idea allows a business to use different styles of music in

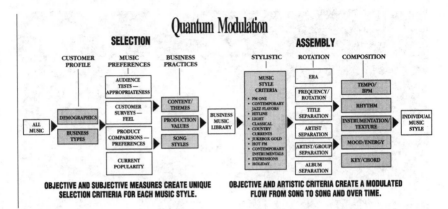

Figure 9-6. Muzak's Quantum Modulation. Courtesy of Muzak Limited Partnership.

different areas. For example, a department store could use one style of music in its young adults clothing departments and another in its dining room.

Broadcast In-Store Messaging

The corporate headquarters of a chain may wish to interrupt the business music of its stores from time to time to play commercial spots. This is called Point-of-Purchase (P-O-P) audio advertising. From the satellite customers in each of the stores will simultaneously hear the same ad. Some store chains even try to give the impression they are operating their own radio "network," including ID music, commercial spots, and "public service" announcements of the helpful hint type. Muzak has been particularly successful in this area with its Muzak/P-O-P Radio service. Although used chiefly in supermarket and drug store chains, P-O-P advertising has been effective as far afield as the banking business. Another satellite-addressable medium is the LED board. Like voice messages, LED programming can be sent to multiple locations via satellite.

Information Broadcasting

Related to the P-O-P Radio concept is Muzak's exclusive NewsCast[SM] service. Brief, half-hourly, national and international headline news interrupts the music program. Produced by the Data Transmission Network, DTN Wallstreet brings up-to-date stock quotations and financial news to a subscriber's personal computer from the satellite.

Data Transmission

In our age of communication, business communications are essential. Thus, an important service of DBS environmental music providers has become data trans-

Music Application Chart

Image + Energy + Demographics = Atmosphere

IMAGE \ ENERGY	PASSIVE BACKGROUND Mild Tempo	RELAXED BACKGROUND Mild / Medium Tempo	CASUAL FOREGROUND Medium / Mixed Tempo	ACTIVE FOREGROUND Mixed Tempo / Uptempo
SOPHISTICATED ELEGANT	Classical Guitar	Lite Classical	Chamber Music	Symphonic / Opera
PROFESSIONAL	New Age / Environmental Sounds	Contemporary Instrumentals		
CONSERVATIVE TRADITIONAL	Beautiful Instrumentals	Folk Music	Classic Jazz / Traditional Country / Great Singers	Bluegrass / Big Band / Swing / Traditional Blues
RELAXED CASUAL		Love Songs / Soft Hits	Adult Contemporary / Urban Adult Contemporary / Contemporary Blues	Classic Rock
CURRENT POPULAR		Lite Jazz	Contemporary Christian / Jazz / Vocal Blends	Hottest Hits / R&B / Rap Hits / Dance / Modern Country / Album Rock / Power Hits
TREND SETTING LEADING EDGE			Reggae / Folk Rock	Alternative Rock / New Music / Rap / U.K. Hits / World Beat / Euro Hits / Heavy Metal
FUN ENTERTAINING			Children's / Christian Inspirational / Movie Sound Tracks	50's Oldies / 60's Oldies / Euro Oldies / Motor City Sound / Gospel / Show Tunes
FESTIVE ETHNIC			French Hits / Ranchera / Tejano / Mariachi / Brazilian Music / Latin Contemporary / German Oldies / Schlager / Italian Hits	Dixieland / Cajun / Salsa / Polka / Dutch Hits / Holiday Music

DEMOGRAPHICS: Children 0 - 12 | Young Adult 12 - 24 | Adult 25 - 45 | Mature Adult 45+ | All Ages

© ICT® Sept. 1994

Figure 9-7. DMX's Music Application Chart. Courtesy of DMX, Inc.

mission via satellite. In its simplest form this could be a credit card verification system. More powerful, however, are point-to-multipoint delivery systems by which time-sensitive information can be received simultaneously by all locations. Such information might be a new promotional program or a special pricing announcement. Typical applications of such data transmissions are:

Corporate headquarters to branch offices or stores

Manufacturers or distributors to member retailers

Regional offices to decentralized stores

Central sales and marketing to field locations

Data and messages are generated and received using a personal computer and printer running special software, connected to the user's DBS music system.

Music Licensing and Fees

Business music, like any other music, is subject to the copyright law. Through the business music industry writers, publishers, record companies, artists, and recording musicians all stand to benefit from their efforts in ways similar to normal radio airplay and CD/tape distribution. The copyright owner's basic exclusive rights are well protected for environmental usage. As in the recording industry, most business is done through licensing and contracts, and most fees are collected through organizations, such as ASCAP, BMI, SESAC, and the Harry Fox Agency (see Chapter 2).

Each time a song is played in a public place (such as a place of business), it is considered a "performance" of that song which must be licensed. Thus, the copyright law restricts restaurants and retail stores from simply piping radio or taped music throughout their establishments. A famous court case tested this issue in the early 1980s. The Gap, a national chain of clothing stores, was using FM radios in all their locations. ASCAP brought suit against The Gap, claiming that performance royalties should be paid by any commercial establishment using music for listening by the public. ASCAP won its suit, which was upheld by the U.S. Court of Appeals in New York. The Gap subsequently employed a leading foreground music service to supply music in its stores.

There are four severe restrictions which, if all met, *would* exempt an establishment from licensing responsibility and allow a radio to be used:

1. The floor area must not exceed 500 square feet.

2. The radio must be a "home"-type receiver and not a commercial type.

3. Customers may not be charged for the music program.

4. The sound may not be distributed over a multiple-speaker system.

Both background and foreground services ensure that all licensing requirements are fulfilled for each of their clients. However, particular licensing requirements vary according to the type of music service, and these need to be discussed one at a time.

Since business music involves the "performance" of copyright music, all types of environmental music services (DBS and tape) must pay performing license fees to performing rights organizations (ASCAP, BMI, and SESAC). These organizations represent the publishers and writers of the music in the area of performing rights only. Each music service obtains a "blanket" license from each of the organizations. The blanket license fee is based on a percentage of the service's gross income (just as it is for broadcasters). A portion of the fee comes from each end-user account.

Environmental Music by Muzak® service makes new recordings ("sound recordings") of existing songs ("works"). For each of these a "transcription" license is obtained from the copyright owner. Muzak normally negotiates a flat fee for a period of time, usually four years. The Harry Fox Agency handles most of these "mechanical" transcription licenses.

Foreground music services, since they use existing "original artist" recordings, must obtain a master duplication ("new use") license for duplicating each master "sound recording." Since the recording is a separate copyright from the song it embodies, such licenses are obtained from the label of each recording. Normally, this business is administered through the Harry Fox Agency. Fees are based on the number of copies of a recording in circulation during a given period. Because of the Special Payments Fund Agreements between individual record companies and the AFM (musicians' union), license fees paid by foreground music services include a slight additional amount which will go to the union.

The fees from licensing business music services add up to a significant amount of income for copyright owners and collecting agencies. One foreground music service has estimated that 25 percent of its budget is devoted to paying licensing fees. Due to the divisibility of rights and the separate copyright coverage for songs ("works") and recordings ("sound recordings"), the patterns of licensing requirements for the various forms of business music may seem rather complex. To clarify this picture, Figure 9–8 shows a table of the various types of licensing required for environmental music services.

Business music has grown into a large and important industry. With the widespread growth of foreground music's popularity, music has found its way into

	License/Fee Type:	1	2	3	4
DBS Broadcast	Environmental Music by Muzak®,	Yes	Yes	No	No
	3M, and DMX	Yes	No	No	No
On-Site Playback	Muzak Tones and AEI Music	Yes	No	Yes	Yes

Figure 9-8. Types of licenses and fees required for environmental music.

types of establishments where environmental music was previously unknown. In commercial environments business music is considered a marketing tool. However, managers must analyze the demographics of their clientele, the precise nature of their operation, and the exact function of music within the environment. The experiences of business music dealers with similar clients has also proven helpful in selecting appropriate music.

The place of business music in contemporary life is undeniably important. Muzak reaches over 80 million people daily, and other music services reach perhaps 20 million more. In addition, there are the millions of us who use the radio as a form of background or foreground music as we go about our daily routine. Through these sources music touches the lives of most people in our society daily.

Review Questions

1. When did functional mood music first come into existence?

2. Who first tried out the idea of "wired" background-music? Did it succeed? What company made it a success?

3. Is Environmental Music by Muzak® intended to be listened to directly? Explain.

4. About how many recordings does Environmental Music by Muzak® keep in its *current* library?

5. Explain the meaning of Stimulus Progression® and how Environmental Music by Muzak® programming uses it.

6. Cite and briefly explain the results of business Music by Muzak® research studies in the following areas:

   (a) Error Reduction

   (b Productivity

   (c) Stress Reduction

   (d) Sound Masking

7. In addition to Muzak, what are some other business music services?

8. Briefly describe the Direct Broadcast Satellite (DBS) system of music delivery.

9. What is the main feature typifying foreground music?

10. Is there a relationship between foreground music styles and radio broadcast formats (see chapter 6)? Discuss.

11. What are some factors a music user must consider when deciding on a background or foreground music style?

12. In what ways can environmental music be considered a marketing tool?

13. Discuss two ways in which a music system's ancillary services can be used to carry marketing messages.

14. If you wished to play a radio in a commercial establishment without paying licensing fees, what four criteria would you have to meet?

15. Discuss the differences in fees the Muzak Limited Partnership has to pay for the following:

   (a) Environmental Music by Muzak®

   (b) Muzak Tones

10

The Retail Music Store

One of the healthiest signs that music is alive and well in our society is the presence of the familiar retail music store. In major shopping malls, in neighborhood strip malls, along metropolitan avenues, and elsewhere can be found stores featuring musical instruments, printed music, sound equipment, accessories, and so forth. The clientele one finds in these establishments is a broad cross section of the public, ranging from professional musicians to students to prospective amateurs who have never before touched a musical instrument or read a note of music.

Why is this a sign of health? It indicates that many people want to make music and not merely listen to it passively. Music stores exist to serve those people by offering instruments, music, education, and service. Most of the present chapter concerns the instrument/equipment business, sometimes called the "music trades." Toward the end of the chapter is a section on the print music business which complements the discussion of music publishing in Chapter 2.

Business Operations

Organization

In many ways retail music stores may be viewed in the context of general retail business. They are faced with exactly the same problems and solutions as stores which handle entirely different types of merchandise: cash flow, financing, personnel, inventory control, promotion, and so forth. Retail music stores are also organized, started up, and run in much the same way as are other retail operations. Basically, there are three types of business organization in use today: sole proprietorship, partnership, and corporation.

The sole proprietorship is by far the most widespread method of organizing a music company. It is the least complicated to start and the most flexible to run. The owner (proprietor) alone dictates store policy and may keep whatever profits the store makes. On the other hand, the owner must raise the capital to start and operate the store, and he has sole financial responsibility if the business should fail. Actually, many music stores operating as sole proprietorships are family businesses. A typical pattern includes a father-owner and one or more grown children who help to operate the business by becoming sales people or administrative staff. As the business grows, the children move into managerial positions. The owner hopes that when it is time for him to retire, the children will carry on the business and build it further.

Partnership organization is similar to sole proprietorship, except that two or more people share the responsibilities, liabilities, and profits. One initial advantage to the partnership arrangement can be a larger start-up capital with which to get the business off the ground. (In fact, sometimes a "partner" is actually just the business's financier.) The best active partnerships are created when the partners' talents complement one another. For example, one partner may be a good salesman with fine merchandising ideas, while the other may be experienced in administration, with banking connections and a proven record of maintaining financial performance.

Corporations are not common in the retail music business. Most of the existing ones are closely held and, as such, are merely extensions of the family business concept. The changeover from a sole proprietorship to a corporation can be a signal that a business is in the process of expanding and requires additional capital to carry out its plans. However, music stores operating as sole proprietorships often find it possible to expand while maintaining their original pattern of organization. Successful owners of individual stores will expand their operations by opening branch stores that reach new markets. The totality of these stores become, in effect, a local or regional chain.

Personnel

Hiring and retaining good personnel is an ongoing challenge to music store managers. The retailers who have been most successful in this area are also the ones with the clearest personnel policies, usually spelled out in writing and reinforced during meetings. Some of the areas deemed necessary to cover are working hours, absence and leave policies, vacations and holidays, raise and promotion reviews, insurance and other benefits, educational opportunities, and rules of conduct.

The staff of a large music store may be varied and specialized. Aside from repair/service and teaching staff, personnel are divided between the administrative staff and the sales force. The administration of a music store includes general management and planning, finance, bookkeeping/accounting, buying, and inventory control. The sales manager and sales force are concerned with merchandising, promotion, selling, education, and follow-up services. In smaller stores with few personnel there may be little or no division between administration and sales, and individual employees may be required to perform a variety of duties.

A large part of the success of a music store can be attributed to the ability of its sales force to produce. In recent years there has been a growing awareness of the need for sales training specific to the music trades. Interest in sales training in music has reached the point that material on sales techniques is available not only in printed form but also in videotape courses available from the National Association of Music Merchants (NAMM). NAMM also publishes a recommended checklist for evaluating sales personnel. The major points on this checklist are customer relations, salesmanship, follow-up, product knowledge, personal appearance, store appearance, clerical, and ability to learn.

There are several standard methods of compensating music store personnel. Strictly administrative staff are normally paid a straight salary plus possible bonuses and other incentives. Sales people may be paid by one of three methods: straight salary, straight commission on their sales, or salary plus a commission on sales (generally, sales exceeding some minimum figure). If studio teachers instruct on the premises, they are paid the fees collected for lessons less 15 or 20 percent for the store's space and for handling student bookings.

Instrument Financing

Credit and rentals are two areas of finance that are fundamental to the retail music business. Studies in other businesses have shown how valuable credit cards and charge accounts can be in stimulating extra business and in establishing regular customers. This is no less true of a music store, where a credit service can enable customers to make larger purchases than they could for cash. Most of a music store's credit sales fall under the category of "incidental credit." Here, the customer does not use a credit card, does not pay finance charges, and must pay the balance of the account in four installments or less. Payments over thirty-, sixty-, or ninety-day periods are most common, with a cash down payment given at the time of purchase. Despite its commercial benefits, credit service is not entirely a blessing for the music merchant. There are always problems collecting overdue accounts. Handling these is a delicate matter, where it is necessary to make the collection without sacrificing customer goodwill. On larger purchases and those requiring more than four payments, some stores prefer to turn credit accounts over to a bank or other lending institution, while some larger stores have discovered a new profit center through self-financing.

Instrument rental is a long-standing tradition in the retail music business. In reality, most of the rental arrangements made are not purely rental or leasing agreements. They are rental-purchase agreements, technically termed "credit sales." Under current federal law this is an important distinction, since credit sales are subject only to the disclosure requirements of the Truth-in-Lending Law but are exempt from those of the Consumer Leasing Law. The former is simpler and less prohibitive. Under the rental-purchase plan the customer agrees to rent the instrument for a sum substantially equivalent to the value of the instrument (possibly in addition to a nominal finance charge). The customer then has the option to become the owner of the instrument within a specified time, or he may continue renting. Rental-purchase agreements are commonly made with individuals, schools, and organizations that support school music.

Merchandise and Merchandise Distribution

The merchandise manufactured and sold for music-making can reach the consumer in several ways. The simplest is for the manufacturer to sell directly to the consumer through magazine advertising or direct mail. This is called direct distribution, which is generally carried out in the form of mail order business. Most musical merchandise sold in this manner is offered by smaller manufacturers and suppliers of instruments, accessories, printed music, or other items connected with music. The most common system of distribution is the one-step distribution pattern, in which suppliers receive orders from dealers, and merchandise is then shipped to them. Most larger manufacturers and importers use this system. A two-step distribution pattern is used principally for accessories and for instruments produced by smaller domestic and foreign manufacturers. In this case, each manufacturer ships goods to a regional distributor, who then gives "one-stop" service to dealers in the area.

Under the one-step plan, suppliers and dealers are usually engaging in interstate commerce and are, therefore, governed by a number of federal laws. Chief among these are the Sherman, Clayton, and Federal Trade Commission acts, but certain court and Federal Trade Commission rulings also apply. Some typical concerns involve such matters as:

1. a dealer who wants exclusive distribution of a line (or part of a line) in the local area;

2. a dealer who is attempting unsuccessfully to compete with a discounter who is cutting prices on some of the lines also handled by the dealer;

3. a manufacturer who wishes a dealer to sell his line exclusively (in that type of merchandise); and

4. a manufacturer who cuts off shipments to a dealer because the dealer's orders are too small or infrequent.

Under some circumstances each of these could be accomplished legally, while in other cases federal law would be violated. Space here does not permit a full discussion of the legalities involved, but the spirit of the present law concerns

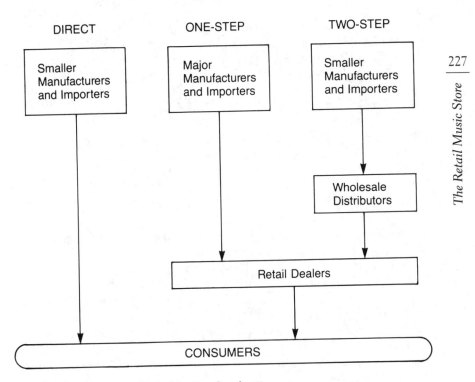

Figure 10-1. Patterns of merchandise distribution.

a prohibition against two parties acting "in concert" (or as a conspiracy) to create a boycott against a third party. For example, a large dealer (or chain) may not coerce a manufacturer into freezing out a smaller local dealer on the basis of greater buying power. The "single trader" doctrine governs suppliers in their choice of distribution outlets as well as retailers in their choice of supply sources.

In today's market there is a wide variety of merchandise offered by retail dealers, ranging from traditional musical instruments to electronic synthesizers, and from recording equipment to printed music. For a grasp of the full spectrum, here are the major categories of musical merchandise:

1. *Pianos*—all sizes, but mostly instruments used in the home;

2. *Organs*—chiefly electronic church instruments;

3. *Band and orchestral instruments*—strings, woodwinds, brass, and related percussion;

4. *Fretted instruments*—guitars of all types, mandolins, and the like;

5. *Instrument amplifiers, sound reinforcement equipment, recording equipment*—guitar/bass amplifiers, mixing boards, microphones, p.a. and monitor speakers, tape recorders, and so forth (some of which constitutes a crossover with the "audio" retail market);

6. *Electronic keyboards, signal-processing devices, synthesizers*—electric pianos, portable and stationary electronic keyboards, electronic drums, MIDI devices, digital and analog synthesizers, and software (some of which constitutes a crossover with the "personal computer" retail market);

7. *Print music*—in instrument stores, chiefly music for piano, organ, keyboards, or guitar; and

8. *Accessories*—mostly small items, such as guitar strings, instrument cases, reeds, drum sticks, and electronic accessories.

Types of Stores

The categories of merchandise given above are useful in identifying areas of manufacture. However, retail music stores are not at all restricted to just one type of merchandise. In fact, probably the oldest type of music store is the multifaceted, full-line store described below. The need for specialty stores became apparent in our century as music in public schools flourished, as the "combo" and Rock band trend set in, and, more recently, as newer types of electronic instruments and equipment made their first appearance. Many retailers have found innovative ways of combining various types of music and sound merchandise. However, there are four main categories of music retail outlets, according to the National Association of Music Merchants. Here is a brief description of each:

1. *Piano*—stores which derive at least 80 percent of their annual sales volume from pianos, organs, and electronic keyboards;

2. *School music*—stores which sell primarily band and orchestra instruments, but may also deal in percussion instruments, guitars, amplifiers, electronic keyboards, and combo-sound reinforcement and recording equipment;

3. *Rock/Combo-sound reinforcement*—stores which carry primarily acoustic guitars, electronic guitars, instrument amplifiers, electronic keyboards, synthesizers, drum sets and other percussion equipment, accessories, recording equipment and sound reinforcement equipment (including p.a. systems);

4. *Full-line*—stores which sell pianos, organs, band and orchestra instruments, percussion instruments, guitars, amplifiers, electronic keyboards, sound reinforcement equipment, print music, and accessories. In smaller markets these stores may also carry radios, TVs, stereos, CDs/cassettes, and similar products.

The full-line store can be a kind of combination of the other three types of stores and is generally quite sizable. Separate departments are needed to properly display and sell the varied merchandise. In large metropolitan centers the leading full-line music stores are often situated in freestanding multistory buildings where each entire floor contains just one or two individual departments. The location and amount of floor space devoted to each department is based on several factors, including the practical space required for the type of merchandise, the portion of the store's income generated in each department, and the current customer demand. For example, portable electronic keyboards might be prominently displayed on the street-level floor because of their popularity, but they will not be given as much space as pianos, which could require an entire floor (or more) to themselves. The size of the sheet music (print music) department could vary considerably from store to store, depending on local demand and competition. In some stores, print music might be a very small item, perhaps a few instruction books supplied by a local jobber. Other stores might carry a complete line of print music, especially if there is an opportunity to sell choral, band, and orchestral music to the local schools with little or no competition. Figure 10-2 shows the organization of a hypothetical full-line music store.

Service and Education

Two necessary adjuncts to retailing musical instruments are service and education. The term "service" incorporates tuning and repair. Education is usually specified as lessons, classes, or entire educational programs. When a dealer offers these types of support to his customers, he sharply distinguishes his store from hundreds of mail order houses and smaller dealers who cannot offer such personal attention.

Service

The area of service falls into three general categories: pianos, acoustic instruments, and electronic instruments/devices. Piano technicians are a breed apart

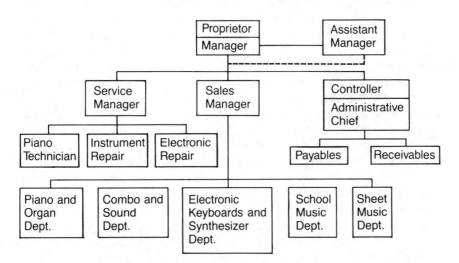

Figure 10-2. Organizational chart: full-line retail music store (hypothetical).

from other instrument repairmen. The field requires special training in tuning, repair, and maintenance. Normally, a piano technician works only on conventional pianos. When a dealer sells a new piano, usually a series of periodic tunings is part of the contract. A store's piano technician is kept busy with these jobs, together with tuning and maintaining previously sold pianos and with keeping the pianos in the showroom in good tune and working order.

Instrument repairmen who work on other traditional instruments must be more versatile (though often less formally trained) than piano technicians. An instrument repairman must be able to perform work on band and orchestra instruments (brass, woodwinds, and strings), fretted instruments (chiefly acoustic guitars), and occasionally on percussion instruments (especially the tuned ones). This type of service is tremendously important to school music retailers who are selling and giving support to bands and orchestras in the secondary schools of their region.

Electronic instrument/device repair is distinctive as the branch of instrument service requiring the greatest amount of technology but the least amount of musical acumen. Normally, only stores which specialize in synthesizers and other electronic instruments and larger full-line stores will keep a full-time electronic repair specialist. Other stores may have a salesperson or repairman who can perform minor work, but they must send out their major repairs of electronic instruments.

Astute dealers view service of all types as a marketing opportunity. A new contact is made when an unfamiliar face appears with an instrument in need of repair. New or old customers whose instruments are becoming old or obsolete are all prime prospects for selling new, higher grade instruments.

Education

Many purchasers of musical instruments are first-time owners with no knowledge or experience with music. The need for instruction is, therefore, an obvious opportunity to follow up a sale. Young band/orchestra players usually receive instruction at school, but the need for in-store musical instruction is particularly strong among purchasers of pianos, organs, small keyboards, and guitars. Often with the purchase of an expensive instrument, the dealer will contribute a short free course of lessons with an in-store instructor.

Income from regular studio instruction can be substantial in itself. In-store instruction is also a marketing tool for the dealer. Negotiated free lessons with an instrument purchase is a sales inducement which can help to increase sales volume. In addition, many dealers use education as part of a strategy to encourage purchasers to upgrade their beginning instruments to more expensive ones, generating further sales for the store. One of the newest applications of this strategy applies to the currently popular portable keyboards. Dealers try to see that each purchaser of a small keyboard becomes proficient enough (through lessons, software, or self-instruction) to feel that he has outgrown his first instrument. This gives the dealer an opportunity to encourage that customer to step up to a more sophisticated keyboard instrument, either electronic or acoustic.

Music retailers and music educators alike are aware that giving young children opportunities to participate in music activities is beneficial to all concerned. Some dealers find that running a "musical kindergarten" is a valuable activity. Musical kindergartens are a form of preschool education in which organized musical instruction is offered in a cheerful, nondemanding atmosphere. Published teaching materials are normally followed. The dealer enjoys the income which the tuition generates. But there is also the prospect that as these children grow older, their interest in music will also grow, and that they and their parents will continue as customers.

Advertising and Promotion

Managers of successful retail music stores everywhere understand the value of advertising. The effectiveness of a good advertising program is provable in increased sales volume. There is a point of diminishing returns, however, and a continually increasing advertising budget does not ensure that volume will continually grow proportionally. Store managers normally budget advertising and promotion as a percentage of gross volume. The proper figure varies and promotion as a percentage of gross volume. The proper figure varies according to store type, but full-line stores typically spend 3 to 4 percent of gross income on advertising and promotion.

The main media for music store advertising are print ads and broadcast spots. However, there is a wide variety of possibilities. Here is a list of advertising media used by members of the National Association of Music Merchants: newspaper display advertisements, newspaper classified advertisements, radio spots, television spots, direct mail, Yellow Pages display advertisements, and billboards and transit advertisements.

There are several factors which a music store manager takes into consideration when planning advertising. One is the amount of budgeted funds in relation to the cost of the various forms of available advertising. For example, in a large city the cost of radio or local TV advertising may be prohibitive for the smaller store. Another consideration is to aim the advertising at the target audience—the segment of the public most likely to become store customers. Not only the choice of advertising media but also the exact advertising copy must be carefully planned to appeal to that audience. A third basic consideration is timing. Some instruments are sold mainly at a certain time of year. For example, band and orchestra instruments are purchased prior to each school year, while the market for pianos and organs livens considerably just before Christmas. Retailers who want a competitive edge normally plan a significant percentage of their annual advertising budgets around important market timing points.

The money for a store's advertising does not come solely from the company's own income. Cooperative advertising involving a manufacturer and a dealer is common in the retail music business. Under such an arrangement the manufacturer pays for a percentage of print advertising (ranging from 25 to 100 percent) either by reimbursement or by giving the dealer a discount allowance on the next order. In return the manufacturer requires that a fixed amount of the print space (generally 25 to 50 percent) must be devoted to the product or product line. Manufacturers usually supply advertising artwork and copy for their lines, and they require the dealer to supply documentation (newspaper tear sheets, billings, and so forth) showing that the advertisements were run and that the terms of the cooperative agreement have been met.

Besides straightforward advertising, music merchants consider various forms of promotion to be valuable in keeping the store name and image before the public. The following is a list of some of the most widely used promotional media and activities:

1. a newsletter mailed out from the store periodically to announce store events and promote new products;

2. promotional gifts;

3. promotional events, for example, a "Guitar Night" in connection with National Guitar Week;

4. free clinics on instruments sold in the store;

5. demonstration programs for service clubs;

6. sponsoring performing contests;

7. becoming a sponsor of a musical organization or concert series; and

8. providing a piano to the local civic or professional orchestra.

Finally, exhibiting is one form of "outside exposure" in which actual selling takes place. Keyboard dealers are particularly active in this enterprise. Shopping malls, shows, and fairs are prime locations for outside demonstrating and selling. Often the dealer will offer some form of "show pricing" to induce on-the-spot sales. Aside from making outright sales, the sales staff can obtain many names of interested sales prospects who can be approached later by phone. Since only a limited amount of merchandise can be displayed at the remote site, a customer will often decide to step up to a more elaborate instrument when he visits the store to finalize the transaction. Sales made away from the store location during fairs, shows, and the like are subject to Federal Trade Commission regulations on "door-to-door" selling. This includes a three-day "cooling off period," in which the customer may reconsider the purchase and cancel if he wishes.

The Impact of Imports

The United States has always imported a portion of the musical instruments sold in this country. Pianos and band/orchestra instruments have been regularly brought in from European countries for resale since at least the nineteenth century. When the guitar became tremendously popular during the 1960s, several Japanese companies began to sell relatively inexpensive guitars to U.S. dealers. The success of these instruments soon prompted the importation of pianos, organs, and band/orchestra instruments. At the same time, many U.S. manufacturers found it more economical to have their own instruments fabricated in oriental countries and then shipped to the United States and other countries for marketing.

The oriental importation trend intensified during the late 1970s and through the 1980s with the quickly spreading popularity of electronic keyboards of all types. The importation of increasing amounts of pianos and band/orchestral instruments brought about the demise of several U.S. manufacturing giants of the past.

At the same time the United States has been able to export a respectable quantity of most types of instruments. As a point of interest, the leading import sources for musical instruments and parts are Japan, Korea, Taiwan, West Germany, Italy, France, and Mexico; while our leading customers are Canada, Japan, the United Kingdom, Australia, Holland, and Mexico.

The Print Music Business

Chapter 2 contains extensive information on music publishing, including a section on "Songs in Print." That section outlines the printing of sheet music and song folios from the point of view of the song publisher. The present section takes up where Chapter 2 leaves off by discussing the distribution and retailing of these formats and by treating the other principal types of contemporary publishing. The major categories of print music are popular sheet music and folios, educational and church music, and "serious" music.

Popular Sheet Music and Folios

A piece of sheet music is a print copy of a single song, while a folio is a collection of related songs printed under one cover. In either case the format of each song is a piano-vocal arrangement with guitar chords indicated. Not all popular songs appear in print. Some (particularly hard rock) do not lend themselves to print arrangements. Most sheet music and folio publications are MOR, Easy Listening, Country, Folk, or Broadway. (Note: Music merchants use the term "sheet music" as a generic expression meaning any type of print music.)

The distribution of sheet music and folios is accomplished by either the one-step or two-step method. Discounts from the publisher depend on the size and type of the order. At the low end is the "daily" order, placed because of momentary demand; and the higher discounts are given for "stock" orders, which usually represent a six-month supply of one or more titles.

> One-Step Distribution: Publishers may maintain five hundred or more direct retail accounts. Discounts are normally 20–50 percent of the retail selling price or better. Larger discounts may depend on the dealer's willingness to purchase and display new issues.

Two-Step Distribution: A jobber/distributor acts as middleman, serving the many retailers not sold directly. (These include book and record stores along with music instrument dealers.) There are rack jobbers as well as conventional jobber/distributors. Some discounts from publisher to jobber can be a little greater than large retailers obtain by buying direct. The range is 20–60 percent, depending, of course, on the size of the order and overall purchasing power. Retailers buying from jobber/distributors usually earn a smaller margin than those buying direct, and they may carry a relatively small inventory of music just as a service to customers.

A technological innovation that has been added to the print music business is computerized sheet music on demand. Any store (not just music stores) can have a computer kiosk where customers may search through a vast database of song titles. When a song is selected, the computer can transpose it to any key the customer chooses. On command, the computer instantly generates the sheet music on a laser printer in the store.

Educational and Church Music

Instruction methods, music composed for educational purposes, and church music represent a significant portion of all print music sold today. The most important categories within the educational field are choral music, band scores (including jazz and stage band arrangements), and orchestra music. The elementary and secondary school markets are deemed most important, since college sales are potentially much smaller in volume. Strictly speaking, church music consists of print music to be performed by a choir or an organist. (Hymnals for congregational use are not considered part of this business.) Much sacred choral music is also purchased for school choirs. The two newest, fast-growing subdivisions of church music are Gospel (originating around Nashville and marketed principally in the South) and Contemporary Christian (running parallel to the Christian radio format introduced in Chapter 6).

There is a great deal of crossover between the educational and church markets, particularly in choral music. For that reason the patterns of distribution and methods of promotion in these two areas is nearly identical. Distribution is mostly one-step. Larger music dealers generally buy direct from publishers at a discount of 20 to 50 percent or slightly greater. In isolated cases publishers sell directly to educational institutions at retail.

Promotion is extremely important in the educational and church print music business, since the promotional tools and methods associated with recorded popular music (and, by extension, popular sheet music and folios) do not exist here. Four of the chief promotional methods employed in the educational/church music field are the following.

1. Publishers send direct mail announcements to educators announcing new issues, sometimes with a one-page sample of each. Most choral houses send sample copies to selected choir directors.

2. A publisher sponsors a series of workshops (choral, band, piano) in which guest clinicians introduce lines of music and new issues and demonstrate their use. The local retailer is usually present to take orders.

3. An educational or church-related organization sponsors new-music workshops. The local retailer provides samples and takes orders.

4. Publishers and retailers exhibit merchandise at educational conventions, such as the Music Educators National Conference.

"Serious" Music

A small but culturally important corner of the print music business deals in what can be collectively termed "serious" music. This field is roughly parallel to what the record business calls "Classical." It encompasses the European and American art music traditions, and its chief print music subdivisions are vocal/opera, piano, chamber, and symphonic. Most music imported from Europe falls into the serious category. Vocal/opera scores and piano and chamber music, as well as miniature symphonic scores, are distributed and retailed through the conventional distribution channels described above. Full-size symphonic scores and parts to older, standard literature are usually purchased outright, while the music for newer symphonic works is most often rented.

Trade Organizations

Divisions of the music industry that involve the manufacture and sale of instruments and print music are extremely organization-oriented. There are several groups whose members consist of manufacturers of some specific type of instrument (for example, the National Piano Manufacturers Association). Beyond these are the major organizations of a general nature whose memberships encompass large segments of the industry. Three of them are introduced below as the National Association of Music Merchants (NAMM), the American Music Conference (AMC), and the National Music Publishers Association (NMPA). The services of these nonprofit organizations are very broad, ranging from government lobbying to publishing training publications. Here is a brief profile of each.

NAMM and AMC

The majority of NAMM members are retail dealers in musical instruments and sound equipment. There is also an important group of "commercial members" who are manufacturers and other suppliers. NAMM's most lavish services are its annual International Music Market held in Anaheim, California every winter

NAMM International Music Market exhibit area. Photo courtesy of National Association of Music Merchants.

and its Summer Session show held in Nashville, Tennessee. These feature extensive exhibits and many information/education sessions. NAMM also offers a large catalog of print and video publications on all aspects of the music and sound business. The NAMM *Playback* is a monthly magazine containing feature articles and showing marketing trends for the various classifications of merchandise. While NAMM's mission is not promotion and public relations, it does support groups and projects which promote music to the public. Chief among these is the National Coalition for Music Education. The Coalition played a key part in shaping the National Standards for Arts Education, one of the foundations of the Goals 2000: Educate America Act of 1994.

The promotion and public relations arm of the instrument and print music business is the American Music Conference, an activity of NAMM. This organization is "dedicated to promoting the importance of music, music-making, and music education." AMC publishes surveys, brochures, books, and videos. A special service to the industry is the annual publication of *Music USA*, a report on the previous year's sales of instruments, accessories, and print music.

NMPA

Although membership in the NMPA numbers only about two hundred, many of its services extend to the several thousand active American music publishers. Chief among these services is the Harry Fox Agency, which is wholly owned by the NMPA. Over the years the NMPA has been effective as a collective voice, notably concerning copyright legislation and enforcement. The time-honored objectives of the association have been "to maintain high standards of commercial honor and integrity among its members, to promote and inculcate just and equitable principles of trade and business, and to foster and encourage the art of music and songwriting." While NMPA serves chiefly popular music publishers, a separate and much smaller organization, the Music Publishers Association (MPA), incorporates the publishers of "serious" music.

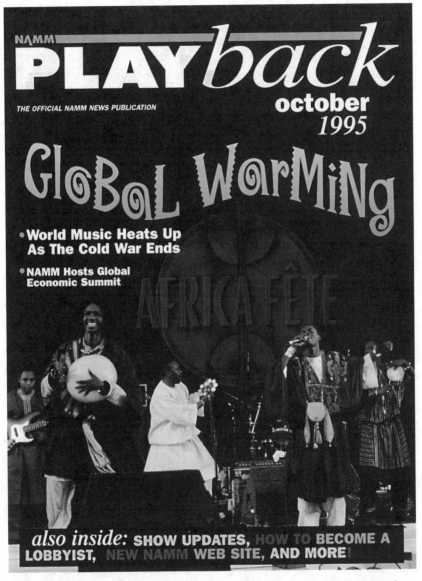

Cover of an issue of the *NAMM Playback*. Used by permission of National Association of Music Merchants.

Retail music is a vibrant, dynamic business which has been given a great boost by the development of affordable electronic technology. At first, the explosive growth of newer electronic instruments adversely affected the conventional instrument trade. However, the markets for these subsequently stabilized, allowing for an orderly adjustment.

There is reason for optimism concerning the future outlook of the musical instrument industry. Amateur group music-making (Rock bands and school music) continues to thrive in today's music scene. In addition, the National Coalition for Music Education now gives music education and the musical instrument business a previously unknown advocate's voice. Over the years the retail music business has proven itself to be an indispensable service to the musical amateur and professional alike. Due to their ability to adapt to changing trends, the retail merchants' place in our contemporary and future musical life appears to be ensured.

Review Questions

1. What are the three types of business organization? Which one is most common in retail music operations?

2. Name the main divisions of a music store staff.

3. What are the advantages of in-store financing of instruments?

4. Name the three patterns of merchandise distribution and the types of suppliers typically found in each.

5. What are the departments usually found in a "full-line" music store?

6. Do piano technicians or electronic instrument repair personnel normally work on other types of instruments? Explain.

7. Discuss some reasons why in-store music education is a good idea.

8. Explain cooperative advertising.

9. Describe a few methods music stores use to promote themselves.

10. Have imported goods completely eliminated U.S. manufacturing of musical instruments? Explain.

11. What are some differences between popular sheet music, educational/church music, and "serious" music.

12. What is the main purpose of NAMM, and what are two of its other activities?

13. What is the chief service that the NMPA performs for music publishers? Can you name another service?

Part 4

Music in Theatrical and Concert Traditions

11

American Musical Theater: History and Musical Trends

In the mid-1950s Leonard Bernstein published an essay dealing with composing for the American musical theater. It was titled "Whatever Happened to That Great American Symphony?" and was an imaginary exchange of correspondence between Bernstein and a fictional Broadway producer. In it the producer tries to convince Bernstein to write another musical show, while the composer resists, insisting that he has committed himself to completing a symphony. The article's thrust was to compare the condition of American musical theater with that of American concert music and to draw the conclusion that the public is infinitely more interested in new musical theater than in new symphonic music, even if it were a symphony by one of the country's best-known composers.

The point is well taken. Symphonies belong closest to the European musical tradition. On the other hand, musical theater—along with jazz—is one of the few forms of musical expression that can be claimed more or less exclusively by American composers and artists. It has even been said that musical theater is "America's classical music." With the Broadway musical stage's solid history of more than one hundred years, the truth of this statement can be appreciated. The principal purpose of the present chapter is to survey that history. However, before plunging into the stream, it will be valuable to review the nomenclature of chief forms in musical theater which have been seen on the professional American stage in our century. These are ordered from the simplest and least organized (revue) to the most carefully planned and executed (opera).

Types of Musical Theater

Musical Revue

The simplest and loosest form of musical theater is a type of musical revue known as the "variety show." It is no more than a succession of songs, skits, and dance routines. American vaudeville, derived from British music hall shows, was a tradition of just such revues, entirely modular and containing no story line whatever. Later, higher-class revues often had a theme running through the show. The series of Ziegfeld Follies were mostly theme reviews.

Musical Comedy

Most traditional musical comedies were little more than song-and-dance shows. It is true that a musical comedy has a book (that is, script or libretto) with a definable story line, but the substance of the story is usually light and fanciful, even unrealistic at times. Lerner and Loewe's *My Fair Lady* (1956) is an example of musical comedy.

Musical Play

This form has more depth than the musical comedy. The story is generally more significant and complex, and higher dramatic values, such as character development, are usually present. Leonard Bernstein's *West Side Story* (1957) and Stephen Sondheim's *A Little Night Music* (1973) are examples of the musical play.

Play with Music

In all the previous types there is an important place for spoken dialogue, but the main focus is on music. The play with music, on the other hand, is mostly talk and action. Songs are interspersed, and there is little or no dance. The story is normally serious, often historical. An example of the play with music is Sherman Edwards' *1776* (1969).

Popular Opera

There are two characteristics which distinguish popular opera from musicals. One is the musical idiom, which avoids the typical Broadway style in favor of popular or folk style. The other is the treatment of dialogue, which is nearly all sung. Examples are George Gershwin's *Porgy and Bess* (1935), which borrowed black folk idioms, Andrew Lloyd Webber's *Jesus Christ Superstar* (1971), a Rock opera, and Claude-Michel Schönberg's *Les Misérables* (1987), which employs both popular and classical elements.

Operetta

The United States inherited operetta from Europe, and with it came a more "classical," complex musical idiom than that found in home-grown musicals. Operetta employs large amounts of spoken dialogue, but the vocal music requires trained singers, rather than singing actors, to do it justice. A classic example of American operetta is Sigmund Romberg's *The Student Prince* (1924), but a show of more recent vintage is Sondheim's *Sweeney Todd* (1979).

Opera

The most sophisticated musical idioms are found in opera. Because of economic considerations, there have been relatively few new full-length operas staged in our century. The golden age of opera was the nineteenth century, with its broad repertoire from Italy, France, and Germany and its full range of styles from the comic to the epic. Some comic opera utilizes spoken dialogue, but most "grand" opera is sung throughout by classically trained singers. Gioacchino Rossini's *The Barber of Seville* (1816) is an example of Italian comic opera; Georges Bizet's *Carmen* (1875) is an example of serious French opera; and Richard Wagner's *Tristan and Isolde* (1865) is a type of grand opera which the composer termed "music drama." Opera in English has come into its own in the twentieth century. Carlisle Floyd's *Susannah* (1955) and John Corigliano's *The Ghosts of Versailles* (1991) are American examples.

Birth of American Musical Theater

Like the earliest settlers on the eastern seaboard, the earliest musical stage productions in North America came from England. In 1735 the citizens of Charleston, South Carolina, gathered to hear *Flora*, a recent English ballad opera. The production was done without scenery, costumes, or lighting, but it was nevertheless a unique experience for the Charlestonians, who were witnessing the first performance of musical theater ever given in the colonies. English ballad opera was the national comic opera of its day, a lowbrow (sometimes vulgar) form of theater which used both original songs and parodies of operatic tunes. The ballad opera tradition was one of the early forerunners of operetta, and it was perhaps historically significant that American musical theater was launched with a simple ballad opera rather than with a more elaborate Italian *opera seria*, which was a thriving form in Europe.

Theatrical performances of all types were sporadic during the eighteenth-century colonial period and the early years of the Union. By the early nineteenth century the ballad opera had died out entirely, but in 1828 a new form of musical comedy was born: the burlesque. Burlesques were parodies of serious literature known to the audience, and the first one was a treatment of Shakespeare's *Hamlet* created by John Poole. Burlesques remained in vogue for about fifty years, but continued sporadically for another fifty. One of the last great burlesques was E. E. Rice's *Evangeline,* a production of 1874 which satirized Longfellow's poem in an uproarious, slapstick style.

Another form of musical entertainment which helped to shape early American musical theater was the minstrel show. This form of musical revue was virtually invented in 1842 by Dan Emmett, a talented blackface performer. Emmett's Virginia Minstrels were an immediate sensation, imitated by minstrel troupes all across the country. The leader of one of these, Ed Christy, was credited with having standardized minstrel shows into three sections: vaudeville, free acts, and burlesque. Emmett's contributions to minstrelsy extended to song composition, including "Dixie," "Old Dan Tucker," and "The Blue-Tail Fly." Stephen Foster also contributed songs to minstrel shows.

Ballad opera, burlesque satires, minstrel shows—all were theatrical and all were musical. However, the truly American form of musical theater had to wait until the end of the Civil War for its birth. It came in the form of a show titled *The Black Crook,* which premiered in New York on September 12, 1866. The show was a real spectacle. Audiences came to see onstage hurricanes, flying chariots, and demonic rituals—all executed with music. There were numerous songs interspersed, some of which were suggestive (for example, "You Naughty, Naughty Men"). There was also a line of chorus girls (a feature left over from burlesque), which became a staple ingredient of later shows. *The Black Crook* was criticized and denounced by the guardians of morality, but people flocked to it night after night. The first production played an unprecedented 400 performances, and the show was revived and updated every few years for a total of more than 2,000 performances.

The Age of Operetta

Spectacular shows in the style of *The Black Crook* inevitably came and went on the American stage during the last third of the nineteenth century. Also, as burlesque died another form arose to take its place: the musical farce. Farcical plots involved national or racial groups known in New York, such as Irish, Germans, and "Negroes." Their songs often employed dialect, and the lyrics revealed characters who were ordinary people with ordinary problems, trying to blunder their way through life. The most famous of the farces was a series by Ed Harrigan and Tony Hart involving the fictional Mulligan family and their "colored" maid. The "Mulligan Guard" farces ran from 1879 to 1885.

Another vogue in the last quarter of the century was the importation of European musical comedies. One type was the French farce known as *opéra bouffe,* of which Jacques Offenbach was the acknowledged master. For ten years, from 1867 to 1877, Offenbach's comedies were presented on the American stage. The next wave of popularity favored Gilbert and Sullivan, who wrote in a style derived to a degree from the French *opéra bouffe.* The Boston premiere of *H.M.S. Pinafore* in 1878 triggered a string of other performances of the show that season in various parts of the United States. Gilbert and Sullivan operettas became a craze in this country at the same time as in England. As a result, simultaneous world premieres of *Iolanthe* took place in London and New York on November 25, 1882. *The Mikado*, first performed in New York in 1885, even succeeded in fostering a popular American imitation, *The Little Tycoon* (1887) by John Philip Sousa.

Operetta's influence on American musical theater came not only from London, but also from Vienna. Viennese/German operettas began being played in the United States during the 1870s. They proved very durable, for as late as World War II works in this tradition were still being mounted occasionally on the American stage. Probably the most famous imported work in this form was Franz Lehár's *The Merry Widow*, introduced on American soil in 1907. The immense success of this work served not only to strengthen the popularity of European-style operetta; it also bolstered interest in an American school of operetta writing, which was emerging at that time.

The first important American operetta was *Robin Hood*, produced in 1890. Reginald de Koven's score to this ultimately included the song "Oh, Promise Me," which became popular to sing at weddings. Despite de Koven's pioneering work, the front line of American operetta composers became traditionally reserved for the three giants of the form: Victor Herbert, Rudolf Friml, and Sigmund Romberg. (All three of them, incidentally, were European-born.)

Victor Herbert got his start in the American musical theater in 1894 with an operetta called *Prince Ananias*. The delicate song "Amaryllis" was part of this work. He followed this with several more successes, notably *Babes in Toyland* (1903), *Mlle. Modiste* (1905), *The Red Mill* (1906), and *Naughty Marietta* (1910). The last named introduced the song "Ah, Sweet Mystery of Life." Herbert died in 1924.

Rudolf Friml became an operetta composer in 1912 through circumstances involving Victor Herbert. When Herbert could not be persuaded to write a new operetta for a temperamental diva, the producer turned to Friml, an up-and-coming composer with some published songs and piano pieces. The result was *The Firefly*, a show containing several hit songs, such as "Sympathy" and "Love Is Like a Firefly," ("The Donkey Serenade" was added for the 1937 film adaptation.) Friml's heyday came in the 1920s, the last decade of European-style American operettas. *Rose-Marie* (1924) gave audiences a refreshing change of scene with its setting in the Canadian Rockies and with such atmospheric songs as "Indian Love Call." Friml's last two operettas, *The Vagabond King* (1925) and *The Three Musketeers* (1928), had historical French settings.

Sigmund Romberg was introduced to Broadway in 1913 through his revue music. In 1915 he received his first opportunity in operetta when he adapted a European work as *The Blue Paradise*. This was followed by *Maytime* (1917), and in 1921 Romberg wrote *Blossom Time*, based on melodies by Franz Schubert. Like Friml, Romberg finished his operetta-writing career in the late 1920s following a trilogy of his best works. *The Student Prince* (1924) gave audiences the song, "Deep in My Heart" and the famous choral "Drinking Song." This was followed in 1926 by *The Desert Song*, whose theme music and song "One Alone" are counted among Romberg's finest pieces. Finally, *The New Moon* (1928) brought to a close a long-running native trend of European-style operetta, which was at last replaced for good by the newer American-born, American-bred form: the American musical comedy.

Comedy and the Yankee Doodle Boy

Before the 1890s musical comedies, such as the Mulligan Guard series, were pastiches made up of new musical material together with tried-and-true songs from previous shows, including popular revues. The first mostly original musical comedy was *A Trip to Chinatown* (1890). Its musical and production style—farcical plot, big-town background, and razzle-dazzle dialogue and pacing—pointed the way to many later shows. *A Trip to Chinatown* contained several hit songs, three of which are still somewhat familiar today. "The Bowery" and "Reuben and Cynthia" (also known as "Reuben, Reuben") were part of Peter Gaunt's score, and "After the Ball" by Tin Pan Alley composer-publisher Charles K. Harris was interpolated later. "After the Ball," a wistful waltz, became such a tremendous hit that nearly thirty years later it was revived for insertion into *Show Boat*.

Comedies in the style of *Chinatown*, comic operas, American operettas, revues, burlesques of successful plays and musicals—these were the Broadway fare of the first decade of the twentieth century. But there was only one person with the ability to synthesize the most important elements from each of these and incorporate them into fresh, "All-American" shows: the true father of musical comedy, George M. Cohan. Cohan did it all: songwriting, playwriting, singing, dancing, even managing and occasionally producing. He was the first to humorously admit that not all of his work was of equal quality. ("I can write better plays than any living dancer.") But he did what he did with sincerity and enthusiasm, and he relished his success immensely. ("I'll never be really happy now until I own a part of Broadway. Just a little part, mind you. The top part.")

Cohan had his hand on the pulse of the American public. His stories were generally set against an urban or industrial background, and they reflected the flush of national pride which the United States was experiencing during that decade. Oscar Hammerstein II once stated that "Cohan's genius was to say simply what everybody else was subconsciously feeling." Cohan was at his best when waving the American flag, and his two most successful shows shamelessly exploited patriotism and what passed for "Americanism." *Little Johnny Jones* (1904) gave the world "The Yankee Doodle Boy" ("I'm a Yankee Doodle Dandy") and "Give My Regards to Broadway." *Forty-Five Minutes from Broadway* (1906) is remembered for "Mary's a Grand Old Name." The peak of this trend was the song "You're a Grand Old Flag," written for the 1906 show *George Washington, Jr.*

Between about 1906 and the end of World War I in 1918 Cohan shows appeared on Broadway with unprecedented regularity. The only name which could compete on his level during that time was not a songwriter but a performer: Al Jolson. Jolson's act featured blackface makeup (in the manner of nine-

GEO. M. COHAN
in
"Little Johnny Jones"

George M. Cohan in *Little Johnny Jones*. Photo courtesy of the Theater Arts Library, Harry Ransom Humanities Research Center, The University of Texas at Austin.

teenth-century white minstrel shows), an inimitable voice, and a bit of dance— all the ingredients of vaudeville. In fact, Jolson was chiefly a vaudeville performer and made a great deal of his living there, but at his height he appeared in Broadway shows for thirty-eight weeks each year. Most of these were now-forgotten productions scored by Sigmund Romberg. However, Jolson was given free rein to interpolate any song which struck his fancy, and that was the way he introduced his most famous numbers: "Rock-a-bye Your Baby with a Dixie Melody," "Toot, Toot, Tootsie," "California, Here I Come," "April Showers," and "Swanee" (music by Jolson and George Gershwin).

Musical Theater in the Jazz Age

The 1920s brought an economic boom which was matched in every way by the opulence of the musical theater of the time. Probably the most conspicuous example was the yearly revue *Ziegfeld Follies*. Florenz Ziegfeld had been producing the *Follies* since 1907, and each year's production was a spectacle that attempted to top all previous ones. A full pit orchestra, lavish production numbers, a girl's chorus line (adapted from burlesque), satire, and featured solo numbers—all these and more were packed into each production. Ziegfeld was not without competition, however. *The Passing Show*, a revue produced in 1894, was revived, rewritten, and reproduced each year beginning in 1912. Earl Carroll, a Broadway songwriter, initiated the *Earl Carroll Vanities* in 1922, a show which would have yearly sequels for more than ten seasons. George White, who had been a headliner in *The Passing Show of 1914* and the *Ziegfeld Follies of 1915*, decided to produce his own revue in 1919. White's *Scandals* came the closest to equaling the vast popularity of Ziegfeld's shows and ran yearly until 1939, outlasting the *Follies*, which appeared only sporadically after 1927.

In 1920 George White was one of the few producers capable of recognizing the immense talent and potential of a little-known, twenty-two-year-old songwriter named George Gershwin. He was already becoming known when White engaged him. A year earlier Gershwin had scored a smash hit with "Swanee," a song which had sold 1 million copies of sheet music and more than 2 million Al Jolson records. *Scandals of 1920* introduced the first of Gershwin's enduring ballads, "Somebody Loves Me." Gershwin continued to write most of the music for the *Scandals* through 1924, when he left the show to devote himself to musical comedy and concert music. (*Rhapsody in Blue* was written in 1924, and the Piano Concerto in F came two years later.)

George Gershwin brought to the American musical stage the one element that clearly distinguished that style of music from European music: *jazz*. His impact on the theater and on Tin Pan Alley alike was meteoric, changing forever the face of American popular music. Gershwin's first full-length musical was *Lady, Be Good!* (1924), for which the composer's brother, Ira, wrote all the lyrics. The show, which featured the dance team of Fred and Adele Astaire, was a tremendous success. Besides the title song, the show introduced the jazzy, syncopated "Fascinating Rhythm." The touching ballad "The Man I Love" was intended for *Lady, Be Good!* but had to be dropped for reasons of dramatic timing; it was reintroduced several years later.

Oh, Kay! (1926) was another Gershwin hit of the Roaring Twenties. That show gave the world a song which many consider to be the definitive Gershwin ballad: "Someone to Watch over Me." In 1927 Gershwin's very durable *Funny Face* was premiered, starring the Astaires and comedian Victor Moore. The show is best remembered for "S'Wonderful" and "My One and Only."

During the early 1930s Gershwin musicals reached a new high. *Girl Crazy* (1930) featured Ethel Merman in her Broadway debut singing the hit "I Got Rhythm," during which she held a high note for sixteen measures. Ginger Rogers also starred in *Girl Crazy*, introducing two other Gershwin blockbusters, "Embraceable You" and "But Not for Me." The pit orchestra for that show was stacked with many of the future stars of jazz, notably Glenn Miller and Benny Goodman. The year 1930 also brought another brilliant Gershwin show, *Strike up the Band!*, a humorous satire on war with a book by George S. Kaufman.

Although *Strike up the Band!* contained some memorable songs, such as "I've Got a Crush on You," it was actually the prelude to an even finer show by the same creators: *Of Thee I Sing* (1931). This musical was a bright sequence of sketches and song-and-dance numbers which satirized political life in Washington, DC, in particular the plight of the oft-forgotten vice president. Gershwin's score was his most ambitious to date, and it included snippets from such well-worn political and patriotic fare as "A Hot Time in the Old Town Tonight," and "The Stars and Stripes Forever." Most of the musical numbers were topical, and few memorable tunes emerged from it. However, *Of Thee I Sing* had the longest run of any Gershwin musical, and it became the first musical show to win the coveted Pulitzer Prize for drama.

Let 'Em Eat Cake (1933) completed the trilogy of political satire musical comedies by the team of Gershwin, Kaufman, and Gershwin. The show was a sequel to *Of Thee I Sing*, but not a very successful one. Apparently the satire was too biting for Depression audiences, and reviewer Brooks Atkinson remarked of the show's authors that "their hatred had triumphed over their sense of humor."

George Gershwin's career in the American musical theater reached its ultimate peak in 1935, not with a musical comedy but rather with a more serious piece: the popular folk opera *Porgy and Bess*. The story, dealing with life in a poor black fishing village on an island off Charleston, South Carolina, was adapted from a novel by DuBose and Dorothy Heyward. Gershwin was so taken with the story that he persuaded DuBose Heyward himself to adapt it for the stage. Naturally, all the song lyrics were written by Ira Gershwin. George Gershwin's quest for authenticity in the opera led him to spend time among the islands where the story takes place.

Unlike Gershwin's musical comedies, *Porgy and Bess* employs continuous music, that is, all dialogue is sung. The influence of jazz, black spirituals, and southern blues can be heard on nearly every page of the score, and these serve to establish the atmosphere of the story and the individual characterizations in an exact, superbly theatrical manner. Many of the songs and "arias" from this folk opera became established as popular standards, including "Summertime," "I Got Plenty o' Nuthin'," "It Ain't Necessarily So," and "Bess, You Is My Woman Now."

Show Boat

Even though many of George Gershwin's musical comedies had great success in the 1920s, the leading composer of the American musical theater during that decade was Jerome Kern. Kern had been involved in musicals since 1903. By 1914 he was being hailed as the most gifted stage composer since Victor Herbert. In fact, that year Herbert heard Kern's song "They Didn't Believe Me" and declared, "This man will inherit my mantle." During the years 1915–1918 Kern teamed up with dramatist Guy Bolton and lyricist P. G. Wodehouse to write a string of acclaimed musical comedies known collectively as the Princess Theater Shows. These witty, sophisticated musicals gave theatergoers a classy alternative to George M. Cohan's vaudevillian-style productions.

Between 1920 and 1925 Kern turned out musical comedies which employed

Show Boat. Photo courtesy of the Theater Arts Library. Harry Ransom Humanities Research Center, The University of Texas at Austin.

most of the formulas and conventions of the times: chorus lines, gag comedians, lavish sets, routines, and songs which were merely light and diverting.

Perhaps that explains why Kern's idea to transform *Show Boat,* Edna Ferber's 1926 novel, into a musical was thought insane at first by nearly everyone, including the author herself. However, Kern was not thinking of making it a conventional song-and-dance show. Rather, he was conceiving a new form of musical theater, one which would utilize the finer characteristics of operetta and bypass the purely "entertainment" conventions of musical comedy. The new form would fuse musical comedy and operetta into something unique. It would be the first "book" musical: *the first musical play.* At that time the librettist/lyricist Oscar Hammerstein II also had a dream of reforming the American musical theater, and Kern had no difficulty in convincing him to collaborate on the project. Author Ferber was persuaded to grant Kern dramatic rights to the story of *Show Boat.* Florenz Ziegfeld, who always admired the unique and ingenious, became the show's producer despite his misgivings about the appropriateness of the story for the musical stage.

After many out-of-town tryouts and much delay (mostly on the part of Ziegfeld) *Show Boat* finally opened in December 1927 in the new Ziegfeld Theater. Although there have been several longer-running shows in the history of musicals, *Show Boat's* run was quite respectable. It ran on Broadway for nearly two years, and a road company made a successful national tour of the major cities. The show has been revived several times, the latest in 1994, and there were three different film adaptations: in 1929, 1936, and 1951.

Quite simply, *Show Boat* was the turning point in the history of the American musical theater. Its story was a sweeping saga of life on the Mississippi River between the 1880s and the 1920s. This setting was novel, being placed in America's heartland rather than in New York. The quality of the libretto itself was far above anything yet produced on the Broadway musical stage. Hammerstein's script and lyrics were built around a cohesive story instead of the usual arbitrary song numbers and dance routines. Rather than Broadway's ubiquitous stock characters and "cardboard," predictable types, *Show Boat* featured believable, flesh-and-bones characters with which the audience could readily identify.

Kern's score made use of atmospheric "source" styles as background to the various time frames in the story. Minstrel olio style, story ballads, ragtime, and other idioms could be easily identified in the music. In one scene Kern even inserted an authentic early song. "After the Ball" by Charles K. Harris, drawn from *A Trip to Chinatown* (1890). This piece had the effect of adding a nostalgic flavor to the scene.

The songs of *Show Boat* were integrated closely into the story and contributed to its progress in several ways. Some of them were there to create mood. Others revealed and developed characters. Still others contributed to the advancement of the plot. *Show Boat* contained more lasting songs than any musical of its time, or perhaps of any time. The better-known original songs from this show are "Make Believe," "Ol' Man River," "Bill," "Can't Help Lovin' Dat Man," "You Are Love," and "Why Do I Love You."

Sophistication and Social Commentary

The leading musical theater composer of the 1930s is generally acknowledged to have been Cole Porter. Porter came to musical comedy not by way of Tin Pan Alley, as Gershwin had done, but rather by way of Yale and Harvard universities, the French Foreign Legion, the Social Register, and the high-living American expatriates in Paris during the 1920s. Porter wrote his own lyrics, and by 1924 the provocative, sophisticated, and often suggestive style of his unique songs had been forged. That year his first important exposure came when some of his work was included in the revue *Greenwich Village Follies*. Four years later his career began gaining momentum with the production of *Paris*, which included the mildly suggestive song "Let's Do It." That was followed by *Fifty Million Frenchmen* and *Wake Up and Dream*, shows from 1929 which gave the world "You Do Something to Me" and "What Is This Thing Called Love?"

The 1930s saw the production of several successful Cole Porter musicals and the writing of most of his immortal songs. *The New Yorkers* (1930) included "Love for Sale," the lyrics of which were banned from radio for at least three decades. *The Gay Divorce* (1932) starred Fred Astaire and introduced "Night and Day." *Anything Goes* (a phrase which could be used to describe Cole Porter's own life-style) was produced in 1934, and besides the title song the show presented "Blow, Gabriel, Blow," "You're the Top," and "I Get a Kick Out of You," all belted out by Ethel Merman. *Leave It to Me* (1938) gave Mary Martin her

Broadway debut, coyly singing "My Heart Belongs to Daddy." Even Porter's unsuccessful musicals of the time could boast hit songs, such as "Begin the Beguine" and "It's De-Lovely."

Following a horseback-riding accident in 1937, Porter was unable to recover sufficiently to complete a show for more than ten years. However, in 1948 he reemerged on Broadway with the most successful musical comedy of his career, Kiss Me, Kate, based on Shakespeare's The Taming of the Shrew. After that, Porter created two more musicals: Can-Can (1953) and Silk Stockings (1955).

In contrast with Cole Porter's light, sophisticated, ironic style, the spirit of the Great Depression was captured in Irving Berlin's 1932 revue, Face the Music. One typical scene showed Wall Street bankers reduced to eating in a New York automat, during which the song "Let's Have Another Cup of Coffee" is sung. This show represented an enormous comeback for Berlin. The composer, who had made a fortune in Tin Pan Alley and vaudeville, experienced a great financial setback with the stock market crash of 1929. The success of Face the Music gave Berlin the confidence he needed to rise to another highpoint in his career. In 1933 his revue As Thousands Cheer was a major hit. In it Ethel Waters sang a steamy rendition of "Heat Wave," but the real blockbuster was the Act One finale, "Easter Parade."

Numerous Berlin hit shows followed during the decade, but a new wave of success crested after the outbreak of World War II. Berlin, who had at one time collaborated with George M. Cohan, was a noted patriot. During World War I, while serving in the army, he wrote an "all-soldier show" called Yip, Yip, Yaphank, the proceeds from which were given to building a new camp service center. Berlin's patriotic flame was rekindled when the United States entered World War II. He contributed another "all-soldier show," This Is the Army (1942), and also brought out "God Bless America" for Kate Smith to sing. Proceeds from the show and the song were donated to the war effort and to charities. After the war Berlin wrote a string of musical comedies based on American themes: Annie Get Your Gun (1946), Miss Liberty (1949), Call Me Madam (1950), and Mr. President (1962).

During the 1930s successful Broadway writers, composers, and lyricists often found themselves in Hollywood writing individual songs and entire musicals for the screen. Gershwin had moved to Hollywood after Porgy and Bess (1935) and wrote for films there until his death two years later. Both Cole Porter and Irving Berlin were also active in film musicals. Some of Porter's finest work was done for films, including the songs "I've Got You Under My Skin," "Easy to Love," "In the Still of the Night," "You'd Be So Nice to Come Home To," "Don't Fence Me In," and "True Love." Irving Berlin's most notable contributions to films included the songs "Cheek to Cheek" and "White Christmas," the latter winning the 1942 Academy Award for best song and becoming an American Christmas standard.

The Depression prompted a few musicals which dealt with the social and economic concerns of the day. Irving Berlin wrote Pins and Needles (1937), a hit revue which featured the theme of unionization. In 1938 Marc Blitzstein completed the book, lyrics, and music for The Cradle Will Rock, an eloquent but heavily socialist statement on social and political exploitation. The premiere of the work, which was scheduled for the WPA Theater, had to be moved at the last minute because of government pressure on the theater's management. The ensuing premiere performance, given without scenery or costumes and accompanied only by a piano, was itself a comment added to the show's message.

Another composer associated with social commentary, Kurt Weill, emerged on the American musical stage during the 1930s. Having fled Nazi Germany in 1933, he came first to France and then to the United States with a reputation for cabaret-style operas. *The Threepenny Opera* (1928) and *The Rise and Fall of the City of Mahagonny* (1930) were controversial works whose biting, left-wing librettos had been authored by Bertolt Brecht. Weill made his bow on the American musical stage with *Johnny Johnson* (1936), an antiwar, antifascist piece with a book by Paul Green. This was followed in 1937 by *The Eternal Road*, a pageant of Jewish history based on a work by Franz Werfel. Although neither of these shows was a financial success, they demonstrated Weill's great versatility and adaptability. He avidly studied the English language and the American musical theater, and in 1938 he was able to synthesize these efforts into a truly American musical show for Broadway, *Knickerbocker Holiday*. If there had been any doubt that Weill could produce a classic American tune, it was dispelled by the show-stopper "September Song."

Weill continued writing for the musical stage throughout the 1940s. His most outstanding shows included *Lady in the Dark* (1941), *Street Scene* (1947), *Lost in the Stars* (1949), and the 1948 American folk opera, *Down in the Valley*. In 1954, four years after Weill's death, *The Threepenny Opera* was revived in a new English-language production for an off-Broadway theater. The translation was provided by Marc Blitzstein, and Kurt Weill's widow, Lotte Lenya, starred as Jenny Diver, the role she had created for the original production in Germany. The show ran for 2,250 performances, longer than any off-Broadway production up to that time, and it generated the popular hit "Mack the Knife."

The Golden Age: Rodgers and Hammerstein ———————

The "musical play" concept which had been born in *Show Boat* was not immediately taken up by Broadway writers. In fact, it took more than fifteen years to be fully realized again. The show was *Oklahoma!* and, like *Show Boat*, it made history in several ways.

Oklahoma! was the first professional collaboration between Richard Rodgers and Oscar Hammerstein II. Hammerstein had had his successes (notably, *Show Boat*) and his failures. Rodgers had been teamed with Lorenz Hart since the 1920s, and while not every one of their shows had been a hit, they could boast a string of successes. Rodgers occasionally experimented, giving audiences something unexpected but tremendously effective. One example was the use of ballet. In musical comedy, serious ballet was unheard of and thought to be bad for the box office until Rodgers and Hart introduced it in *On Your Toes*, a dance show of 1936. The number, choreographed by George Balanchine, was a jazz ballet called "Slaughter on Tenth Avenue." It portrayed in stylized movement the flight of a dancer and his girlfriend from gangsters and the subsequent murder of the girl. "Slaughter on Tenth Avenue" became a hit by itself and was the most durable aspect of the show.

Ballet music came to be a hallmark of many Richard Rodgers musicals, notably the first Rodgers and Hammerstein collaboration, *Oklahoma!* (1943). However, Laurie's dream sequence ballet was not *Oklahoma!*'s only revolutionary feature. Right from the opening curtain audiences knew they would experience something novel in the musical theater. Normally, a musical show would begin with a big production number involving a girls' chorus line. *Oklahoma!* boldly defied that tradition by starting simply with one character on stage and the distant sound of "Oh, What a Beautiful Mornin'." The reason: the play did not call for a crowd until much later in the act, and in this musical play the creators were firmly committed to dramatic values rather than to musical comedy conventions. In scenes where the dance company was featured, Agnes De Mille's choreography avoided traditional Broadway routines in favor of folk and western dance movements. Many of the songs, too, had the freshness of the frontier about them, notably "The Surrey with the Fringe on Top," "The Farmer and the Cowman," "Kansas City," and the title song. The only song harking back to traditional Broadway/Tin Pan Alley style was the show's love song, "People Will Say We're in Love."

The boldness of Rodgers and Hammerstein paid off in box office records, too. The original production of *Oklahoma!* ran five years on Broadway. There were two national touring companies which worked over a ten-year period, and the show was produced in many foreign countries. The original-cast record album (78 rpm) of *Oklahoma!* was the first of its kind, and it sold over a million copies. In 1955 a lavish film version was released, grossing over $8 million. *Oklahoma!* effectively defined the principal characteristics of musicals for some time to come and served to establish Rodgers and Hammerstein as the dominant writing team in the 1940s and early 1950s.

Around the time of *Oklahoma!* there developed a trend in selecting musical stage stories which was to last through the 1950s. The idea was to base a show on some proven piece of literature: a modern play, short story, novel, or classic. *Oklahoma!* was based on the Lynn Riggs play *Green Grow the Lilacs*. Prior to that time, Rodgers and Hart had written *Pal Joey* (1940), based on a series of short stories by John O'Hara. The trend was not a sure formula for success, as *Pal Joey* proved during its initial run. However, after Rodgers and Hammerstein began collaborating, they led the trend with their greatest accomplishments.

In 1945 Rodgers and Hammerstein mounted their second work together: *Carousel*, based on the Ferenc Molnár play *Liliom*. Here, the team brought a new dimension to the American musical theater: humanity. And with humanity came the need for expanded expression. "Soliloquy" from this show was a musical narrative that took on the dimensions of a full operatic aria. Lyrics and music for "If I Loved You" and "You'll Never Walk Alone" set a new, elevated tone in

Oklahoma!. Photo courtesy of Billy Rose Theater Collection, the New York Public Library at Lincoln Center, Astor, Lenox, and Tilden foundations.

theatrical songs. The show contained its dance element in the form of the memorable "Carousel Waltz," heard first as the overture. There were light moments, too, as in the songs "June Is Bustin' Out All Over" and "When I Marry Mr. Snow."

James Michener's Pulitzer Prize-winning book, *Tales of the South Pacific*, became the basis of Rodgers and Hammerstein's classic musical, *South Pacific* (1949). The popularity of this show was immediate and permanent. Some critics have gone so far as to say that it was a flawless creation and to call it the finest musical show ever to open on Broadway.

There was a mixture of musical styles in *South Pacific*, but they reflected the cultural mix of the main characters, and somehow it all worked as a unified creation. Rodgers had flirted with operatic style in the "Soliloquy" of *Carousel*, but now he had an opportunity to compose for the operatic voice of Ezio Pinza, who was making his Broadway debut. Pinza sang "This Nearly Was Mine" and the ingratiating "Some Enchanted Evening." Exotic, non-Broadway music was heard in such "native" songs as "Bali Ha'i" and "Happy Talk." More American in flavor were "I'm Gonna Wash That Man Right out of My Hair," "I'm in Love with a Wonderful Guy," "Younger than Springtime," and the ensemble number "There Is Nothing Like a Dame."

Exoticism was taken a step further in Rodgers and Hammerstein's next musical, *The King and I* (1951). Based on the British novel *Anna and the King of Siam* by Margaret Landon and a film adaptation of that book, the musical show became a challenge to all involved. It was a spectacle for the eye as well as the ear. Large, luxuriant oriental sets were complemented by costumes made from Thai silk. The traditional pit orchestra was augmented by oriental percussion instruments, and the score was magnificently orchestrated by Robert Russell

Bennett, Richard Rodgers' exclusive orchestrator. The story emphasized contrasts between Eastern and Western cultures, and the wide variety of songs in the show reflected that theme. For example, in the same act appeared the "March of the Siamese Children" and Anna's song "Hello, Young Lovers." The gentle, friendly personality of Anna shown in "Getting to Know You" was sharply differentiated from the stiff formality of the King in his song "Shall We Dance?" In the original Broadway run Yul Brynner made his major role debut as the King, and Gertrude Lawrence bade her theatrical farewell in the role of Anna.

During 1958–1959 Rodgers and Hammerstein had a modest success with *Flower Drum Song*, but the following season they completed *The Sound of Music*, which represented the pinnacle of their collaboration. It was a record-breaker, beginning with advance ticket sales of more than $3 million, through its three-year Broadway run, its record-grossing motion picture, and its recorded movie sound track sales of more than 8 million albums. As usual, Rodgers and Hammerstein were full of surprises, beginning with the opening music. Instead of the traditional overture, the curtain went up on a convent scene and the singing of a choral "Praeludium." *The Sound of Music* was the story of the singing Trapp Family, led by Maria Rainer and Baron von Trapp, and their eventual flight from Nazi-occupied Austria.

The Austrian setting suggested European forms to the composer, and it was not surprising to find the music to be on the brink of operetta at times. This was particularly apparent in the show's principal song, "Climb Ev'ry Mountain." Echoes of the Austrian countryside appeared in the folksong-like melody of "Edelweiss" and the yodelling motives of "The Lonely Goatherd." The Broadway musical style was not entirely absent from this show, however. "Do, Re, Mi," "Sixteen Going on Seventeen," and the immortal "My Favorite Things" were very much in the Rodgers and Hammerstein mainstream style.

The Sound of Music was both the pinnacle and, regrettably, the final collaboration between this incredible duo. After the death of Oscar Hammerstein II in 1960, Richard Rodgers went on to compose *No Strings* (1962), using his own lyrics, and *Do I Hear a Waltz?* (1965), in collaboration with Stephen Sondheim, among other shows. But these were pale next to the brilliance and unerring theatrical power of the five or six great musicals written by the all-time giants of American musical theater, Rodgers and Hammerstein.

Fantasies, Fair Ladies, and Fast Talk

By 1947 the Golden Age of Rodgers and Hammerstein was in full swing, eclipsing nearly every other Broadway effort. However, in that year two musicals generated by other writers set new standards for fantasy in American musical theater. One of these shows was *Finian's Rainbow*, by Burton Lane, E. Y. Harburg, and Fred Saidy. The other was *Brigadoon*, the first stage success of Alan Jay Lerner and Frederick Loewe.

Finian's Rainbow was a satire on Irish folklore, juxtaposing it with the problems of modern rural American society. The show's two hit ballads were "How Are Things in Glocca Morra?" and "Look to the Rainbow," but the satirical side of the story was revealed in such numbers as "The Begat" and "When the Idle Poor Become the Idle Rich."

Lerner and Loewe's fantasy *Brigadoon*, set in Scotland, concerns an eighteenth-century town which comes back to life for one day every hundred years. It was a delicate, sensitive fairy tale. The show boasted several memorable hit ballads, notably "Almost Like Being in Love," "The Heather on the Hill," and "Come to Me, Bend to Me."

Lerner and Loewe would again return to the domain of pure fantasy in 1960, but not before making musical theater history with *My Fair Lady* (1956). This show, based on G. B. Shaw's play *Pygmalion*, had all the theatrical perfection of a Rogers and Hammerstein creation, but also had a most individual charm and character. Much of the music had strong tinges of British style, often associated with the social class of the character(s) performing it. Doolittle, a cockney, sings the music hall-style songs "With A Little Bit of Luck" and "Get Me to the Church on Time." The show's famous pantomime "Ascot Gavotte" was a perfect reflection of Edwardian manners and attitudes. Much of the remaining music of *My Fair Lady* displayed a continental, period-style flair. Eliza (sung by Julie Andrews in her first starring role on Broadway) sang the exhilarating "I Could Have Danced All Night," and young Freddie crooned the puppy-love song "On the Street Where You Live."

My Fair Lady was, to say the least, a blockbuster. It became the longest-running Broadway show, breaking *Oklahoma!*'s previous record. Its national tour set box office records everywhere, and it was produced in many foreign countries, including the Soviet Union. The original cast recording sold 3 million copies, and the film rights were sold for $5.5 million, the highest price paid up to that time for a musical.

My Fair Lady. Photo courtesy of the Theater Arts Library. Harry Ransom Humanities Research Center, The University of Texas at Austin.

Lerner and Loewe's *Camelot* (1960) was both a return to the realm of fantasy and an attempt to create a second *My Fair Lady*. Based on T. H. White's King Arthur novel, *The Once and Future King*, the story concerned the love triangle among Arthur (Richard Burton), Guenevere (Julie Andrews), and Launcelot (Robert Goulet). Although *Camelot* was not the equal of *My Fair Lady*, it did contain some durable songs, notably "How to Handle a Woman" and "If Ever I Would Leave You," both containing delicately ironic lyrics.

For several years following World War II, there appeared shows which stood out in contrast to fantasies (*Finian's Rainbow*; *Brigadoon*) and exotic settings (*South Pacific*; *The King and I*). They were shows set back in good old New York City, and they had the fast pacing and urbane wit associated with musical comedies of the 1920s and 1930s. However, since that earlier time experience had taught Broadway to base its book musicals on solid literary turf.

One of the first of such shows was *On the Town* (1944), Leonard Bernstein's debut as a theatrical composer. Book and lyrics were by Betty Comden and Adolf Green. The story, about three sailors on shore leave in search of girls, became something of a model for a new breed of musical comedy set against a New York backdrop. The dynamic opening production number, "New York, New York," became a classic of its type. Nine years later Bernstein followed up that show with *Wonderful Town*, based on the successful Fields and Chodorov play *My Sister Eileen*. This time the protagonists were two midwestern young ladies living in Greenwich Village. Although the music of *Wonderful Town* did not become especially popular (with the possible exception of "O-H-I-O"), the show was a notable success, running for two years on Broadway and garnering several awards.

If there were an award for the classic New York musical, it would have to go to Frank Loesser's 1950 show, *Guys and Dolls*. The plot and unique characters were drawn from stories by Damon Runyon dealing humorously with the shady fringe of the underworld. The genius of composer-lyricist Loesser was characterization. Probably no other musical show has defined and developed the main characters through song as adeptly as did *Guys and Dolls*. Here are the principal examples:

Sky Masterson, a high roller but sensitive inside: "Luck, Be a Lady Tonight" and "My Time of Day"

Sarah, Salvation Army missionary who falls for Sky: "If I Were a Bell"

Sky and Sarah: "I'll Know" and "I've Never Been in Love Before"

Nathan Detroit, Sky's fellow crap-shooter, and *Miss Adelaide*, nightclub entertainer engaged to Nathan for fourteen years: "Sue Me"

Miss Adelaide alone: "Adelaide's Lament"

Nicely-Nicely, a racetrack tout: "Sit Down, You're Rocking the Boat"

Perhaps the most ingenious touch, however, was the way the opening scene communicated the entire flavor of the show. The scene was "Runyonland"

Guys and Dolls. Photo courtesy of the Theater Arts Library, Harry Ransom Humanities Research Center, The University of Texas at Austin.

(Broadway), where various "types" of guys and dolls passed and pantomimed selected slices of life. In the midst of this scene, Nicely-Nicely and two other racing form readers were making their picks for the day. This trio sang the very clever round, "Fugue for Tinhorns" ("I've got the horse right here . . . ").

The *Guys and Dolls* method of opening a show may well have been the inspiration for the opening scene of Meredith Willson's *The Music Man* (1957). Here, the bouncy rhythm of a moving train was used as the background to a cleverly

Robert Preston in *The Music Man.* Photo courtesy of the Theater Arts Library, Harry Ransom Humanities Research Center, The University of Texas at Austin.

written rhythmic dialogue between traveling salesmen, "But He Doesn't Know the Territory." *The Music Man* was set in Iowa in 1912, the time and place of Willson's own boyhood. It concerned a fast-talking musical instrument salesman ("Ya Got Trouble"), "Professor" Harold Hill, who sells the town on the idea of a high school band. Willson's versatile musical craftsmanship was apparent throughout this show. The boisterous march "Seventy-Six Trombones" was magically transformed into the wistful ballad "Goodnight, My Someone," sung by Marian, the town librarian. "Period" music (by Wilson) was introduced in the form of a barbershop quartet song, "Lida Rose," and the operetta-like "Will I Ever Tell You"; then the two songs were cleverly combined. In terms of its energy, time setting, and "American-ness" *The Music Man* was somewhat reminiscent of the work of George M. Cohan. At the same time the show had considerable originality and contemporary appeal, which was further demonstrated by the success of the film version, released in 1962.

Broadway Opera

The stylistic range of American musical theater has always been broad. There has been as much room for "class" as for crass commercialism. At the classy end of the spectrum there was operetta at first, and touches of operetta's European refinement later found their way into the musicals of such writers as Rodgers and Hammerstein, and Lerner and Loewe. There were also some attempts to mount even more highbrow operatic efforts on the New York stage, and a few of these met with success.

In 1949 Marc Blitzstein's opera *Regina* opened on Broadway. The show was based on Lillian Hellman's *The Little Foxes*, and it ran for only fifty-six performances. Although *Regina* failed to attract large Broadway audiences, it was produced by the New York City Opera Company in 1953 and subsequently became part of that group's regular repertoire.

The following year *The Golden Apple*, by Jerome Moross and John La Touche, opened off-Broadway. This show was a modern satire on the Homeric legend of Ulysses and Helen set in an American town. Although the treatment was light, the work was sung throughout, qualifying it as a kind of opera. The show was so successful off-Broadway that after five weeks it was moved to a Broadway theater for a good run. One song from *The Golden Apple* that may be remembered was "Lazy Afternoon."

Frank Loesser followed *Guys and Dolls* with a work in 1956 that had strong operatic overtones. The show was called *The Most Happy Fella*, and it was based on Sidney Howard's 1925 Pulitzer Prize-winning play, *They Knew What They Wanted*. Although *The Most Happy Fella* contained almost continuous music, Loesser did not consider it an actual opera, preferring to dub it an "extended musical comedy." The composer had good reason, since the show's wide gamut of musical styles extended well into Tin Pan Alley and Broadway traditions. Examples were spirited songs like "Standing on the Corner" and "Big D," along with the ballad "Joey, Joey, Joey." However, the main character, Tony, was an Italian vineyard owner in Northern California. This fact called for some European touches, such as the Italianate songs "Abbondanza" and "Benvenuta," and the lovely waltz "How Beautiful the Days." The part of Tony (created originally by Robert Weede) required a trained baritone voice, and his principal song, "My Heart Is So Full of You," verged on operetta.

In the same year as *The Most Happy Fella*, Leonard Bernstein's *Candide* was produced. Perhaps due to its "classical" subject matter and intellectual thrust (book by Lillian Hellman), it was not a box office success. However, the rich variety and quality of Bernstein's score for this musical play was highly praised. The fact that the score became as popular as it did despite the absence of any "catchy" hit tunes was puzzling to all. Bernstein has depicted this puzzlement in his essay "Why Don't You Run Upstairs and Write a Nice Gershwin Tune?"

Although there have been many modern adaptations of Shakespeare's tragedy *Romeo and Juliet*, none has been able to rival Leonard Bernstein's *West Side Story* for overall quality, social impact, and sheer power of expression. In place of Montagues and Capulets, the book by Arthur Laurents substituted rival teenage street gangs, one Anglo ("Jets") and the other Hispanic ("Sharks"). The star-crossed lovers, Tony and Maria, were from the neighborhoods where the two gangs were centered.

Modern dance and ballet were employed in new and effective ways in the choreography of Jerome Robbins, who originally conceived the idea for the show. In "The Dance at the Gym" and "The Rumble" the hostilities and violence between the gangs were expressed in stylized modern dance. A ballet sequence in the second act involving Tony and Maria gave way to a processional and the song "Somewhere."

West Side Story. Photo courtesy of the Theater Arts Library, Harry Ransom Humanities Research Center, The University of Texas at Austin.

Bernstein's music, coupled with the masterful lyrics of young Stephen Sondheim, perfectly expressed the surly bravado of the Jets ("Jet Song" and "Gee, Officer Krupke") as well as the sarcasm of the Sharks' girls ("America"). Bernstein's complete absorption of the American jazz idiom was heard clearly in the modern dance numbers as well as in the song "Cool."

Several features of *West Side Story* were operatic. Most obviously, the part of Maria (Carol Lawrence in the original cast) required a trained voice and enough vocal agility to bring off "I Feel Pretty." The show also incorporated several duets and ensemble numbers employing the principal characters, notably "Tonight" (Tony and Maria in the balcony scene; later Tony, Maria, Anita, Riff, and Bernardo); "One Hand, One Heart" (Tony and Maria); "A Boy Like That/I Have a Love" (Anita and Maria); and "Finale" (Tony and Maria). These were handled somewhat in an operatic manner, yet it was an American brand of opera.

One further feature of the score borrowed from opera and concert music was the use of a recurring melodic motive. It could be heard prominently during dance sequences such as the "Prologue," "The Dance at the Gym," and "The Rumble"; and in altered form at the beginning of the songs "Something's Coming," "Maria," and "Cool."

Both the stage and film versions of *West Side Story* were hailed as resounding artistic successes, and some critics even felt that the show had made history on the musical stage. One London critic declared that with *West Side Story* began "a new age in the theater," and American writer David Ewen called the show "one of the crowning masterworks of the American musical theater."

"Little Shows" and Off-Broadway

Inflation in the 1960s caused the producers and creators of Broadway musicals to change their focus. The number of openings was reduced and, as with films of the same period, the blockbuster mentality took hold. A Broadway producer, instead of attempting to build up a string of hits, would try for one, long-running blockbuster. Also, because of inflation, producers sought ways to reduce production overhead. One method was to reduce the size of the main cast; another was to reject show proposals which required many large production numbers.

Richard Rodgers was one of the first major creators to bring a startling artistic economy to Broadway. His *No Strings* (1962) utilized an orchestra with no string section and, rather than beginning with an overture, plunged directly into the most important song of the show, "The Sweetest Sounds." Dance was kept to a minimum, and the small cast was required to move scenery around the stage to suggest new settings.

Another conception of Richard Rodgers, but one which he did not finally compose, was *On a Clear Day You Can See Forever* (1965) by Alan Jay Lerner and Burton Lane. The main cast consisted of little more than the main characters: a young clairvoyant woman, her psychiatrist, and her boyfriend. Settings were limited, and there was no dance, although the show did require a large chorus.

The Apple Tree (1966), by Jerry Bock and Sheldon Harnick, was a triptych of one-act musical plays involving various sides of a woman's personality: "The Diary of Adam and Eve," "The Lady and the Tiger," and "Passionella." The principal cast consisted of one woman and two men, and the style of production was austere except for the presence of a chorus. However, such sparseness was counterbalanced by great imagination, for example, the final playlet in which a film projection of the heroine was shown simultaneously with live action.

The classic example of such "little" shows was *I Do! I Do!* (1966), by Harvey Schmidt and Tom Jones, based on the Jan de Hartog play *The Fourposter*. The story portrayed the fifty-year married life of Michael and Agnes ("He" and "She"), and the cast consisted of Robert Preston and Mary Martin. That was all—no subordinate characters, no chorus, no dancers.

The cost of renting a Broadway theater was also a substantial part of a musical's budget. One method of dealing with the rental expense and cutting financial risk was to open a show in an off-Broadway theater, often in Greenwich Village. If the show was a success, it might be moved to Broadway, as with *The Golden Apple*. Or, the producer might decide that the show was more suitable to the theater in which it opened. Such was the case with *The Fantasticks*, the first show by Harvey Schmidt and Tom Jones.

In 1960 *The Fantasticks* opened in a small Greenwich Village theater with a seating capacity of under 150. It received lukewarm reviews, and the show limped along, losing a little money for the first three months. Then, suddenly, the show became chic and New York audiences began flocking to it. This off-Broadway show has run continuously for over three decades, far outdistancing its nearest competitor as the longest-running American musical in history.

The Fantasticks was freshness, youth, and simplicity personified. Its ladder-and-chair settings required the audience to use their imagination, and the plot was designed to signify different things to different people. The cast consisted of only five main members, and the "pit orchestra" was made up of only two pianos, harp, percussion, cello, and contrabass. *The Fantasticks* song "Try to Remember" has become a standard, and Barbra Streisand popularized "Soon It's Gonna Rain" through her 1963 recording.

New Settings

The decade of the 1960s was one of the most exciting ones of the century for entire fields of music. New styles, such as rock, country, and soul, became known to the general public for the first time. Electronically produced music found a place in several domains. Civil rights, ethnic awareness, the war in Vietnam, the youth culture—all these developments and more had a distinct impact on all the arts, but especially on music. There was a spirit of adventure and exploration in the air, and this was equally felt and shown in the American musical theater during the 1960s and early 1970s. Off-Broadway shows and even shows originating outside New York proved that the market for musical theater had grown considerably. Broadway musicals also concerned themselves less with adapting tried-and-true literary vehicles in favor of exploring new terrain: people, places, and time settings.

The Business World

Two shows in the early 1960s used the world of business as a backdrop. *How to Succeed in Business Without Really Trying* (1961) was a Pulitzer Prize-winning comedy with music and lyrics by Frank Loesser (his last show). It satirized big business and all the personal attributes deemed necessary to climb the corporate ladder. The show's most memorable song was "I Believe in You." In 1962 *I Can Get It for You Wholesale* was brought to the Broadway stage, and it may be remembered as the debut of nineteen-year-old Barbra Streisand, who stole much of the show. The story was a bittersweet comedy about life in the New York City garment industry during the Depression.

Exotic People, Places, and Times

Rodgers and Hammerstein had blazed the trail to exoticism, first with *South Pacific* (1949) and then with *The King and I* (1951). They proved that a genuinely American musical could be written on non-American subject matter. In the former show both the place and secondary characters were exotic; in the latter, people, place, and even time setting were all rather remote from the contemporary American milieu. Considering the immense success of those two shows, it seems strange that for more than ten years Broadway's creative talents rarely ventured further than Europe or earlier than 1912 for their setting. Notable exceptions were *Once Upon a Mattress* (1959) and *Camelot* (1960), both fantasies.

The ice was broken in 1962 with Stephen Sondheim's satire on Rome in the time of Plautus, *A Funny Thing Happened on the Way to the Forum*. This show was a raucous burlesque, replete with double meanings and anachronistic gags. Most of the Broadway cast, featuring Zero Mostel, was engaged for the film version, released in 1966.

Zero Mostel returned to the Broadway stage in 1964 to play another exotic character. This time it was Tevye, the milkman of the tiny village of Anatevka, drawn from Yiddish stories by Sholom Aleichem. The title of the show, *Fiddler on the Roof*, was taken from an image in a Marc Chagall painting and was used to symbolize the precarious life of Polish/Russian Jews living in a Christian world around the turn of the century. The music by Jerry Bock and lyrics by Sheldon Harnick were perfect illustrations of that remote culture, and the story, with its rich humor and pathos, utterly captivated audiences. This was entirely fresh material—no Broadway clichés, no surefire audience pleasers. The show was built largely around the character of Tevye, and he was given the most characteristic (and attractive) songs: "If I Were a Rich Man," "L'Chaim—To Life," and "Do You Love Me?"

Zero Mostel in *Fiddler on the Roof*. Photo courtesy of the Theater Arts Library, Harry Ransom Humanities Research Center, The University of Texas at Austin.

Another musical built largely around one character was the 1964 "show that has become a legend," Jerry Herman's *Hello, Dolly!*. The character of Dolly Levi was created by Carol Channing, who went on to make a career of Dollies in revivals and road show productions. *Hello, Dolly!* was pure entertainment and spectacle directed masterfully by Gower Champion. Set in the 1890s, the musical's title number was purposely written as a sort of "Lillian Russell turn-of-the-century production number." The show and the song both enjoyed a huge success. *Hello, Dolly!* ran for more than three years on Broadway and was produced in several foreign countries. An all-black cast version was presented on Broadway in 1967. The song "Hello, Dolly!" became one of the all-time show tune pop hits also, largely through the recording made by Louis Armstrong. (The only taint on the song's phenomenal success was a copyright lawsuit brought against composer Jerry Herman. It was settled out of court for a sum estimated at half a million dollars, and Herman retained exclusive rights to the song.) In 1969 a film version of *Hello, Dolly!* was released, with Barbra Streisand replacing Miss Channing in the title role.

While *Hello, Dolly!* was not really very "exotic," *Man of La Mancha* (1965) was. This musical play was based on the classic novel *Don Quixote* by Miguel Cervantes. The music was by Mitch Leigh, a relative newcomer to Broadway, and several others involved in the show were fairly unknown as well. This remarkable musical revealed the best reason for choosing a remote or classic sub-

Carol Channing in *Hello, Dolly*. Photo courtesy of the Theater Arts Library, Harry Ransom Humanities Research Center, The University of Texas at Austin.

ject: to communicate a universal message. The show was a panorama of humankind—with its vulnerability, heroism, and highest aspirations. While the music contained its share of Spanish flavor, *Man of La Mancha*'s message was never obscured. It came across most clearly in the hit number "The Quest" ("The Impossible Dream").

A very different sort of exoticism was explored in the 1966 musical *Cabaret*. The setting was Berlin around 1930, and much of the music by John Kander for scenes set in the Kit Kat Club was reminiscent of Kurt Weill's *Threepenny Opera* (1928). The cast even included Lotte Lenya, who had starred in the original *Threepenny Opera*. Although the main story line deals with Sally and Clifford, two American expatriates, the show was stolen by Joel Grey in the part of the cabaret's decadent master of ceremonies. Against a background of rising Nazism ("Tomorrow Belongs to Me"), an intimate, tense love story was told. Scenes on the stage of the Kit Kat Club provided necessary relief and were a natural setting for production numbers. The film version of *Cabaret*, released in 1972, starred Liza Minnelli as Sally and retained Joel Grey in his original part.

John Kander explored ethnicity more deeply in his score for *Zorba* (1968). Audiences were already familiar with the best-selling novel and motion picture entitled *Zorba the Greek*. The story dealt with life in a Greek mining village. More particularly, it had to do with a big, lovable bumbler named Zorba, a character who had been created by Anthony Quinn for the screen version. The musical version featured Hershel Bernardi, but in the 1983 revival Quinn re-created the role. The show's message and spirit—a zest for living—came across particularly well in Zorba's closing number, "I Am Free."

History and Biography

Other Broadway creators turned to the retelling of historical events and famous lives. In 1969 the play with music *1776* was brought to the stage. Book, music, and lyrics were written by Sherman Edwards. The story, of course, dealt with the first Continental Congress and the forging of the Declaration of Independence. It may seem odd to imagine Thomas Jefferson and Benjamin Franklin singing on a Broadway stage, but the entire show was conceived and executed with such mastery that the music served only to heighten the momentous event. *Pippin* (1972), with quasi-rock music by Stephen Schwartz, was built around the son of Charlemagne. Dance was the real focus of the show, however, thanks to the dynamic choreography of Bob Fosse and the electrifying dancing of Ben Vereen.

The portrayal of the lives of twentieth-century personages was another direction taken in the book musicals of the 1960s and 1970s. Three of these were built around famous performers in show business. In the vanguard of this trend was *Gypsy* (1959), with music by Jule Styne and lyrics by Stephen Sondheim. The book was based on the autobiography of Gypsy Rose Lee, famous burlesque queen. Ethel Merman, playing a stage mother, was the hit of the show, which was also remembered for "Everything's Coming Up Roses."

Next came another musical about a famous lady of entertainment, Fanny Brice. *Funny Girl* (1964), with music by Jule Styne and lyrics by Bob Merrill, gave Barbra Streisand her first Broadway lead in the title role. Her portrayal of the Broadway and vaudeville comedienne was considered by the critics to be phenomenal. A number of Streisand's songs from the show became popular, including the Fanny Brice song, "Second-Hand Rose," as well as "Don't Rain on My Parade" and "People."

George M! (1968) was the nostalgic, razzmatazz dance musical about George M. Cohan. All thirty-two songs in the show were authentic Cohan pieces. (See the section "Comedy and the Yankee Doodle Boy," above.) Joel Grey captured Cohan's jaunty, cocky personality, and Grey's singing and dancing were lauded by the critics.

The trend toward biography appears to have been brought to a close with *Evita* (1979) by Andrew Lloyd Webber and Tim Rice. This show, with its nearly continuous music, bordered on opera. The book was based on the unlikely subject of Eva Perón, the wife of an infamous Argentine dictator. "Don't Cry for Me, Argentina" was the show's most prominent song.

Rock on the American Stage

Once the style of Rock music had superseded Tin Pan Alley in the arenas of radio and the record business, its appearance in the American musical theater was fairly predictable. Only the timetable was in doubt, since the market for live and recorded American musicals has always been an older age group than that of "youth music," such as Rock. The first introduction of the newer style was actually a satire on the Rock 'n' Roll craze of the late 1950s. *Bye Bye Birdie* (1960), a show with songs by Charles Strouse and Lee Adams, concerned a singer of the Elvis Presley type who was about to enter the army (as Presley did around that time). The singer, Conrad Birdie, was the only character in the show to be given anything like rock to sing, and then it was a ballad, "One Last Kiss." *Bye Bye Birdie* was Gower Champion's debut as a director, and the show's most memorable song was not the rock ballad but a Broadway-style tune, "A Lot of Livin' to Do."

Rock Musicals

The introduction into a musical of a more genuine type of Rock had to wait another seven years until the first production of *Hair* (1967). The famous "tribal love-rock musical" first opened in a theater in lower Manhattan for a limited run, but was subsequently moved to Cheetah, a large Broadway discotheque. In a revised version, *Hair* opened on Broadway in 1968. The show had such a thin plot and such a wide variety of songs and singers that it was almost a revue. The songs dealt with the concerns of the young during the 1960s: military service, drugs, sex, money, religion, activism, and so forth. *Hair* was iconoclastic in many ways, the most notorious being an imaginatively lighted, symbolic "nude" scene. The tremendous success of *Hair* on Broadway sparked some concurrent productions in major U.S. cities, notably Los Angeles.

The score of *Hair* consisted of songs with music by Galt MacDermot and lyrics by Gerome Ragni and James Rado. Several of these were recorded singly and made into popular hits, notably "Aquarius," "Let the Sun Shine In," "Good Morning, Starshine," and "Easy to Be Hard." The show was a tremendous hit abroad, particularly in London, where it was given nearly 2,000 performances. Oddly, the film version of *Hair* did not appear until 1979, by which time its style and topical interest seemed faded.

In the same year that *Hair* reached Broadway a second Rock musical was produced. *Your Own Thing*, by Hal Hester and Danny Apollinar, was an adaptation into a contemporary setting of Shakespeare's *Twelfth Night*. In place of the traditional mistaken identity the authors substituted the long-haired "unisex" look of the time. *Your Own Thing* was an off-Broadway show, and it had the distinction of being the first such musical to win the New York Drama Critics' Circle Award.

A second Rock musical adaptation of Shakespeare, *Two Gentlemen of Verona*, made its bow in 1971. The show was created for the New York Shakespeare Festival, held in Central Park during the summer, and it proved so popular that it moved to Broadway in the fall. This represented Galt MacDermot's second Rock musical score (*Hair* being the first), and he collaborated on it with lyricist John Guare. *Two Gentlemen of Verona* and its creators won several awards, including the Tony for best musical score.

During the 1970s a revival of interest in the Rock 'n' Roll culture of the 1950s generated a ready-made audience for the musical *Grease*. The show originated in a Chicago community theater in 1971, but in 1972 it was somewhat revised and moved to New York for a phenomenal Broadway run of over 2,500 performances. The characters in this musical were "greasers" and their "chicks," high school adolescents of the James Dean/Sandra Dee era, and the story involves teenage dating and social mores of that time. While no particular song from the show became popular, the musical itself was enormously successful. A film version of *Grease*, featuring John Travolta and Olivia Newton-John, was released in 1978, and *Grease 2*, a film sequel, appeared in 1982.

The musical style of the Rock shows mentioned thus far was of a "mainstream" sort: generally rather "white," with a sprinkling of rhythm and blues or latin influence. However, in early 1975 Broadway was taken by storm by a completely black-style musical score which animated a most unusual production: *The Wiz*. The book of *The Wiz* was a travesty on L. Frank Baum's *The Wonderful Wizard of Oz* (1900) and its subsequent film adaptation (1939). The story was set in Harlem, and the entire cast was black. The attractive score by Charlie Smalls became immediately infectious. Opportunities for dance were natural and frequent in the show, seen particularly in its most popular number, "Ease on Down the Road." A film adaptation was made of *The Wiz* (1978), featuring performances by Diana Ross, Michael Jackson, Sidney Lumet, Nipsey Russell, Mabel King, Lena Horne, and Richard Pryor.

Rock Operas

In 1968 *Tommy* was hailed as the first "Rock opera." Written by Peter Townshend and other members of The Who, a British Rock group, *Tommy* was undoubtedly the longest and most ambitious Rock music undertaking of any type up to that time. It was operatic to the extent that it did contain a vivid story and continuous music. However, the work was originally conceived for The Who to perform in semistaged concert settings. Thus, it originated as something between an oratorio and an opera. Most of *Tommy*'s audiences first became acquainted with it through The Who's 1969 recording. The following year history was made when The Who gave two performances of *Tommy* at New York's Metropolitan Opera House. The tremendous appeal of this work generated a second complete recording, utilizing the London Symphony Orchestra and featuring such popular artists as Ringo Starr, Richard Harris, and Rod Stewart, *Tommy* was filmed in 1975 by Ken Russell in the manner of a true grand opera—no spoken dialogue and continuous music. The film featured members of The Who along with Ann-Margret, Jack Nicholson, and rock stars Eric Clapton, Tina Turner, and Elton John (who sang the very popular "Pinball Wizard").

Jesus Christ Superstar followed somewhat in the footsteps of *Tommy* by becoming popularly known first as an LP recording. However, this British work by Andrew Lloyd Webber and Tim Rice was intended to be a theatrical spectacle, and so it was mounted on Broadway in 1971. On its own merits the show became a great success, but it was helped by the religious controversy which also attended it. The story was that of the Passion, a dramatic enactment of the last days of Christ. Biblical characters such as Judas and Mary Magdalene sang songs that portrayed them in a human, emotional manner easily perceived in songs like "I Don't Know How to Love Him." Critics gave the New York production mixed reviews, but a subsequent presentation in London lasted over six years, becoming the longest-running musical in British theater history. A motion-picture version of *Jesus Christ Superstar* was released in 1973, and there have been stage revivals and a television production since that time. With its continuous music, unique character development, and broad variety of numbers, *Jesus Christ Superstar* ranks as a true Rock opera.

One other theatrical Rock creation should be mentioned in this context, because it was based on the same story as *Jesus Christ Superstar* and it was produced in the same year, 1971. The show was *Godspell*, and it featured a musical score by Stephen Schwartz, who had been the composer of *Pippin*. *Godspell* was a "clown" revue, and Jesus was portrayed as a kind of innocent clown. The style of the music was quite mild compared with previous Rock musicals and consisted principally of the Folk and Folk-Rock genres associated with "Contemporary Christian" popular music. In spite of adverse criticism, *Godspell* had a long New York run and a successful original cast recording.

Stephen Sondheim

In nearly every decade of the American musical theater one or two preeminent figures have emerged. Around World War I Irving Berlin was the undisputed master of revue song material. During the 1920s George Gershwin's jazzy style blazed new trails, while Jerome Kern became the dominant composer. Cole Porter owned the 1930s. The leaders during the 1940s were Rodgers and Hammerstein, but in the course of the 1950s they had to share that position with Lerner and Loewe. There was no single figure representing the 1960s, since that was a time of rapid change, reform, and new production methods. However, during that decade there emerged a composer-lyricist who would go on to dominate the scene during the 1970s: Stephen Sondheim.

Sondheim received his first exposure to professional musical theater while he was a graduate student at Columbia University studying composition under Milton Babbitt. Arthur Laurents, who was writing the book for *West Side Story* at the time, heard some of Sondheim's theatrical songs. Laurents brought Sondheim's work to Leonard Bernstein, who was enthusiastic and immediately made Sondheim the lyricist for the new show. Following *West Side Story*, Sondheim was engaged to write the lyrics for *Gypsy*.

Sondheim's continuing desire to compose led to *A Funny Thing Happened on the Way to the Forum*, which opened in May 1962 and ran for more than 1,000 performances. In *Anyone Can Whistle* (1964) Sondheim first experimented with using the orchestral accompaniment of a song to ironically belie a character's inner feelings. During the following two years he contributed the lyrics to Richard Rodgers' *Do I Hear a Waltz?* and the Mary Rodgers musical *The Mad Show*.

In 1970 Sondheim returned to Broadway as composer-lyricist for *Company*, the first of several collaborations with director-producer Harold Prince. These would all be "concept" shows, in which the exposition of a central theme would take precedence over the story line. In *Company* the theme was urban living with its stresses, loneliness, and compulsive but superficial friendships.

The next of Sondheim's works, *Follies* (1971), was given the Drama Critics' Circle Award. It concerned a reunion of ladies who at one time performed together in a series of Ziegfeld-style follies shows. The concept behind the show was the conflict between illusion and reality.

Sondheim's *A Little Night Music* (1972), a musical play, was based on Ingmar Bergman's 1955 bedroom farce film, *Smiles of a Summer Night*. The underlying themes of this turn-of-the-century story were the problems of aging and marital fidelity. *A Little Night Music* contained "Send in the Clowns," the first hit song for which Sondheim had written both music and lyrics.

Pacific Overtures (1976) followed more experimental and epic routes than any previous effort by Sondheim. The concept entailed tracing the westernization of Japan from Commodore Perry's arrival in 1853 up to the present-day commercialized society. The form of the play was a Western adaptation of traditional Japanese Kabuki theater, and the style of the music also bore Japanese traits.

Sondheim has been quoted as saying, "I *have* to go for something I haven't done before. The result is people don't know what to expect from show to show." That certainly was true of the operetta *Sweeney Todd*, staged in 1979. The story, set in nineteenth-century Dickensian England, was the grisly tale of "The Demon Barber of Fleet Street," involving revenge, murder, and cannibalism. Musically, this was Sondheim's most adventurous score. Vocal lines given to the demented Sweeney were often jagged and expressionistic. The somewhat contrapuntal orchestral score was generously peppered with modern dissonance, recalling the composer's academic training. The show ran on Broadway for more than 550 performances and was videotaped for broadcast over cable TV.

Merrily We Roll Along opened in 1981. The show's retrogressive twenty-five-year story line, derived from a 1934 play by Moss Hart, is reflected in the musical treatment as well. The composer has spoken of "musical motifs which could be modified over the course of the years, extended and developed, reprised, fragmented, and then presented to the audience in reverse: extensions first, reprises first, fragments first."

Next came *Sunday in the Park with George* (1984). The framework of the show is a series of vignettes based loosely on the work of pointillist painter Georges Seurat. The show is an inquiry into the creative forces that drive the artist. (For painter Seurat, read composer/writer Sondheim.) The musical won the Pulitzer Prize for drama and has been videotaped for cable TV. *Into the Woods* (1987), which also won several awards, revises the endings of traditional fairy tales, showing that the characters do not necessarily "live happily ever after."

During the first half of the 1990s Sondheim became a culture hero. (*The Sondheim Review*, a quarterly journal even appeared, focusing on productions and record reviews of his music.) He wrote two musicals during that time. *Assas-*

sins (1991) echoed the dark, macabre side of Sondheim's approach. It dealt with the men and women who have attempted, successfully or not, to take the lives of American presidents between the years 1865–1981. Savagely satirical and often grotesque, the show sought to explore the psychology of the assassins without sounding any clear moral. The story of *Passion* (1994) came to Sondheim from Ettore Scola's 1981 film, *Passione d'Amore*, which is based on a 19th-century Italian novel. In it, an ugly and sickly Italian woman persuades a handsome army captain to write a love letter to her, the musical setting of which is the show's centerpiece. For the love triangle that develops, Sondheim provides a different, more rhapsodic music than ever before. The *New York Times* noted that "Sondheim's usual sophisticated cool has been replaced by unembarrassed commitment."

The shows of Stephen Sondheim, with their musical experimentation and psychological probing, have frequently made audiences uncomfortable. Sondheim has had to pay a price for his innovations, since none of his musicals have become long-running blockbusters. Nevertheless, he has won a preeminent position in the American musical theater. And, because of the artistic doors which Sondheim has dared to open, he has inspired younger composers to strike out in newer, more contemporary directions, often far outside the mainstream traditions of Broadway.

New Composers and New Directions

Following the "concept" formula, several composers during the 1970s attempted to replicate the success of Stephen Sondheim. The most successful of these shows was *A Chorus Line* (1975), with music by Marvin Hamlisch and lyrics by Edward Kleban. This musical (played without intermission) explores the lives and psyches of its characters, who are auditioning for the chorus line of a fictional Broadway show. *A Chorus Line* won the Pulitzer Prize and became the longest-running Broadway show of all time. A film version was released in 1985.

The blockbuster approach to producing musicals became, for economic reasons, more rampant than ever during the 1970s and 1980s. Producers, looking for the "sure thing," chose musicals which followed a number of supposedly tried-and-true routes. The feature these shows all had in common was familiarity—either in musical style or in subject matter. One trend was to make a new musical by piecing together songs and other musical material written by some famous jazz-oriented composer. Probably the earliest of these revues was *Ain't Misbehavin'* (1977), based on the music of pianist Fats Waller. The songs of Duke Ellington were featured in *Sophisticated Ladies* (1981), with Ellington's descendants helping to prepare the production. This was followed in 1983 by a collection of Gershwin melodies made into the book musical *My One and Only*. A relative of these was the play with music, *Ma Rainey's Black Bottom* (1984), which employed songs originally sung by the great blues singer in a dramatic context, and which won several awards.

The search for familiarity also resulted in the comic-strip musical. This approach had been tried successfully as early as 1956 with *Li'l Abner*. A far bigger success was achieved in 1977 with the production of *Annie*, based on the perennial comic strip "Little Orphan Annie." Music for this show was composed by Charles Strouse to lyrics by Martin Charnin, and the song "Tomorrow" was the show's hit tune. A lavish film version of *Annie* was released in 1982. A far less successful attempt at a comic-strip musical was *Doonesbury* (1983).

One of the freshest-sounding shows produced during the 1970s was *The Best Little Whorehouse in Texas* (1978), by newcomer composer-lyricist Carol Hall. The book (by Larry L. King and Peter Masterson) was based on a magazine article concerning the heyday of the "Chicken Ranch" brothel near Austin. Hall, who was from Abilene, incorporated elements of country and western music into the overall style of the show. This captivating musical was adapted for film in 1982, featuring Dolly Parton and Burt Reynolds. Another "down-home"-style show, but one built more on contemporary country music styles, was *Pump Boys and Dinettes* (1982).

The new era was not without its razzle-dazzle and its nostalgia. *Chicago* (1975) was billed as "a musical vaudeville" by John Kander and Fred Ebb, the team that had written *Cabaret* nearly ten years earlier. *Chicago* was based on a late 1920s play about jazz, flappers, and gangsters. The life and times of circus king P. T. Barnum during the period 1835–1880 served as the basis for *Barnum* (1980), with music by Cy Coleman. The settings for *Dreamgirls* (1982) were the early 1960s and early 1970s, and the featured characters were a trio of black soul singers à la The Supremes.

If there were a single formula for a successful musical in the 1980s, it would have to have been the combination of a creative, familiar-sounding vehicle coupled with expert direction and seasoned performers. Undoubtedly the most typical execution of this formula was the musical play *42nd Street* (1980). The book was based on a 1933 Hollywood musical. The music by Harry Warren to lyrics by Al Dubin consisted of a revival of older Tin Pan Alley and Broadway classic songs. Veteran success-maker Gower Champion directed, and the show starred Tammy Grimes, Jerry Orbach, and Carole Cook. *42nd Street* ran until early 1989.

The biggest hit of 1989 was *City of Angels* with a jazzy score by Cy Coleman and lyrics by David Zippel. Its original script was smart, sexy, and funny, spoofing both the private-eye novel and its movie counterpart in the 1940s. While *City of Angels* kept its distance from the audience, people took *The Secret Garden* (1991) right to their hearts. Based on Frances Hodgson Burnett's 1911 children's book, Marsha Norman's script and lyrics depicted a world where life's joys and sorrows have been suspended. Songs by Lucy Simon (sister of Carly Simon) enhanced the show's expression of spiritualism/mysticism.

In a spectacular marketing ploy, Disney studios brought its movie-musical blockbuster, *Beauty and the Beast*, to the Broadway stage in 1994. Pouring $14 million into the production itself and an additional $29 million into refurbishing the theater (for this and future Disney transformations), the studio successfully reversed the traditional process of taking Broadway musicals to Hollywood. This production also brought the work of composer Alan Menken and lyricist Howard Ashman back to the theater (*Little Shop of Horrors:* stage, 1982; film 1986). Costuming and stage design were particularly impressive in this show.

The European Connection

The number of musical hits and, indeed, the number of musical openings both on and off Broadway decreased significantly from the late 1970s to the mid-1990s. The main causes were spiraling production costs and attendant financial risks. Another factor has been the public's shifting entertainment habits, particularly with the impact of video media. The paucity of American shows was somewhat aided, however, by productions brought to Broadway from the London stage. These were dominated by the work of two composers—one British, the other French—Andrew Lloyd Webber and Claude-Michel Schönberg. The blend of European classicism and American popular culture is an extraordinary feature in the music of both. In fact, their shows, called "faux operas" by one critic, are actually popular operas written in a blend of contemporary and romantic idioms.

Lloyd Webber, who had made such an impact on the American musical theater with *Jesus Christ Superstar* and *Evita,* returned to the American stage in 1983 with the premiere of *Cats.* This work represented a totally new direction for Lloyd Webber, since its "book" was not a theatrical script at all but rather a collection of witty poems by T. S. Eliot titled *Old Possum's Book of Practical Cats.* Since *Cats* incorporated far more dance movement and ensemble singing than Lloyd Webber's previous efforts, the show was more rhythmic and more intricately choral. As with many musicals since about 1970, the overall effect and success of *Cats* was largely attributable to its designer/director, in this case Trevor Nunn. The show has run on Broadway into the 1990s.

Lloyd Webber followed the homey simplicity of *Cats* with the soulless technology of *Starlight Express* (1985). Ostensibly based on the children's story, "The Little Engine That Could," this show dazzled audiences by numbers that included performers on roller skates gliding along a suspension bridge, cantilevered tracks on the theater walls, three video screens, a light show, and a variety of music from fifties rock to traditional gospel. Also coming to Broadway in 1985 was *Song and Dance,* Webber's revision of two earlier short works. The show was a variant of the familiar girl-meets-boy love story, focusing on Emma (played by Bernadette Peters), a new-wave English groupie, and Joe (Christopher d'Amboise), a nice kid from Nebraska. The first act featured Emma's singing the second Joe's dancing. Pursuing their ambitions in New York, the couple finally unites after suffering disillusionment in a hard world.

The phenomenal success of Lloyd Webber's *Phantom of the Opera* (1987) has been due in great part to its innovative production design. This is not to degrade the music, which is impressive. Composer and designer succeeded in transforming a 1911 thriller into a macabre romance, a musical love story with the sweeping style of European opera. *Phantom* has enjoyed huge success both on Broadway and through road shows.

Lloyd Webber's next two shows have been successful, though not to the degree of *Phantom*. *Aspects of Love* (1989), based on a David Garnett novel from the 1950s, followed five lovers across three generations. The score, which made more use of recurring melodies than any previous Lloyd Webber show, was described by one critic as "old romanticism with a new sincerity." Based on Billy Wilder's 1950 film classic, *Sunset Boulevard* (1994) was Lloyd Webber's stage adaptation about a demented, retired silent movie star who still believes she is famous. With Glenn Close playing the lead, *Sunset Boulevard* scored a dramatic and musical success. Critics hailed the show's music, which contains two notable songs, "With One Look" and "As If We Never Said Goodbye."

Transforming the Victor Hugo classic, *Les Misérables*, into a three-act popular opera libretto was risky business for writer Alain Boublil. Nonetheless, that is what he did for composer Claude-Michel Schönberg. The Paris production was mounted in 1980. Two years later the team began to revise the show for its 1985 London smash run. The Broadway production opened to enormous acclaim in 1987. *Les Misérables* the musical, like *Les Misérables* the book, has reached a worldwide audience, having played in more than twenty countries to about twenty million people.

Schönberg and Boublil followed that triumph with the adaptation of an opera from the standard repertoire, Puccini's *Madame Butterfly*. Boublil updated the story, placing it in Viet Nam during the fall of Saigon. Opening in London in 1989 and on Broadway in 1991, *Miss Saigon* was the story of a Vietnamese bar girl who falls in love with an American marine, a "two-bit hustler" who deals in fake Rolex watches. Amid the nightmare of war, the drama focused on the unlikely relationship between lovers who exist worlds apart. As with many shows of recent vintage, spectacular stage effects were the rule, including a helicopter that actually took off.

It has been cynically suggested that the American musical theater has become dominated by directors and choreographers since the 1970s. One corollary to that idea is that composers, lyricists, and theatrical writers have become no more than artisans, turning out rough vehicles for production people to mold into finished shows. There are even those pessimistic enough to declare the American musical theater virtually dead.

However, if we reflect on the work of the truly outstanding creators in the American musical theater during recent years, gross exceptions to the theory are readily apparent. Shows composed by the likes of Sondheim, Lloyd Webber, and Hall display that spark of superb creativity that illuminates every aspect of their best works. As long as that spark continues to be nurtured we can surely look to a continued life for the American musical theater.

Year	Title	Composer	Lyricist
1735	Flora (British ballad opera)		
1828	Hamlet (burlesque)		
1866	The Black Crook (adaptation of songs)		
1874	Evangeline (burlesque)		
1879	The Mulligan's Guard's Ball	Braham	Harrigan
1887	The Little Tycoon	Sousa	Spenser
1890	A Trip to Chinatown	Gaunt	Hoyt
	Robin Hood	de Koven	Smith
1903	Babes in Toyland	Herbert	MacDonough
1904	Little Johnny Jones	Cohan	Cohan
1905	Mlle. Modiste	Herbert	Blossom
1906	Forty-five Minutes from Broadway	Cohan	Cohan
	George Washington Jr.	Cohan	Cohan
1906	The Red Mill	Herbert	Blossom
1907	Ziegfeld Follies (revue: first year)		
1912	The Firefly	Friml	Harbach
	The Passing Show (revue: revival)		
1915	The Blue Paradise	Romberg	Reynolds
1917	Maytime	Romberg	Johnson Young Wood
1918	Yip, Yip, Yaphank	Berlin	Berlin
1919	George White's Scandals (revue: first year)		
1921	Blossom Time	Schubert Romberg	Donnelly
1924	Lady Be Good	G. Gershwin	I. Gershwin
	Rose-Marie	Friml	Harbach Hammerstein
	The Student Prince	Romberg	Donnelly
1925	The Vagabond King	Friml	Hooker Post
1926	The Desert Song	Romberg	Harbach Hammerstein
	Oh, Kay!	G. Gershwin	I. Gershwin

Figure 11-1. Table of selected American musicals.

Year	Title	Composer	Lyricist
1927	Funny Face	G. Gershwin	I. Gershwin
	Show Boat	Kern	Hammerstein
1928	The New Moon	Romberg	Hammerstein
			Mandel
			Schwab
	The Three Musketeers	Friml	Grey
			Wodehouse
1930	Girl Crazy	G. Gershwin	I. Gershwin
	Strike up the Band	G. Gershwin	I. Gershwin
1931	Of Thee I Sing	G. Gershwin	I. Gershwin
1932	Face the Music	Berlin	Berlin
	Gay Divorce	Porter	Porter
1933	As Thousands Cheer	Berlin	Berlin
	Let 'Em Eat Cake	G. Gershwin	I. Gershwin
1934	Anything Goes	Porter	Porter
1935	Porgy and Bess	G. Gershwin	I. Gershwin
1936	Johnny Johnson	Weill	Green
1938	The Cradle Will Rock	Blitzstein	Blitzstein
	Knickerbocker Holiday	Weill	Anderson
1942	This Is the Army	Berlin	Berlin
1943	Oklahoma!	Rodgers	Hammerstein
1944	On the Town	Bernstein	Comden
			Green
1945	Carousel	Rodgers	Hammerstein
1946	Annie Get Your Gun	Berlin	Berlin
1947	Brigadoon	Loewe	Lerner
	Finian's Rainbow	Lane	Harburg
	Street Scene	Weill	Hughes
1948	Kiss Me, Kate	Porter	Porter
1949	Lost in the Stars	Weill	Anderson
	Regina	Blitzstein	Blitzstein
	South Pacific	Rodgers	Hammerstein
1950	Call Me Madam	Berlin	Berlin
	The Golden Apple	Moross	La Touche
	Guys and Dolls	Loesser	Loesser
1951	The King and I	Rodgers	Hammerstein
1953	Can-Can	Porter	Porter
	Wonderful Town	Bernstein	Comden
			Green
1955	Silk Stockings	Porter	Porter

Figure 11-1. Continued.

American Musical Theater: History and Musical Trends

Year	Title	Composer	Lyricist
1956	Candide	Bernstein	Wilbur
	The Most Happy Fella	Loesser	Loesser
	My Fair Lady	Loewe	Lerner
1957	The Music Man	Willson	Willson
	West Side Story	Bernstein	Sondheim
1959	Flower Drum Song	Rodgers	Hammerstein
	Gypsy	Styne	Sondheim
	Once Upon a Mattress	Mary Rodgers	Barer
1960	Bye Bye Birdie	Strouse	Adams
	Camelot	Loewe	Lerner
	The Fantasticks	Schmidt	Jones
	The Sound of Music	Rodgers	Hammerstein
1961	How to Succeed in Business Without Really Trying	Loesser	Loesser
1962	A Funny Thing Happened on the Way to the Forum	Sondheim	Sondheim
	I Can Get It For You Wholesale	Rome	Rome
	No Strings	Rodgers	Rodgers
1964	Anyone Can Whistle	Sondheim	Sondheim
	Fiddler on the Roof	Bock	Harnick
	Funny Girl	Styne	Merrill
	Hello, Dolly!	Herman	Herman
1965	Do I Hear a Waltz?	Rodgers	Sondheim
	Man of La Mancha	Leigh	Darion
	On a Clear Day You Can See Forever	Lane	Lerner
1966	The Apple Tree	Bock	Harnick
	Cabaret	Kander	Ebb
	I Do! I Do!	Schmidt	Jones
1967	Hair	MacDermot	Ragni Rado
1968	George M! (revival of songs)	Cohan	Cohan
	Your Own Thing	Hester	Apolinar
	Zorba	Kander	Ebb
1969	1776	Edwards	Edwards
1970	Company	Sondheim	Sondheim

Figure 11-1. Continued.

Year	Title	Composer	Lyricist
1971	Follies	Sondheim	Sondheim
	Jesus Christ Superstar	Lloyd Webber	Rice
	Two Gentleman of Verona	MacDermot	Guare
1972	A Little Night Music	Sondheim	Sondheim
1975	A Chorus Line	Hamlisch	Kleban
	The Wiz	Smalls	Smalls
1976	Pacific Overtures	Sondheim	Sondheim
1977	Ain't Misbehavin' (revival of songs)	Waller	(various)
	Annie	Strouse	Charnin
1978	The Best Little Whorehouse in Texas	Hall	Hall
1979	Evita	Lloyd Webber	Rice
	Sweeney Todd	Sondheim	Sondheim
1980	42nd Street (revival of songs)	Warren	Dubin
1981	Merrily We Roll Along	Sondheim	Sondheim
	Sophisticated Ladies (revival of songs)	Ellington	(various)
1983	Cats	Lloyd Webber	Eliot
	My One and Only (revival of songs)	G. Gershwin	I. Gershwin
1984	Sunday in the Park with George	Sondheim	Sondheim
1986	The Mystery of Edwin Drood	Holmes	Holmes
1987	Into the Woods	Sondheim	Sondheim
	The Phantom of the Opera	Lloyd Webber	Hart
	Les Misérables	C.-M. Schönberg	Boublil/Kretzmer
1989	City of Angels	Coleman	Zippel
	Aspects of Love	Lloyd Webber	Black/Hart
1991	Assassins	Sondheim	Sondheim
	Miss Saigon	Schönberg	Maltby/Boublil
	The Secret Garden	Simon	Norman
1994	Beauty and the Beast	Menken	Ashman
	Passion	Sondheim	Sondheim
	Sunset Boulevard	Lloyd Webber	Black/Hampton

Figure 11-1. Continued.

Review Questions

1. Name and describe three or four types of musical theater. Give one example of each from the repertoire.

2. Who were some famous composers of American operetta?

3. Name one famous song by George M.Cohan.

4. What were some characteristics of the songs of George Gershwin?

5. Name the "folk opera" with which Gershwin reached his peak.

6. Why was *Show Boat* the turning point in the history of American musical theater?

7. Compare features in shows by Cole Porter, Irving Berlin, and Kurt Weill, beginning in the 1930s.

8. Discuss some ways that *Oklahoma!* was innovative or revolutionary.

9. Name and discuss other shows written by Rodgers and Hammerstein.

10. Compare and contrast *My Fair Lady* and *The Music Man* as "period" pieces.

11. Compare and contrast *On the Town* and *Guys and Dolls* as shows with a New York setting.

12. Describe some features of *West Side Story* that may have led one critic to say that it began "a new age in the theater."

13. What was the effect of rising production costs on the style of musical theater during the 1960s?

14. Name the longest running musical show in history. The longest running *Broadway* musical?

15. What were some of the "exotic" places treated in musicals of the 1960s? Who were some of the historical personage in other shows?

16. Make a comparison between *Hair, Tommy,* and *Jesus Christ Superstar* as stage vehicles featuring Rock musical style.

17. Name and discuss a few of Sondheim's "concept" shows.
    Is *Passion* a concept show?

18. What were some of the new musical directions of the 1970s and 1980s?

19. Discuss musicals made from movies: *Beauty and the Beast* and *Sunset Boulevard.*

20. Discuss the work of Andrew Lloyd Webber from *Jesus Christ Superstar* to *Sunset Boulevard.*

21. Discuss *Les Misérables* and *Miss Saigon* as representing a new breed of popular opera.

12

Musical Shows: Creation, Production, Business

The American musical theater is one of the most collaborative fields in the arts. To begin, a creative collaboration must take place between a playwright, a lyricist, and a composer. Once a musical show is in rehearsal (and throughout its run), further collaboration must occur between these three, the producer, the performers, and all the production staff. The musical show also represents a collaboration between the arts. It is a true synthesis of drama, verse, music, design, and dance. The purpose of this chapter is to explore the synthesis and the process of musical theater, as well as to outline the business aspects of producing musical shows.

Creative Elements of a Musical Show

The Book

The script of a musical is called the "book." Another term meaning the same thing is "libretto." The latter term is derived from the long tradition of operatic librettos, which are the scripts of operas. Thus, the playwright who creates the book for a musical show is generally called the show's librettist.

The book must come first. Without a book the show's lyricist and composer would have no idea of what types of musical numbers to write or where they should be placed. Most books are derived from some existing source; very few are entirely original. In adapting an existing work, the librettist is compelled to discipline his work in several ways. One is that the dramatic action must be compressed to allow room for lyrical/musical expansion. The librettist must also create credible opportunities for the music (and dance) to be able to "open up" the story. Because of the need for economy, many of the subtleties of spoken plays must be put aside. A book must be simple, direct, and at times even obvious. Each important idea must be projected so that the audience picks it up at once. There simply is no time for recurrent statements.

A two-act structure is a tradition in comic musical theater that stretches back as far as the Italian comic *intermezzi* of the early eighteenth century. That tradition continues to be maintained in most American musical shows of all types, even when it overlengthens the second act. The Act I finale is crucial to the show's structure, since it must bring the problems in the story to a peak and convince the audience to return for the second act. Act II then proceeds to unravel and resolve those problems.

The book itself is made up of several elements. The most basic of these is the show's *concept*. The concept embodies the theme of the show, what the show represents or what it is all about. *Plot* and *action* may be considered a composite element. This element is really a sequence of situations (miniplots) which move the story forward and may generate opportunities for song or dance. The element of *characters* is essential to the plot/action of the book. The main characters must possess qualities which would interest and involve the audience. The successful book causes the audience to become so engrossed in the problems of the characters and plot that it dares not leave the theater until all has been resolved. Finally, the element of *dialogue* reveals the personality as well as the "sound" of each character. Attention must often be given to dialects, as well as to the rhythm and general pacing of speech between characters.

The Score

The totality of music in a show is called the score. This generally consists of an overture, songs, dance and production numbers, and special material. The composer's original draft of the score is generally a "piano-vocal" version written for the purpose of auditions and rehearsals. Generally, the full orchestral version will be developed later, during the rehearsal period. The overture to a show is often merely a pastiche of tunes from the show's songs and other music, arranged for the orchestra. Dance numbers are purely instrumental compositions, while production numbers are composed for chorus, dancers, and orchestra. Often production numbers contain parts for the principal characters as well. Some form of special orchestral material is usually required for a show. Common examples are the musical cues played while a change of scenery is in progress. If a show were to contain a pantomime scene accompanied by music, that part of the score would also be grouped with the "special material."

The Songs: Lyrics and Music

As explained in Chapter 2, a song has two basic components, words and melody. The poetic words of a song are called its lyric, and a writer of lyrics for the musical stage is called a lyricist. Because of the need for continuity between the dialogue of a show's book and its lyrics, it is not unusual for the author of the book to also function as lyricist. Oscar Hammerstein II and Alan Jay Lerner are prominent examples. It is less common for the composer of the show's score to also be its lyricist. Only a few composers have been sufficiently talented in both music and literature to perform these tasks equally well. Stephen Sondheim is a living example of a composer-lyricist.

Naturally, the main attractions of any musical show are its songs. Although originality and freshness of approach are highly valued, many songs can be placed in one (or more) of the traditional categories associated with theatrical tradition.

To start, the *opening number* of a show is frequently a production number designed to capture the audience's attention and interest them in what is to follow. This number must also project or suggest the overall concept of the show, which is as much a problem for the lyricist as for the composer. When done well, the opening number instantly expressed the show's concept and its general spirit. One prominent example is "Twenty Fans Were Turning" (*The Best Little Whorehouse in Texas*). Occasionally, the production number tradition for show openers has been replaced by something simpler. As mentioned in Chapter 11, this was carried out with great success by Richard Rodgers in his musicals *Oklahoma!* and *No Strings*.

Romantic love is probably the most popular theme in musical theater, and the *ballad* is its usual vehicle. Ballads are slow songs full of lyric richness. They sometimes help to expose the main characters of a show in an indirect way. On the other hand, the "I am" and "I want" categories expose inner feelings in a very direct, open manner. For example, the song "I'll Know" (*Guys and Dolls*) informs the audience about the hidden romantic desires of two principals, and a humorous approach to the "I am" type is found in the song, "I Cain't Say No" (*Oklahoma!*).

Some songs in musical shows are there chiefly for entertainment value. At least one *charm song* is included in nearly every traditionally constructed musical comedy. The function of the charm song is simply what the name suggests, to be charming and delightful. A prominent example of the charm song is "My Favorite Things" (*The Sound of Music*). Another entertaining category is the *comedy song*. Older musical comedies and revues would normally contain several of these. *West Side Story*, an otherwise completely serious show, contains just one of out-and-out comedy relief in the satirical song "Gee, Officer Krupke." Rhythmic propulsion is frequently a strong element in theatrical songs designed for entertainment, and the *rhythm song* is a category which exploits this feature. Most rhythm songs are written to be performed in a fast tempo, such as "Trouble" (*The Music Man*). However, the moderate speed and steady clip-clop rhythm of a horse's hooves helped to generate the rhythm/charm song, "Surrey with the Fringe on Top" (*Oklahoma!*).

Occasionally, a situation in the book of a musical will require that extensive music be used. The result is either a *musical scene* or an *ensemble*. In a musical scene the orchestra loosely underscores a sequence of spoken dialogue, perhaps interrupted at times by singing, and the scene generally climaxes with the singing of a duet. *Carousel* contains such scenes. A scene may also be sung from beginning to end in a tightly organized ensemble involving two or more characters. The "Tonight" scene from *West Side Story* is an outstanding example.

Theoretically, a hit song can originate at any moment in a musical show. However, very near the end of the evening is a favorite spot to place a possible hit. A song in that position is called an *eleven o'clock song*. Often this will be a ballad or at least in ballad tempo. A classic eleven o'clock song is "Send in the Clowns" (*A Little Night Music*).

Dance

The element of dance encompasses a wide range extending from a singer's simple movements to large production numbers involving the entire cast. The gamut of dance styles in the American musical theater is also extremely broad. Classic ballet, modern dance, jazz, ethnic, tap, ballroom, and acrobatic dance have all been used in one Broadway show or another. Some musicals (especially the "Play with Music" category) contain only a minimal amount of movement or no dance at all. In recent years, however, there has been a reemergence of "dance shows" with as much verve as seen in their stage and screen forerunners of the 1920s, 1930s, and 1940s. Shows such as *Cats* (1983) and *Song and Dance* (1985) owe a great deal of their success to the prominence of dance in the production.

Large dance production numbers are sometimes included for the purpose of pure *spectacle*, which is one reason audiences attend musicals. *Comedy* is another reason to include dance, since humorous dialogue can be easily extended into sight humor through dance routines.

However, there are also several functions of dance which are more meaningful. A dance number, such as may appear at the opening of a musical, is one of the best and most direct ways to express the *theme* and *style* of the show. The dance styles employed in two contrasting shows, say *West Side Story* and *Fiddler on the Roof*, give the audience an immediate picture of the cultural background of the characters involved in each of the shows. By extension, the *mood* and *atmosphere* of an individual scene can often be projected better through dance than through dialogue or song lyrics. That is because dance movement can take up where dialogue leaves off. It can expand a dramatic moment when words would be inappropriate; it can continue telling the story on a more purely symbolic level than words will allow. As an old French saying goes, "What can be spoken can be sung; what can be sung can be danced."

Design

A show's design concerns its visual impact and the integration of the physical aspects of the show with its book, lyrics, music, and dance. There are three areas of design: sets, costumes, and lighting. Designers are responsible to see that the style and overall concept of the show are carried out in every detail. A set designer must create stage sets that are both aesthetically "right" for the show and also practical. The acting and dancing spaces must be carefully planned, and account must be taken of the order and manner of scene changes. If the musical is a period piece or a show employing some exotic setting, set designers must perform research to work out a good stage representation of the time and place the book demands. Costume designers, likewise, must be concerned with authenticity. Their designs must be at once attractive, authentic, and practical. Costumes, especially for dancers and principal players, must be able to withstand many strenuous wearings. The lighting of a show is perhaps the most subtle area of design. Fundamentally, the lighting must show the set to its fullest advantage and must provide properly lighted acting and dancing spaces. Less obvious is the lighting designer's responsibility to create exact shadings of mood for individual scenes and to give emphasis to the presence of one or more characters when needed. While the element of design would appear to merely support the overall concept of a show, the work of an outstanding designer can actually influence one or more of the other elements.

Getting Started

As mentioned above, the musical show begins with a book. It is possible for a book to be an entirely original creation by the librettist. However, by far the majority of musicals that reach Broadway or off-Broadway are adaptations of preexisting material. Show writers (librettist, lyricist, and composer) who wish to have the musical rights to such material will need to request an "option" on it. That means that they will pay the copyright owner (or author) a fee, in return for which they will be granted exclusive rights to develop a musical adaptation. Options have a time limit, generally one year. Since an option can be costly, and getting a musical accepted for production is risky, some writers proceed without obtaining an option. They reason that if their work is accepted, the producer will obtain an option, and that will cover their efforts adequately. Alternatively, a producer may hold an option on some property and may put together the creative team himself, assigning work to a librettist, lyricist, and composer.

Finding a Producer and Backers

Writers without a producer may work on the musical for months or even years before they consider it ready for a hearing. Once that point is reached, it is time to find a producer. This is accomplished by making *presentations* of the show to all the producers who might be interested. The presentation itself is a compact, miniature version of the show designed to show off its best songs and other material. Putting together an effective presentation is an art in itself. In effect, a presentation is a merchandising "package," or sales tool. It generally runs less than an hour and is done in an informal style designed for a producer's office or living room.

Presentations are normally given by the composer and lyricist, with the possible assistance of one or two vocalists and perhaps a pianist. The most effective presentations are given live rather than on tape or videotape. The presence of and immediate contact with the writers is considered essential to stirring interest in a producer. Around eight songs are included in a presentation. These are sung with only a rough indication of the storyline narrated in between, and normally dialogue is avoided. A producer may initially audition a show presentation by himself, but if he becomes interested in the show, he may ask that the presentation be given again, this time in the presence of his advisers or business/creative associates.

Once a producer is found, another round of presentations follows. These are called backers' auditions. The producer invites potential investors to presentations of the show. After seeing it, they all discuss the show's possibilities. Backers' auditions continue until enough money has been raised to put the show through rehearsals, tryouts, and the first few weeks of the main run. Occasionally some producers, such as Harold Prince, have such an outstanding record of successes that backers wait to invest in one of their shows.

At the same time that the producer is working on capitalizing the show, he and his office staff begin making arrangements to proceed with production. If an option on preexisting material is necessary, that is obtained first. The producer must also option the actual musical from the writers. This reserves the property for the producer in return for a small stipend which helps the writers get by until the show opens and (hopefully) begins earning some real money. A few further business arrangements are made at this time, including renting a theater for rehearsals and the run of the show. A budget must be sketched, including rehearsal, tryout, and run periods. A promotional strategy may be worked out at this time, and this normally involves a press agent and perhaps also an advertising agency. Finally, and most importantly, the producer hires the remainder of the show's creative staff.

The Creative Staff

As mentioned above, the American musical theater is one of the most collaborative of art forms. Once the writers have fashioned the musical, it is subject to further adaptation, elaboration, and sometimes radical revision. These changes come about during rehearsal, tryout, and even occasionally during the run, and they are due to decisions made by the show's creative staff.

Figure 12–1 is an organizational chart showing the various areas of creative effort and the relationship between them. It may be noticed that, outside of the writers, the key staff members are the director, the musical director, and the production designer. Also, some staff positions have other functions included with them. For example, the choreographer has been placed with the director

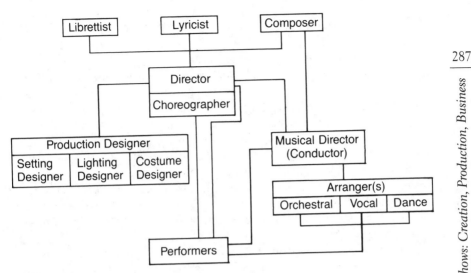

Figure 12-1. Creative staff for a Broadway musical theater production.

because of a trend for these functions to be handled by the same person, notably the case with Jerome Robbins, Bob Fosse, and Gower Champion. Grouped with the production designer come the designers of settings, lighting, and costumes. Again, these may be all different people, or the jobs may be combined—possibly into a single position. The arranging staff, which is supervised by the musical director, has the job of converting the composer's piano-vocal score and sketches into a finished orchestral score. Some scores may require three different arrangers, while others may be arranged by one person, and smaller productions may combine the arranging task with that of musical director. All members of the creative staff are hired with the approval of the writers.

Although the director handles or arbitrates most decisions during rehearsals, writers' contracts usually include a veto clause. This allows the writers to turn down any new suggestion from the rest of the creative staff. However, this provision is not a guarantee that all of the writers' new ideas will be accepted. Bringing a musical show to the stage requires a tremendous amount of give-and-take, and members of a show's creative staff are sometimes replaced because of insolvable disagreements.

The director is at the hub of the creative staff. The writers and the producer normally go through the director when introducing or responding to ideas for the show. The composer may be an exception to this rule when working with the musical director or arrangers on technical details in the score. There may also be times when the writers may need to confer with the choreographer or production designer about the practicality of an idea before discussing it with the director. However, the regulations of Actors Equity (the actors' union) forbid anyone but the director, the choreographer, or the musical director to deal directly with the performers in the show.

Rehearsals and Tryouts

The protocol and relationships mentioned above must be dealt with every day of a show's rehearsal period. Normally, this period lasts five weeks and is divided into two segments. The first week is devoted to dancers alone, and the remaining four weeks involves the total cast. During the hectic second phase, rehearsals may take place in several locations at once, not necessarily just in the theater. Dancers may be working in one rehearsal hall, while a few principal performers rehearse musical numbers in another. Meanwhile, staging rehearsals are taking place in the theater. Gradually, more and more of the show is put together on stage, culminating in the first run-through. This reveals the flaws, holes, and complete derailings which will need to be fixed before the tryout. Until then, rehearsal time will be divided between going over bits and pieces and running larger segments of the show.

At last the scheduled tryouts begin. For a Broadway production, these traditionally take place somewhere near New York. Boston and New Haven have been popular places for tryouts. Broadway shows normally also preview in New York before opening night. During tryout and preview performances, the producer and key members of the creative staff try to gauge the show. Often rewrites in the book must be done. Sometimes songs or even entire musical scenes need to be replaced quickly. The purpose of the tryout and preview is to iron out as many flaws and miscalculations as possible, so that the official New York opening will be received with favor by the public and the critics.

The "Run" and Follow-Up Productions

A show must usually be a critical success to attract audiences, and acceptance by audiences is necessary to a show's financial success. The initial success of a show can be measured by simple arithmetic. If income from ticket sales exceeds the total "running" expenses (see below), then the show has shown a profit. The total weekly overhead for a show is usually projected long ahead of time by the producer. Due to unforeseen circumstances, however, this figure must often be increased, sometimes alarmingly. If a sufficient profit margin can be realized, the production expenses incurred before the opening of the show will also be covered sooner or later, the backers may begin to see a good return on their investment. Five hundred consecutive performances has been a benchmark traditionally used to determine whether a show is a hit. Few shows today can break even in less than a year.

Once a show becomes (or promises to become) a hit, further theatrical productions usually follow. A long-running show usually generates one or more road companies which tour major U.S. cities. Prominent regional theaters and summer stock companies may also wish to produce the show sometime during or after the original run. Subsequent foreign productions of the most successful Broadway musicals are common, especially in London, where several long runs have taken place.

Business Aspects of Theatrical Production ———————

The rights of ownership in a musical show are covered by the copyright law in much the same way that the law covers individual songs. Initially, all rights reside with the "author(s)" (writers), who may license or assign the various rights to others. For musicals the right to perform is most important. Performance licensing for musicals is handled differently from individual songs or nondramatic works. Musical shows are considered "dramatic works," and the rights to present them in that form are called *grand rights*. The field of dramatic works, including musical shows, has its own group of performance licensing agents. Nondramatic performance rights to individual songs are called *small rights*, and these are normally handled like other songs—through ASCAP, BMI, or SESAC (see Chapter 2).

The right to dramatic performance is placed in the hands of the producer under the terms of a Dramatists Guild Minimum Basic Production Contract. While the guild is not a union for writers, it is an extremely powerful organization which has established several standard minimum fees and royalty rates which serve to protect writers. Several of the areas covered by the contract include optioning, royalties after opening, subsidiary rights, foreign productions, original cast recording, publishing, and film rights.

Optioning the Musical Show

Although the terms for optioning a nonmusical property for musical adaptation can be entirely negotiable, the Dramatists Guild provides certain hard minimums when it comes to the producer optioning the musical show itself. This option is generally for a one-year period, effective from the date the completed book and score are delivered. If the producer fails to mount the show within that period (or to fulfill all of the other contract provisions), the option is canceled and all rights revert to the writers. There are two possible methods for making option payments. The producer may make level monthly payments to be divided among the writers. Or, he may use a graduated scale. These funds are considered an advance against eventual royalties but are nonrefundable in case the producer defaults on the contract. Provisions for extending the option for an additional six months are sometimes included.

Royalties During the Initial Run

Writers' royalties are calculated on the basis of gross receipts for ticket sales, including receipts from tryouts. The writers as a group are given a minimum of 6 percent (but negotiable up to 8 percent). The show's director may earn 2 to 2½ percent (more if he is also the choreographer), while the choreographer and production designer each receive about 2 percent. If preexisting material was used for the book or the concept of the show, an additional 1 percent royalty is normal. A star performer's contract may also call for a percentage of gross receipts.

Other "Running" Expenses

Royalties are just a part of the enormous expenses connected with maintaining a show on stage. Long before the opening the producer will have had to project a weekly budget. This is constantly subject to adjustment as the actual costs are incurred. Figure 12–2 represents areas of the weekly "running" expenses of a musical show (excluding royalties).

The theater rental can take the form of a straight percentage, around 25 to 30 percent, or a combination of actual operating expenses plus a percentage (around 10 percent). Salaries for supporting actors, dancers, production personnel, and musicians are mostly set by unions. The producer's "management fee" is generally in the 1 to 2 percent range. Payments to backers of the show are not figured here. These are somewhat more complicated and can involve payments from both gross and net income.

Subsidiary Rights

Once a musical show has opened in New York and has played for twenty-one consecutive performances, the Dramatists Guild contract permits the producer to activate a group of potentially lucrative activities known as "subsidiary rights." Initially, the producer's share of income from these is 40 percent and the writers' share is 60 percent, but the producer's share will begin to decline after ten years. Sources of subsidiary income include touring companies and subsequent productions of it by companies other than the original New York cast and authorized touring companies. Additional subsidiary uses of a show could be adaptations for radio, TV, and film; foreign language productions; recordings; and commercial uses in which the name of the show and its characters may be used to manufacture games, toys, figures, and other novelties.

THEATER RENTAL
SALARIES
   Stars
   Leading Players and Supporting Players
   Dancers
   Creative Staff (some against royalties)
   Stage Director and Production Crew
   Pit Musicians
ADMINISTRATION
   Production Assistants
   Office Staff
   Producer's "Management Fee"
PROMOTION
   Public Relations
   Advertising

Figure 12-2. Areas of weekly "running" expenses of a musical show.

Domestic Productions

There is a variety of theater activity other than the New York stage. The most prestigious type is *regional theater*. This is usually a noncommercial endeavor that takes place in a prominent metropolitan theater. One example is the Mark Taper Forum in Los Angeles. Casts are professional, and productions are supported by ticket sales, donations, and foundation grants. Several Broadway shows were first presented in regional theaters and then moved to Broadway.

Another type of theatrical activity which operates in a regional area is the *dance and opera company*. Often a production will be mounted in the company's home theater and then toured through other cultural centers in the region. A very successful example is the Los Angeles Civic Light Opera, which regularly takes its productions to San Francisco. Such companies are generally non-profit enterprises.

Summer stock is a type of commercial theater activity which can be found in summer vacation spots and resort areas. It gives the public a chance to see high-quality shows (often outdoors), and it gives many professional performers an opportunity to work during New York's off-season. While most shows produced in summer stock are in the well-known, "stock" repertoire, audiences may occasionally see new, Broadway-bound productions.

A novel theatrical development has been *dinner theater*. For the price of admission audiences are treated to a full-course meal followed by a show, which they see from their tables. Besides plays, the repertoire of these houses includes musicals from the mainstream repertoire (for example, *South Pacific* and *The Music Man*). Sometimes the length of the show is reduced slightly to allow time for eating and drinking. The dinner-theater circuit is entirely professional, and usually features well-known older performers from stage and films. Many dinner theaters are part of a chain.

There is also wide variety of amateur theater activity in the United States. This category includes *community (grass-roots) theater, showcase theater, children's* and *educational theater*, and *university theater*. Although musical productions mounted by these companies do not usually pay their personnel, a licensing fee must be paid for each performance given of a copyrighted show.

Foreign Productions

Several successful Broadway musical shows have gone on to long runs in London. For that reason, the Dramatists Guild treats productions in the British Isles differently from other foreign productions. The original producer normally has the right to produce the show in the British Isles himself or, with the consent of the writers, may assign production to another party. The writers' collective royalty from such a run is set at 6 percent. The writers themselves have control over any other foreign productions, but they must pay the original producer 40 percent of net proceeds from those productions.

Publishing and Original Cast Recording

Nonstage usage of a hit musical is sometimes even more lucrative than the original run. Sooner or later a music publisher and a record company will become involved. These often obtain rights to a score by becoming initial investors in the show. Other shows have to be "sold" to publishers, usually before the show reaches the New York stage. In that case, the publisher's function will be similar to popular music publishing. The publisher will commercially exploit the music in any way possible and manage the royalty income that results. Print music sales are one possibility (see Chapter 10). However, the publisher can also be influential in obtaining recordings of individual songs from a show or even the original cast album.

An original cast album will be released following the opening weeks of a successful Broadway or off-Broadway show. Occasionally, the reputations of the writers, director, and star(s) are sufficiently strong to justify the simultaneous release of the recording. In addition to writer and producer royalties, the record company pays the publisher a "mechanical" licensing fee for each musical number on the album to the publisher of the musical score. Unlike pop songs, compulsory licensing does not apply to dramatic music. The copyright owner (publisher or publisher/writers) has the exclusive right to grant or refuse permission to make recordings, use the music on jukeboxes, and produce it over public broadcasting.

Film Rights

The sale of film rights to Broadway musicals has become quite rare in recent years, but when it happens, negotiations are the producer's job. The exclusive film rights to a musical show are contracted for an outright, fixed amount. In addition, there may be other contracts or riders to cover such matters as the soundtrack recording from the film. Today, film rights are sold for extremely high prices because film producers will not take on anything less than a blockbuster. For example, film rights to the show *Annie* were sold for a record $9.5 million.

The production of musical theater is a tremendously high-risk activity. Until a show has been firmly accepted critically, there is risk at every step. Writers, especially new ones, must sacrifice time (and money) in order to take the chance that their show will be optioned by a producer. In turn, the producer and his backers invest their resources in the show, following the best information and advice they can obtain, but mixing these with a large amount of pure faith. The creative staff, performers, and crew go into a show with high hopes for its success but also with the realistic knowledge that the show could easily close after opening night.

Compounding these risks are the ever-rising costs connected with producing a show. Not only have union scales increased, but the costs of materials, services, and theater operation have shot up dramatically each year since the 1950s. This is the principal reason that the number of Broadway and off-Broadway openings—plays as well as musicals—have steadily declined during the past few decades.

Nevertheless, the musical stage is still a vibrant, thriving part of twentieth-century show business. Writers, producers, performers, and production staff continue to take the risks. Perhaps that is because there is still a hungry market for clearly outstanding talent on the New York stage and elsewhere in the American theater. Superior dramatic-musical talents, who are willing to pay the price of sacrifice and risk, can still be heard and given their chance to succeed.

Review Questions

1. What are the main elements of a show's "book"?

2. What different types of music can the score of a show contain?

3. Describe some of the types of show songs.

4. What purposes can dance serve in a show?

5. Briefly describe the three areas of show design.

6. What is an option? Who normally asks for and who normally grants options for original material? For a musical show?

7. How much of a show takes place during a backer's audition?

8. Briefly describe what a director does.

9. What is the purpose of tryout and preview?

10. Without considering advance ticket sales, how long does it usually take before a show breaks even?

11. How much of the show's gross receipts can the writers expect to receive?

12. For most subsidiary rights, what is the usual split between writers and producer?

13. What is the difference between normal compulsory licensing of pop songs and the licensing of theatrical music?

14. What was the largest sum ever paid for the film rights to a Broadway musical? What was the name of that musical?

13

American Concert Life and Opera: History and Musical Trends

Much of the material in this book thus far has been concerned with the world of "popular," or "commercial," music. While many consider the music for films and Broadway musicals to be somewhat more elevated, none of those areas of American music are part of the long-standing European tradition of *concert music*, often called "art music" or, more generically, "classical music." The American concert and operatic stage have a distinctive history, and their contemporary audiences differ demographically from the core audience for most segments of the popular field.

Portions of Chapter 1 discussed classical music and opera in the recording industry; Chapter 4 alluded to specialization in management for classical artists; and Chapters 5 and 6 referred to the place of concert music and opera in broadcast history and programming practices. The principal thrust of the present chapter will be the history of live performance.

The Beginnings

When the earliest settlers reached Jamestown in 1607 and Plymouth in 1620, a cultivated concert life was probably farthest from their minds. Survival and the development of new colonies took top priority. It is true that the early New England Pilgrims and Puritans had a great love of music, as shown in their tradition of psalm singing. But theirs was an austere tradition, one in which the participation of instruments was strictly forbidden. Throughout the seventeenth century there was virtually no "art music" of any consequence in the new colonies.

By the beginning of the eighteenth century four main cultural centers had developed: Boston, Philadelphia, New York, and Charleston. Williamsburg, Virginia, also became an active center for amateur music-making during the eighteenth century. However, the first paid public concert in the colonies took place in Boston on December 30, 1731. Newspaper advertisements for the event placed it in "Mr. Pelham's Great Room," part of the home of an engraver and part-time musician. The program was probably all instrumental, and the concert is noteworthy for being both paid and public, since events of this type were just coming into fashion in London at the time. A concert was given in Charleston the following year, and New York heard its premiere concert in 1736. In Philadelphia, the beginning of concert life had to wait until 1757.

The Moravians

The year 1741 saw the arrival in Pennsylvania of a group of immigrants who were the most highly cultured, musically, that the colonies had yet seen. These were the Moravians, a cluster of Protestants from Central Europe who possessed not only a liturgy rich in musical heritage but also a strong tradition of secular music-making that employed the latest styles of composition. The first Moravian settlement, in Pennsylvania, was called Bethlehem. (To this day, an elevated musical tradition continues there in the form of a famous annual Bach festival.) It has been estimated that one-third to one-half of Bethlehem's population participated in its musical life. From the 1760s there were reports of concert music performances, and by 1780 prints and manuscripts of contemporary symphonies and chamber music were already part of the community's music holdings. The symphonies of Haydn, Mozart, J. C. Bach, and others were catalogued along with Haydn string quartets and Mozart trios.

The Moravians later built a southern settlement as well, located in what is now Winston-Salem, North Carolina. From both locations a great deal of original sacred music (which included orchestral instruments) originated, and also some original chamber music. The most important Moravian composer was Johann Frederick Peter (1746–1813). It is regrettable that, due to the isolation caused by religious differences, the Moravians exerted very little influence over the musical life of the main American cultural centers.

Revolutionary Times

In Philadelphia prior to 1750 dilettante chamber music concerts were frequently held in the homes of well-to-do citizens. There, the music of European composers such as Handel, Corelli, Vivaldi, and Purcell could be heard. From about 1750

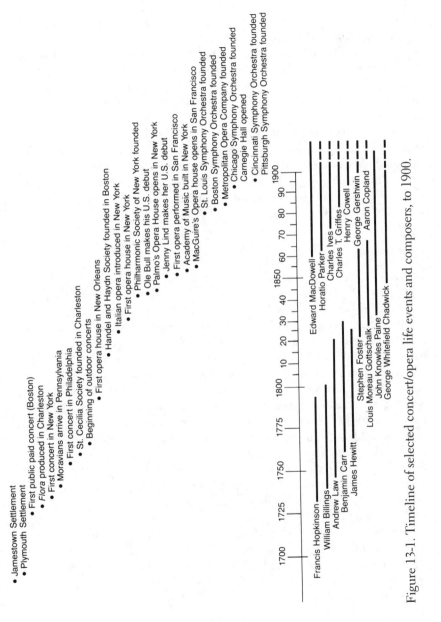

Figure 13-1. Timeline of selected concert/opera life events and composers, to 1900.

on, there began a notable influx of musicians to Philadelphia, and from 1757 concert activity was strong in that city. One concert given that year was attended by none other than George Washington. By 1769 a regular orchestra seems to have been formed in Philadelphia for the purpose of playing subscription concerts.

New York and Charleston began to enjoy a regular concert life about the same time, featuring both visiting foreign artists and resident ones. In 1765 New York heard its first outdoor concerts (modeled on England's Vauxhall series). Charleston established America's first musical society, the St. Cecilia Society, in 1762. The society, patronized by the city's wealthy gentry, was able to support a paid orchestra (of partly professional musicians) which performed concerts in subscription series.

However, the coming of the American Revolution inhibited the natural development of all the performing arts in the colonies. In 1774, as a measure to support the war effort, the Continental Congress passed a resolution against personal spending on extravagances and frivolities, such as music and theater. Thus, cultured musical development had to be curtailed, and concert music gave way to "Yankee Doodle" for a time.

Composers

During the later eighteenth century, especially in Pennsylvania and Virginia, there grew to be a number of musical dilettantes, including such notable figures as Benjamin Franklin, Thomas Jefferson, and Patrick Henry. This period also saw the emergence of the first native American composers. Francis Hopkinson (1737–1791) was a member of the circle of Philadelphia musical amateurs who went on to write vocal music dedicated to George Washington, published in 1788, as well as sacred settings. Hopkinson's most ambitious work was the oratorio *The Temple of Minerva*, premiered in 1781. William Billings (1747–1800), a Boston tanner, was also a creator of vocal music (as well as poetry), and his inspiring "fuging tunes" contained more enthusiasm than polished compositional technique. Billings' rousing hymn "Chester" became a revolutionary hit sung by many of the troops, and his last publication was the memorable *The Continental Harmony* (1794).

In the postrevolutionary years concert music again began to flourish, outdoor concerts again became fashionable, and America recommenced its former cultural development. This encouraging state of affairs prompted Benjamin Franklin to remark that "'Tis said the Arts delight to travel Westward, and there is no doubt of their flourishing on our side of the Atlantic." During the last fifteen years of the eighteenth century, there was a great influx of foreign musicians, and through their dominance of the musical scene, they helped to reawaken concert life after the Revolution.

Patriotism and Heroism

Toward the turn of the nineteenth century program music became quite fashionable, particularly when it contained political, patriotic, or military/heroic subject matter. The English immigrant composer James Hewitt (1770–1827), an exact contemporary of Beethoven, was particularly successful in New York with this type of music. Hewitt's piano sonatas, *The Battle of Trenton* (1792) and *The Fourth of July* (ca. 1795), were enthusiastically received as the type of topical fare popular at concerts in the late 1790s. Among other leading American composers of the day were Andrew Law (1749–1821) and Benjamin Carr (1768–1831). Law was chiefly a hymn writer. However, Carr was more versatile, as seen in his *Federal Overture* (1794), a patriotic/heroic potpourri for orchestra (including, of course, "Yankee Doodle").

Opera in the New World

Part of Charleston's fame as a colonial musical center rests on the fact that the first performance of an opera on American soil took place there. The year was 1735, and the opera was Colley Cibber's *Flora*, an English ballad opera. Ballad operas had come into existence in London in 1728 with the first production of *The Beggar's Opera*, by Samuel Pepusch and John Gay. This work and its followers were lowbrow entertainments, consisting of spoken dialogue punctuated frequently by simple songs, most of which were street ballads with new words or English parodies of Italian operatic arias. *The Beggar's Opera* itself became popular in the colonies about midcentury, playing in New York in 1750, Philadelphia in 1759, and Williamsburg in 1768. The American Company, a Williamsburg-based theatrical company, introduced many more ballad operas to the colonies and eventually monopolized the production of ballad opera until the Revolution.

Following the war, the great influence of English immigrant musicians resulted in a rebirth of interest in ballad opera and other light musical stage fare. In New York James Hewitt produced *Tammany* in 1794, and Benjamin Carr's *The Archers*, based on "William Tell," was staged there in 1796. These may be considered the first American ballad operas.

In New Orleans, the "Paris of America," opera began to flourish while George Washington was still president. In 1791 Louis Tabary arrived with his troupe from Europe, and in the following year he opened the city's first theater. Comic operas were a regular feature there. Beginning in 1806, records indicate that American premieres were given in New Orleans theaters of several operas by prominent French stage composers, including Grétry, Méhul, and Boieldieu. By 1810 the city could boast three theaters and America's first permanent opera company.

Grand Opera Debuts in New York

During the first quarter of the nineteenth century, New York's opera-going audience was accustomed to hearing productions only in English—either American ballad operas or translated versions of European works. However, in 1825 a full

Italian company was brought in to perform Rossini's *Il barbiere di Siviglia* in Italian and in the authentic, original style. This was New York's introduction to European opera on the "grand" scale. Among the audience for this momentous occasion were James Fenimore Cooper and Lorenzo da Ponte (Mozart's famous librettist). The event was so enthusiastically received that it triggered a rash of productions of other Rossini operas, mounted over the next several years.

This popularity also became an invitation for many other opera companies, including that of New Orleans, to play in New York. The net result was that New York had an opportunity to hear much of the operatic repertoire which was at that time just becoming established on the continent. Presented in the original language or in translation, this body of works included Mozart's *The Magic Flute*, Weber's *Der Freischütz*, Beethoven's *Fidelio*, Auber's *La dame blanche*, and Rossini's opéra comique, *Le comte Ory*, to name only a few.

New York's first opera theater, the Italian Opera House, was inaugurated in 1833 with a performance of Rossini's *La gazza ladra*. An eighty-performance season ensued, featuring the works of Rossini and some lesser Italian composers. The second season was a financial failure for the company, and the project was abandoned. In 1844 Palmo's Opera House was opened with the American premiere of Bellini's *I Puritani*, and three years later a syndicate of 150 well-to-do New Yorkers opened the Astor Place Opera House with Verdi's *Ernani*. Unfortunately, both enterprises eventually failed.

Growth in the Mid-Nineteenth Century: New York —

Earlier in the century Boston had gained a great reputation for choral music with the successful establishment of the Handel and Haydn Society in 1815. What Boston did for choral music, New York later did for orchestral music. Beginning around the turn of the century, New York newspapers reported sporadic subscription series of orchestral concerts. After the Erie Canal was opened in 1825 and New York became the leading U.S. port, cultural growth became inevitable, and this included the musical arts.

In 1842 the Philharmonic Society of New York was inaugurated, establishing America's oldest permanent orchestra and the third oldest in the world. The orchestra's first concert consisted of Weber's Overture to *Oberon*, Beethoven's Fifth Symphony, and an assortment of chamber and shorter vocal pieces. The first season was rounded out by two more concerts. During the second season of four concerts the American premiere of Beethoven's Third Symphony ("Eroica") was given. The orchestra continued to give four concerts per year until 1859, when a fifth program was added. Ten years later the season was expanded to six concerts. The main conductor during the first twenty-five years was Theodore Eisfeld, who directed from 1852 to 1865. Eisfeld was also responsible for organizing and performing in many chamber music concerts in New York.

Beginning in 1856, the New York Philharmonic Orchestra made its home in the Academy of Music, which had been built two years before. The Academy was an opera/concert hall boasting the largest stage in the world and an audience capacity of 4,600. Aside from concerts, the Academy filled the gap in opera houses until the Metropolitan Opera was founded in 1883. The American premiere of Verdi's *Aida* was given at the Academy in 1873, before it was heard in either London or Paris.

The New York Philharmonic Orchestra was not the only orchestra heard during this time. The orchestra of Louis Antoine Jullien, a French conductor, made its first appearance in New York in 1853. It performed programs which mixed light music with serious symphonic fare. At that time, hearing a complete symphony performed in one evening was a novelty in America. Jullien made a habit of performing in this manner. He also made a habit of cheap theatrical effects during his concerts, but he can be credited for increasing interest in serious concert music in New York.

Jullien, as a leading musical personality, was somewhat unusual at the time because of his French origin. Throughout the century, German artists dominated the American musical scene. This tendency was typified by Carl Zerrahn, a flutist who toured America in 1848 with the "Germania Orchestra" but stayed on in Boston. There, he conducted the Handel and Haydn Society for over forty years and established an orchestra which became the forerunner of the Boston Symphony Orchestra. German influence in American concert life continued to intensify until the end of the nineteenth century and, beginning in 1850, American music students poured into Germany for training.

Opera at Midcentury

Outside the chief eastern cities it was opera, not orchestral music, which flourished at mid-century. In Chicago the first operatic performance took place in 1850, and the work was Bellini's *La Sonnambula*. This was given by a small touring company, and visits like this would become a trend over the next several years. From 1858 opera companies touring the United States generally spent about two weeks in Chicago. The first opera house in Chicago was built in 1865.

In San Francisco opera was also the first musical love. La Somnambula was performed there in 1851. The following year San Francisco held its first opera "season," consisting chiefly of Italian operas. Frontier opera houses were viewed by local citizens as an "ennobling temple of art and refinement," and MacGuire's Opera House, opening in 1856 in San Francisco, was prototypical.

Early Virtuosos

The expanding United States furnished a near-perfect marketplace for touring musical virtuosos. Smaller cities usually had no musical establishment, and in the larger ones there was great demand for new faces and fresh talent. Virtuoso

Jenny Lind's American debut at the Castle Garden Theater, New York. Photo courtesy of the Theater Arts Library, Harry Ransom Humanities Research Center, The University of Texas at Austin.

performers, particularly those who had already established a reputation in Europe, were strong attractions in America's concert halls. Three figures stand out sharply: Ole Bull, Jenny Lind, and Louis Moreau Gottschalk.

Ole Bull was a Norwegian violinist following in the footsteps of Paganini. He first toured the United States in 1843 and then again in 1852–1857, when his stops included towns in the Middle West and California. To entertain the somewhat uncultivated audience who attended his concerts, Bull performed violinistic tricks (sound effects and the like) along with legitimate music.

Jenny Lind, the "Swedish Nightingale," was brought to America by P. T. Barnum for a two-year tour beginning in 1850. Barnum paid Lind a phenomenal $1,000 for each appearance, which, thanks to Barnum's crass promotional techniques, always drew a capacity crowd. The audience and the press alike were ecstatic. *The New York Tribune* reported that "the enthusiasm of the moment, for a time beyond all bounds, was at last subdued . . . and the divine songstress, blending a childlike simplicity and half-trembling womanly modesty with the beautiful confidence of Genius and serene wisdom of Art, addressed herself to song."

Louis Moreau Gottschalk (1829–1869) was not only an American-born virtuoso pianist and conductor but was also this country's leading composer of concert music in the mid-nineteenth century. Born in New Orleans, Gottschalk was a child keyboard prodigy. At age thirteen he was sent to Paris for advanced musical education. There, he became the composition student of Berlioz, and Chopin predicted a huge success for him. This subsequently came to pass as Gottschalk became a culture idol of women, very much in the image of Franz Liszt. Gottschalk developed early as a composer; he was only fifteen when his music was first published. During the 1850s and 1860s he toured extensively in the United States and Latin America, giving literally hundreds of concerts and recitals—eighty of them in New York alone. His concerts, whether he was conducting or performing as a pianist, featured his own compositions. These were written mainly in the lowbrow "salon" tradition of the Victorian times in which he lived. But, through his music, Gottschalk became the first American composer to achieve a foreign reputation.

Another famous composer of the time, Stephen Foster (1826–1864), devoted his energy strictly to songwriting. A true master of melody and sometimes called "America's Schubert," Foster wrote over two hundred songs, most of which were settings of this own words. Foster was not exactly a "concert music" composer. In fact, many of his song texts were in Negro dialect and were first performed in minstrel shows (notably those of Ed Christy). Foster's most productive decade was 1850–1860. Some of his most famous songs were "Old Folks at Home," "Oh! Susanna," "Camptown Races," "My Old Kentucky Home," "Jeannie with the Light Brown Hair," and his last published song, "Beautiful Dreamer."

Other American composers of the mid-nineteenth century included William Henry Fry (1813–1864) and George Frederick Bristow (1825–1898).

Toward the Turn of the Century

Following the Civil War, the country's mushrooming expansion in industry fostered growth in the arts as well. New orchestras came into being, new operatic ventures were tried, and the training of a professional class of American musicians became a reality for the first time.

There had been pioneering efforts at placing music in higher education as early as 1835 at Oberlin College, and Harvard had instituted music courses in 1862. However, the full force of the movement was felt in the years immediately following the Civil War as America's first independent music schools became established. The mission of these institutions would be to prepare their students for work as concert artists and studio teachers. The following is a table of the schools with their opening dates:

Oberlin Conservatory	Oberlin, OH	1865
Chicago Musical College	Chicago	1867
Cincinnati Conservatory	Cincinnati	1867
New England Conservatory	Boston	1867
Peabody Institute	Baltimore	1868
American Conservatory	Chicago	1886

New York Orchestras

One of the most significant American musical figures in the last forty years of the century was Theodore Thomas, a violinist who turned conductor around 1862. Although he believed that only a resident orchestra could produce the best results, Thomas organized an orchestra to tour the country from New England to the West Coast. His group also concertized consistently in New York, where, beginning in 1868, its performances began to overshadow those of the Philharmonic. His concerts in Chicago also took attendance away from the local orchestra. In 1878 Thomas was named conductor of the New York Philharmonic, but was allowed to continue conducting his own orchestra, which now performed chiefly lighter music. Then, in 1891 Thomas was named the first conductor of the newly formed Chicago Symphony Orchestra. Completely underwritten by the Symphony Board, this resident orchestra brought the best symphonic music to the Midwest. Thomas remained conductor in Chicago until his death in 1905.

One of Thomas' chief rivals during the New York years was Leopold Damrosch, who formed his own orchestra in 1878 under the sponsorship of the New York Symphony Society. This organization contributed significantly to concert life in New York with such events as the American premiere of Brahms' First Symphony. It continued to be a strong rival of the New York Philharmonic Orchestra until 1928, when it was absorbed by the latter. Leopold's son, Walter Damrosch, was conductor of the New York Philharmonic (1902–1903) and in his later years was known to radio audiences as a broadcast conductor and commentator.

Theodore Thomas and his orchestra (after 1876). Photo courtesy of the Theater Arts Library, Harry Ransom Humanities Research Center, The University of Texas at Austin.

Boston

The Boston Symphony Orchestra was established in 1881 through a million-dollar endowment from banker/music lover Henry Lee Higginson. This unprecedented move protected the future of the orchestra for many years to come, ensuring its position as one of the city's cultural attractions. The inaugural concert program consisted of

Beethoven, *Consecreation of the House Overture*

An aria from Gluck's *Orfeo*

Haydn, Symphony No. 12

Schubert, Ballet Music from *Rosamunde*

Bruch, *Odysseus*

Weber, *Festival Overture*

The Boston Symphony's first season was composed of an ambitious twenty-four pairs of concerts. In the early years its conductors were a distinguished group of German musicians. The orchestra received its permanent home in 1900, when Symphony Hall was completed.

During the last two decades of the century, other new orchestras were established in the industrial and trade centers of St. Louis (1880), Cincinnati (1895), and Pittsburgh (1895).

The Metropolitan Opera

New York's Metropolitan Opera Company was initiated as the plaything of nouveau riche industrialists who were having difficulty obtaining boxes at the Academy of Music. The new opera house on Broadway was built to be close to the homes of its investors, and it opened in 1883 with a production of Gounod's *Faust*. This non-Italian first effort would become an emblem of the Met's programming practices over the next ten years.

After a financially unsuccessful first season competing head-to-head with the Academy, a string of German operas featuring European stars was planned for future seasons. There would be a sprinkling of French and Italian works, but the mainstays would be heavy, mostly Wagnerian, operas. The impact of this newer style of programming can be seen in the repertoire of an American touring company organized in the wake of the Met's success:

Goetz, *The Taming of the Shrew*

Nicolai, *The Merry Wives of Windsor*

Delibes, *Lakmé*

Mozart, *The Magic Flute*

Wagner, *The Flying Dutchman* and *Lohengrin*

This trend was largely the result of efforts by Leopold and Walter Damrosch. They also imported Anton Seidl, Wagner's protégé, who by 1892 had introduced New York to every Wagnerian opera except the last, *Parsifal*. Seidl went on to become conductor of the New York Philharmonic Orchestra from 1891 to 1898, during which time he premiered Dvořák's *New World Symphony*.

During the early 1890s there was a reaction against heavier operatic works, and the emphasis at the Met shifted to fine singing rather than momentous repertoire. Imported voices continued to command the stage, and by 1900 only sixteen Americans had sung leading roles at the Met.

The chief event of the early 1890s for the New York Philharmonic was the building of Music Hall (later renamed Carnegie Hall). The opening music festival in 1891 ran five days and featured Tchaikovsky conducting several of his own works.

Composers

The most celebrated and widely performed American composer of the late nineteenth century was Edward MacDowell (1861–1908). Like so many other musicians of his day, MacDowell received his musical education in Europe, first in Paris and later in Frankfurt. He became well known on the continent as a pianist-composer and even had the endorsement of Franz Liszt. After returning to the United States, MacDowell took over the new music department at Columbia University (New York) in 1896. He remained at that post until 1904. MacDowell's best-known compositions are *Indian Suite* (1895) and *Woodland Sketches* (1896), containing "To a Wild Rose."

The New England group of composers was headed by John Knowles Paine (1839–1906), often called the first Dean of American Composers. Following his education in Berlin, Paine joined the Harvard faculty in 1862. He established basic music courses there, leading gradually to the development of a department of music. There, Paine taught many of the turn-of-the-century American composers, notably Arthur Foote (1853–1937), Frederick Converse (1871–1940), Daniel Gregory Mason (1873–1953), and John Alden Carpenter (1876–1951). Paine's music is chiefly orchestral and heavily German-Romantic in style. His "Prelude" to Sophocles' *Oedipus Tyrannus* (1881) won international acclaim.

George Whitefield Chadwick (1854–1931), like Paine, was a New Englander and an orchestral composer. He obtained a musical education in Boston and Berlin and became a teacher, both privately and in colleges. Chadwick's orchestral ballads, which he called "overtures," are his best works. One example is *Rip Van Winkle* (1879).

In 1894 the Munich-educated Horatio Parker (1863–1919) became head of the Yale University Music Department, where he was the teacher of Charles Ives. Parker achieved fame in America and England with his cantata *Hora Novissima* (1892).

From 1900 to 1920

The Philadelphia Orchestra, founded in 1900, became the first American major orchestra established in the new century. The Minneapolis (now Minnesota)

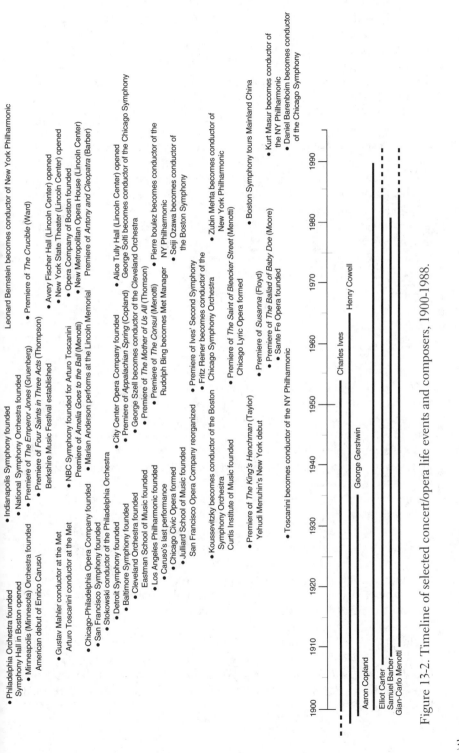

Figure 13-2. Timeline of selected concert/opera life events and composers, 1900–1988.

Symphony Orchestra soon followed in 1903. Prior to that time, there had been only about half a dozen American orchestras of any importance.

The new century also ushered in a period of opera in the United States which has been called the "Golden Years." The new age in the Metropolitan Opera began in 1903 with a change in management, the American debut of Enrico Caruso, and the American premiere of Wagner's *Parsifal* (against the wishes of Wagner's widow). Then, the 1906–1907 season saw the debut of Geraldine Farrar and the American premiere of Puccini's *Madame Butterfly*.

That season a rival opera house opened: Oscar Hammerstein's Manhattan Opera House. It survived only four years in the shadow of the Met, but during that time the Manhattan brought important new productions to America, notably Debussy's *Pelléas et Mélisande*, Charpentier's *Louise*, Offenbach's *Tales of Hoffmann*, and Richard Strauss' *Elektra*.

An ailing Chicago Opera picked up Hammerstein's company and formed the Chicago-Philadelphia Opera Company. Its opening production in 1910 was Verdi's *Aida*. Mary Garden (the creator of the role of Mélisande in Debussy's opera) became its main star and later its manager. The company, as the Chicago Civic Opera Company, grew to be one of the foremost opera companies in the world.

New Conductors

Back in New York, Gustav Mahler became principal conductor at the Met in 1908 with a brilliant performance of Wagner's *Tristan und Isolde*. The following year Mahler was elected conductor of the New York Philharmonic Society, a position he held for two years before returning to Europe. However, there was a general veering away from using strictly German conductors during this period. In 1908 Arturo Toscanini was brought to America to conduct at the Met. He continued to conduct opera and symphony orchestras variously until 1928, when he was named principal conductor of the newly reorganized New York Philharmonic Orchestra. In 1937 the NBC Symphony Orchestra would be formed especially for him.

The year after Toscanini's arrival, Leopold Stowkowski was given his first conducting assignment, the Cincinnati Orchestra. Then, in 1912 Stokowski moved to the Philadelphia Orchestra to begin a period when that orchestra's scintillating sound made it one of the foremost orchestras in the world. Looking forward, Serge Koussevitzky would become conductor of the Boston Symphony in 1924 and would hold that post for an unprecedented twenty-five years.

These three conductors, and others who followed in their footsteps, perfected the playing technique of their orchestras and gave them unique sound personalities. Civic enthusiasm for orchestral music also spread during the second decade of the century, when new orchestras were established in these centers: San Francisco (1911), Detroit (1914), Baltimore (1916), Cleveland (1918), and Los Angeles (1919).

Arturo Toscanini. Photo courtesy of the Theater Arts Library, Harry Ransom
Humanities Research Center, The University of Texas at Austin.

Performers

The geographical broadening of concert audiences brought a new crop of trav-
eling virtuosos to American concert halls. Violinists Fritz Kreisler, Mischa
Elman, and Efrem Zimbalist, as well as cellist Pablo Casals, were in the forefront. Pianists who appeared during this time included Alfred Cortot, Ferruccio
Busoni, Josef Hofmann, and Ignace Jan Paderewski. Sergei Rachmaninoff
played his Third Piano Concerto with Walter Damrosch's New York Symphony
Society in 1910 and returned in 1917, eventually making America his home.
The development of the phonograph made concert artists more widely known to
the American public than was possible from concert appearances alone. By
1910, every prominent singer and several well known instrumentalists had
recorded.

Concert Music and the War

The U.S. entry into World War I in 1917 set off a wave of patriotism and anti-
German sentiment which, unfortunately, had repercussions in American concert life as well. For example, German opera was suspended from the Chicago
Opera until 1920. The New York Philharmonic and New York Symphony established a boycott against works by living German composers. There was even sen-

timent among some patrons (notably in Philadelphia) against the music of Beethoven and Wagner. Karl Muck, the Boston Symphony's permanent conductor since 1912, became the hapless victim of this wave of feeling. Because of his pro-German sentiments, his programming choices were misinterpreted as a refusal on his part to perform "The Star-Spangled Banner." Ultimately, he was arrested as an enemy alien and interned in a military prison camp until 1919, at which point he was deported to Germany. After the war, musical leadership of the Boston Symphony shifted sharply toward French conductors with Henri Rabaud, 1919–1920, and Pierre Monteaux, 1920–1924.

Composers and New Music

During the first two decades of the twentieth century very little headway was made in American concert halls toward performing progressive works by American composers. The most embarrassing oversight was the case of Charles Ives (1874–1954). Most of Ives' works stem from the first three decades of the century (because of his later illness). However, in that short span Ives utilized or anticipated nearly every twentieth-century compositional technique that has been developed for conventional instruments. A total patriot, Ives is known for incorporating American popular, religious, and patriotic tunes into his otherwise unconventional scores. His genius was not fully recognized until the 1940s. Among his works are four symphonies, several symphonic poems (notably *Three Places in New England*), piano sonatas, chamber music, and 114 songs.

Another iconoclast of the period was Henry Cowell (1897–1965). In 1912 Cowell introduced his famous "tone clusters" on the piano at a performance before the San Francisco Music Club. The clusters were produced by striking the keyboard with the fist, palm, or forearm. Most of Cowell's works are for piano.

A new composer, but less experimental than Ives or Cowell, was Charles T. Griffes (1884–1920). Griffes was chiefly an orchestral and piano composer, writing in an impressionistic vein. His best-known work is probably *The White Peacock*. Other American composers of the period included Amy Beach (1867–1944), Henry Hadley (1871–1937), Arthur Farwell (1872–1952), Edward Burlingame Hill (1872–1960), Rubin Goldmark (1872–1936), Charles Wakefield Cadman (1881–1946), and Arthur Foote (mentioned above).

Between the World Wars ——————————

Three major Eastern music schools opened during the 1920s. In 1919 Augustus G. Juilliard died and left $20 million for the development of music in the United States. This endowment enabled the start of the Juilliard School of Music (New York City) in 1923, soon to become the best-known American conservatory. Almost simultaneously, George Eastman (inventor of the Kodak camera) gave a gift of $3 million (which he later augmented) for the establishment of the Eastman School of Music (1918), which later became part of the University of

Rochester. In 1924 Mary Louise Curtis Bok founded the Curtis Institute of Music in Philadelphia. In 1929 tuition fees at Curtis were abolished and, after that, students were admitted exclusively on scholarship.

Paradoxically, several later-prominent American composers went to France in the early 1920s for the completion of their musical education. Most studied under the legendary Nadia Boulanger. Notable among these composers were Aaron Copland, Virgil Thomson, Roy Harris, and Walter Piston.

Opera

Opera flourished during the 1920s. In 1921 Sergei Prokofiev was brought to Chicago to conduct the world premiere of his *Love for Three Oranges*. The reorganization of the Chicago company in 1922 as the Chicago Civic Opera led to the most brilliant period of opera in that city. The company's own singers included Mary Garden, Claudia Muzio, Lotte Lehmann, and Alexander Kipnis. From New York, Chicago brought in such names as Amelita Galli-Curci, Toti dal Monte, and Feodor Chaliapin.

On the New York scene, Caruso gave his last performance in 1920 and died the following year. Rosa Ponselle made her name at the Met in this decade as one of the finest American voices heard to date. Other durable Met stars introduced in the course of the 1920s included Lauritz Melchior, Ezio Pinza, and the Americans Grace Moore and Laurence Tibbett.

In 1923 the newly reorganized San Francisco Opera Company gave its first season with such ambitious undertakings as Puccini's *La Bohème* and *Tosca*, as well as Giordano's *Andrea Chénier*, Gounod's *Romeo and Juliet*, and Boito's *Mefistofele*. Well-known opera stars were brought in to sing the major roles, while local singers were trained to sing the supporting parts. This opera company became symbolic of San Francisco's cultural leadership on the West Coast.

Summer opera festivals became popular during the 1920s, led by enterprises in Chicago and Cincinnati. During the 1930s some new festivals sprang up. The first Festival of Contemporary Music was given at Saratoga Springs (Yaddo), New York, in 1932. The Berkshire Music Festival originated in 1934, when Henry Hadley conducted members of the New York Philharmonic in a concert series given in Stockbridge, Massachusetts. By 1936 the Boston Symphony had been engaged for the festival, and the following year the property at Tanglewood was donated to become the permanent home of the festival (also of a prestigious musical summer school).

Conductors and Soloists

The three great conductors of the 1920s and 1930s were Arturo Toscanini (New York Philharmonic), Leopold Stowkowski (Philadelphia Orchestra), and Serge Koussevitzky (Boston Symphony). Each made a unique contribution to the musical scene. Toscanini's discipline and temperamental devotion to executing the composers' intentions became an inspiration to his players. Stowkowski's personal interpretations, showmanship, and dashing stage appearance (especially his hand motions) made him the musical equivalent of a matinee movie idol. Koussevitzky became distinguished for championing contemporary music, particularly that of American composers. Somewhat to the credit of phonograph recordings, orchestral conductors (especially these great three) became the new stars of serious music, replacing the opera stars of the past.

Concert soloists could still be expected to draw a crowd, however. Violinist and child prodigy Yehudi Menuhin made a spectacular debut at Carnegie Hall in 1927. During the 1930s pianists were particularly popular. Among the front line were Artur Rubinstein, Robert Casadesus, and José Iturbi. Marian Anderson, the very gifted black contralto, drew the most attention of any vocalist with a legendary concert in 1939. Anderson had been engaged to sing a concert in Philadelphia's Constitution Hall, but the Daughters of the American Revolution (DAR) soon succeeded in barring the performance. Amid the ensuing publicity and racial controversy, Eleanor Roosevelt resigned from the DAR. Ultimately, the concert was given on the steps of the Lincoln Memorial in Washington, DC, before a crowd of 75,000 listeners.

Tour Circuits

"Organized audiences" was a development in the 1920s which had far-reaching implications. This was a culture-marketing scheme that had originated out of the Chautauqua and Lyceum cultural circuits of the nineteenth century. The musical version was started in 1920 by Harry P. Harrison, a Chicago Chautauqua and Lyceum bureau chief. Under Harrison's plan, advance men would go into small cities and outlying communities throughout the United States. In each location they would organize a "Civic Music Association," book a series of artists, set up the sale of subscription tickets, and then move on to another town to repeat the formula. Thus, audiences were "organized" and waiting for artists when they came to town as part of the local series. Tour circuits became established, and the business grew increasingly larger throughout the 1920s and early 1930s. This system established a new, modern method of booking concert artists.

Young Artists

During the 1920s new methods were established for American-born aspiring concert artists wishing to break into the field professionally. The usual manner of choosing one of these artists was (and still is) through a performing competition, the winner of which has the opportunity of giving a debut concert, often with a hired orchestra. One means of carrying out such competitions was through foundation grants administered by such organizations as the National Music League and the National Federation of Music Clubs. Another was through annual standing awards sponsored in part by commercial companies. One of the first of these was the Schubert Memorial award set up in 1928 (the centennial of Schubert's death) under the joint sponsorship of the Victor Talking Machine Company and the Juilliard Foundation.

The Great Depression

The stock market crash of 1929 and the resulting economic Great Depression of the 1930s took their toll in the arts just as they did in other quarters of society. Although concert halls experienced a loss of patronage, opera was hit even harder, because an opera season was so much more expensive to mount. In 1932 the Chicago Civic Opera was forced into bankruptcy, and the following year the Metropolitan Opera was in danger of dissolution. Fortunately, a well-organized appeal to the public (including the listeners of weekly radio broadcasts which had been a regular feature since 1931) brought in sufficient contributions to continue operations at the Met. Opera in Chicago struggled to exist during the Depression with abbreviated seasons and artists borrowed from the Met. In New York, however, in spite of difficulties, bright new operatic singing stars were introduced throughout the decade. Lili Pons made her spectacular debut in 1931, and in 1935 the Swedish Wagnerian soprano, Kirsten Flagstad, was introduced as Sieglinde in Wagner's *Die Walküre*.

Despite the Depression, the operatic efforts of several American composers were presented on the professional operatic stage during the 1930s. Deems Taylor's *The King's Henchman* (libretto by Edna St. Vincent Millay) had been comissioned and staged by the Met in 1927. Taylor followed this in 1931 with *Peter Ibbetson*. *The Emperor Jones* (based on Eugene O'Neill's play) by Louis Gruenberg was produced at the Met in 1933, and the following year that company staged Howard Hanson's *Merry Mount*. Virgil Thomson's controversial *Four Saints in Three Acts* (libretto by Gertrude Stein) was mounted twice during 1934, first in Hartford, Connecticut, and then in the 44th Street Theater in New York. Gian-Carlo Menotti's first opera, *Amelia Goes to the Ball*, was premiered in Philadelphia in 1937, and the following year performances of it were given elsewhere, including at the Met.

The fiftieth anniversary of the Boston Symphony in 1930 was the occasion of several commissions of new orchestral music from prominent American and European composers. Noteworthy scores included Howard Hanson's Symphony No. 2 ("Romantic") and Igor Stravinsky's *Symphony of Psalms*.

With the Depression came a slowing of public cultural growth, and fewer new orchestras were established than in previous decades. The Indianapolis Symphony was founded in 1930, and National Symphony Orchestra in Washington, D.C., offered its first season in 1931.

The loss of concert audiences during the Depression prompted imaginative musicians to seek methods of creating new audiences. The most notable result was the so-called "music appreciation" movement, in which a speaker would "explain" concert music to listeners, hoping to stimulate interest and an "appreciation" for works of fine music. Although this cause brought out some charlatans who felt they had to attach a "story" to virtually every work in the repertoire, there were a few genuinely helpful lecturers. Conductor Walter Damrosch and music commentator Deems Taylor, known through radio, were notable examples. However, the most famous contributor to the movement was Olga Samaroff, pianist, critic, and Juilliard instructor. Samaroff's lectures, focusing on listening as an *active* experience, grew to be so popular that they had to be given in New York's Town Hall. Aided by the phonograph, Samaroff and her many imitators all over the country began a national tradition of listeners' courses and concert preview series that continues to this day in the universities, civic organizations, and concert associations of the United States.

Another stimulus to music during the Depression was the Federal Music Project of the Works Progress Administration (WPA). The aim of the program was to provide employment and to preserve the skills of unemployed professional musicians who were on relief. Over ten thousand persons had received benefits from the project by the end of the 1930s. The program shared the sponsorship of musical projects with universities, civic parks and recreation boards, chambers of commerce, school boards, the American Federation of Musicians (AFM), the National Federation of Music Clubs, and many other organizations. Orchestras, concert bands, dance bands, choirs, and opera units were established and manned by participants in the program. American composers were also affected, and nearly six thousand compositions were written with WPA aid.

Composers

A new breed of composer emerged in the 1920s and 1930s, imbued with European concert traditions, yet composing in a truly American spirit. That spirit took into account the purely American musical styles of jazz, folk, and Broadway.

George Gershwin (1898–1937) was originally a songwriter and gained his biggest successes on the Broadway stage. (See Chapter 11 for more details.) However, a chance to perform an original piano work with the famous Paul Whiteman Orchestra in 1924 prompted Gershwin to compose his *Rhapsody in Blue*, drafted in only ten days. His idea was an attempt to incorporate the idiom and feeling of jazz into a concerto-like work which would be crafted in the European concert tradition. The phenomenal reception of *Rhapsody in Blue* led Gershwin to compose several other orchestral works in this vein during the next few years. Notable among these are his Concerto in F and *An American in Paris*.

As the twentieth-century "Dean of American Composers," Aaron Copland (1900–1990) was granted nearly every conceivable form of recognition, including the Pulitzer Prize and the Medal of Freedom. After his years of training in the United States and France, Copland embarked on a brilliant career as composer, pianist, conductor, teacher, and writer. His music from the 1920s to the mid-1950s often utilized the idioms of American folk music or jazz. Many of these works were for orchestra, notably the ballets *Billy the Kid, Rodeo,* and *Appalachian Spring*. His jazzy Clarinet Concerto was commissioned by Benny Goodman. Among Copland's most familiar music are *Appalachian Spring* and *Fanfare for the Common Man*.

Other prominent native composers of the period included Howard Hanson (1896–1981), Roger Sessions (1896–1985), George Antheil (1900–1959), Carl Ruggles (1876–1971), Frederick Converse (1871–1940), Roy Harris (1898–1979), Virgil Thomson (1896–1989), Randall Thompson (1899–1984), Paul Creston

(1906–1985), Norman Dello Joio (1913–), William Schuman (1910–1992), David Diamond (1915–), Douglas Moore (1893–1969), Walter Piston (1894–1976), Samuel Barber (1910–1981), Marc Blitzstein (1905–1964), Ruth Crawford Seeger (1901–1953), and William Grant Still (1895–1978).

Several eminent European composers emigrated to the United States during the 1930s or after the start of World War II. The presence of these creative forces in our culture made an impact on both American concert life and young American composers. Edgard Varèse (1883–1965) had lived in the United States since 1915. Prominent composers who arrived later included Ernest Bloch (1880–1959), Ernest Toch (1887–1964), Igor Stravinsky (1882–1971), Paul Hindemith (1895–1963), Arnold Schoenberg (1874–1951), Darius Milhaud (1892–1974), and Béla Bartók (1881–1945).

The 1940s and 1950s

After Arturo Toscanini left the New York Philharmonic in 1936, the orchestra worked until 1950 under a series of individual and joint directors (John Barbirolli, Artur Rodzinski, Bruno Walter, and Leopold Stokowski). This detrimental situation was remedied by Dimitri Mitropoulos, who was the orchestra's conductor from 1950 until 1958. That year Mitropoulos' associate conductor, Leonard Bernstein, took over the orchestra and held its directorship for the next eleven years, a longer tenure than any preceding director of that orchestra.

An important and popular chamber orchestra was formed in New York in 1947. The Little Orchestra Society, under the leadership of Thomas Sherman, performed and recorded neglected early concert and operatic works and was a champion of contemporary music as well.

Leopold Stokowski and Eugene Ormandy shared the directorship of the Philadelphia Orchestra during the 1936–1938 seasons. After that, Ormandy became the orchestra's permanent director until his retirement in 1980—after forty-four years of continuous service. Under Ormandy, the Philadelphia Orchestra continued to produce the warm sound developed by Stokowski, and it grew more prominent internationally.

The Chicago Symphony, led by Frederick Stock, stressed contemporary music during the 1940s. One significant event, and part of the orchestra's fiftieth anniversary in 1941, was the premiere of Igor Stravinsky's Symphony in C with the composer conducting.

Elsewhere in the nation major orchestras were developing with vigor. The Cleveland Orchestra engaged George Szell in 1946, and by the mid-1950s he had developed that orchestra into a world attraction. Vladimir Golschmann deserves credit for building the St. Louis Symphony during his 1931–1958 tenure. In Los Angeles, Alfred Wallenstein took over the orchestra in 1943. By the end of the decade the Los Angeles Philharmonic Orchestra had achieved national prominence and was the leading orchestra in contemporary music programming. Orchestras in New Orleans and Denver made significant strides dur-

Leonard Bernstein. Photo courtesy of the Theater Arts Library, Harry Ransom
Humanities Research Center, The University of Texas at Austin.

ing this period, and in Texas major symphony orchestras in Dallas, Houston, and
San Antonio had been firmly established by the end of the 1940s. In the early
1950s the Louisville Orchestra, under director Robert Whitney, initiated a com-
mission-performance-recording series in which new symphonic works were created. The project was aided in part by the Rockefeller Foundation.

Opera

At mid-century, opera in New York and Chicago was rejuvenated. In 1950
Rudolf Bing became manager of the Metropolitan Opera, ushering in a period
of reforms extending from artistic integrity to budget.

   While the Met's artist roster was international in the extreme, the rival New
York City Opera Company (formerly the City Center Opera Company founded
in 1943) employed chiefly American singers. This company produced its share
of operas from the standard repertoire, but it also mounted many lesser-heard
works, such as Prokofiev's *Love for Three Oranges*, Mussorgsky's *Khovanshchina*,
and Cherubini's *Médée*.

   In 1954 opera in Chicago was revitalized in the form of the Chicago Lyric
Opera. Under the guidance of manager Carol Fox, the company established
itself firmly in its first three seasons and became distinguished for a number of
unique events, including the debut of American soprano Maria Callas.

During the 1940s and 1950s the somewhat controversial practice of per-forming opera in English was given new attention. The San Francisco Opera performed Puccini's *The Girl of the Golden West* in English in 1943. Better and better singing translations written during the 1950s were a factor in bringing more opera in English to the New York City Opera as well as to the Chicago Lyric Opera and even at times to the Met. The main repertoire heard in English was that of comic operas, with Mozart's works in the vanguard.

New Concert Music and Ballet

Several American composers wrote concert music during the war years, either independently or as part of their military duties. These works seemed to docu-ment the American experience in World War II and had great morale value as well. Here are some representative works:

Samuel Barber, *Commando March*
Robert Russell Bennett, *The Four Freedoms*
Paul Creston, *Fanfare for Paratroopers*
Walter Damrosch, *Dunkirk*
Roy Harris, *March in Time of War*
Walter Piston, *Fugue on a Victory Tune*
Bernard Wagenaar, *Fanfare for Airmen*

In the years during and following World War II the United States saw a great flowering of native ballet. New companies such as the New York City Ballet and Ballet Theatre, as well as new choreographers such as Jerome Robbins, Agnes De Mille, and Martha Graham, were responsible for commissioning and stimu-lating the creation of numerous new works. Although dance is an art in itself, the adoption of several of the new balletic works into the concert repertoire invites us to view American ballet also as an extension of American concert life. A few works which have continued in the orchestral repertoire are:

Aaron Copland, *Rodeo* (1942)
Aaron Copland, *Appalachian Spring* (1944)
Leonard Bernstein, *Fancy Free* (1944)
Leonard Bernstein, *Facsimile* (1946)
Samuel Barber, *The Serpent Heart* [Medea] (1946)
William Schuman, *Night Journey* (1947)
Morton Gould, *Fall River Legend* (1948)

American Opera

Opera by American composers likewise came into its own from the 1940s to the early 1960s. The year 1947 saw the premieres of Virgil Thomson's *The Mother of Us All* and Roger Sessions' *The Trial of Lucullus*, both performed in academic settings. Kurt Weill's *Down in the Valley* (1948) and William Grant Still's *Trou-bled Island* (1949) were latter-day nationalistic operas utilizing folk-song material, and Carlisle Floyd's *Susanna* (1955) adapted the folk and gospel idiom of the Tennessee mountains into a moving stage work. Robert Ward's awarding-winning opera *The Crucible* (based on Arthur Miller's play) was commissioned by the New York City Opera and produced in 1961.

The leading American opera composer of this era, however, was Gian-Carlo Menotti (1911–), who produced an extremely successful string of operas based on his own librettos. Following early successes at the Met, his comic-tragic double bill, *The Telephone* and *The Medium* (1946/47), was staged on Broadway. In 1950 Menotti followed this with another tragedy, *The Consul*, which also ran on Broadway and won the Pulitzer Prize. *Amahl and the Night Visitors* is the work best known to most people. It was commissioned by NBC in 1951 for TV broadcast and has been rebroadcast at Christmas time every year since. *The Saint of Bleecker Street* (1954) won Menotti a second Pulitzer Prize, but *Maria Golovin* (1958), written for television, was not very successful. During the 1960s and 1970s Menotti continued to compose comic, serious, and church operas. *Vanessa* (1958), with libretto by Menotti and music by Samuel Barber, is considered one of the major American operas.

Among the prominent names of concert music composers around the 1950s are the following: Ulysses Kay (1917–), Alan Hovhaness (1911–), Peggy Glanville-Hicks (1912–), Carlisle Floyd (1926–), Wallingford Riegger (1895–1961), John Cage (1912–1992), Milton Babbitt (1916–), Irving Fine (1914–1962), Arthur Berger (1912–), Lou Harrison (1917–), George Rochberg (1918–), William Bergsma (1921–), and Leonard Bernstein (1918–1990).

From the 1960s to the Present

In the early 1960s a new center for performing arts was established, piece by piece, in New York. This was the famed Lincoln Center, brain-child of John D. Rockefeller III. Philharmonic Hall (later renamed Avery Fisher Hall) was inaugurated in 1962, followed by the New York State Theater, the Metropolitan Opera's new home, and the two theaters to be occupied by the Lincoln Center Theater Company, the Vivian Beaumont and the Mitzi Newhouse. Alice Tully Hall, used primarily for smaller recitals, was opened in 1969.

The Met bade farewell to its old house in the spring of 1966, despite the reluctance of its manager and a furtive grass-roots campaign to "Save the Met." The Met's new quarters were not the only breath of fresh air felt by opera-goers during this decade. Several new voices were also introduced, beginning with Leontyne Price and Franco Corelli in 1961. Aside from its otherwise traditional repertoire, the Met produced several newer operas during this period. Alban Berg's *Wozzeck* had been given in 1958, the year that Samuel Barber's *Vanessa* was premiered. *Vanessa* was revived in 1964, and Barber's *Antony and Cleopatra*, commissioned by the Met, inaugurated the new Met home in Lincoln Center in 1966. Productions were also given of Gian-Carlo Menotti's *The Last Savage* (1963), Marvin Levy's *Mourning Becomes Electra* (1967), and Benjamin Britten's *Peter Grimes* (1968).

Under a new management and reorganization, the Met became even more adventurous during the 1970s. Somewhat obscure operas, such as Berlioz's *Les Troyens* and Rossini's *The Siege of Corinth*, received hearings along with newer works like Britten's *Death in Venice* and the 1927 Kurt Weill-Bertolt Brecht piece *The Rise and Fall of the City of Mahagonny*.

The New York City Opera, operating in Lincoln Center's New York State Theater, continued to develop productions of newer or infrequently heard works without sacrificing the standard repertoire. The company's inaugural production at Lincoln Center was of Alberto Ginastera's *Don Rodrigo*. Other new works given there have included Benjamin Britten's *Albert Herring*, Hans Werner Henze's *The Young Lord*, and Robert Ward's *Hedda Gabler*. The company has also mounted the seldom-heard Tudor trilogy by Donizetti: *Roberto Devereaux*, *Maria Stuarda*, and *Anna Bolena*.

The Chicago Lyric Opera, like the New York companies, has, since the 1960s, seasoned its standard repertoire with a sprinkling of fresh, new additions. Novel attractions have included Bizet's *The Pearl Fishers*, Janáček's *Jenufa*, Bartók's *Bluebeard's Castle*, Prokofiev's *Flaming Angel*, Britten's *Billy Budd*, and Verdi's *I due Foscari*.

Under the management of Kurt Herbert Adler, beginning in the 1950s, the San Francisco Opera became an even more sophisticated operation than before. A cycle of rarely heard Richard Strauss operas was complemented by older novelties, like Meyerbeer's *L'Africaine*. Annual productions of twentieth-century operas have also become a hallmark of this company. Works by Carl Orff, Benjamin Britten, Gottfried von Einem, Norman Dello Joio, and others presented by the San Francisco Opera have helped to create the truly cosmopolitan atmosphere associated with this company.

In 1965 the Opera Company of Boston was founded after years of effort by its director, Sarah Caldwell. The company has studiously avoided the strictly traditional repertoire in favor of contemporary works or operas which are older but slightly offbeat. In its first two years of existence, the Boston company staged Luigi Nono's *Intolleranza* and Arnold Schoenberg's two-act fragment, *Moses und Aron*. Works from the more distant past have included *Boris Gudonov* by Mussorgsky, *Semiramide* by Rossini, and *Les Troyens* by Berlioz.

Opera companies in urban centers across the nation have sprung up since World War II. With new, speedier travel these companies have been able to fly in talent for leading roles, while supplying the supporting cast and means of production locally. Notable among these companies are the Dallas Civic Opera, the Houston Grand Opera, the Opera Society of Washington, D.C., Philadelphia's two opera companies, and similar companies in Baltimore, Miami, New Orleans, San Diego, and elsewhere.

Festivals

Summer opera festivals have, likewise, grown in recent decades, thriving on a diversified repertoire. The Cincinnati Summer Opera is the oldest of these festivals. Colorado's Central City Opera, functioning in a historical opera house and located in a rebuilt mining town, is a unique attraction. Although nineteenth-century works are the core of repertoire in this authentic theater, a few contemporary works have been performed there, notably the world premiere of Douglas Moore's *The Ballad of Baby Doe* (1956), an opera based on the historical personages and events of Central City.

One of the most famous American summer opera festivals takes place annually near Santa Fe, New Mexico. The Santa Fe Opera, in existence since 1957, has balanced its repertoire between traditional and contemporary music. For example, in one season productions were given of both Puccini's *Madame Butterfly* and Berg's *Lulu*.

American Orchestras

Orchestral concert life in New York thrived during the 1960s as Leonard Bernstein led the New York Philharmonic in both standard and lesser-known music. Bernstein's tenure from 1958 until 1970 was characterized by an element of showmanship and marked attention to American music of the twentieth century. The same conductor who had rediscovered and premiered Charles Ives' Second Symphony in 1951 also programmed works by such composers as Randall Thompson, William Schuman, and Daniel Pinkham (1923–). For the inaugural program at Lincoln Center, Bernstein's program included Aaron Copland's *Connotations for Orchestra* and Samuel Barber's prizewinning Piano Concerto, both of which had been commissioned for the occasion.

After Bernstein's retirement, French composer-conductor Pierre Boulez became the New York Philharmonic's director from 1971 until 1978. Boulez gave considerable attention to twentieth-century repertoire without losing sight of the standard works and lesser known music of the Romantic period. Boulez's "rug concerts" in Avery Fisher Hall were a unique series of programs, informal yet uncompromising in their quality.

Following Boulez, Zubin Mehta moved from the Los Angeles Philharmonic to become music director of the New York Philharmonic in 1978, and he continued in that position for 13 seasons. In 1992 Kurt Masur became music director in time for the orchestra's 150th anniversary. In the New York area, other than the Philharmonic, there are more than twenty active orchestras. Several of these are amateur or community groups, while others are fully professional.

Fritz Reiner led the Chicago Symphony from 1953 to 1963. Reiner was followed by Jean Martinon (1963–1968), and Georg Solti was music director of the orchestra during 1969–1993. Solti brought the Chicago Symphony to new heights. Its recordings have won more Grammy Awards than any other orchestra, and Time magazine has called it the world's greatest orchestra. Upon Solti's retirement, Daniel Barenboim became music director.

Erich Leinsdorf came from the New York City Opera to become music director of the Boston Symphony following Charles Munch's retirement in 1962. Leinsdorf remained with the orchestra until 1969, at which point William Steinberg took over until 1972. In that year Seiji Ozawa came from the San Francisco Symphony to become Boston's music director, and he has since continued in that position. Ozawa led the Boston Symphony on an epochal tour of mainland China in 1979, and for the orchestra's centennial celebration during the 1981–1982 season, no fewer than twelve new works (eight of them by Americans) were commissioned and premiered.

One of the brightest stars on the American (and world) concert scene today is conductor-composer-pianist Michael Tilson Thomas. He was the youngest assistant conductor of the Boston Symphony Orchestra in 1969 (associate conductor, 1970). From Boston his career developed through overlapping positions as music director of the Buffalo Philharmonic, principal guest conductor of the Los Angeles Philharmonic, music director of the New York Philharmonic's Young People's Concerts, summer conductor of the Pittsburgh Symphony Orchestra, and artistic advisor of the New World Symphony Orchestra (Miami). In 1988, he became principal conductor of the London Symphony Orchestra with which he has made superlative recordings.

Composers

While the standard repertoire continues to dominate America's concert and recital halls, the contemporary composer has not been entirely forgotten. Many major orchestras and arts organizations on federal, state, and local levels continue to subsidize new music through fellowships, grants, and commissions. Many

Year	Composer	Title
1974	Donald Martino (1931–)	*Notturno*
1975	Dominick Argento (1927–)	*From the Diary of Virginia Woolf*
1976	Ned Rorem (1923–)	*Air Music*
1977	Richard Wernick (1934–)	*Visions of Terror and Wonder*
1978	Michael Colgrass (1932–)	*Déjà Vu for Percussion and Orchestra*
1979	Joseph Schwantner (1943–)	*Aftertones of Infinity*
1980	David del Tredici (1937–)	*In Memory of a Summer Day*
1981	(not awarded)	
1982	Roger Sessions (1896–)	Concerto for Orchestra
1983	Ellen T. Zwilich (1939–)	Three Movements for Orchestra
1984	Bernard Rands (1934–)	*Canti del Sole*
1985	Stephen Albert (1941–)	*Symphony, River Run*
1986	George Perle (1915–)	Wind Quintet IV
1987	John Harbison (1938–)	*The Flight Into Egypt*
1988	William Bolcom (1938–)	*12 New Etudes for Piano*
1989	Roger Reynolds (1934–)	*Whispers Out of Time*
1990	Mel Powell (1933–)	*Duplicates:A Concerto for Two Pianos and Orchestra*
1991	Shulamit Ran (1949–)	Symphony
1992	Wayne Peterson (1927–)	*The Face of the Night, The Heart of the Dark*
1993	Christopher Rouse (1949–)	Trombone Concerto
1994	Gunther Schuller (1925–)	*Of Reminiscences and Reflections*
1995	Morton Gould (1913–)	*Stringmusic*

Figure 13-3. Pulitzer Prizes in music, 1974–1995.

works written under these forms of patronage are performed and, thus, reach audiences who might otherwise not experience new orchestral music.

There are many fine American composers at work today. It is difficult to cite a broad sampling of them. However, since annual awards are one measure of critical acceptance, a list of winners of the Pulitzer Prize in music from the mid-1970s to mid-1990s is shown in Figure 13–3 as way of further recognizing this prestigious group of composers.

Review Questions

1. What cities were the main cultural centers in Colonial North America?

2. Who were the Moravians? What was their contribution to musical culture on this continent?

3. Name one work associated with patriotic or military subject matter following the Revolutionary War.

4. In what city was America's first permanent opera company?

5. When did New York develop a taste for opera?

6. When and where was America's oldest symphony orchestra established?

7. Who was Louis Antoine Jullien?

8. When did opera develop in Chicago and San Francisco?

9. Who were Ole Bull, Louis Moreau Gottschalk, and Jenny Lind? Who brought Jenny Lind to the United States?

10. Who was Stephen Foster? Name a few of his songs.

11. Who was Theodore Thomas?

12. When and how was The Boston Symphony Orchestra established?

13. How did the Metropolitan Opera begin? What type of operas did it favor at first?

14. Who was Edward MacDowell?

15. Name two New England composers around the turn of the 20th century.

16. Who were Arturo Toscanini, Leopold Stokowski, and Serge Koussevitzky?

17. Name one or two virtuoso performers from around the second decade of the 20th century.

18. What is the importance of Charles Ives?

19. Name the three major Eastern music schools.

20. When did summer festivals start to flourish?

21. What was Marian Anderson's most significant performance and how did it come about?

22. What were some of the American operas staged during the 1930s?

23. What and when was the "music appreciation" movement?

24. Who was George Gershwin?

25. Who was Aaron Copland?

26. Name two composers who emigrated from Europe to the United States during the 1930s or after the start of World War II.

27. Who is Gian-Carlo Menotti?

28. What is Lincoln Center, and what organizations are housed there?

29. Name two or three prominent conductors of American orchestras today.

30. Identify two or three recent recipients of the Pulitzer Prize in Music. Name the work that won and the year.

31. Place each of the following composers in his/her correct historical position: Horatio Parker, Ruth Crawford Seeger, Samuel Barber, Benjamin Carr, William Henry Fry, Elliott Carter, Francis Hopkinson, Amy Beach, Howard Hanson, Leonard Bernstein.

14

Arts Management: Symphony Orchestras and Opera Companies

Unlike commercial enterprises, production in the musical arts is normally organized within permanent institutions, such as symphony orchestras and opera companies. These stand both as forms of American culture and as forms of higher entertainment, and they differ infinitely from the previously discussed commercial forms of music in contemporary life. Orchestras and opera companies rarely make a profit, and they depend upon donations and other forms of outside funding to make up their losses. The approach to marketing and other business aspects, likewise, differs widely between commercial music and art music, since popular styles are a part of mass entertainment, while concert music and opera appeal to a smaller audience. In both the United States and Europe these have nearly always depended on a system of patronage to sustain them and preserve their traditions.

This chapter will explore some of the artistic workings of symphony orchestras and opera companies, but will also discuss institutional management, funding, and other business aspects of concert music and opera. Toward the end of the chapter there is a brief review of the conductor's world and the solo artist's world.

The American Symphony Orchestra League

The major organizational force in the world of American orchestras is the American Symphony Orchestra League (ASOL). Originating in 1942 as a grass-roots organization of civic orchestra managers and symphony officials, the ASOL has grown to encompass and serve orchestras of all sizes and budget ranges. Its membership consists chiefly of U.S. orchestras. However, there are also several Canadian members and even a few members as remote as Bolivia and Russia.

The league offers a number of services to its members. Most of these focus on information exchange and data gathering. The primary service is the bimonthly *Symphony Magazine*. The ASOL's annual report is a valuable source of data on the current financial trends among symphony orchestras. Other ASOL publications include separate quarterly newsletters for conductors, youth orchestras, and the ASOL Volunteer Council, as well as printed guides on aspects of orchestral management. Additional services provided by the league include consulting and an employment referral service. The league's general activities are rounded out with an annual National Conference.

The ASOL's educational program is exemplary. Each year the league offers a full range of regional and national seminars and workshops on management, conducting, new music, fund raising, and marketing. The ASOL's Orchestra Management Fellowship Program is an extended educational-vocational opportunity. It is a twelve-month paid period of training and internship in which each fellow receives:

1. a two-week introduction to the music industry;

2. a one-week assignment with an urban or community orchestra;

3. three separate fifteen-week assignments with major, regional, and/or metropolitan orchestras;

4. a three-week assignment with the league, including exposure to the league's headquarters, the National Conference, and an orchestra management seminar; and

5. assistance and counseling in job placement.

Orchestra Classifications

The American Symphony Orchestra League has identified approximately 1,500 orchestras in the United States and Canada. Of these, over 800 are members of the ASOL. The league classifies orchestras according to their approximate annual budgets or educational purpose. There are five categories:

A Greater than $1 million
B Between $250,000 and $1 million
C Less than $250,000
U University, college, or conservatory orchestra
Y Youth orchestra

Figure 14–1 lists the orchestras that fall within the "A" category.

Orchestra	Location
Phoenix Symphony Orchestra	Phoenix, AZ
Tucson Symphony Orchestra	Tucson, AZ
Arkansas Symphony Orchestra	Little Rock, AR
Long Beach Symphony Orchestra	Long Beach, CA
Los Angeles Chamber Orchestra	Los Angeles, CA
Los Angeles Philharmonic	Los Angeles, CA
Pacific Symphony Orchestra	Santa Ana, CA
Pasadena Symphony Orchestra	Pasadena, CA
Philharmonia Baroque Orchestra	San Francisco, CA
Sacramento Symphony Orchestra	Sacramento, CA
San Diego Symphony Orchestra	San Diego, CA
San Francisco Symphony Orchestra	San Francisco, CA
San Jose Symphony	San Jose, CA
Santa Barbara Symphony Orchestra	Santa Barbara, CA
Colorado Springs Symphony	Colorado Springs, CO
Colorado Symphony	Denver, CO
Hartford Symphony Orchestra	Hartford, CT
New Haven Symphony Orchestra	New Haven, CT
Delaware Symphony Orchestra	Wilmington, DE
National Symphony Orchestra	Washington, DC
Florida Orchestra	Tampa, FL
Florida Philharmonic Orchestra	Fort Lauderdale, FL
Florida West Coast Symphony Orchestra	Sarasota, FL
Jacksonville Symphony Orchestra	Jacksonville, FL
The Naples Philharmonic	Naples, FL
New World Symphony	Miami Beach, FL
Atlanta Symphony Orchestra	Atlanta, GA
Savannah Symphony	Savannah, GA
Hawaii Symphony Orchestra	Honolulu, HA
Chicago Symphony Orchestra	Chicago, IL
Grant Park Symphony Orchestra	Chicago, IL
Music of the Baroque	Chicago, IL
Evansville Philharmonic Orchestra	Evansville, IN
Fort Wayne Philharmonic	Fort Wayne, IN
Indianapolis Symphony Orchestra	Indianapolis, IN
Cedar Rapids Symphony Orchestra	Cedar Rapids, IA
Des Moines Symphony Orchestra	Des Moines, IA
Quad City Symphony Orchestra	Davenport, IA
Wichita Symphony Orchestra	Wichita, KS
The Louisville Orchestra	Louisville, KY
Baton Rouge Symphony	Baton Rouge, LA
Portland Symphony Orchestra	Portland, ME

Figure 14-1. Category "A" Orchestras in the United States (by state).

Orchestra	Location
Baltimore Symphony Orchestra	Baltimore, MD
Boston Symphony Orchestra	Boston, MA
Springfield Symphony Orchestra	Springfield, MA
Ann Arbor Symphony Orchestra	Ann Arbor, MI
Detroit Symphony Orchestra	Detroit, MI
Grand Rapids Symphony	Grand Rapids, MI
The Minnesota Orchestra	Minneapolis, MN
Saint Paul Chamber Orchestra	Saint Paul, MN
Kansas City Symphony	Kansas City, MO
Saint Louis Symphony Orchestra	Saint Louis, MO
Omaha Symphony Orchestra	Omaha, NE
Atlantic Symphony Orchestra	Atlantic City, NJ
New Jersey Symphony Orchestra	Newark, NJ
New Mexico Symphony Orchestra	Albuquerque, NM
American Composers Orchestra	New York, NY
Brooklyn Philharmonic Orchestra	Brooklyn, NY
Buffalo Philharmonic Orchestra	Buffalo, NY
Long Island Philharmonic	Melville, NY
New York Philharmonic	New York, NY
New York Pops	New York, NY
Rochester Philharmonic Orchestra	Rochester, NY
Syracuse Symphony Orchestra	Syracuse, NY
Charlotte Symphony Orchestra	Charlotte, NC
Eastern Music Festival	Greensboro, NC
North Carolina Symphony Orchestra	Raleigh, NC
Winston-Salem Piedmont Triad Symphony	Winston-Salem, NC
Akron Symphony Orchestra	Akron, OH
Cincinnati Symphony Orchestra	Cincinnati, OH
The Cleveland Orchestra	Cleveland, OH
Columbus Symphony Orchestra	Columbus, OH
Dayton Philharmonic Orchestra	Dayton, OH
Youngstown Symphony Orchestra	Youngstown, OH
Oklahoma City Philharmonic	Oklahoma City, OK
Tulsa Philharmonic	Tulsa, OK
Oregon Symphony	Portland, OR
Erie Philharmonic Orchestra	Erie, PA
Northeastern Pennsylvannia Philharmonic	Avoca, PA
The Philadelphia Orchestra	Philadelphia, PA
Pittsburgh Symphony Orchestra	Pittsburgh, PA
Puerto Rico Symphony Orchestra	Santurce, PR
Rhode Island Philharmonic Orchestra	Providence, RI
Greenville Symphony Orchestra	Greenville, SC
Chattanooga Symphony	Chattanooga, TN
Knoxville Symphony Orchestra	Knoxville, TN

Orchestra	Location
Memphis Symphony Orchestra	Memphis, TN
Nashville Symphony Orchestra	Nashville, TN
Austin Symphony Orchestra	Austin, TX
Dallas Symphony	Dallas, TX
Fort Worth Symphony Orchestra	Fort Worth, TX
Houston Symphony	Houston, TX
San Antonio Symphony	San Antonio, TX
Utah Symphony Orchestra	Salt Lake City, UT
Richmond Symphony	Richmond, VA
Roanoke Symphony Orchestra	Roanoke, VA
The Virginia Symphony	Norfolk, VA
Seattle Symphony	Seattle, WA
Spokane Symphony Orchestra	Spokane, WA
West Virginia Symphony Orchestra	Charleston, WV
Wheeling Symphony	Wheeling, WV
Milwaukee Symphony Orchestra	Milwaukwee, WI

Orchestras: Artistic Activities

The main activity of larger orchestras is a series of "subscription" concerts. The length of this series and the number of different programs it entails is extremely variable, depending on the local audience, the orchestra's budget, the availability of musicians, and similar considerations. Many programs in the main series may feature an instrumental or vocal soloist, but often the program consists solely of music from the orchestral repertoire. The conductor for each of these programs may be the orchestra's own music director, the assistant or associate conductor, or a guest conductor.

A common adjunct to the main subscription series is a group of pops concerts. These feature light classics and popular music from such sources as operettas and film scores. Often, for these concerts, the size of the orchestra is reduced and the conductor is not the orchestra's regular music director. He may be the assistant or associate conductor or an entirely different series conductor. The Boston Pops, an adjunct of the Boston Symphony Orchestra (BSO), is the most famous American Pops orchestra. Its series runs in the spring, following the BSO's regular subscription series. The musicians are partly from the BSO and partly other local professionals.

Youth concerts signify a symphony orchestra's role as a viable and valuable educational institution. Introducing children to fine music and cultural experiences is considered the responsibility of those involved in educational and musical leadership. Concerts in the schools themselves or in central locations to which students are bused are arranged between the orchestra and individual schools or their school district offices. Larger orchestras often have an educational director to help make these arrangements, and that person may also have conducting duties in the youth concerts themselves. Televised youth concerts have also been tried.

Additional performing opportunities for an orchestra sometimes materialize in the form of festivals and summer concert series. Local or regional music festivals running several days, or even weeks, normally depend on a resident orchestra for the core of the festival's programming. The orchestra may be featured in concerts of its own, but it is also needed when festival events include operas, ballets, and concert artists. Several American orchestras run summer concert series, usually performed in an outdoor setting. These are extremely popular with audiences and have the added benefit of extending the contract year for the musicians. (The additional weeks of employment, which increases salaries, can also attract finer musicians to audition for the orchestra, thus building its quality.) Two of the most acclaimed summer series are those given by the Chicago Symphony Orchestra in Ravinia Park and by the Los Angeles Philharmonic in the Hollywood Bowl. On a smaller scale, many orchestras present occasional free concerts in public parks. In most cases funding for these programs comes from municipal resources.

For several of the major symphony orchestras recording is an important activity. Although "live" orchestral recordings before an audience are rare, the orchestra normally uses its own hall to record. Recordings are a significant tool for exposing, publicizing, and enhancing the image of the orchestra, and they also provide some extra income to the orchestra's conductor and its musicians.

Performing outside the home venue is a frequent activity for many orchestras. Larger orchestras engage in tours, sometimes on a regular, regional basis and less often on a national or international scale. In arranging longer, more complicated tours an orchestra normally works through a talent agency, such as Columbia Artists.

Orchestral Repertoire and Programming Considerations

One of the prime responsibilities of a conductor is the choosing of repertoire for the programs he will conduct. In the case of concerts in which a soloist is to appear, the artist (or his management) provides a limited list of works that the artist has prepared for the season in question. However, the remaining purely orchestral works are normally selected at the discretion of the conductor.

Programming is more complex than it may seem at first, since there are several competing factors involved, and not all of them are musical issues. A prime consideration is the matter of balance. Within a single program balance should be maintained with reference to historical periods, weight, and what is sometimes described as the pattern of psychological "tension." There is no pat formula for programming a concert, but the late conductor Charles Munch once offered the following suggestion as a point of departure:

1. a classical symphony or a baroque concerto or an overture;

2. a difficult work (possibly twentieth century); and

3. a big symphony.

The idea of this pattern is that the first work would "sharpen the receptivity." In the second the conductor would "try to make the public love music whose tartness may still be disturbing." And the third (presumably a sort of reward for tolerating the second), "rich and solid, relaxes the atmosphere." If a soloist appears on the program, his work would normally occupy position number 2.

The problem of balance is more complicated when the orchestra's music director (principal conductor) must plan the programs for an entire season. He must be certain not to replay too many familiar works which have been heard in recent years. Although audiences may be expecting a large dose of the standard repertoire, most conductors feel an obligation to also educate their audiences to new or unfamiliar works. The trick is to strike the necessary delicate balance between the familiar and the new/unfamiliar which will work for that orchestra's particular audience. If the conductor goes too far afield in presenting new music or unfamiliar older works, he runs the risk of losing part of his regular, loyal audience, some of whom may be major contributors. This could endanger the orchestra financially. At the other extreme, constantly programming old "warhorses" and "chestnuts" is stifling to the orchestra. It is also the quickest route to disfavor among critics, which, in turn will discourage concert-goers.

Surveys conducted over the years by Broadcast Music, Inc. (BMI), by the ASOL, and by individual researchers have shown a preponderance of older music in the repertoires of most American orchestras. However, as the twentieth century has ripened, the percentage of twentieth-century works has steadily grown. Many of these have been the music of American composers. If pops concert programs are included, the figure for twentieth-century music begins to approach 50 percent of all concert music performed. "American Music Week," launched in 1985, has given a further boost to the cause of American music. During the first week in November concerts are presented nationwide, featuring American "classical" music, ethnic music, experimental music, and jazz. During the inaugural American Music Week, over four hundred concerts were given.

Such efforts are still special occasions, however, and many critics continue to characterize American concert halls as "museums" for dead masters. (This claim is countered by the argument that only with the passing of time can a true masterpiece be identified; therefore, all truly great music is old.)

Programming also entails other considerations, such as resources. With certain works the conductor must consider whether there is an available choral ensemble and whether that chorus is capable of a good performance of the work he has in mind. If the orchestra has a limited budget, the conductor may be restricted from performing too many works which require hiring extra musicians or paying high music rental fees. These and other local factors must be weighed in selecting works for an individual concert or for an entire series.

Opera in the United States

The world of American opera performance is not quite as well organized as that of orchestral concert music. The closest parallel to the ASOL is Opera America. This fine organization fosters close association among opera companies and opera workshops. The Opera America Information Service has become the "principal national source of information and analysis on the field of opera." Chief areas are:

1. *Repertory:* complete annual American and Canadian repertory, as well as major foreign repertories;

2. *Translations:* those available, where performed, and rights;

3. *Performances:* when, where, and by whom;

4. *Musical materials:* availability of scores, parts, and orchestrations, as well as publishers;

5. *Scenery, costumes, props:* rental, sale, or exchange opportunities, as well as new production devices;

6. *Company statistics:* schedules, auditoria, staff positions, budgets, and ticket prices;

7. *Academic opera departments:* personnel, degrees, cooperative programs with professional companies; and

8. *Annual opera statistics and career assistance:* competition and performance opportunities for young singers, apprentice programs for singers, and competitions for composers and librettists.

There is a tremendous amount of operatic activity in this country. There are no "official" guidelines for categorizing opera companies, but, as with orchestras, divisions may be made by using operating income and scope of operations as rules. Using those guidelines, four opera company categories emerge: major, regional, civic, and college.

There are only five major opera companies: the Metropolitan Opera Company, the New York City Opera Company, the Lyric Opera of Chicago, the San Francisco Opera Company, and the Seattle Opera Company. The Metropolitan Opera and the New York City Opera have been discussed in Chapter 13. The Lyric Opera of Chicago has grown tremendously since the mid-1950s. Presently, it offers a season that spans more than four months. The San Francisco Opera, under the guidance of Kurt Herbert Adler from 1953 to 1981, attained international prominence. It has engaged its own orchestra, and its program incorporates activities of the Western Opera Theater and the American Opera Theater.

The Seattle Opera Company was established in 1964 and now presents a six-month season, generally including over thirty performances.

Two examples of regional companies, are the Houston Grand Opera Company and the Minnesota Opera Company. The enormous cultural growth in the United States during the 1960s and 1970s led to the establishment of a number of "arts centers" which have become the homes for many of the nation's regional and civic opera companies. The nation boasts over 200 of these centers, whose activities included over 80 professional opera companies. Sixteen of these are regional companies.

The total number of U.S. opera companies exceeds 550. In addition to these, there are over 400 college opera theaters and workshops. It has been estimated that one third of the total number of opera performances given in the United States are presentations by college opera theaters and workshops.

Opera Repertoire

The choice of repertoire for an opera company is more of a collaborative effort than in the orchestral field, but it is based on several of the same factors: a balanced season, audience preferences, conductor/performer preferences, and economics. A balanced season takes into consideration the inclusion of operas from several languages (chiefly Italian, German, French, and English) and the avoidance of too many works by the same composer. Since ticket sales are opera's major source of income, audience preference must be considered carefully. The standard repertoire can usually be counted on to draw good-size audiences. However, unlike orchestral music, a lesser-known opera by a standard composer (for example, Verdi, Wagner, Puccini, Mozart) is likely to attract substantial crowds as well, especially if big names can be obtained to sing the lead roles.

The personal preferences of opera conductors and singers are also strong factors. Certain conductors have established reputations for their exemplary performances of a specialized area of the repertoire. Their own wishes to perform these works may very well coincide with the audience's desire to hear that music. Star performers, likewise, are known for the operatic roles they have created and recorded. A major company's repertoire for any given season is at least partially influenced by the availability of "stars" to sing the major roles.

"Name" artists who can draw an audience are also an important economic consideration, but repertoire decisions must rest on other economic factors as well. Many of the standard works require extremely high production costs, Verdi's *Aida* for example. The season's budget may be able to withstand one or two of these productions, but the losses they entail must be counterbalanced by a few surefire low cost hits. New works have an economic impact as well, since they require extra rehearsals for which the artists and orchestra must be paid. For reasons of economics and problems of coordinating productions with the schedules of international artists, the burden of programming in a major opera company rests ultimately on the shoulders of its general manager.

Trends in opera repertoire in the United States run reasonably parallel to those in orchestral music. The established standard works are still the main attractions. Performances of contemporary operas by Europeans once led those by American composers. However, since the 1960s the Americans have pulled ahead, so that by 1980 American companies were performing over 200 American contemporary operas, but less than 50 European contemporary works. The current standard repertoire, numbering nearly 250 works, continues to outstrip the newer repertoire, however. Among the most performed standard composers are Verdi, Wagner, Puccini, Mozart, Rossini, Gounod, Bizet, Donizetti, and Richard Strauss.

Management in the Musical Arts

The two most important components in the management of a symphony orchestra or opera company are its governing board (board of directors) and its general manager, sometimes called the "managing director." Between them most decisions regarding operations, planning, and budget are made and general policies for the organization are formed. In order to sketch out the area of management, the following discussion gives brief profiles on governing boards and general managers in both the orchestral and operatic fields. For illustrations of the overall organization of a symphony orchestra and an opera company, see Figure 14–2 (orchestra) and Figure 14–3 (opera).

Symphony and Opera Boards

Board members are, for the most part, musically nonprofessional. They are volunteers from the community who have a mutual interest in music and in developing and promoting their organization as a culturally vital force. Business executives predominate as board members. Persons active in civic or nonarts social service organizations and professional individuals are next most numerous. Some members of a board are chosen for their expertise in certain areas, such as financial management or fund-raising, while others may be actual or potential donors to the organization.

The main responsibilities of an orchestra's governing board are financial planning for the organization and engaging permanent artistic and administrative personnel. Helen M. Thompson (important force behind the ASOL since the 1950s) has concluded that the financial success or failure of a symphony orchestra is in the hands of its governing board. Strong boards which require sound financial planning and management generally produce continual success, while weak boards with little or no expertise in financial planning and management generally fail hopelessly year after year. A commitment to the arts and a willingness to work hard are also the hallmarks of successful governing boards.

The governing board of an opera company has very much the same charge of responsibilities. It determines the financial framework within which the com-

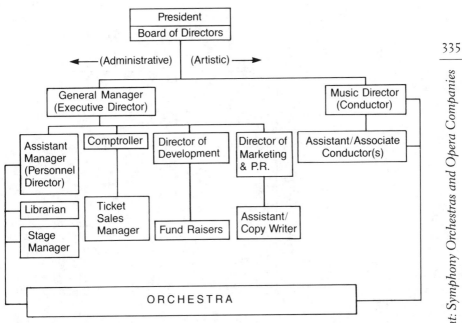

Figure 14-2. Organizational chart: a symphony orchestra (hypothetical).

pany can operate. This is accomplished by making clear policy decisions and general guidelines, by controlling finances, and by allocating funds for new productions and for the advertising and promotion necessary to draw audiences to them.

General Managers

An orchestra's general manager, or managing director, oversees all aspects of the operation, coordinates units and staff members with one another, and coordinates the orchestra's membership campaigns and other general efforts. The main duty areas of the general manager are:

1. *Long-range Planning.* Provides board with facts and figures concerning local and national trends which help the board to adopt realistic artistic and financial goals.

2. *Budgeting and Finance.* Coordinates with comptroller to develop yearly budgets and income projections. Makes recommendations to the governing board.

3. *Grantsmanship.* Draws up and submits grant proposal to federal, state, and civic agencies on behalf of the organization.

4. *Fund-Raising and Ticket Sale Campaigns.* Works with directors of develop-

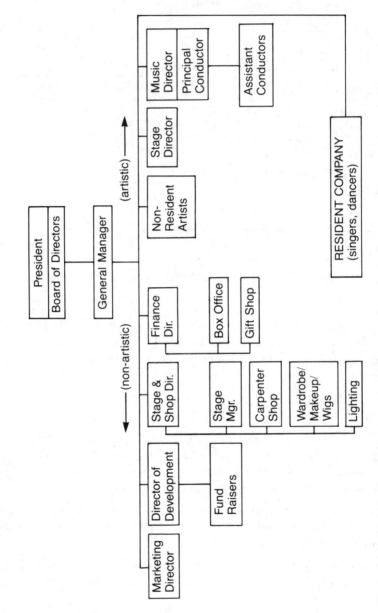

Figure 14-3. Organizational chart: an opera company (hypothetical).

ment and marketing to plan and execute strategies for increasing local patronage.

5. *Promotion and Publicity.* In coordination with the marketing director, supervises promotion and publicity efforts. These may include newspaper and magazine articles, a radio or TV series, and material connected with record releases.

6. *Personnel and Logistics.* Works with assistant manager and music director concerning personnel vacancies, rehearsal and production details, tour planning, and so forth.

7. *Labor Negotiations.* With completely or partially professional orchestras, an AFM labor contract is usually involved. The general manager is normally the chief negotiator in contract renewals.

The general manager of an opera company is often looked upon as the hero of the organization, particularly when the organization experiences artistic triumphs and positive development. Likewise, this individual is viewed as a villain when there are problems and he must get tough with artistic personnel, particularly star artists and conductors. Such matters are nearly always controversial and emotional. The operatic general manager does the contract negotiations and hiring of opera stars, and thus is much more exposed to public criticism than is the general manager of a symphony orchestra. The areas of responsibility for an opera company's general manager are structured somewhat differently from those of his orchestral counterpart, reflecting the productional and organizational uniqueness of opera. The following are the main duty areas:

1. *Artistic Operations.* Negotiates contracts with managers of singers and conductors, union representatives, ballet and chorus personnel, and stage director. Manages rehearsal times. Resolves artistic and stylistic issues.

2. *Technical Responsibilities.* Coordinates the operation of the opera house. Allocates space for rehearsals. Coordinates stage and shop operations with artistic operations.

3. *Financial Operations.* Makes budget analyses and projections. Monitors income and expenses. Prepares reports for the governing board.

4. *Stage Management.* Coordinates rehearsal schedules. Provides transportation for stars and ensures that all artists are on stage at the proper time. Ensures that prompters, coaches, and other support personnel are present when needed.

Funding

A descriptive term for arts organizations is "not-for-profit." Most of the nation's formally established musical arts organizations have some form of official nonprofit status. The major symphonies, major opera companies, and several smaller groups are chartered nonprofit corporations and maintain tax-exempt status.

The expectation of yearly deficits is so strong and deeply rooted that the governing board of a musical arts organization might even grow suspicious if a profit were shown in any given year. In that unlikely event, the nonprofit status of the organization would not be threatened as long as the profit was carried over into the next budget year and not distributed. The economic problem is that the potential audience for the arts is small compared to mass media and commercial music, too small to completely support the activities of local and regional arts organizations. A major orchestra or major opera company will have to maintain a payroll of approximately two hundred professionals from sales of only a few thousand seats per performance. Here, for example, are the seating capacities of the major U.S. opera houses:

Metropolitan	3,600
Chicago	3,500
San Francisco	3,000
Seattle	2,875
NY City	2,500

The situation is further dramatized if one considers the size of these venues next to the stadiums and arenas of professional sports, such as baseball, basketball, football, and soccer.

Thus, there is a need for outside funding in order to maintain musical arts organizations. Arts administrators must spend a considerable portion of their time raising the necessary funding to enable continuation of their programs. Time must be spent planning and executing campaigns, working with potential donors, meeting with government officials, and writing grant proposals. Funding support can come from a variety of sources, the principal areas being private/corporate/foundational, civic, state, and federal.

Private/Corporate/Foundational Funding

Private donations are the bread and butter of a musical arts organization. Although many of these are relatively small, most communities have at least a few wealthy supporters of the arts. The donations of these individuals can be sizeable, particularly if their money is to be targeted for some specific project. Local business leaders, often members of the governing board, can be counted on as potential donors, and they are generally capable of persuading other business executives to contribute as well.

Several of the larger corporations are committed to supporting the arts. Through some office established specifically for the task, these industrial patrons consider grant requests and dispense funding to those arts organizations they deem most worthy. Many foundations exist to aid the arts and other nonprofit enterprises, and a great number of these are extensions of industry. Following the lead of the Ford Foundation and the Rockefeller Foundation in the 1950s and

1960s, a large number of endowed foundations have sprung up. Many of these consider requests on a national basis, but a number of them operate on a regional or statewide level only. Local foundations are often of the "community-foundation" type, which have proliferated in recent years due to increased tax advantages for themselves and their donors.

Public Funding

Civic support for musical arts organizations can come through community foundations, through the efforts of a civic arts council, or directly from the city budget. The nominal purpose of a civic arts council is to foster cooperation among the various arts organizations in the community and provide a central means for promoting the arts locally. However, in practice, councils have often been used as a vehicle for promoting the largest arts organization on the council, usually the local symphony orchestra. The civic arts council may operate membership drives and other fund-raising activities to aid its constituent organizations. Larger projects carried forth by civic arts councils are often focused on establishing a community arts center, which all of its member organizations will be able to use. If the city has allocated a portion of its budget to support the arts, the civic arts council is normally the clearinghouse for funding requests.

The state-level counterpart of the civic arts council is the state arts council. Beginning with the New York State Council on the Arts, established in 1960, states have established a council to recognize and promote the arts within the state, manage and distribute state funds earmarked for the arts, and manage and distribute federal funds granted to the state for use in the arts.

NEA

At one time the United States was the only major nation in the Western world which, because of its philosophy of private enterprise, did not provide official support to the arts. Then, in 1965 Congress established the National Foundation for the Arts and Humanities, which contained two agencies: the National Endowment for the Arts (NEA) and the National Endowment for the Humanities (NEH). The Congress stated that "while no government can call a great artist or scholar into existence, it is necessary and appropriate for the Federal Government to help create and sustain not only a climate encouraging freedom of thought, imagination, and inquiry, but also the material conditions facilitating the release of this creative talent. . . ."

The mission of NEA is "to foster the excellence, diversity, and vitality of the arts in the United States" and "to help broaden the availability and appreciation of such excellence, diversity, and vitality." The Endowment is committed to:

1. demonstrate national recognition of the importance of artistic excellence;

2. provide opportunities for artists to develop their talents;

3. assist in the creation, production, presentation/exhibition of innovative and

diverse work that has potential to affect the art form and directly or indirectly result over time in new art of permanent value;

4. assure the preservation of our cultural heritage;

5. increase the performance, exhibition, and transmission of art to all people throughout the nation;

6. deepen understanding and appreciation of the arts among all the people nationwide;

7. develop international interchange that benefits American artists, arts organizations, and/or audiences;

8. encourage serious and meaningful art programs as part of basic education;

9. stimulate increasing levels of non-Federal support of the arts;

10. improve the institutional capacity of the best of our arts organizations to develop, produce, present, and exhibit bold and varied fare; and

11. provide information about the arts, their artistic and financial health, and the state of their audiences.

Another part of the NEA mission statement reads:

> The Endowment, in conjunction with private and public partners, carries out its mission through grants programs and a wide range of leadership and advocacy activities. The Endowment also serves as a national forum to assist in the exchange of ideas and as a catalyst to promote the best developments in the individual, project, and longer term institutional support.

NEA maintains national panels which develop guidelines and evaluate grant applications. The Endowment provides three major types of financial assistance:

1. nonmatching fellowships to artists and composers of exceptional talent;

2. matching grants to nonprofit, tax-exempt organizations of national or regional significance; and

3. matching grants to state and local arts agencies and regional arts groups.

"Music" and "Opera-Musical Theater" are just two of the twelve arts programs supported by the endowment. As the NEA states, "The Music Program provides support for the performance and creation of music, with an emphasis on assisting the growth of American music and musicians." Currently, grant awards are in the following categories:

Chamber/Jazz Ensembles

Jazz Special Projects/Jazz Services to the Field

Choruses

Orchestras

Composer in Residence

NEA's Opera-Musical Theater program "recognizes the distinct structures, responsibilities, and institutions of various components within the opera-musical theater field, which encompasses traditional opera and musical theater, operetta, Broadway musical comedy, non-traditional music-theater, and still-evolving forms." Currently, grant awards are in the following categories:

Professional Opera-Musical Theater Companies

New American Works

Professional Artist Development

Artist Fellowships

With the nation's economic boom during the 1960s, funding for the arts was relatively plentiful. However, as inflation snowballed and the economy grew worse in the course of the 1970s and 1980s, subsidies had less and less purchasing power. As a result, the 1980s and 1990s have seen a series of reductions in the annual budget of the National Endowment for the Arts.

The Conductor's World

The conductor—absolute master of the orchestra, glamorous figure of the art world, member of the jet set, darling of society matrons, TV and radio star—such are the images we might conjure up. However, the real, less glamorous nature of conducting as a career is not generally known.

First, the conductor must be the most complete of all musicians. That means that his musical background and training must be thorough and impeccable. He must have a masterly grasp of music theory, history, performance practices, baton technique, score reading, and the art of performance itself. This last normally means that he must have mastered at least one instrument. For most conductors the piano is that instrument, although violinists also often become conductors. A conductor's knowledge of the classical musical literature must be vast and comprehensive. It is not enough to know the symphonies of Beethoven and Brahms and all the standard operas. A conductor must be acquainted with the most remote corners of orchestral music and musical theater, since balanced programming encompasses considerably more than just the mainstream works. Reputations are frequently ensured by the introduction on a concert of an obscure but high-quality piece, which then becomes the specialty of that conductor.

Many conductors have risen from the orchestral ranks. Toscanini was a cellist and Koussevitzky was a contrabass player. It is also common for an orchestra's concertmaster (first chair, first violin section) to assume some conducting duties, and this has sometimes led to a full-time career as a conductor. A conductor's advanced education normally takes place at a conservatory, either in the United States or in Europe.

Getting work in the conductor's world requires both talent and politics. The talent will be evident once the conductor is given a chance to perform. That chance sometimes comes in the form of a summer orchestral workshop, such as those held at Tanglewood, Interlochen, or the series sponsored by the ASOL.

Conductors have seldom been able to become associated with major orchestras early in their careers, even as assistant or associate conductors. The first few positions a young conductor obtains are likely to be either in the field of education (college or university orchestras) or with low-budget "community" or "urban" orchestras. An occasional conductor, after garnering some initial credits, is enterprising enough to start his own small orchestral organization, replete with manager, board, and donors.

Moving up through the political and artistic trenches of the orchestral world is an arduous task, and conductors can remain at various levels for indefinite lengths of time. The obvious goal for most is to become music director of the most prestigious orchestra possible. However, this is not always realized in a linear, sequential manner. For example, one individual might arrive at the musical directorship of a "regional" orchestra after having conducted "urban" and "metropolitan" groups. Another individual may land a job as assistant conductor with a major symphony orchestra, which he may hold for several years before being appointed music director of a regional orchestra. Music directorships of the major U.S. orchestras are chosen from the ranks of music directors of other major orchestras, worldwide; associate and assistant conductors of major U.S. orchestras; and sometimes music directors of regional U.S. orchestras.

The career pattern of major orchestra conductors today is diverse. Most have a contract with a management agency for the purpose of arranging guest conducting engagements. Some have recording contracts, while others may record for several labels. (Most major orchestras, themselves, are not signed to a record label.) A pattern which has become widespread with the ease of jet air travel is guest conducting on a worldwide basis. Individual conductors' contracts may vary widely concerning the number of home concerts they are required to conduct. The rest of the time they are free to accept engagements with other orchestras. In some cases, the demand for a particular conductor has been so great that he will be permitted to become music director of two orchestras at once, normally one in the United States and one in Europe. These "stars" must divide their time between their two orchestras and a few guest appearances elsewhere, a situation which is further complicated by the amount of time they must spend traveling between orchestras.

Many conductors have talents for both the concert stage and the opera. However, only a few conductors, such as the music directors of the major opera companies, devote most or all of their time to opera. Generally, conductors become directors with the major companies for only short periods. On the other hand, operatic guest conducting has become extremely widespread. In the field of traditional opera, "star" conductors are the rivals of "star" artists. In the performance of newer American opera, however, the composer is considered to be the real "star," and some critics view the conductor as the composer's "prophet," with the singing artists constituting a third rank.

The Solo Artist's World

The work of a classical artist is similar in many respects to the work of a popular artist. Both are concerned with establishing and building an audience of devotees who will attend performances and buy records. Both wish to have an international reputation and to continue performing as long as they are physically able. Both take the same risks when they enter their profession, but both are in fields where there is the potential to earn large sums of money.

A classical solo artist's list of long-term and short-term associates is relatively short, and his world is perhaps less complex than that of the pop performer, but it is just as fraught with toil and difficulties. The classical artist does not have to develop a uniquely new image, since concert dress, overall appearance, and performance style in this field are quite traditional and slow to change. Most of the musical literature the classical artist records is standard, so promotional tours are unnecessary. Since the typical audience for classical music is older than the core market for pop styles, and its standards of judgment are quite different, the popularity of established classical artists tends to remain strong until the artist either dies or chooses to retire. (The main restriction here is on the singer, whose voice, like an athlete's body, may experience a fateful decline.)

On the other hand, the rigors of maintaining technique and learning new repertoire are astonishingly heavy. Most artists must practice many hours a day, *every* day, to remain in top shape, and the preparation of new musical material, such as a concerto or an operatic role, can take many months of work.

The educational preparation and training of a classical performer is protracted and highly concentrated. Instrumentalists may begin studies from childhood, while singers normally can begin serious study during middle or late adolescence. At college age and after years of private study the performer often attends a major school of music or conservatory. Private study normally continues alongside general studies in music similar to the training of a conductor. Instrumentalists obtain experience in school giving recitals, while singers can perform both in recitals and in opera workshops. Once the instrumental performer reaches the early twenties, full potential is generally known. It often takes longer for a singer to exhibit potential, because the voice may not mature physically until the early thirties. Those who are of concert or operatic caliber will normally take one route, while those who are not will be best advised to take another. Orchestral work is the normal course for fine string players who would have difficulties attempting a career as a concert soloist. Performers on other instruments and vocalists who do not pursue concertizing or opera full time normally expect to divide their efforts between teaching and performing on a local or regional basis. Becoming a performer with a touring ensemble is another possibility.

The first professional step for the aspiring solo artist is a kind of apprenticeship period. For instrumentalists this generally takes the form of entering a number of performing contests and trying to obtain performing engagements with low-budget orchestras. For solo singers, the only potentially lucrative career area is in opera, and there are two main postgraduate routes in that field. One is to become associated with one of the "schools" connected with a major opera company, such as those run by the Metropolitan Opera and the Lyric Opera of Chicago. The other route is to go to Europe and audition for work with one of the many opera companies there. The former choice will give the singer additional coaching and the possibility of singing an occasional minor role in one of the company's productions. The latter is a form of employment which produces much the same professional result, but lacking the benefits of further training. Both routes can become powerful springboards for the start of an operatic career.

For an American artist the importance of a New York debut cannot be overemphasized. Although a successful New York debut does not lead automatically to a brilliant career, the critics there are the toughest and most authoritative, and the important artist's managers discover much of their talent there.

That first New York recital will probably be arranged through what is known as a "concert manager" (roughly the equivalent of the rock concert promoter). The concert manager takes care of all the details of the presentation from booking the hall to ticket sales, publicity, and promotion. Some concert managers work for a flat fee, while others may be willing to accept a percentage of ticket sales. Arrangements involving a combination of flat fee and percentage are also possible.

The artist normally deals directly with concert managers until he is represented by a management firm. Following the debut (or later) the up-and-coming artist will sign with a firm which books engagements for the artist after that. The normal term for a classical artist management contract is four years, including option periods. (See Chapter 4 for more on talent agents.)

Once the successful instrumental concert artist's career has been launched, offers to make recordings may follow, and a recording contract with a major classical label (U.S. or European) is a possibility. However, the major portion of the artist's time will be taken up with touring and the preparation of new repertoire. Tour appearances will be chiefly as a soloist with symphony orchestras, but solo recitals by pianists are also popular.

For most American opera singers all roads lead, hopefully, to the Met. One of these roads is the annual Metropolitan Opera Auditions, held regionally and nationally. Top singers from this competition are given a berth at the Met school and a chance to sing one or more roles in actual Met productions. Other singers have been capable of launching successful careers before Met appearances. Some simply remain in Europe after their apprenticeship period there. Others choose to pursue contracts with major or regional U.S. opera companies other than the Met. The upward mobility possible in the conducting profession has its counterpart among operatic artists, and many of those starting in grassroots companies can build on that experience when they are ready for work with larger organizations.

Besides work during the normal concert and opera seasons, the sizable number of summer music festivals in the United States extends additional performance and exposure opportunities to solo artists. For those artists versatile enough to also perform on pops concerts or in summer performances of Broadway musicals, yet another career dimension is open.

Aspiring conductors, concert artists, and operatic singers should not be mislead by the smoothness of the generalizations and theory outlined above. In the real world it takes a tremendous amount of talent even to be heard professionally. Unlike commercial music, promotion and hype cannot create a successful classical artist. Achievement in concert life or opera requires a person with superior artistic gifts and the grit to overcome any disappointment or setback that may occur. To most of us, that may seem superhuman. However, for the greatest talents who are willing to work hard and never allow their determination to waver, the rewards can be great. As the successful operatic soprano Evelyn Lear has put it:

> There are four ingredients for a career. The first one . . . is talent . . . any ability you have. The second quality is hard work. . . . The third thing is timing and luck, as in any profession. The fourth point is the most important: it's having sheer unmitigated gall and the skin of an elephant on the outside and the heart of a dandelion on the inside—vulnerability with a hard shell. That's what it takes to make a career.

Concert life and opera in the United States have often been underrated by professionals involved in the various phases of commercial music. This is partially because the promotion and publicity surrounding a fine classical artist rarely reaches the proportions of the hoopla and hype associated with the most popular stars. It is also partially because the commercial professional views the classical field as a far smaller business (and therefore much less significant) than his own. After all, for one concert appearance, a top classical star like Luciano Pavarotti earns nowhere near, say, Dolly Parton. Also, the concert and opera field is generally conducted on a not-for-profit basis, and that is inconsistent with the profit motive associated with commercial music.

However, if one considers the amount of money which actually changes hands in the classical field, it is not such a small corner of music after all. One must take into consideration the operating budgets of every orchestra and opera company. One must also consider the subsidies which are given at the private, foundational, corporate, civic, state, and federal levels to classical musical activities and artists of all types.

The musical arts can be seen to occupy a significant economic position within music in contemporary life. However, more important than that is their place in the cultural life of this country. The grass-roots and regional arts organizations and projects are proof of the depth of public commitment to the traditions of art music. The major U.S. orchestras, the country's major opera companies, and its top performing artists reflect our most serious cultural intentions. Those all carry a high intangible value and may be numbered among our national treasures.

Review Questions

1. What is the ASOL? What are its orchestra classifications?

2. Give a few details of ASOL's Orchestra Management Fellowship Program.

3. Discuss the main activity of an orchestra and some of its adjunct activities, such as a pops series, youth concerts, summer festivals, and recording.

4. Discuss the problem of programming "warhorses" versus programming newer music.

5. Name a few of the areas of information available through the Opera America Information Service.

6. Name the five "major" opera companies.

7. Are "name" artists more important in opera than in concert music? Explain.

8. What are the purposes of symphony and opera boards?

9. Compare the job of a symphony's general manager to that of an opera company's general manager.

10. Why can musical arts organizations *not* support themselves from the sale of tickets, while professional sports organizations can?

11. Describe Private/Corporate/Foundational Funding.

12. Name and describe the three levels of public funding. Why is this form of funding called "public."

13. Name a few of the "commitments" of the National Endowment for the Arts.

14. What are the three major types of financial assistance offered by NEA?

15. Name a few of the categories within NEA's "Music" and "Opera-Musical Theater" funding programs.

16. Describe how a conductor might build a career.

17. Are there some similarities between classical and popular artists? Also, identify some of the differences.

18. What opportunities do young classical artists have for entering the profession? Describe some routes that may be taken by (1) a singer, (2) a concert pianist, and (3) an orchestral player.

Further Reading

The Music Industry: General References

Baskerville, David. *Music Business Handbook & Career Guide*, 6th edition. Los Angeles: Sherwood Publishing Co., 1995.

Brabec, Jeffery and Brabec, Todd. *Music, Money, and Success*. New York: Schirmer Books, 1994.

Krasilovsky, M. William and Shemel, Sydney. *More About This Business of Music*, 5th edition. New York: Billboard Books, 1994.

Passman, Donald S. *All You Need to Know About the Music Business*, 2nd edition. New York: Simon & Schuster, 1994.

Shemel, Sydney and Krasilovsky, M. William. *This Business of Music*, 7th edition. New York: Billboard Books, 1995.

Recording Industry History

Bart, Teddy. *Inside Music City, U.S.A.* Nashville: Aurora Publishers, 1970.

Benjaminson, Peter. *The Story of Motown*. New York: Grove Press, 1979.

Gellatt, Roland. *The Fabulous Phonograph: From Tin Foil to High Fidelity.* Philadelphia: Lippincott, 1954.

Hamm, Charles. *Yesterdays: Popular Song in America.* New York: W.W. Norton, 1979.

Palmer, Robert. *A Tale of Two Cities: Memphis Rock and New Orleans Roll.* ISAM Monograph No. 12, New York: Institute for Studies in American Music, 1979.

Sanjek, Russell. *American Popular Music Business in the 20th Century.* New York: Oxford University Press, 1991.

Stuessy, Joe. *Rock and Roll: Its History and Stylistic Development.* 2nd edition. Englewood Cliffs, NJ: Prentice-Hall, 1993.

Songwriting and Song Publishing

Dranov, Paula. *Inside the Music Publishing Business* (White Plains, NY: Knowledge Industry Publications, 1980.

Nashville Songwriters Association International. *The Essential Songwriter's Contract Handbook.* Nashville, TN: NSAI, 1994.

Copyright and Licensing

Althouse, Jay. *Copyright: The Complete Guide for Music Educators.* East Stroudsburg, PA: Music in Action, 1984.

Copyright Office. "Copyright Registration of Musical Compositions and Sound Recordings." Circular R56a.

Creus, Kenneth, *Copyright, Fair Use, and the Challenge for Universities.* Chicago: University of Chicago Press, 1993.

Kohn, Al and Kohn, Bob. *The Art of Music Licensing.* Englewood Cliffs, NJ: Prentice-Hall, 1992.

Recording

Eargle, John. *Sound Recording,* 2nd edition. New York: Van Nostrand Reinhold, 1991.

Gillett, Charlie. "The Producer as Artist," pp. 51–56 in *The Phonograph and Our Musical Life,* ed. by H. Wiley Hitchcock, ISAM Monograph No. 14, New York: Institute for Studies in American Music, 1980.

Rappaport, Diane Sward. *How to Make and Sell Your Own Record,* 2nd edition. New York: Quick Fox/Crown Publishers, 1991.

Waram, John M. and Kefauver, Alan P. *The New Recording Studio Handbook.* Commar, NY: Elar Publishing Company, 1989.

Artist Relations

Davidson, John and Casady, Cort. *The Singing Entertainer*. Los Angeles: Alfred Publishing Co., 1979.

Frascogna, Xavier M. and Hetherington, H. Lee. *Successful Artist Management*, revised edition. New York: Billboard Books, 1990.

Halloran, Mark, editor-compiler. *The Musician's Business and Legal Guide*. Englewood Cliffs, NJ: Prentice-Hall, 1991.

Maisel, Eric. *Staying Sane in the Arts*. New York: G.P. Putnam, 1992.

Papolus, Janice. *The Performing Artist's Handbook*. Cincinnati: Writer's Digest Books, 1984.

Pettigrew, Jim, Jr. *The Billboard Guide to Music Publicity*. New York: Billboard Books, 1989.

Weissman, Dick. *Making a Living in Your Local Music Market*. Milwaukee: Hal Leonard Publishing Corp., 1990.

Radio Broadcast History

Barnouw, Eric. *A History of Broadcasting in the United States*, 3 vols. New York: Oxford University Press, 1968–1970.

Eberly, Philip K. *Music in the Air: America's Changing Tastes in Popular Music, 1920–1980*. New York, Hastings House, 1982.

Music Broadcasting

Broadcasting & Cable Yearbook. New Providence, NJ: R.R. Bowker, yearly.

Halper, Donna L. *Radio Music Directing*. Boston: Focal Press, 1991.

MacFarland, David T. *Contemporary radio programming strategies*. Hillsdale, NJ: L. Erlbaum Associates, 1990.

Wilby, Pete. *The Radio Handbook*. New York: Routledge, 1994.

Music Criticism

Graf, Max. *Composer and Critic: Two Hundred Years of Musical Criticism*. New York: W.W. Norton, 1946.

Laurence, Dan H. *How to Become a Music Critic*. New York: Hill and Wang, 1961.

Schonberg, Harold C. *Facing the Music*. New York: Summit Books, 1981.

Thompson, Oscar. *Practical Musical Criticism*. New York: Witmark Educational Publications, 1934.

Films and Film Music

Bernstein, Leonard. "Interlude: Upper Dubbing, Calif.," in *The Joy of Music*. New York: Simon & Schuster, 1959.

Hagen, Earle. *Scoring for Films*, updated edition. Los Angeles, Alfred Publishing Co., 1989.

Karlin, Fred. *Listing to Movies: The Film Lover's Guide to Film Music*. New York: Schirmer Books, 1994

Karlin, Fred and Wright, Rayburn. *On the Track: A Guide to Contemporary Film Scoring*. New York: Schirmer Books, 1990.

Mast, Gerald. *A Short History of the Movies*, 5th edition. New York: Macmillan, 1992.

Business Music

Bernstein, "The Muzak Muse." In *The Infinite Variety of Music*. New York: Simon & Schuster, 1966.

Business Music: A Performance Tool for the Office/Workplace, Special Report. Seattle, WA: Muzak Limited Partnership, 1991.

Jarvis, Jane. "Notes on Muzak." In *The Phonograph and Our Musical Life*, pp. 13–18. Ed. by H. Wiley Hitchcock, ISAM Monograph No. 14. New York: Institute for Studies in American Music, 1980.

Lanza. *Elevator Music*. New York: St. Martin's Press, 1994.

Van-Summers, W.; Pisoni, David B.; Bernacki, Robert H.; Pedlow, Robert I.; and Stokes, Michael A. "Effects of Noise on Speech Production: Acoustic and Perceptual Analyses." *Journal of the Acoustic Society of America*, 84/3 (1988), 917–928.

Retail Music Stores

American Music Conference. *Music USA*. Carlsbad, CA: National Association of Music Merchants, yearly.

Dranov, Paula. *Inside the Music Publishing Industry*. White Plains, NY: Knowledge Industry Publications, 1980.

NAMM Senior Music Merchants Group. *So You Want to Open a Music Store*, 2nd edition. Carlsbad, CA: National Association of Music Merchants, 1996.

History of American Musical Theater

Bernstein, Leonard. "Whatever Happened to That Great American Symphony?" and "Why Don't You Run Upstairs and Write a Nice Gershwin Tune?" in *The Joy of Music*. New York: Simon & Schuster, 1954.

Bordman, Gerald. *American Musical Theatre: A Chronicle*, 2nd edition. New York: Oxford University Press, 1992.

Ewen, David. *The New Complete Book of American Musical Theater*. New York: Holt, Rinehart and Winston, 1970.

Mast, Gerald. *Can't Help Singin': The American Musical on Stage and Screen*. Woodstock, NY: The Overlook Press, 1987.

Musical Show Production

Bennett, Susan. *Theatre Audiences: A Theory of Production and Reception*. New York: Routledge, 1990.

Engel, Lehman. *The Making of a Musical*. New York: Macmillan, 1977.

Harris, Andrew B. *Broadway Theatre*. New York: Routledge, 1994.

Langley, Stephen. *Theatre Management and Production in America: Commercial, Stock, Resident, College, Community, and Presenting Organizations*. New York: Drama Book Publishers, 1990.

Rosenberg, Bernard. *The Broadway Musical: Collaboraton in Commerce and Art*. New York: New York University Press, 1993.

History of American Concert Life and Opera

Davis, Ronald L. *A History of Music in American Life*, 3 vols. Malabar, FL: Robert Krieger, 1980–82.

A History of Opera in the American West. Englewood Cliffs, NJ: Prentice-Hall, 1965.

Opera in Chicago: A Social and Cultural History, 1850–1965. New York: Appleton-Century, 1966.

Hart, Philip. *Orpheus in the New World: The Symphony Orchestra as an American Cultural Institution*. New York: W.W. Norton, 1973.

Kolodin, Irving. *The Metropolitan Opera, 1883–1966. A Candid History*. 4th ed. New York, A. A. Knopf, 1966.

Schonberg, Harold C. *The great conductors*. New York: Simon & Schuster, 1967.

Arts Management

DiMaggio, Paul. *Managers of the Arts: Careers and Opinions of Senior Administrators of U.S. Art Museums, Symphony Orchestras, Resident Theatres, and Local Arts Agencies,* 2nd ed. Washington, DC: Seven Locks Press, 1988.

Martorella, Rosanne. *The Sociology of Opera.* New York: Praeger, 1982.

Shore, Harvey. *Arts Administration and Management: A Guide for Arts Administrators and Their Staffs.* New York: Quorum Books, 1987.

Whittingham, Nik-ki. *Arts Management in the '90s: The Essential Annotated Bibliography.* Chicago: ENAAQ, 1990.

Inside the Music Industry

Glossary

A & R Artists and Repertoire. The department of a record company responsible for scouting talent and songs, coordinating record producers and artists, record production, and often artist development.

ABC American Broadcasting Company, radio and TV networks.

acoustic A category of instruments which do not require electronic amplification.

Adult Contemporary A radio broadcast format featuring recent popular songs with a few oldies.

affiliate See *network*.

AFM American Federation of Musicians, a union.

AFTRA American Federation of Television and Radio Artists, a union.

Album-Oriented Rock A format of radio broadcasting in which most of the program material comes from Rock albums rather than single records. Often called "AOR."

AM Amplitude Modulation. The oldest commercial radio broadcast method, subject to electrical interference, and limited in both dynamic and frequency range (q.v.). *See* FM.

amplitude Loudness. See also *dynamic range*.

analog A method of recording and playback in which the frequency (q.v.) and amplitude (q.v.) of sound waves is reflected in an analogous way on a magnetic tape or phonograph record.

AOR See *Album-Oriented Rock.*

ARB See *Arbritron.*

Arbitron A radio rating service of the American Research Bureau (ARB).

aria A section of an opera, cantata (q.v.), or oratorio in which a solo singer is featured, normally with orchestral accompaniment.

arrangement An enhancement of any basic song or piano score done by writing and assigning instrumental parts and by imposing an overall form (routine). Sometimes original material by the arranger is added.

ASCAP American Society of Composers, Authors and Publishers. A performing rights organization.

automation Broadcasting by means of prerecorded tapes played on machines that are programmed electronically.

BMI Broadcast Music, Inc. A performing rights organization.

baroque A period of music extending from approximately 1600 to approximately 1750.

book In management, to schedule one or more performances. In musical theater, see *libretto.*

broadcast To electrically transmit sound (radio) and images (video) which can be reproduced with receivers. TV broadcasting is often called "telecasting." Cable TV broadcasting is often called "cablecasting."

© Part of the copyright notice of a work, meaning "Copyright," found on a published copy. Next to this appears the year of publication and the name of the copyright claimant.

cantata A vocal or vocal/choral work in several sections, normally with instrumental accompaniment.

CBS Columbia Broadcasting System, radio and TV networks.

CD See *digital.*

CD-ROM A compact disc in Read-Only-Memory format. Such discs may contain printed data, graphics, sound, and motion pictures.

chamber music Music for a small ensemble of instruments in which each player performs a distinct part (as opposed to orchestral music in which several players—particularly strings—may perform from the same part). Examples of chamber music include string quartet, piano trio, and so forth.

channel A distinct, discreet electronic route for analog signals or digital data.

chart The ranking of records, based on sales and frequency of airplay, published in trade periodicals and elsewhere.

classical (1) A generic term meaning "art music" in the European tradition. (2) A period of music extending from approximately 1750 to approximately 1820.

clip (1) Originally, an excerpt from a motion picture. (2) A form of music video (q.v.) featuring one song and usually lasting three to five minutes.

combo A small ensemble of instruments used to perform jazz, pop, or rock music; or, the group of musicians who make up the ensemble itself.

commercial spot A prerecorded radio or TV commercial.

compression The reduction of an audio signal's dynamic range. A certain amount of compression is necessary in the mastering of conventional phonograph records. See also *dbx*.

concerto (1) A classical work for soloist and orchestra, notably piano concertos and violin concertos. (2) A baroque (q.v.) work for a small group of soloists and a small orchestra.

conservatory A college of music, traditionally concentrating on the training of concert and operatic performers and composers.

contemporary (1) A widely used term in the music and broadcasting industries to indicate any one of a number of styles of popular music current at the time. (2) A radio format, usually synonymous with Top 40 (q.v.).

copy The words which make up a printed communication, especially in journalism, advertising, and public relations.

copyright Literally, the right (q.v.) to copy or reproduce one's own artistic or intellectual property. In practice it is the body of exclusive rights granted by law to the owners of such property.

CPB Corporation for Public Broadcasting.

crossover In record sales, the quality of appealing to more than one established market.

crosstalk Interchannel interference or leakage between tracks (q.v.) on a disc or a magnetic tape.

cue In theater and films: (1) the beginning of an event, such as a line of dialogue, a sound, or a visual effect; (2) a written device or symbol for that event. In film music, one piece or several pieces of music intended to become part of a film's soundtrack (q.v.).

DAT See *digital*.

dB Decibel. The standard unit of loudness measurement. It is relative and is used to compare two loudness levels. (E.g., "-5 dB" means 5 dB softer than some particular 0 dB reference.)

DBS Direct Broadcast Satellite. A system by which data, video, and audio can be uplinked from a transmitter to a satellite, which directly distributes the signal to subscribers coded to receive it.

dbx A patented noise-reduction system in which sound is encoded onto tape or disc using a 2:1 compression (q.v.) ratio format, then reconstructed during playback using a 1:2 ratio of expansion.

DCC See *digital.*

delay In recording, the effect of immediate, close repetition of a signal (q.v.). Delay is produced electronically by either analog (q.v.) or digital (q.v.) devices.

demo Demonstration.

digital In recording, a system whereby sound is sampled and transformed into high-speed binary pulse code, as in computer technology. Digital "information" may be stored on magnetic tape and transferred to discs, such as the digital compact disc (CD). Professional tape formats include Super-VHS and High-8 for multitrack (q.v.) recording and Digital Audio Tape (DAT) for two-track mixdowns (q.v.). Newer magnetic formats for portable consumer use employ compression technology. These formats include the Digital Compact Cassette (DCC) and the MiniDisc (MD).

disc jockey An announcer who hosts a radio show that features the playing of records. Also called a "DJ."

disc mastering Preparing a glass master compact disc which will be used for electroplating and ultimately CD pressing.

Disco Abbreviation for "discothèque" or dance club musical style popular around 1980.

distortion In recording or playback, any change in sound from the recorded source. The most common type is harmonic distortion, which affects the tonal qualities of music.

DJ See *disc jockey.*

DMX Digital Music Express. A multichannel business music service delivered by DBS (q.v.).

Dolby/Dolby A, B, C systems, Dolby Stereo® Tape noise reduction systems developed by Dr. Ray Dolby and his laboratories. Dolby A is intended for professional recording studios; Dolby B is commonly found in home recorders. Both reduce high-frequency hiss (q.v.). Dolby C, now available in home recorders, reduces noise throughout the audible frequency range. A six-track Dolby Stereo® has been used for the sound tracks (q.v.) of many films since 1978.

doughnut A form of commercial spot (q.v.) in which music is featured at the beginning and end, but recedes in the middle under the voice of an announcer.

drum machine Not a machine at all, but rather a piece of electronic equipment designed to reproduce the exact sounds of drums and their typical rhythmic patterns in popular music.

dub, dubbing (1) In films, the blending the recordings of all sound sources (voice, music, sound effects) into a unified sound track. (2) Making a copy of any finished recording. See also *overdub*.

dummy machine In films, any machine which plays back a sound source for the purpose of synchronizing it with other sound sources during dubbing (q.v.).

dynamic range The width between the loudest and softest sounds which can be recorded or played back using a given system, generally expressed in dB (q.v.). See also *signal-to-noise ratio*.

echo In recording, a controlled effect in which sound is enhanced by countless indistinct repetitions. This is generally achieved by means of a "chamber," a spring device, or an electronic device. See *pre-echo/post-echo* and *delay*.

editing (tape) After mixdown (q.v.), the splicing of leader tape onto the beginning and end of a song. Also, the assembling of songs into the order they will be heard on an LP record or prerecorded tape.

engineer Technician involved in the recording process. Recording engineers make tapes in a studio; mastering engineers cut lacquer disc masters.

equalization (EQ) Adjusting the recorded frequency response in any part of the audio range (bass, midrange, treble range, or finer gradations) by raising or lowering selected amplitudes (q.v.).

equalizer An electronic device that raises or lowers the amplitude of selected frequency bands. See *equalization (EQ)*.

FCC Federal Communications Commission, government regulatory agency for all broadcasting and telephone communications.

filter An electronic device which suppresses certain frequencies and allows others to pass through unaffected. The three most common types are high-pass, low-pass, and band-pass filters.

flutter See *wow and flutter*.

FM Frequency Modulation. A radio-broadcast method better suited to high-fidelity music transmission than AM, because of its wider dynamic and frequency range (q.v.). See AM.

frequency The speed of sound wave vibrations for a given musical sound. See *Hz*.

frequency range The entire spectrum of frequencies from lowest to highest. The frequency range of the human ear is approximately 20 Hz to approximately 20,000 Hz. The frequency range (or response) of tapes and records, and of the machines that play them, may vary considerably.

fuging tune A form of hymn or psalm tune from the late eighteenth century.

grand rights The right to perform a dramatico-musical composition on the staged, normally licensed from the copyright owner.

harmonic(s) Overtone(s); upper partial(s). Pitch(es) produced naturally above a fundamental pitch which form part of its sound and determine its tone quality.

hiss/tape hiss A range of high-frequency noise inherently included in analog (q.v.) tape recordings. This fault can be reduced below the level of audibility by applying a noise reduction system. See *Dolby* and *dbx*.

Hz Hertz. The standard measurement of pitch, expressed in cycles or complete sound vibrations per second. 100 Hz = 100 cycles per second.

impresario One who sponsors or produces concerts or operatic performances.

intermezzo (-i) In the eighteenth century, a light or comical theatrical entertainment played between the acts of a serious play or opera. Since the play or opera was generally in three acts, an intermezzo consisted of two scenes. This practice led to the two-act structure of Italian *opera buffa* and later forms of musical comedy.

jingle A song intended to advertise a particular product over radio or TV, generally found in a commercial spot (q.v.).

label (1) Nearly synonymous with "record company," although one record company may release and/or distribute records under more than one label. (2) The physical label on a compact disc.

libretto, librettist In opera and any form of American musical theater a libretto (literally, "little book") is a script showing all dialogue, stage directions, and suggestions for scenery. The writer of a libretto is a librettist.

long form A form of music video (q.v.) longer than five minutes or consisting of several songs, sometimes up to the length of a feature motion picture.

master (tape/disc) (1) The final, two-track stereo tape which carries the final mixdown (q.v.) version of a recording. (2) The lacquer disc which is cut using the master tape. (3) In recording contracts, a recording of one song.

MBS Mutual Broadcasting System, a radio network.

MD See *digital*.

Met Nickname for the Metropolitan Opera Company.

Middle-of-the-Road (MOR) A generalized style of popular music and radio programming which overlaps somewhat with soft rock, Broadway show music, "golden oldies," and "easy listening."

MIDI Musical Instrument Digital Interface. The de facto standard for connecting digital electronic musical instruments to one another, to computers, and to software.

mixdown/final mixdown Mixing down means combining two or more tracks on a multitrack (q.v.) tape into one or two tracks, such as mixing down the various rhythm instrument tracks into one or two. The final mixdown encorporates all the final tracks of a multitrack recording into a two-track master tape (q.v.).

MOR See *Middle-of-the-Road.*

"Mother" In record manufacture, the electroplated positive disc copy used to produce stampers, which will then press the vinyl records.

Motown Black dialect expression, meaning roughly "Motor Town," or the city of Detroit, used as the name of a record label.

MTV A cable broadcaster whose programming features music videos (q.v.) in contemporary (q.v.) rock style.

multiplex A method of FM (q.v.) broadcasting in which two (or more) separate signals (q.v.) are broadcast simultaneously from one transmitter on the same frequency.

multitrack A system of recording in which between four and twenty-four tracks (q.v.) are recorded side by side in synchronization on one tape.

musicology Music as a branch of scholarship. The term used by itself usually connotes the field of historical musicology, which is focused on aspects of music history.

music video A form of "visual radio" in which a musical performance or audio recording is synchronized with moving images.

NAB National Association of Broadcasters.

NBC National Broadcasting Company, radio and TV networks.

network (1) A group of radio or TV stations or cable systems ("affiliates") linked (usually by satellite) to a host company providing programs to the group. (2) The host company that supplies programming to its affiliates.

NPR National Public Radio.

opéra comique A style of French opera composed from the late eighteenth century to the late nineteenth century which focuses on a few characters and uses spoken dialogue. The plot may be serious or comic.

option A contract requiring fulfillment before a stated deadline. Options common in the American theater include the use of existing material for a play or musical, the right to produce a musical on the stage, and the right to make a film version of a play or musical.

oratorio A narrative or dramatic concert work, normally involving vocal soloists, a chorus, and an orchestra.

Oscar Nickname for a motion picture Academy Award or the trophy associated with such an award.

overdub To add one or more new tracks of sound to a tape that contains previously recorded material. See also *dub, dubbing.*

overlay In film music, any track which is added to a cue (q.v.) after the cue has been recorded, as in overdubbing (q.v.).

overture A piece of music performed by an orchestra, usually preceding an opera or play. Independent concert overtures also became popular during the nineteenth century. Many of these may be classified as program music (q.v.).

(P) Part of the copyright notice of a sound recording, meaning "Phonorecord Copyright." Next to this appears the year of release and the name of the copyright claimant.

piece (1) In music, an individual selection. (2) In journalism, an article.

pitch The perceived location of a musical sound within the audible frequency range (low to high); a function of frequency (q.v.).

playlist A radio station's ranked list (or system of lists) showing which recordings make up the chief programming material for a given week.

pre-echo/post-echo On a tape, a faint echo of sound about to be heard or just heard caused by magnetic "print-through" of sound from an adjacent wrap of the tape.

program music Instrumental concert music in which the composer intends to tell a story, paint a picture, impart poetic images, or express a philosophy.

psychedelic A type of popular art and music of the late 1960s which emphasized intensified colors, uninhibited imagery, and wild improvisation, in the manner of "heightened consciousness" or drug-induced halucination.

R&B Rhythm and Blues. A style of Black urban music first made popular during the 1950s.

Rap From the slang expression meaning to talk or discuss. An urban style (originally Black) of rhymed metrical/rhythmic speaking performed to the accompaniment of rhythm instruments. Melodic-harmonic refrains are sometimes interspersed.

recital A performance of classical music normally performed by a soloist or a series of soloists.

reverberation (1) The echo sound characteristics, or ambience, of a room. (2) In recording, an electronic sound enhancement similar to echo (q.v.), but more distinct and with greater depth.

RIAA Recording Industry Association of America. Organization of record companies and related interests that gives gold and platinum awards for sales of recorded products. RIAA is also an information clearinghouse and a political advocate for the recording industry.

rights Legal privileges.

rococo A light, elegant, and simplified style in the arts which superseded the heavier, more complex baroque style in the early eighteenth century.

rpm Revolutions per minute; the standard of speed measurement for phonograph records and compact discs. The standard speeds are: 78 rpm (older phonograph records); 45 rpm (modern single records); 33 1/3 rpm (LPs); and 400 rpm (compact discs).

SAG Screen Actors Guild, a union.

score, scoring The fully orchestrated version of a musical work. Alternately, any piece of music in finished written form (for example, a piano-vocal score). In film, the musical part of the sound track (q.v.); composing and orchestrating the music for a film.

sequence In film music, a series of musical cues (q.v.) which are composed to overlap one another slightly and which will sound like one cue after dubbing (q.v.).

SESAC Society of European Stage Authors and Composers. A performing-rights organization.

shellac In older record manufacturing, the chemical composition used to make records before the advent of vinyl.

signal The electrical waveform, or pattern, representing sound.

signal-to-noise ratio (S/N) A comparison of the level of interference (noise) with the signal (q.v.) level in a sound system, usually expressed in dB (q.v.). A S/N of 50 dB means that the level of interference (noise) is 50 dB lower than that of the signal at a given output level. See also *dynamic range*.

Singspiel German comic opera with spoken dialogue developed in the eighteenth century.

small rights The right to perform a nondramatic musical work, such as a song or a piece of concert music, normally licensed through one of the performing rights organizations (ASCAP, BMI, or SESAC).

sound recording In copyright law, a particular recorded performance, considered as an artistic work and therefore qualifying for copyright protection.

sound track In films: (1) the total sound component of a film, consisting of voices, music, and sound effects; (2) the stripe running alongside the frames of a film on which the total sound component has been recorded. On records, a "sound track recording" normally consists of only music.

source music In films, music for which a literal source is visible on the screen. Nightclub and theater scenes are typical examples.

spot See *commercial spot.*

standard A song, concert work, or opera which has become a "standard" piece of the repertoire in its style.

stereophonic sound, stereo Sound (chiefly music) in which two or more tracks (q.v.) have been used to record the program and an equal number of speakers are required to reproduce it.

sweetener A track of overdubbed (q.v.) sound added as an enhancement to a multitrack (q.v.) tape recording.

symphony A musical composition for orchestra, normally consisting of several movements.

synchronization The concurrent recording (on film or videotape) of images with sound, particularly music.

syndication The distribution and local broadcasting of prepackaged radio or TV programs.

synthesizer An electronic instrument, generally controlled by a keyboard, capable of producing a wide variety of sounds and effects.

take In recording, one version of, or attempt at, a recorded performance. A take may involve one or more tracks (q.v.) of the tape.

tempo Speed. In music, the rate of speed is usually calculated in beats per minute.

Top 40 A radio broadcast format in which the music programming consists largely of the forty most popular records of the week. These are generally rotated from three ranked lists: 1–10, 11–20, and 21–40.

track (1) One of the several side-by-side magnetic paths on a recorded tape; or, the music recorded on one such track. (2) On a CD (q.v.) an individually recorded selection.

traffic In a radio station, the function of scheduling commercial spots (q.v.) and reporting these for billing purposes.

video An electronic audiovisual medium. Transmission may be by cable or airwaves (TV); viewing is by TV set or monitor; and storage is usually on videotape or videodisc (q.v.).

videodisc A recorded disc containing video (q.v.) programming. The most common type is "read" optically by laser illumination. Also called "laser disc."

video jockey An announcer who hosts a TV show that features the playing of music videos (q.v.). Also called a "VJ."

virtuoso A concert or operatic performer who possesses outstanding technical abilities.

VJ See *video jockey*.

Index